Queer Studies

An Interdisciplinary Reader

edited by

Robert J. Corber
and Stephen Valocchi

Blackwell
Publishing

350 Main Street, Malden, MA 02148-5018, USA
108 Cowley Road, Oxford OX4 1JF, UK
550 Swanston Street, Carlton South, Melbourne, Victoria 3053, Australia
Kurfürstendamm 57, 10707 Berlin, Germany

First published 2003 by Blackwell Publishing Ltd

Library of Congress Cataloging-in-Publication Data

Queer studies : an interdisciplinary reader / edited by Robert J. Corber and Stephen
Valocchi.
    p. cm.
  Includes bibliographical references and index.
  ISBN 0-631-22916-7 (alk. paper) – ISBN 0-631-22917-5 (pbk. : alk. paper)
  1. Gay and lesbian studies.   2. Homosexuality – Research.   I. Corber, Robert J.,
1958–   II. Valocchi, Stephen M., 1956–

HQ75.15 .Q48 2003
305.9'0664'07 – dc21

                                                                          2002026250

A catalogue record for this title is available from the British Library.

Set in 9.5 on 11.5 pt Ehrhardt
by SNP Best-set Typesetter Ltd., Hong Kong

For further information on
Blackwell Publishing, visit our website:
http://www.blackwellpublishing.com

Contents

Contents

Acknowledgments

The idea for this volume grew out of discussions with our colleagues in the Women's Studies Program at Trinity College about designing a curriculum that combined the perspectives of both women's studies and lesbian and gay studies. We would like to thank the members of the Faculty Working Group in Queer Studies, where many of those discussions took place: Janet Bauer, Renny Fulco, Joan Hedrick, Jane Nadel-Klein, Beth Notar, Margo Perkins, Kat Power, and Barbara Sicherman. The group's activities were generously funded by Trinity's Center for Collaborative Teaching and Research, and we are very grateful to Michael Niemann, the Center's director, for making possible precisely the kind of dialogue across the humanities and the social sciences with respect to gender and sexuality that we hope this volume will promote on a larger scale. We owe a special thanks to Robyn Wiegman, whose incisive comments on an early draft of the introduction led us to reframe our account of the emergence of queer studies, although we alone are responsible for its short-comings. We would also like to thank Judith Halberstam for allowing us to publish her essay on the Brandon Teena archive, which she presented as part of Trinity's annual Lesbian and Gay Studies Lecture Series. Finally, we are deeply indebted to Jayne Fargnoli, our editor at Blackwell Publishing, whose editorial acumen made this a much stronger volume than it would otherwise have been.

The editors and publisher gratefully acknowledge the permission granted to reproduce the copyright material in this book:

1 Martha M. Umphrey, "The Trouble with Harry Thaw," pp. 8–23 from *Radical History Review* 62:8 (1995). © 1995 by MARHO, the Radical Historians' Organisation. All rights reserved. Reprinted by permission of Duke University Press.
2 Cheryl Chase, "Hermaphrodites with Attitude: An Emergence of Intersex Political Activism," pp. 189–211 from *GLQ* 4:2 (1998). © 1998, Duke University Press. All rights reserved. Reprinted with permission.
3 Cathy J. Cohen, "Contested Membership: Black Gay Identities and the Politics of AIDS," pp. 362–94 from Steven Seidman (ed.), *Queer Theory/Sociology*. Oxford: Blackwell, 1996.
4 C. Jacob Hale, "Leatherdyke Boys and Their Daddies: How to Have Sex without Women or Men," pp. 222–36 from *Social Text* 15:3–4 (Fall–Winter 1997). © 1997, Duke University Press. All rights reserved. Reprinted with permission.
5 Lisa Duggan, "The Trials of Alice Mitchell: Sensationalism, Sexology, and the Lesbian Subject in Turn-of-the-Century America," pp. 791–814 from *Signs* 18:4 (Summer 1993).
6 Jennifer DeVere Brody, "The Returns of Cleopatra Jones," pp. 91–121 from *Signs* 25:1 (1999).

7 Laura Kipnis, "(Male) Desire and (Female) Disgust: Reading *Hustler*," from Lawrence Grossberg, Cary Nelson, and Paula A. Treichler (eds.), *Cultural Studies Vol. 5.* New York: Routledge, 1991. Reproduced by permission of Taylor & Francis Ltd (http://www.tandf.co.uk).

8 Nayan Shah, "Perversity, Contamination, and the Dangers of Queer Domesticity," pp. 77–104 from Nayan Shah, *Contagious Divides: Epidemics and Race in San Francisco's Chinatown.* Berkeley and Los Angeles: University of California Press, 2001.

9 John Howard, "The Talk of the County: Revisiting Accusation, Murder, and Mississippi, 1895," pp. 191–218 from W. Fitzhugh Brundage (ed.), *Where These Memories Grow: History, Memory, and Southern Identity.* Chapel Hill and London: University of North Carolina Press, 2000.

10 Judith Halberstam, "The Brandon Teena Archive." © 2003 by Blackwell Publishing Ltd.

11 Lauren Berlant and Michael Warner, "Sex in Public," pp. 547–66 from *Critical Inquiry* 24:2 (Winter 1998).

12 Jennifer Robertson, "Dying to Tell: Sexuality and Suicide in Imperial Japan," pp. 1–35 from *Signs: Journal of Women in Culture and Society* 25:1 (1999).

13 Gayatri Gopinath, "Nostalgia, Desire, Diaspora: South Asian Sexualities in Motion," pp. 467–89 from *Positions* 5:2 (Fall 1997). © 1997, Duke University Press. All rights reserved. Reprinted with permission.

14 Tom Boellstorff, "The Perfect Path: Gay Men, Marriage, Indonesia," pp. 475–510 from *GLQ* 5:4 (Winter 1999). © 1998, Duke University Press. All rights reserved. Reprinted with permission.

15 Don Kulick, "A Man in the House: The Boyfriends of Brazilian *Travesti* Prostitutes," pp. 133–60 from *Social Text* 52–53 (Fall–Winter 1997). © 1997, Duke University Press. All rights reserved. Reprinted with permission.

Every effort has been made to trace copyright holders and to obtain their permission for the use of copyright material. The publisher apologizes for any errors or omissions in the above list and would be grateful if notified of any corrections that should be incorporated in future reprints or editions of this book.

Introduction

Queer Studies: An Interdisciplinary Reader brings together previously published essays in queer studies, a rapidly developing field that since its emergence a decade ago, has transformed the study of gender and sexuality in both the humanities and the social sciences. Focusing in particular on sexual and gender practices such as sadomasochism, transvestism and hermaphroditism that cannot be reduced to the categories of either homosexuality or heterosexuality, queer studies scholars have shown that desires, identities, and practices do not always line up neatly. In so doing, they have unsettled many of the intellectual assumptions and methodological conventions guiding the study of gender and sexuality in a number of disciplines. Although in some disciplines such as history and sociology the term queer is often used as a kind of shorthand for "lesbian, gay, bisexual, and transgendered," queer studies understands the term somewhat differently. For scholars influenced by queer theory, "queer" names or describes identities and practices that foreground the instability inherent in the supposedly stable relationship between anatomical sex, gender, and sexual desire. Such identities and practices have the potential to expose the widely held belief that sex, gender, and sexuality have a causal or necessary relationship to each other as an ideological fiction that works to stabilize heterosexuality. For this reason, queer studies is especially interested in nonnormative forms of identity, or forms in which sex, gender, and sexuality do not line up in the socially prescribed way.

This understanding of the category of queer first emerged in the humanities, and its deployment has transformed many key elements of the humanist project – everything from the analysis of literary and filmic texts to the imagining of historical subjects. Not surprisingly, the interdisciplinary fields of women's studies and lesbian and gay studies were quick to take up the category as they recognized the limits of identity-based thought but nevertheless remained committed to producing knowledge about minoritized groups as an emphatically political project. Although for reasons discussed below, the social sciences were more reluctant to incorporate queer approaches and remain somewhat skeptical of their value, much current research dealing with gender and sexuality in anthropology, sociology, political science, and history, for example, routinely draws on queer theoretical insights. As a result, issues of gender and sexuality are now being interrogated from a queer perspective at a variety of disciplinary sites.

But even as it has transformed the study of gender and sexuality, the category of queer has generated a series of debates, as it has traveled across the disciplines, that reflect the different ways the disciplines organize and produce knowledge. The most important of these debates concern the limitations of identity-based knowledge, which until the emergence of queer studies dominated the study of gender and sexuality; queer theory's relationship to feminism, which again until the emergence of queer studies provided the most sophisticated theoretical framework for analyzing the category of gender; the strengths and weaknesses of the post-structuralist conception of power underlying much queer scholarship; and the value of psychoanalytic models of subject formation, which have dominated queer scholarship in the humanities. To map the boundaries of this still emerging field, we briefly sketch these debates and trace the disciplinary geneologies that gave rise to them. Our goal is to make the readings that follow as accessible as possible, as they are drawn from a variety of disciplines and have emerged out of these debates.

Identity and Its Discontents

In the wake of the gay liberation movement of the early 1970s, gay scholars in the United States and Great Britain, many of whom had no academic affiliation, published a series of groundbreaking studies that transformed the study of sexuality, which until then was divided primarily between a tradition of sociology concerned with understanding how subcultural groups like homosexuals managed the stigma attached to their "spoiled" identities and a tradition of sexology centered on quantifying sexual behavior.[1] Following in the footsteps of British sociologist Mary McIntosh whose pioneering work on "the homosexual role" in the 1960s shifted the focus of sociological inquiry from deviance to the ways in which the stigmatized category of the homosexual served to maintain the boundaries between the normal and the abnormal, these studies, which included Jonathan Ned Katz's *Gay American History* (1975), Jeffrey Weeks's *Coming Out* (1977), and John D'Emilio's *Sexual Politics, Sexual Communities* (1983) challenged the assumption that sexuality is a natural or a biological instinct existing outside of social institutions. Taking for granted that the meanings attached to same-sex eroticism vary historically and across cultures, these studies asserted that lesbian and gay identities are socially constructed, that they are products of historically specific economic, political, and social conditions. Ironically, these studies demonstrated the *in*ability to recover an unbroken or continuous history of a subordinate group. Instead, they showed that the categories homosexual and het-

erosexual were inventions of late nineteenth-century Western societies, that they had their roots in the dramatic social transformations that accompanied the rise of industrial capitalism and the emergence of the nation-state, and that they were struggled over and eventually transformed by self-identified gays and lesbians.

In stressing the historicity of lesbian and gay identities, these and similar studies written from a social constructionist perspective existed in tension with the quasi-ethnic, or minoritarian model of homosexuality that in the 1970s and '80s came to dominate the lesbian and gay movement and subculture. According to this model, gays and lesbians constitute an oppressed minority similar to other oppressed minorities such as Jews and African Americans, and they have their own distinct history and culture that can be traced to the ancient Greeks. But in sketching the historical and social processes by which the minoritarian model gradually became dominant, social constructionist studies showed that that model was not a given but was a site of struggle and that it eventually displaced other models of homosexuality. At the same time, however, many of these studies implicitly asserted that the minoritarian model was the end point of the development of a modern homosexual identity, and thus they tended to legitimate the subculture's claim that to be lesbian or gay was akin to being Jewish or African American.

One of the reasons for this contradictory effect was methodological in nature. Historians doing this kind of research often drew on the assumptions, conventions, and techniques deployed by social historians for recovering the histories and cultures of racial and ethnic minorities. Such studies narrated the formation of a collective lesbian and gay identity with its attendant processes of culture making, institution building, and political activism and argued that this identity was crucial to the struggle of gays and lesbians to gain political and social legitimacy. One of the unintended effects of this approach was to accept without challenging the binary organization of sexuality. Even as the studies showed that lesbian and gay identities were socially constructed, they implied that those identities were stable and coherent as they took for granted that the boundaries between homosexuality and heterosexuality were fixed and impermeable.

Queer studies emerged partly as a reaction against this approach, which despite its limitations began to define lesbian and gay studies scholarship in the 1980s.[2] While queer studies is deeply informed by the social constructionist perspective developed by lesbian and gay scholars in history and sociology, the most influential scholars in queer studies, such as Judith Butler, Eve Kosofsky Sedgwick, Teresa de Lauretis, David Halperin, and Michael Warner, are humanists who have absorbed, albeit not uncritically, the post-structuralist critique of identity that came to dominate humanistic inquiry in the 1980s. Influenced by the work of Louis Althusser, Jacques Derrida, Michel Foucault, and Jacques Lacan, many scholars working in the humanities began rejecting the notion of the subject that had informed humanistic inquiry since the Renaissance. One of the underlying assumptions of such inquiry was that the subject was unified, coherent, and self-determining. But scholars influenced by post-structuralism argued that this notion of the subject was an ideological fiction that worked to conceal, and thereby perpetuate, modern relations of power. For them, the subject does not exist prior to social structures but is constituted in and through them, and thus it is neither autonomous nor unified but contingent and split. Subjectivity is not a property of the self but originates outside it and therefore is unstable.

Influenced by this critique, queer studies scholars claim that desires, practices, and identities do not line up as neatly as lesbian and gay studies scholarship implies. For these scholars, lesbian and gay identities are provisional and contingent rather than fixed and coherent. "The homosexual" is not a stable or autonomous category but a supplement that works to stabilize heterosexuality by functioning as its binary opposite. As such, homosexuality enables heterosexuality to go unmarked, to function as a social norm from which homosexuality deviates. In other words, heterosexuality depends on homosexuality for its coherence and stability. Queer studies scholars also claim that the minoritarian model that has determined the lesbian and gay movement's strategies and goals has more disadvantages than advantages. For

them, the assertion of a collective identity, rather than a prerequisite for political and social intervention, marginalizes and excludes those who are unable or unwilling to conform to it and requires lesbians and gays to gloss over the racial and class differences among them.

This stress on the limitations of identity-based scholarship and activism reflected developments outside as well as inside the academy. In the 1980s, as the lesbian and gay movement came to embrace the quasi-ethnic status of "gay people" and to institutionalize that status in both a political community and a commercial subculture, various conflicts and tensions emerged that reflected the biases and exclusions embedded in that status. These conflicts and tensions centered on issues of race and class, as well as the policing of sexual practices, gendered modes of embodiment, and political identifications. The movement increasingly saw itself as an advocate for lesbian and gay identity rather than for dissident sexualities, and lesbians and gays of color resisted the expectation that they would subordinate their race and class to their sexuality. Moreover, as AIDS ravaged gay male communities throughout the 1980s, identity-based political activism proved ill-equipped to deal effectively with the cultural backlash and intense homophobia triggered by the epidemic. This was partly because the AIDS crisis focused renewed attention on gay sexual culture, which even many lesbian and gay activists repudiated as the source of the epidemic, thereby stigmatizing certain forms of gay identity as "promiscuous" and "irresponsible." In response to these developments, AIDS activist organizations such as ACT UP (AIDS Coalition to Unleash Power) argued that the focus needed to be on the types of practices that put people at risk of contracting HIV, the virus that causes AIDS, rather than the types of people considered most likely to engage in those practices, especially because there are many men who have sex with other men but who do not identify as gay.

The theorist most responsible for the queer critique of identity-based activism and scholarship is Judith Butler. In her frequently cited book *Gender Trouble*, published in 1989, Butler extended the feminist claim that gender is socially constructed by asserting that identity is performative. For Butler, rather than an expression of a core self or an essence that defines the individual, identities are the effect of the repeated performance of certain cultural signs and conventions. There is no original from which gender and sexual identities are derived; rather, they are copies of copies. One implication of this argument is that lesbian and gay identities are performatively constituted by the very expressions of gender and sexuality that are thought to be produced by them. Despite how her claims have often been interpreted, this does not mean that identity for Butler amounts to a form of role playing, which would assume that the subject already exists and is capable of assuming and controlling its performances. Such a misinterpretation reinscribes the notion of the subject critiqued by post-structuralists. Rather, it is through the repeated performance of certain significations of gender and sexuality that the subject comes into being. In complicating the social constructionist perspective, this understanding of how identity is constituted radically destabilized the humanist project underlying lesbian and gay studies. Because lesbian and gay identities are no different from other identities, they cannot be understood as an expression of a core or "true" self but are constituted through a regularized and constrained repetition of social norms.

Queer scholars have not limited their critique of lesbian and gay studies to the minoritarian model of lesbian and gay identities. Influenced by the work of Michel Foucault, which we discuss in more detail below, they have attempted to unsettle without overturning the master categories of lesbian and gay studies by shifting the field's focus from identities to practices. Following Foucault, they define sexuality as a historically specific organization of power, discourse, bodies, and affectivity. For them, sexuality is a regime of knowledge and power that structures the economic, political, and social life of modern societies. Sexuality is at once constituted by society and a vehicle for regulating and controlling it. Thus queer scholars contend that the focus of lesbian and gay studies on the making of lesbian and gay identities and communities tacitly accepts the binary organization of sexuality underlying the dominant position of heterosexuality in society. More problematic, the field's narrow focus cannot accommodate or account

for practices such as crossdressing, sado-masochism, and transsexualism not defined by the gender of object-choice; as a result, the field fails to address the full range of nonnormative genders and sexualities. For these reasons, queer scholars argue that the field's object of study should instead be the institutions, discourses, and practices that maintain the heterosexual/homosexual binary so that the field can contribute to the dismantling rather than the reproduction of that binary. Although lesbian and gay identities remain a focus of queer studies, they are not the only focus; rather, they are one of a variety of possible configurations of desires, practices, and identities studied by the field, and they are explicitly problematized in terms of power relations, including the silences, repressions, and exclusions on which their constitution as a form of ethnicity has depended.

In shifting the focus of scholarly inquiry from identities to practices, queer scholars have introduced an important new concept, heteronormativity, that has proved crucial to understanding structures of domination and patterns of inequality as they relate to sexuality. By heteronormativity, they mean the set of norms that make heterosexuality seem natural or right and that organize homosexuality as its binary opposite. This set of norms works to maintain the dominance of heterosexuality by preventing homosexuality from being a form of sexuality that can be taken for granted or go unmarked or seem right in the way heterosexuality can. As a result, the dominance of heterosexuality often operates unconsciously or in unmarked ways that make it particularly difficult to expose and dislodge. One reason why the concept of heteronormativity is so useful is because it allows for more complex understandings of homosexuality and heterosexuality. It does this by making a distinction between the normative structures privileging heterosexuality and individual patterns of organizing sexual lives. Although they overlap, heteronormativity and heterosexuality are not co-extensive and cannot be reduced to each other. Thus there may be modes of organizing sexual relations between straights that are not heteronormative, just as there may be modes of organizing sexual relations between gays and between lesbians that are, and one of the crucial tasks of scholars working in the field is to identify what these modes are so we can under-stand better systems of sexual stratification and how to disrupt them.

In highlighting the limitations of the identity-based approach that has dominated the study of sexuality, queer studies has problema-tized some of the founding assumptions of lesbian and gay studies, especially those con-cerning the emergence of homosexuality as a distinct form of personhood in the nineteenth century. As we saw above, beginning with the groundbreaking work of Katz, Weeks, and D'Emilio, a historiographic tradition has emerged that has deeply informed lesbian and gay studies scholarship. This tradition has tended to recapitulate on a social and historical scale a process that since the gay liberation movement of the 1970s has been seen as crucial to the formation of lesbian and gay identities on a personal scale. This process involves moving from the closet to public visibility, from isolation to collective action. As a result, lesbian and gay history has often taken the form of the coming out process writ large.

One unintended effect of this recapitulation has been to cast earlier forms of homosexuality such as sexual inversion, the dominant con-struction of homosexual identity in the late nineteenth and early twentieth centuries which defined homosexuality as a form of sex-role reversal, as lesbian and gay identities in the making. But such forms have their own gene-ologies and may have persisted, despite being marginalized or displaced. Another unintended effect is to construct forms of homosexuality that deviate from the white, middle-class, urban lesbian and gay identities that gradually became hegemonic over the course of the twentieth century as pre-modern and by implication culturally backward. These include homosexual identities and practices involving cross-gender identification, especially in men, or persons who engage in same-sex relations but who do not identify as gay or lesbian, or who do not center their lives on their sexuality because other aspects of their identities such as their race or class figure more prominently in their experi-ence. For this reason, this historiographic tradi-tion has tended to reinforce the hegemony of the very lesbian and gay identities whose formation it sets out to explain.

By contrast, historiography undertaken by queer studies scholars has shown that the emergence of the heterosexual/homosexual bi-nary was uneven and was mediated by a complex of factors including race, class, gender, region, and nation. Recent studies such as John Howard's *Men Like That*, for example, argue that in small towns and rural areas homosexual-ity continued to be understood as a set of prac-tices as late as the 1980s, and access to lesbian and gay webs of affiliation and desire depends on circulation through geographically dispersed cruising venues such as rest stops along inter-state highways and internet chat rooms, rather than congregation in urban neighborhoods.[3] Such studies suggest that the focus on commu-nity, which has come to define the historical scholarship on lesbian and gay life, may distort or misrepresent the history of homosexuality in modern societies.[4] Such a focus cannot account for subjects of homosexual desire who exist at the margins of lesbian and gay life or whose relation to urban lesbian and gay communities is transient or touristic. Because of its investment in community history as a methodology and interpretive framework, the dominant form of lesbian and gay historiography indirectly reinforces the claim that the emergence of the modern homosexual depended on processes of industrialization and urbanization. By contrast, queer historiography complicates this claim by exploring how lesbian and gay identities have developed in rural areas and small towns that lack the institutions that support urban lesbian and gay life.

The limitations of identity-based scholarship have been further highlighted by the recent turn to transnationalism in queer studies. One of the most important and exciting developments in the field, this turn has raised some of the same questions about identity-based analyses as has queer historiography.[5] There is now a significant body of queer scholarship in history, anthropol-ogy, and sociology that explores how the circulation of people, commodities, media, discourses, and capital across national borders has transformed the sexual politics and cultures of Western and non-Western nations alike. The most sophisticated of this scholarship acknowl-edges that while its scale and intensity have increased dramatically in the last two decades, this circulation has existed at least since the emergence of capitalism in the sixteenth century. It also stresses that this circulation is never on equal terms, that some social formations have greater material resources than others and that this relation of inequality profoundly affects whether and how the sexual practices, identities, and modes of embodiment flowing across national borders are absorbed, transformed, and/or resisted at the local, regional, and national level.

Scholars working in this area of queer studies focus primarily on the emergence in postcolonial and so-called underdeveloped nations of sex-based social movements whose political rhetoric and strategies incorporate Western forms of sexual desire and identity. They show that even as these movements draw on Western notions of gay and lesbian identities and models of political organizing, they call into question Western notions of sexuality, subjectivity, and citizenship, rooted as they are in a concept of the nation-state increasingly under pressure from the processes of globalization. They have also stressed how the transnational movement of diasporic and immigrant populations is transforming the sexual practices, identities, and politics of both the homelands and the host nations of these populations. Like queer work on regional sexual formations, this scholarship renders problematic histories of lesbian and gay identities and communities that are geographically bounded or that analyze and explain the development of those identities and communities by locating them solely in national histories. Instead, what is needed is historical scholarship that takes into account the coexistence of multiple forms of homosexuality and that recognizes that these forms are never historically static or unchanging but shift over time as they interact with each other and compete for dominance.

Sexing Gender: Queer Studies and Feminism

Queer studies' relationship to women's studies is even more complicated than its relationship to lesbian and gay studies. Although it is deeply indebted to the modes of feminist analysis developed by women's studies scholars in the

1980s – indeed, its emergence as a field would not have been possible without those modes – there are tensions between the two fields. Overlooking a vast body of feminist scholarship that has sought to link a progressive sexual politics to feminism's emancipatory project, many queer scholars believe that women's studies has reinforced the sexist stereotype that women are less sexual than men and are easily victimized and need protection.[6] This is partly because of the theoretical model that came to dominate many women's studies programs in the late 1970s and '80s and that despite the influence of queer studies, continues to inform how some women's studies scholars understand the relationship between gender and sexuality. Women's studies scholars influenced by this model tend to conceive of sexuality as the site where masculinity and femininity are constituted along an axis of domination and subordination. This claim provided the foundation for the anti-pornography campaigns of the late 1970s and '80s orchestrated by Catherine MacKinnon and Andrea Dworkin. In conceiving of sexuality as a realm of coercion and exploitation rather than pleasure, these campaigns deeply divided feminists and as we will see led to the formulation of more nuanced conceptions of the relationship between sexuality and gender that are central to queer studies. But if some queer scholars feel that women's studies does not adequately acknowledge women's sexual agency, some women's studies scholars feel that queer studies does not always acknowledge its debt to feminism. For these scholars, queer studies does not pay sufficient attention to the material consequences of inhabiting a female body in a patriarchal society, and its focus on nonnormative sexualities threatens to displace gender as the primary category of feminist analysis.

As this discussion indicates, the primary disagreement between queer studies and women's studies is over how to theorize the relationship between sex, gender, and sexuality. Unlike queer scholars, who as we will see are careful to make a conceptual distinction between sex, gender, and sexuality, women's studies scholars have tended to conflate the three constructs. This tendency first surfaced in women's studies scholarship of the 1970s that relied on such key feminist concepts as "women's oppression" and "patriarchy." Overlooking the complexity of power relations, this scholarship tended to position men as the oppressor and women as the oppressed. In so doing, it inadvertently reproduced the normative alignment of sex, gender, and sexuality. For women's studies scholars influenced by this strand of feminist theory, maleness, masculinity, and male privilege were inextricably linked.

The limitations of this understanding of male privilege were pointed out as early as 1977 by the Combahee River Collective, a group of black socialist feminists founded in 1974. In its widely influential "A Black Feminist Statement" published in 1977, the Collective argued that feminism needed to develop a more complex understanding of power that could account for how men and women were positioned differently along the axes of race and class. For the Collective, the strand of feminist theory that had come to dominate the women's movement failed to acknowledge that the category of man is not monolithic and that access to male privilege depends on racial and class identity. As a result, the movement could not account for modes of affiliation and collectivity that crossed gender lines; indeed, it actively discouraged them because they supposedly threatened to undermine women's solidarity. Challenging some of the movement's most basic assumptions, the Collective asserted the need for black women to affiliate with black men: "Our situation as Black people necessitates that we have solidarity around the fact of race. We struggle together with Black men against racism, while we also struggle with Black men about sexism."[7] Thus in black feminist thought such as the Collective's, the relationship between maleness, masculinity, and male privilege was complicated by race and class. This theoretical stance not only anticipated but helped make possible that of queer studies. As we will see, one of queer studies' central claims is that masculinity has no necessary link to maleness and the belief that it does serves to legitimate patriarchal social arrangements.

The tendency of women's studies scholars to collapse sex and sexuality into gender was perhaps most pronounced in scholarship influenced by lesbian feminism, which in the 1970s redefined the category of lesbian in part by emptying it of its sexual content. For lesbian feminists, lesbianism was the logical extension of feminism. Any woman, they believed, could become a lesbian simply by making women central to her life and by developing a "lesbian consciousness." In other words, lesbianism was a matter more of "woman-identification" than of sexual desire. One of the most influential formulations of this definition of lesbianism was Adrienne Rich's. In her widely anthologized and often cited essay "Compulsory Heterosexuality and Lesbian Existence," first published in 1980, Rich argued that lesbianism was best understood in terms of the category of gender and that lesbians, despite their sexuality, had more in common with straight women than with gay men. Indeed, gay men, insofar as they were men, were implicated in structures of male domination. Their sexuality supposedly did not affect their access to patriarchal power. Rich further conflated gender and sexuality by arguing that any bond between women that was rooted in solidarity could be called lesbian whether or not it involved sexual relations. This redefinition of lesbianism was strategically useful to the women's movement because it promoted solidarity among women by minimizing differences that had the potential to divide them. At the same time, however, it failed to acknowledge that lesbians were oppressed by homophobia as well as sexism and that like gay men they had a stake in challenging systems of social stratification based on sexuality.

One of the earliest and most signficant critiques of this approach to sexuality was Gayle Rubin's groundbreaking essay "Thinking Sex," first published in 1984. Though indebted to a structuralist rather than a post-structuralist conception of power, Rubin's essay is one of the founding texts of queer studies. Rubin rejected the analysis of women's oppression advanced by anti-pornography feminists such as MacKinnon and Dworkin, arguing that its central claim, namely that sexuality was the site at which women's subordination was consolidated, collapsed the distinction between sexuality and gender. For Rubin, gender and sexuality, though closely related, constituted "two distinct arenas of social practice."[8] For this reason, sexuality required its own theory and politics. Feminism could not explain how sexuality operates as a system of social stratification distinct from gender. Building on but qualifying Michel Foucault's arguments in *The History of Sexuality, Volume One*, which as we discuss below privilege discursive over institutional power, Rubin traced the history of the state regulation of sexuality in Great Britain and the United States beginning in the nineteenth century, and in so doing showed that sexuality operates as a vector of oppression in modern Western societies.

Rubin maintained that in certain historical periods when sexuality is highly contested and overtly politicized, sexual acts become burdened with an excess of meaning, and individuals are divided up according to a "hierarchical system of sexual value."[9] Married heterosexuals who have sex only for the purposes of procreation are at the top of the hierarchy; gays and lesbians, whether monogamous or promiscuous, are in the middle; and persons who engage in the most stigmatized forms of sexuality such as commercial sex or sadomasochism are at the bottom, whether they are heterosexual or homosexual. For Rubin, this hierarchy is not fixed but shifts in response to social conflicts over sexuality. Thus some sexual practices that were once at the bottom or in the middle of the hierarchy have moved up and crossed over into the realm of social acceptability. More importantly, she argued that this system of social stratification cuts across other systems of social stratification such as those based on race, class, and gender and cannot be reduced to them or understood in their terms. Thus even a white middle-class man who engages in stigmatized sexual practices cannot escape sexual oppression, despite his racial, class, and gender privilege.

In *Gender Trouble*, Judith Butler challenged an even more basic assumption of much women's studies scholarship. For many women's studies scholars, the relationship between sex and gender is systemic. Sex is what Gayle Rubin in her classic 1975 essay "The Traffic in Women" called "the biological raw material" that culture transforms into gender.[10] This understanding of the relationship between sex and gender was foundational for the field because it enabled women's studies scholars to argue that the differences between men and women were not biologically determined but culturally constructed. Although Butler agreed

that gender was culturally constructed, she rejected the argument that anatomical sex was "raw material" worked over or processed by culture. Analyzing the experiences of Herculine Barbin, a nineteenth-century French hermaphrodite whose journals Michel Foucault edited and published in 1980, Butler reversed the feminist understanding of the relationship between anatomical sex and gender and argued that "sex itself is a gendered category."[11] For Butler, sex is not gender's biological foundation, but one of its most powerful effects. The category of sex works to naturalize the binary organization of gender by functioning as the seemingly neutral referent of gendered identity. Born with ambiguous genitals, Barbin was given a female sex assignment but was later forced by the courts to change her/his sex to male when her/his sexual involvements with women were discovered, thereby raising the specter of lesbianism. For Butler, the arbitrary way in which the French courts attempted to fix Barbin's gender and sexual identities showed that there is no necessary link between sex and gender, that gendered identity cannot be mapped back onto the body, and that society has an enormous stake in enforcing the belief that it can be.

Rubin's and Butler's theoretical interventions were crucial to the development of queer studies as a field. They enabled queer studies scholars to examine a wide range of nonnormative genders and sexualities from a more sophisticated feminist perspective. Focusing on practices and identities such as transgenderism, queer studies scholars have shown that sex, gender, and sexuality have no causal or necessary relation to each other but are mobile; that is, they can be configured in a variety of ways, none of which is "natural" or biologically mandated. Such an understanding has enabled more nuanced accounts of nonnormative genders and sexualities than either women's studies or lesbian and gay studies has provided. Gayle Rubin and Judith Halberstam, for example, have shown that lesbians exhibit a range of masculinities not adequately described or named by the category of butch.[12] Some butches may experience their masculinity as an essential part of their identity but have no desire to be anatomically male; others may wish to alter their bodies surgically and hormonally to bring them into alignment with their gender; still others may feel that their masculinity is purely an erotic identity they assume only in certain subcultural spaces such as bars and gyms. If such forms of masculinity have been stigmatized as freakish, unnatural, and deviant, that is because they demonstrate that masculinity is not necessarily the property of male heterosexuals. The belief that it is contributes to the consolidation and reproduction of patriarchal social arrangements. In highlighting this aspect of masculinity, this scholarship has made clear the value of the queer project to feminism.

Queer studies scholarship like Rubin's and Halberstam's opens up new ways of thinking about a wide range of subcultural practices and identities (butch lesbians who are bottoms, gay male queens who are tops, female-to-male transsexuals who identify as lesbian, male-to-female transsexuals who identify as gay, and so on) that previously were illegible or may have seemed incoherent insofar as they do not conform to the alignments of sex, gender, and sexuality that are normative in the subcultural contexts in which they emerge. Queer scholars have been particularly interested in transsexualism and intersexuality because they provide graphic illustrations of the institutional and discursive power required to maintain normative alignments of sex, gender, and sexuality. The institutional regulation of these forms of identity also suggests that on some level the dominant society recognizes that there is no natural or biological relationship between sex, gender, and sexuality and that it must vigorously enforce the belief that there is. For example, in the case of intersexuality pediatricians surgically assign infants born with a combination of male and female genitals a particular genital status, depending on their assessment of whether the genitals can be cosmetically altered to appear to be "normal" penises or vaginas.[13] The body of the intersexed baby, in other words, is surgically altered so that it conforms to the dominant understanding of how sex, gender, and sexuality should line up. Activist groups such as the Intersex Society of North America have protested the surgery and renamed it intersex genital mutilation because it can leave deep psychological scars, lasting physical pain, and often a loss of erotic function as an adult. As an alternative, they have proposed delaying the surgery until the intersexed infant is old enough to decide on her/his own or in consultation with parents and doctors whether to undergo it. Because these groups have engaged in strategies and forms of activism traditional to identity politics such as consciousness raising and community and institution building as well as set an agenda centered on gaining recognition of intersexuals as an oppressed group, their project may not seem especially queer. Yet because the identity they are in the process of forming directly challenges dichotomous constructions of sex, gender, and sexuality, it decidedly is.

Work on this and related topics represents the cutting edge of queer studies. But even as this work complicates our understanding of the relationship between sex, gender, and sexuality and the discursive and institutional power brought to bear on maintaining their normative alignment, it raises important questions with respect to race and class that queer studies as a field is only beginning to address. To begin with, what role do race and class play in both normative and nonnormative alignments of sex, gender, and sexualty? Are there ways in which they enable or constrain such alignments? Put another way, how do race and class determine a person's access to the material and cultural resources necessary for aligning sex, gender, and sexuality in both normative and nonnormative ways? Are there configurations of race and class that make it easier for some people than for others to transgress the normative alignment of sex, gender, and sexuality and with what consequences? Another important question involves the extent to which the erotics of nonnormative alignments of sex, gender, and sexuality depend on certain configurations of race and class. For example, does a middle-class Asian-American gay man's butch mode of embodiment have the same erotic purchase in gay sexual culture as a working-class African-American gay man's does? Indeed, is it even legible as butch? Finally, are there alignments of sex, gender, and sexuality that secure, or undermine, racial and class privilege? If so, what are they, and what are the institutional and discursive arrangements that keep them in place?

In some ways, women's studies scholars are better equipped than queer studies scholars to answer these questions. Over the last decade, women's studies has developed a mode of analysis, intersectionality, that has proved particularly useful for elucidating the complexity of identity.[14] In the 1980s feminists of color such as Barbara Smith, Audre Lorde, Cherríe Moraga, and Gloria Anzaldúa criticized the women's movement for deploying the category of woman in ways that elided important racial, class, and sexual differences among women.[15] They argued that women subordinated by one set of oppressions (for example, sexism and classism) might be empowered by another (for example, racism and homophobia). In reconceiving identity as the intersection of various axes of difference and subordination, this approach transformed women's studies, which now routinely examines without subordinating the intertwined categories of gender, race, class, sexuality, and nation. At the same time, however, women's studies scholars have been slow to incorporate the emphasis on the mobility of sex, gender, and sexuality central to queer scholarship. This may be because it is not yet clear whether that emphasis is compatible with intersectionality, which at least as a metaphor implies fixity or stasis. Nevertheless, both fields have much to gain by engaging in dialogue about the similarities and the differences in how they conceive identity. For example, taking into account the mobility of sex, gender, and sexuality might enable women's studies scholars to gain an even more complex understanding of the relationship between various categories of identity, one that does not see them as intersecting at a fixed point. And engaging the strengths as well as the weaknesses of intersectional analysis might help queer studies scholars develop a mode of analysis that extends their emphasis on mobility to race, class, and other crosscutting axes of difference.

Queering Power

Although, as we have already pointed out, much current scholarship on gender and sexuality in history, sociology, political science, and anthropology is written from a queer perspective, the social sciences have been less willing than the humanities to adopt the theoretical framework developed by queer studies scholars. This is partly because that framework depends on the conception of power elaborated by Michel Foucault in his book *The History of Sexuality, Volume One*, the English translation of which appeared in 1978. There Foucault advanced an argument about the formation of the social subject that challenged the dominant understanding of structure and agency in the social sciences, which have not taken up fully the poststructuralist critique of identity and continue to ascribe autonomy and intentionality to the subject. Like Katz, Weeks, and D'Emilio, who pioneered the social constructionist framework central to lesbian and gay studies, Foucault traced the transformation of sexuality in modern societies from a set of practices and relations governed by religious and secular law into a set of identities regulated by norms. Unlike Katz, Weeks, and D'Emilio, however, Foucault situated this transformation not in institutional change or in changes in political economy but in a shift in the regulatory apparatus of social life. Power in the Foucauldian account is discursive in nature and operates through the internalization of norms. For Foucault, the subject is constituted in and through the meaning systems, normative structures, and culturally prescribed taxonomies that circulate in society.

Contrary to what Foucault called "the repressive hypothesis" advanced by many on the political left during the 1960s, the history of sexuality in the modern period is not a history of censorship and prohibition that can be traced to the stultifying or "repressive" effects of capitalism, which supposedly needed to contain sexuality so that it did not interfere with the reproduction of labor. This was the argument made by Herbert Marcuse in his book *Eros and Civilization*, published in 1962, which profoundly influenced the strategies and goals of the gay liberation movement. Instead, the emergence of sexuality as a separate sphere of social life and a distinct domain of personhood was integral to the consolidation of a new and distinctly modern regime of power. For Foucault, power involves more than domination and repression; it is also productive in the sense that it opens up possibilities for action and is constitutive of the self. Individuals internalize the norms generated by the discourses of sexuality as they are circulated by social institutions such as schools, clinics, and the mass media and in so doing become self-regulating subjects, or subjects who police their own behavior so they will appear "normal." Moreover, although power is unevenly distributed and concentrated in various social institutions, it does not operate unidirectionally but is "everywhere." It comes from below as well as from above, and thus there is no escaping its reach. Foucault argues that because of this, power can never be overthrown, only resisted or reversed.

Foucault developed this conception of power partly to overcome what he saw as one of the limitations of the form of Marxism that dominated the radical movements of the 1960s and '70s. In marked contrast to those movements, which tended to advocate the overthrow of the state as the center of power, he argued that there is no single source of power in modern societies and political struggle needs to occur on multiple fronts. For him, discursive formations such as sexology were more important sources of power than the state because they generated the social norms internalized by individuals, especially those pertaining to sexuality.

Foucault's account of the creation of interiority via the discourses of sexuality complicated the tradition of lesbian and gay historiography that was emerging in the 1970s when the English translation of *The History of Sexuality* first appeared. As we saw above, the historical scholarship on lesbian and gay identities and communities curiously reproduced the coming-out process by constructing a modernist narrative that traced the emergence of a form of subjectivity in which desires, practices, and identities lined up neatly. Foucault constructed a more complicated historical narrative, however. For him, the category of the homosexual was a product of both the agents of social control (jurists, sexologists, and psychiatrists) who defined the category in the late nineteenth and early twentieth century and the social actors who "reversed" its deployment by mobilizing politically around it. Although this reversal challenged many of the dominant meanings of homosexuality, it also contributed to the consolidation of the binary organization of sexuality by reifying and further entrenching the category

of the homosexual. This example highlights the complex nature of discursive power for Foucault. Despite the fact that it shifted relations of power, the creation of a positive identity out of the category of the homosexual did not mark the homosexual's liberation from oppression. On the contrary, it created the need for further struggle, as it left intact the regime of power/knowledge that identified sexuality as one of the primary constituents of the self.

For social scientists, one of the limitations of this conception of power is that it minimizes or glosses over the role of institutions in organizing and regulating sexuality. Although social scientists also emphasize the role of discourses such as sexology in the construction of sexual identities, they focus more on the material realities and structural arrangements underlying the organization of sexuality. Foucault's account of the emergence of the modern homosexual, for example, foregrounds the discourses, or meaning systems, circulated by social institutions such as schools, churches, and clinics but it does not consider why those discourses were so influential in the construction of norms in the first place. By contrast, social scientists have argued for the need to analyze the institutional underpinnings of discursive formations, the fact that discourses originate in and are circulated by social institutions and that these underpinnings partly determine how much power they have in society. To cite just one example, the cultural authority of sexology, which created the sexual taxonomies partly responsible for the reorganization of sexuality in the nineteenth century, depended on the consolidation of the medical profession as one of the most powerful institutions in modern society. Social scientists have also shown that the institutional regulation of sexuality, particularly by the state, has had and continues to have a major impact on how sexuality is organized and experienced, especially in the age of AIDS.[16]

Given this emphasis on the importance of institutional analysis, it is not surprising that social scientists have been more reluctant than humanists to take up the category of queer. Indeed, many social scientists have argued that, despite its aspiration to transform lesbian and gay theory into a general theory of social relations, the concept of the social deployed by queer studies remains underdeveloped. As they point out, the primary goal of queer scholars in the humanities, whose scholarship continues to dominate the field, is to produce close readings of high and mass cultural texts, which is hardly surprising given these scholars' training in literary studies.[17] While such readings complicate our understanding of how homosexual desire shapes and is shaped by texts, this approach has been criticized by social scientists for following Foucault and privileging the role of discourse in the construction of sexuality over that of institutions. Because social scientific work on sexuality is more attentive to the ensemble of social relations in which sexuality is embedded, it can broaden queer understandings of the social by encouraging queer scholars to engage the materiality of discourse.

Sociology, for example, has long been concerned with the materialist basis of institutional power. It examines the unequal distribution of material resources among different social formations and analyzes how that unequal distribution affects the structure and functioning of social institutions and their capacity to shape people's lives and experiences. This sociological tradition points to the importance of taking into account the materialist basis of the discursive formations most often invoked by queer scholars in the humanities to elucidate the construction of sexual subjectivity. In arguing for the need to locate these formations in their materialist and institutional contexts, social scientists do not deny the role of the symbolic realm in constituting the social subject; rather, they seek to identify the institutional sources of discursive power, as well as how institutions themselves are in part discursively constructed.

Destabilizing the Subject: Queer Studies and Psychoanalysis

Adopting an approach that is attentive to both institutional and discursive forms of power, as social scientists have proposed, promises to further one of the primary goals of queer studies, to elucidate the social processes whereby sexual subjectivity is constituted. By contrast, queer scholars in the humanities have tended to rely on psychoanalytic models of subject forma-

tion that avoid institutional analysis. Through careful rereadings of Freud, queer theorists Leo Bersani and Teresa de Lauretis have shown in separate studies that psychoanalysis can make a significant contribution to queer studies, despite its normative tendencies and its role, especially in the US, in pathologizing nonnormative genders and sexualities.[18] Psychoanalytic models of subject formation enable queer scholars to address the psychic processes influencing the development of an individual's gender and sexuality. One of the most important insights of psychoanalysis is that the psychic realm has its own history and logic, and that it is in this realm, in addition to the social realm, that the body and our experience of it assumes meaning. What is central to psychoanalysis is the role of the unconscious in shaping sexuality. As the repository of fantasy and desire, the unconscious often conflicts with our conscious construction of our sexual identities, and this conflict between the two different levels may affect the alignment of an individual's sex, gender, and sexuality in ways that cannot be neatly read off the social environment. This may explain why queer studies scholars have been drawn to psychoanalytic models of subject formation. Such models complement the critique of identity-based activism and scholarship that distinguishes queer studies from lesbian and gay studies. Because of the refractory nature of the unconscious, the social subject cannot be understood as unified, self-knowing, or coherent but is always at risk of being destabilized.

By contrast, social scientists have shown little interest in the psychic component of sexuality or in the construction of sexual subjectivity. Instead, their interests primarily lie in elucidating the subcultural elaboration of sexual identities or in the construction of individual sexual identities via "symbolic interaction," an approach that examines how individuals acquire a fairly stable set of roles, commitments, and understandings of themselves as sexual subjects through interaction with others and interpretation of a historically and culturally variable system of sexual meanings.[19] As even many social scientists have recognized, one of the problems with this focus is that it inadvertently normalizes heterosexuality by treating homosexuality as a deviation from the norm that must be explained.[20] Social scientists who adopt this approach do not adequately consider how the coherence and stability of heterosexuality depends on the category of the homosexual.

But, as queer scholars in the humanities have pointed out, there is another problem with this approach. For these scholars, without an understanding of the refractory and contradictory nature of sexuality, the social scientific concept of the sexual seems as underdeveloped as the humanistic concept of the social. Social scientists tend to address the social processes associated with only one aspect of sexuality, sexual identity, and thus they do not fully take into account the messiness of sexuality, its potential to disrupt or unsettle identities. With their understanding of the role of fantasy and desire in the construction of sexual subjectivity, psychoanalytically oriented queer scholars are better equipped to understand this aspect of sexuality. At the same time, however, the contributions of psychoanalytically oriented queer studies scholarship are limited. As social scientists have suggested, psychoanalytic models of subject formation tend to privilege the role of the nuclear family in the construction of gender and sexual identity over that of other social institutions. For this reason, they not only indirectly affirm a normative understanding of child care and the distinction between public and private, but they also overlook the role of sexual subcultures in transforming sexual subjectivity. Moreover, it remains unclear how such models might elucidate the transnational flow of nonnormative genders and sexualities. For example, are the psychic processes queer studies scholars see as underlying the formation of gender and sexual identities universal? Or is the explanatory power of psychoanalysis limited to Western organizations of gender and sexuality?

Unsettling Disciplinary Knowledge: Organization

The primary goal of *Queer Studies* is to promote dialogue across the social sciences and the humanities, as well as women's studies and queer studies. As we have already stated, the debates we have been outlining were provoked by the category of queer as it traveled across the disciplines and encountered the different ways the disciplines approach the study of gender and sexuality. The selections comprising the anthology reflect this journey as well as suggest the distance that still needs to be traveled. As this occurs, the terms of the debates will surely change as well as the rubrics the different disciplines use to organize and produce knowledge about gender and sexuality. One purpose of the anthology, then, is to read the following selections in critical dialogue with the core concepts and current tensions highlighted by our introductory comments on the emergence and development of queer studies. Our hope is that this dialogue will extend, revise, and further complicate those concepts and in so doing resolve some of the intellectual and disciplinary tensions we have described but in the process create others equally as important and provocative. The interdisciplinary work represented in this volume suggests that even at this early stage in the field, the study of gender and sexuality is calling into question the usefulness of narrowly defined disciplinary boundaries and the organizing assumptions of the different disciplines that serve to police those boundaries.

The debates provoked by the category of queer raise the following questions. How might a broader conception of the social, one that takes into account the full range of social locations studied by social scientists, complicate the approach to gender and sexuality taken by queer theory and the humanities more generally? How might queer theory's understanding of sexuality as a fluid, mobile, and permeable terrain deepen and enrich social scientific accounts of sexual identities and subcultures? How might queer histories be written to capture the sometimes stable, sometimes fluid relationships between sex, gender, and sexuality and to situate these relationships in both institutional and discursive formations? How might a broader conception of the social complicate the psychoanalytic model of subject formation underlying queer work in the humanities privileging the discursive construction of sexuality? How might incorporating queer scholarship on nonnormative genders and sexualities help women's studies formulate a less static conception of identity? How might engaging intersectionality help queer studies scholars develop a mode of analysis that clarifies the role of race, class, and nation in determining normative and nonnormative configurations of sex, gender, and sexuality?

These questions have guided our selection of the readings. Although we realize that providing answers to them constitutes an enormous undertaking requiring ongoing conversations among social scientists and humanists, as well as women's studies and queer scholars, we have organized the anthology in such a way as to encourage scholars to begin addressing them. One way we have done this is by balancing essays written from a social scientific, humanistic, queer theoretical, and/or women's studies perspective. In this way, teachers and students with differing epistemological starting points can begin these dialogues with some degree of intellectual comfort. The ultimate goal, however, is to disrupt comfortable, and comforting, disciplinary assumptions.

We have organized the anthology according to the different social locations or sites of power where sexual agency is at once exercised and controlled. This organizational frame reflects a somewhat broader conception of the social than the one usually deployed by queer scholars working in the humanities. This conception recognizes that social influences apart from but constitutive of the subject exist at the level of community, culture, economy, the nation-state, and the global, and that these influences, particularly with regard to gender and sexuality, have different but related effects at each of these levels. This way of organizing the anthology also reflects a somewhat broader conception of the social subject than the one usually deployed by social scientists who study gender and sexuality. This conception makes clear that subjectivity is constituted at multiple social sites and, again, that these sites affect subjectivity in different but related ways. Our hope is that this organizational frame will provide a way to examine, evaluate, and extend the debates and controversies in the field in a way that builds on the field's already strong interdisciplinary orientation.

The anthology's organization also makes clear that sexuality rather than sexual identity is our point of departure. We feel that focusing on the ensemble of acts, expectations, pleasures, identity formations, and knowledges as it is formed at different social locations enables the most productive exploration of the debates and tensions in this still emerging field. Social scientists tend to study these different sites of power in isolation from each other, as though they were discrete entities, and we have deliberately selected readings that could be assigned to more than one of these sites to encourage a more complex approach that takes into account their interconnection. We have also wanted to promote dialogue across as well as within the anthology's different sections. These sites of power will be familiar to students in both the humanities and the social sciences in that they are held together by a general concern with the relationship between structure and agency and its attendant questions concerning the nature of power and the social subject, the stability of communities, and the role of institutions, culture, and history in the organization of social life. We hope that the juxtaposition of essays with different analytic starting points, methodologies, and theoretical frameworks will disrupt, or "queer," the thinking of social scientists and humanists around these questions as they relate to sexuality.

Because of capitalism's pivotal role in the construction of sexuality, everything from the regulation of bodies, desires, and affectivities to the production of new forms of gender and sexual expression, we would have liked to have included a separate section on the complicated relationship between capitalism and sexual agency but space prohibited us from doing so. Despite this omission, however, several of the essays engage capitalism's contradictory effects on the formation of sexual subjectivity either directly (for example, the essays by Kipnis, and Berlant and Warner) or indirectly (for example, the essays by Brody, Halberstam, and Robertson). Taken together, these essays show that capitalism with its profit and consumption imperatives valorizes some forms of sexual and gender expression over others. At the same time, however, they also show that any critique of capitalism must be tempered by an understanding of the opportunities it provides individuals and communities for resisting the dominant organization of gender and sexuality.

The selections are divided among four social sites that correspond to the different levels of society studied by social scientists. "Practices,

Identities, Communities" focuses on the level of community and how nonnormative genders and sexualities are formed at the micro-level of human association and social interaction. Even as these communities provide a vehicle for exercising sexual agency, they generate their own set of norms which in turn come to regulate and control how members resist the dominant organization of gender and sexuality. Despite this understanding of norms as both enabling and constraining, members exercise sexual agency partly beyond the reach of the larger institutional and discursive systems of power that enforce the normative construction of gender and sexuality. Because the level of community enables a focus on sexual agency and, in many instances, group solidarity and collective action, it is the social location at which lesbian and gay studies has traditionally worked.

The remaining social sites shift our attention to these systems of power and how these systems affect the construction of gender and sexuality. "The Cultural Construction of Gender and Sexuality" examines the impact of the cultural sphere on how people internalize, experience, and articulate their understandings of gender and sexuality. Culture, understood as systems of meaning that emerge from a dynamic interaction between sexual subjects and social structures, generates norms, which as we have seen can be simultaneously empowering and disempowering. Whether it be through film, newspapers, or the discourses generated by the state and other social institutions, cultural norms help define the limits of acceptability, the definitions and meanings associated with acceptable and unacceptable genders and sexualities, as well as supply the images we use to understand and construct our own gender and sexual identities. In this latter regard and as testament to the multifaceted and incomplete nature of power, these cultural norms also provide the images or ideas that enable resistance to heteronormative social structures, often in unpredictable ways. This unpredictability is due, in part, to the nature of the social subject, especially because of the role of the unconscious and the ways in which fantasy and desire interact with cultural processess in shaping gender and sexual identities.

The nation-state is another important level at which gender and sexuality are constructed.

"Sexual Citizenship and the Nation-State" focuses on the sexual and gender norms that serve as prerequisites for membership in the nation and how those norms are established, circulated, and transgressed. Not surprisingly, these processes entail not only the use of the legal apparatus of the state but perhaps more importantly the imbrication of political processes with many other forms of institutional and discursive power, those emanating from commercial capitalism, heteronormativity, and the informal policing of gender and sexuality through rumor, innuendo, and scandal. Even as the nation-state establishes and enforces these norms of belonging, spaces open up in which individuals can exercise sexual agency, partly in resistance to these dominant understandings of sexual citizenship. Again, the resistance registered is always incomplete due to the complex nature of discursive power and the constitutive role it plays in the formation of the social subject.

The nation-state has never been completely adequate as the analytical framework for the study of gender and sexuality, especially given the West's long history of colonialism and the circulation of people, goods, and ideas across geographical space and political borders since at least the sixteenth century. "Transnationalizing Sexualities" examines the organization of gender and sexuality in global terms and points to the role global processes play in the construction of gender and sexuality. Not surprisingly, these processes play themselves out in decidedly unequal terms, as those people, goods, and ideologies supported by a preponderance of material resources have more influence in the construction of gender and sexuality than those that do not.

This social site, moreover, throws into sharp relief many of the insights of queer studies, since approaching gender and sexuality from the perspective of transnationalism disrupts many of the assumptions regarding the organization of sexual practices, identities, and communities that have dominated the humanities and the social sciences, as well as the interdisciplinary fields of women's studies and lesbian and gay studies. In this regard, "Transnationalizing Sexualities" further problematizes notions of stable sexual subjectivities and identities, highlights the mobility of sex, gender, and sexuality, and foregrounds the role of race, class, and gender in structuring relations of power across national borders – all core features of queer studies. This social site, as well as the organizational frame of which it is a part, demonstrates the importance of a queer perspective for the study of gender and sexuality. This perspective, represented here by our introductory essay and the selections that follow, challenges conventional thinking about the relationship between sex, gender, and sexuality and moves us onto new terrain from which emerges a host of questions not only about gender and sexual identities but also about the nature of power, the relationship between structure and agency, and the formation, expression, and operation of a variety of modes of social difference.

Notes

1 The recent commercial success of such sexological studies as *Sex in America* and *The Social Organization of Sexuality*, both published in 1994 by the University of Chicago, a major university press, suggests that this tradition of sexology continues to thrive, even if only at the level of mass culture, perhaps because it provides a foil for morally or religiously based pronouncements about sexual behavior.

2 Influential formulations of the queer project and its relation to lesbian and gay studies are Eve Kosofsky Sedgwick, *Tendencies* (Durham, NC: Duke University Press, 1993); Judith Butler, *Bodies that Matter: On the Discursive Limits of "Sex"* (New York: Routledge, 1993), 223–42; Teresa de Lauretis, "Queer Theory: Lesbian and Gay Sexualities: An Introduction," *differences*, vol. 3, no. 2 (1991): iii–xviii; Michael Warner, "Introduction," *Fear of a Queer Planet* (Minneapolis: University of Minnesota Press, 1993), vii–xxxi; and Lisa Duggan, "Making It Perfectly Queer," *Socialist Review*, vol. 22, no. 1 (1992): 11–32.

3 John Howard, *Men Like That: A Southern Queer History* (Chicago: University of Chicago Press, 1999). For more on regional sexual formations, see Richard Phillips, Diane Watt, and David Shuttleton, eds., *De-Centering Sexualities: Politics and Representations Beyond the Metropolis* (London: Routledge, 2000); John Howard, ed., *Carryin' On in the Lesbian and Gay South* (New York: New York University Press, 1997); and

Karen Lee Osborne and William J. Spurlin, eds., *Reclaiming the Heartland: Lesbian and Gay Voices from the Midwest* (Minneapolis: University of Minnesota Press, 1996). For a different example of queer historiography, see Lisa Duggan, *Sapphic Slashers: Sex, Violence, and American Modernity* (Durham, NC: Duke University Press, 2000).

4 In addition to D'Emilio's *Sexual Politics, Sexual Communities*, representative examples of this historiographic tradition also include Elizabeth Lapovsky Kennedy and Madeline D. Davis, *Boots of Leather, Slippers of Gold: The History of a Lesbian Community* (New York: Penguin USA, 1993); George Chauncey, *Gay New York: Gender, Urban Culture, and the Making of the Gay Male World, 1890–1940* (New York: Basic Books, 1994); Esther Newton, *Cherry Grove, Fire Island: Sixty Years in America's First Gay and Lesbian Town* (Boston: Beacon, 1993); Marc Stein, *City of Sisterly and Brotherly Loves: Lesbian and Gay Philadelphia, 1945–1972* (Chicago: University of Chicago Press, 2000); and Brett Beemyn, ed., *Creating a Place for Ourselves: Lesbian, Gay, and Bisexual Community Histories* (New York: Routledge, 1997).

5 For a representative example of this work, see Elizabeth A. Povinelli and George Chauncey, ed., *Thinking Sexuality Transnationally* (Durham, NC: Duke University Press, 2000).

6 An important example of this strand of feminist thought is Carole Vance, ed., *Pleasure and Danger: Exploring Female Sexuality* (London: Routledge, 1984). See also Ann Snitow, Christine Stansell, and Sharon Thompson, ed., *The Powers of Desire: The Politics of Sexuality* (New York: Monthly Review Press/New Feminist Library, 1983).

7 Combahee River Collective, "A Black Feminist Statement," *All the Women Are White, All the Blacks Are Men, But Some of Us Are Brave*, eds. Gloria T. Hull, Patricia Scott Bell, and Barbara Smith (Old Westbury, NY: The Feminist Press, 1982), 16.

8 Gayle Rubin, "Thinking Sex: Notes for a Radical Theory of the Politics of Sexuality," Vance, *Pleasure and Danger*, 274.

9 Ibid., 280.

10 Gayle Rubin, "The Traffic in Women: Notes on the 'Political Economy' of Sex," *Toward an Anthropology of Women*, ed. Rayna R. Reiter (New York: Monthly Review Press, 1975), 165.

11 Judith Butler, *Gender Trouble: Feminism and the Subversion of Identity* (New York: Routledge, 1990), 7.

12 See Gayle Rubin, "Of Catamites and Kings: Reflections on Butch, Gender, and Boundaries,"

The Persistent Desire: *A Femme–Butch Reader*, ed. Joan Nestle (Boston: Alyson Publications, 1992), 466–82, and Judith Halberstam, *Female Masculinity* (Durham, NC: Duke University Press, 1998).

13 For a detailed account of intersexuality written from a queer perspective, see Suzanne Kessler, *Lessons from the Intersexed* (New Brunswick, NJ: Rutgers University Press, 1998).

14 The most influential discussion of intersectionality is Kimberle Williams Crenshaw, "Mapping the Margins: Intersectionality, Identity Politics, and Violence against Women," *Critical Race Theory*: *The Key Writings That Formed the Movement*, ed. Crenshaw, Neal Gotanda, Garry Peller, and Kendall Thomas (New York: New York University Press, 1995), and Crenshaw, "Beyond Racism and Misogyny: Black Feminism and 2 Live Crew," *Words That Wound*: *Critical Race Theory*, *Assaultive Speech*, *and the First Amendment*, ed. Mari J. Matsuda, Charles R. Lawrence, and Richard Degado (Boulder, CO: Westview Press, 1993), 111–32.

15 See, for example, Cherríe Moraga and Gloria Anzaldúa, ed., *This Bridge Called My Back*: *Writings by Radical Women of Color* (New York: Kitchen Table: Women of Color Press, 1984), and Barbara Smith, ed., *Home Girls*: *A Black Feminist Anthology* (New York: Kitchen Table: Women of Color Press, 1983).

16 See, for example, Jeffrey Weeks, *The Regulation of Sexuality since 1800* (London: Longman, 1981).

17 See, for example, Steven Seidman, ed., *Queer Theory/Sociology* (Malden, MA: Blackwell, 1996).

18 Leo Bersani, *Homos* (Cambridge, MA: Harvard University Press, 1995), and Teresa de Lauretis, *The Practice of Love*: *Lesbian Sexuality and Perverse Desire* (Bloomington: Indiana University Press, 1994).

19 Influential symbolic interactionist accounts of sexuality are Ken Plummer, *Sexual Stigma*: *An Interactionist Approach* (London: Routledge, 1975), and William Simon and John Gagnon, "A Sexual Scripts Approach," *Theories of Human Sexuality*, ed. James Greer and William O'Donahue (New York: Plenum, 1987).

20 See, for example, Seidman, *Queer Theory/Sociology*.

Part I

Practices, Identities, Communities

1

The Trouble with Harry Thaw

Martha M. Umphrey

On the one hand, this story is an archetypal tragedy: a heterosexual love triangle gone sour. On June 25, 1906, a young playboy murdered a celebrated New York architect and bohemian over a beautiful girl. Harry Thaw, son of a Pittsburgh railroad and mining magnate, shot Stanford White dead in the rooftop theatre of White's own creation, the old Madison Square Garden, because White had "ruined" Thaw's young wife Evelyn Nesbit, a well-known model and member of the famous Florodora Sextet, by "deflowering" her before marriage, perhaps violently. For the murder scandal of the (young) century Thaw was tried twice, ultimately declared insane in 1907, then released in 1915 – to widespread public approval – as a man of honor pursued unfairly by an overzealous system. Usually the story ends there.

On the other hand, the stock narrative in this melodrama of honor masks a much more complex configuration of sexual relations. If seduction and violence did mark the first sexual encounter between the sixteen-year-old Nesbit and the forty-eight-year-old White (in the form of a much-contested and recanted story of Nesbit's drugging and rape), theirs was a relationship also constituted and ultimately sustained for several years by White's paternalistic concern for Nesbit's health, education, and financial welfare and by an apparently genuine passion between them, fueled by an aestheticized eroticism.[1] And as for Harry Thaw – he was trouble. A man who claimed injury as a wronged husband, his own sexual escapades crossed boundaries of sex and age and often confused tenderness and violence. In this article I would like to muse upon the trouble that Thaw has given me as a historian of sexuality and the trouble he makes more generally for the project of lesbian/gay history.

In her 1934 autobiography *Prodigal Days*,[2] Evelyn Nesbit describes two brushes with male homosexuality. The first concerns Thaw, from whom she had been divorced:

> Then, in New York between seasons, we were shocked to open the papers, one morning, and read the glaring exposure of Thaw's sadistic cruelty to the Gump boy. Thaw had enticed the seventeen-year-old youth – who, the newspapers said, resembled me – to his secluded suite at the McAlpin, and there induced him to take a bath. Then Thaw, whose advancing paranoia had undoubtedly brought him to the stage where girls no longer interested him, had disrobed the hapless youth and beaten him unmercifully. The newspaper photographs of Gump's body were sickening, Thaw had forced the tortured boy to his knees, made him kiss his feet and call him "Master." Gump had tried to hurl himself out the seventeenth-story window.[3]

Only ten pages later Nesbit describes another scene, one involving a "young, gentle boy" named Jackie whom she asks to "park . . . on one of the couches" in her home until she overcomes her nervousness after an attack by thugs. Her second husband Jack Clifford, attempting to find cause for divorce action, has been "spying" on her from across the street.

> Clifford soon detected the fact that Jackie slept somewhere on the premises. One night he broke in with several witnesses. For a few moments there was wild confusion as the witnesses, groping about in the dark, knocked over a table, scattering silverware over the floor, and scaring Jackie half to death. He promptly threw a fit of hysterics, shrieking:

> "My sainted aunt! My reputation is ruined! The boys will swear I've been having an affair with a woman! They'll think I've turned queer! Oh, no! What shall I do?" And he swooned.

> The witnesses laughingly advised Clifford never to produce this "man" as evidence in a divorce action.[4]

In the first scene, male homosexuality is figured simultaneously as a set of attributes (Thaw's sadistic cruelty), a condition of developing perversion emerging from madness (his advancing paranoia), and a series of manipulative and violent acts (enticement, disrobing, beating, forced submission). In the second, male homosexuality is an identity established through social relations: the "pansy," the "quiet, gentle boy," inscribed in a male homosexual milieu built upon reputation and mutual recognition, unrecognizable in the public sphere of legal action as a "man" because he does not participate in a heterosexual economy of affairs, spy raids, and divorce actions.[5]

In the first, attributes, conditions, acts; in the second, identity. Taken together, these scenes pose certain difficult questions about the proper parameters of the practice of lesbian/gay history. What do we look for? What do we see? How might our historical methods produce certain meanings about homosexual identity or behavior, and how might other meanings be excluded in that very process of production? As a matter of lesbian/gay history, how should we approach the far reaches and intermittent eruptions of same-sex acts in any given historical moment?

This article is meant to be a brief theoretical musing, rather than a historical exploration, of the questions and tensions embodied in Nesbit's

vignettes. Within this symptomatic reading of specific moments in her narrative, one might consider Jackie as a historically identifiable gay male subject, self-identified, inscribed within a locatable homosexual subculture, a campy queen, parodying femininity in a self-conscious, recognizable performance. He can fear being "queered" into straightness because his identity *is* stable. As a historian (if I can substantiate Nesbit's account) I can find and recuperate Jackie as a forebear, a sign that "we" as homosexuals were there just as we are here now, perhaps differently constructed (pansy, not queen[6]), but nonetheless historical agents whose sexual lives, once unveiled, in some sense enable and justify our own.[7] Whether homosexuality is innate or socially constructed, Jackie (or someone like Jackie about whom we have more information) can relatively accurately be identified as a gay man in modern New York City.[8]

But what of Harry Thaw? Given that he engaged in same-sex sexualized activity, can or should he be a "proper" object of study for historians of homosexuality, and if so in what way? And what does finding Harry Thaw do to lesbian/gay history? His presence as a sexual outlaw, neither precisely straight nor precisely gay, tests the parameters of lesbian/gay history and even, perhaps, "queer" history (the definition of which I'll take up later). Is he situated sexually and culturally in such a way as to be a part of "our" history? As a rich playboy who married Nesbit, murdered White, escaped execution with an insanity plea, took pleasure in whipping not only Nesbit and Gump but also (at least allegedly) many others, he may be an unsavory ancestor for many, uneasily situated near the project of lesbian/gay history and easily erased (perhaps with relief).

No doubt about it: Harry Thaw was and is trouble. But as Judith Butler has impishly suggested, "trouble is inevitable and the task, how best to make it, what best way to be in it."[9] To countenance Thaw as a legitimate subject for lesbian/gay historians is to pose difficult questions about, and to trouble the assumptions embedded in, our methodological stances. More often than not, lesbian/gay historians participate in a model of history that relies on the recuperation and celebration of homosexual subjectivity and thus implicitly promotes a partial view of the history of sexuality. Where we locate identity, we can find oppression; where we locate oppression, we can find resistance. This analytical move is crucial to the politics of an antihomophobic history, but it remains caught in a binary logic that, if left uncontested, will always and only accord gay men and lesbians "minority" status. By making the marked half of the hetero/homosexual binary visible, we paradoxically gain recognition while constantly reinscribing the terms of our own disempowerment in reified identity categories. As such, the identity politics that has been so crucial to the birth of a specific lesbian/gay history of sexuality, essential as a foundation from which to ask questions about compulsory heterosexuality and homosexual resistance, must be simultaneously supplemented by a critical history of sexuality that unpacks the assumptions that inform the very construction of that foundation.[10] Harry Thaw as the impossible subject of lesbian/gay history refuses the binary politics of identity, calling into question the completeness of a historiographic gesture based upon stable identity categories as epistemological foundations for history.

I say that Thaw is an impossible subject for lesbian/gay history. Yet initially I became interested in the Thaw trials partly *because* Thaw was rumored to be homosexual. Rumor always engenders naive fascination, and once one is in the thick of things, plunged into a project, one then becomes responsible for grappling with conundrums and contradictions revealed as the fog clears. If my recuperable gay man transmogrifies into a site of incoherent and indeterminate sexual identity, that isn't his fault.

But perhaps it is in the end to my benefit that Thaw is so slippery a character; by exploding easy categories, by raising the possibility of a homosexualized subplot, his unstable presence can help to reveal the overdetermined and constructed nature of this very heterosexual melodrama. Having posed that possibility, let me step back to narrate the phenomenological path I followed as I tried to characterize his place in my larger work on the intersections of gender, sexuality, madness, and criminal law; I will then move to a broader discussion of the implications of queer theory for lesbian/gay history.

Harry Thaw as a Gay Man

I didn't exactly go looking for a gay man when I began working on the Thaw trials, but alerted by quiet yet clear allusions in various secondary works to Thaw's interest in "both sexes,"[11] I began envisioning him as gay, as someone whose primary sexual interests might lie with men, whose marriage was a masquerade of those desires. "Gay" in this context functions to some extent as metaphor, making an identity of certain same-sex (but not always same-sex) practices – a projection of desire on my part for a story lost to history, suppressed by the fragile propriety of other historians. The story of Thaw's homosexuality, I naively thought, might be his "true" story, closeted by post-trial public constructions of Thaw as a man of honor avenging his wife's sexual ruin at the hands of a beast. Or it might be the clue that would unlock the puzzle of Thaw's madness: perhaps repressing a shadow-life broke his mind. Even if Thaw weren't Oscar Wilde, weren't truly and completely gay, perhaps he should be labeled bisexual, someone whose desire for other men was partly, if inconsistently, constitutive of his identity.

Much of this was speculative early thinking, making Thaw's same-sex relations into something talismanic, beguiling. Without much evidence, I layered Thaw with displaced identities and insincere actions in the name of antihomophobic history. Further, this tack presupposed certain categories of identity (homosexual, bisexual) as stable and coherent, when in fact Thaw is a prime example of their very instability and incoherence. His obsession with Evelyn Nesbit and his occasional forays into homosexual sadism belie any overreading of his identity as that of "a homosexual," however one might define that term.

Harry Thaw as Sadist

Having discarded sexual object-choice as the best means of understanding Thaw's identity, I began to attend to Thaw's behavior, which more obviously labeled him a sadist than a homosexual. Nesbit herself dwelled upon that behavior at length in *Prodigal Days*, most vividly in her chapter "Nightmare of Sadism," in which she describes Thaw's attack with a horsewhip while the two were staying in the secluded and gothic Schloss Katzenstein, somewhere in Austria.[12] Explicitly invoking the Marquis de Sade, she describes in almost pornographic detail his entry into her room one night, stark naked, his glassy dilated eyes, his lashing of her body, his nails in her flesh. When the attack ended he asserted in words what he had already asserted in deed: "You are too impudent. You are entirely too impudent. I had to punish you. . . . If we were living in ancient times, you would be my slave." Immediately after that scene Nesbit discovers Thaw masturbating (she can only call it a "disgusting habit" or "vicious pleasure"[13]). Nesbit later attributes Thaw's rage to cocaine addiction and suggests that his masturbation might have contributed to his insanity.[14]

In this passage Thaw's sexuality thus seemed to revolve more around assertions of power and the retention of control over his objects of desire, even as those assertions of power required simultaneously a loss of control, a frenzy. His sexuality and his violent disposition thus intertwined, it was easy for me to follow Nesbit in claiming a moral high ground. If Nesbit could easily explain Thaw's sadism with drug addiction, I could just as easily explain it with a feminist analysis of gender relations. Thaw's obsessive jealousy of Nesbit's relations with White and other men, his need to force her submission, his interest in younger, relatively disempowered men (whom he offered to "educate"[15]) all inscribe him within a gendered narrative in which power is related to masculinity and violence. "I would be a prince," he said to Nesbit, "and you would dance and serve me, wearing bracelets and anklets."[16]

This kind of analysis, though, is a kind of photographic negative of my naive recuperative stance in its ethical certainty. If Thaw as a "homosexual" was a positive historical find when viewed only through the lens of lesbian/gay history, someone to be rescued from approbation and situated within "our" genealogy, then Thaw as a sadist was a find in a slightly different sense when captured through the lens of feminism: someone who could be analyzed critically as a man obsessed with power over a woman whose own much-circulated image held extraordinary sway over a fascinated public. Both interpretations make more of Thaw than he himself was. Further, my stance toward this material made it impossible for me to separate artificially a recuperative lesbian/gay from a critical feminist point of view.[17] Gender and sexuality, though by no means coextensive, are in fact inextricably entangled (at least as they are currently constituted).[18] Yet the moral weights of each pulled in opposite directions. Was Harry Thaw a hero or beast? What if he were both? Ironically, hasn't that been the question about Harry Thaw all along, both to his contemporaries and to me?

The Libertine, the Pervert, the Madman

Perhaps to escape the heavy moralism of both positions, I decided to look more closely at historically specific typologies of Thaw's behavior. Thaw seemed to fit well, for example, in the shoes of the eighteenth-century rake or libertine, a manly man interested in both women and boys. According to Randolph Trumbach, libertines who engaged in homosexual intercourse were nonetheless not "homosexual" in the sense of the "molly," the eighteenth-century English precursor to the "queen." In fact, Trumbach argues, "they were secretly held in awe for the extremity of their masculine self-assertion, since they triumphed over male and female alike."[19] His masculinity bolstered by sadistic practices, Thaw surely might have identified more with the libertine than the homosexual, particularly the "homosexual" figured by Jackie.

The "libertine," though a label historically misplaced, is by its very multiplicity and fluidity able to capture more of the sexually transgressive character of Thaw's life. By the early twentieth century, Thaw was described by Nesbit and others not as a libertine but as a pervert.[20] Unlike Jackie, more properly labeled an "invert" in turn-of-the-century medical terminology because of his inherent homosexuality, Thaw could be labeled a "pervert" because his homosexual behavior was lust-driven.[21] More broadly, Nesbit linked Thaw's perversion to his sadism (with both men and women) and masturbation, breezily parroting popular psychoanalytic discourse on "sex abnormalities."[22]

Both the libertine and the pervert are defined by virtue of their excessive sexuality, their polymorphous and uncensored relationship to desire, fantasy, and enactment.[23] It is no wonder, then, that such excess flowed easily into constructions of madness; "the unexplained extravagences of a sexual pervert," wrote Dr. Allan McLane Hamilton in 1896, "may raise the question of insanity."[24] Ironically, although Harry Thaw was indeed acquitted of Stanford White's murder on the basis of insanity, that acquittal was based not on a narrative of Thaw's excesses, but (at least partly) on a narrative of White's. Thaw claimed that he shot "the beast" in order to rid New York of a "moral pervert" who had ravished young girls and ruined his wife,[25] and in his first trial he tried to rely on the "unwritten law" that allowed juries to acquit a wronged husband (the trial ended with a hung jury). Indeed, Thaw became a popular hero in the eyes of many who endorsed his act as a defense of honor.[26]

Harry Thaw as a libertine, a pervert, or a madman – the specificity of these discursive identity categories stands Thaw in oblique relation to the hetero/homo dyad I had initially imposed on him. But if I had not envisioned Thaw as a gay man at the outset, would I have seen these more specific identities that lurk in the shadows of lesbian/gay history? What kind of historiographic stance might both do justice to this specificity of Thaw's excesses and transgressions, while underscoring the ways in which Thaw's practices unravel his own insistence on a particularly normative heterosexuality? It seems to me that Thaw is *not* "obviously" gay in the way lesbian/gay history imagines its objects of recuperation, but that a history of Thaw and his sexual practices could also be a history that, broadly speaking, locates a refusal of compulsory heterosexuality.

QUEER [of doubtful origin]

1 Strange, odd, peculiar, eccentric, in appearance or character. Also, of questionable character, suspicious, dubious.
2 (Thieves' cant.) Bad; worthless.
3 a. To quiz or ridicule; to puzzle. b. To impose on, swindle, cheat.
4 To spoil, put out of order.[27]

Although few instances of the word "queer" exist before 1700, the term long predates the confrontational gay and lesbian politics of the 1980s and 1990s and the insult appropriated by those politics. The word's classic definition is not explicitly political, though it contains an incipient politics by describing a process of making the normal strange. None of the classic definitions is a noun. Rather, as an adjective, "queer" describes a process of "queering," a distorting, a making the solid unstable. Or at most a condition of queerness; when Jackie exclaims "The boys will think I've turned queer!" he means: they will think I've shifted, I've been spoiled, I've become something other to what they thought was my real being.

In that sense, to talk about "queerness" is to talk about a relation between something perceived to be solid or stable and its destabilization into something else. The "solid" need not be the "normal" and the something else need not be the "pathologized." Rather, the solid is the commonly understood, the taken-for-granted in any given context, standing in relation to its distortion. One focuses not on the identities of those labeled normal and those labeled abnormal, but on the oblique relation between two (or more) identities, positions, or practices that have no certain and timeless definition or content. To see Jackie turning queer requires that one perceive a relationship between the supposed stability of his homosexual identity and its distortion by a heterosexual encounter into something else, something not quite heterosexual. Thus, the "queered" position is related to and dependent upon the stable position, rather than being a separate position in itself. It undermines the stability of the primary term and opens up the possibility that the solid has never been solid at all.

To theorize queerness in relation to lesbian/gay history is thus to move away from a history of stable identity categories. On one level, such a project is not new; it is suggested by work in lesbian/gay history that emphasizes the historically contingent and discursive nature of identity categories and the invented nature of "the homosexual." As Foucault has argued compellingly in *The History of Sexuality*, sexual identity is constructed within and by discursive fields; sexuality is (in Judith Butler's formulation) a historically specific organization of power, discourse, bodies, and affectivity.[28] "The homosexual" as such is an invented, not innate, characterization of specific organizations of sexual behavior. In that Foucauldian sense, Harry Thaw could be neither a "true" homosexual nor a "true" heterosexual, naturally and innately; for that matter, neither could Jackie. Rather, Jackie's identity as a "pansy" was a product or effect of certain early twentieth-century medico-legal and popular discourses about homosexuality as a congenital defect or a result of incomplete sexual development.

Even beyond historicizing identity, though, "[t]he task," as Judith Butler formulates Foucault's position, "is to call into question the explanatory gesture that requires a true identity and, hence, a mistaken one."[29] Jennifer Terry, in her article "Theorizing Deviant Historiography," takes up that project in calling for new methodological practices that attempt not to rediscover lost homosexuals, but to trace "deviant subject formation."[30] This deviant history, according to Terry, "exposes not the events and actors elided by traditional history, but instead lays bare the processes and operations by which these elisions occur" to theorize a "counterdiscursive position of history-telling which neither fashions a new coherence, nor provides a more inclusive resolution of contradicting 'events.'"[31]

> Instead of positing a fixed deviant subject position, the archivist finds a provisional position corresponding to a discursively fashioned outlawed or pathologized sexual identity – the location from which a resistant historiography can be generated.[32]

Terry exposes the process of deviant subject formation by reading the texts of elite discourses subversively, attentive to rupture and discontinuity, in search of signs of deviance. Specifically, her readings of a 1930s study of "sex variants" (i.e., homosexuals) emphasize the *process* of identity construction that occurs as medical experts and the objects of their study interact. She analyzes the ways in which expert interpretations of the appearance and behavior of various lesbians and gay men are consciously subverted by the characterizations lesbians and gay men give themselves. As such, although Terry does not use the term, her work explores the ways in which these "sex variants" *queer* the experts' interpretations of them, resist their pathologizing tendencies, and distort their rigidly constructed taxonomies of sex variance. "Deviance" becomes defined implicitly as emerging from the dialogized meanings produced by the intersection of pathologizing medical discourses and the self-consciously resistant counter-discourses of homosexual subjects.

Yet Terry narrows her reading of the "deviant" from the outlawed or pathologized (a definition of deviance she produces that is broad enough to include someone like Harry Thaw) to the homosexual subject that resists pathologization. Thus, she veers back to a politics of identity and resistance that still requires homosexual subjectivity to be imagined as stable and coherent, if differentiated along the lines of gender, race, class, and age. As a result, Terry's formulation of deviant historiography requires a level of self-conscious resistance that Thaw does not and cannot evince because he does not belong to the discursively constructed category "homosexual."

The problem remains: Harry Thaw is a man who engaged in same-sex relations, but cannot be assimilated into even the broadest of current historiographic models. If both lesbian/gay history and deviant historiography explore the history of homosexual subjectivity, then Harry Thaw makes trouble for both those models, destabilizing the discursive categories that either I or his contemporaries might impose upon him. Thaw was, one might say, a queer one: strange, odd, peculiar, eccentric. Unfixable and unidentifiable as a homosexual, both to contemporaries and to historians, he is at best a dubious subject for lesbian/gay history – hardly one to recuperate for his conscious resistance to homophobic oppression. To engage Harry Thaw, one must redirect one's attention from the search for lesbian/gay identity toward a reexamination of the coherence of those discursively constructed identity categories in and of themselves.

Given Thaw's poor fit with heterosexual/ homosexual identity categories, perhaps he should be recharacterized as a sexual outlaw, one outside the law in two senses: he violated social mores by standing outside medico-legal prohibitions against excess in sexuality and violence, and he stood outside the politico-historiographic laws of identity formation, which require a self-conscious association with the group subject to historical excavation. Of dubious character, Thaw made no defense of "the love that dare not speak its name"; he injected the horror of nonconsensual violence into a potentially subversive sexuality; his only self-consciousness was of his own class privilege ("I am Harry Thaw of Pittsburgh," he used to say at every introduction, as if that was justification enough for any behavior). Outside the laws of justice and history, Harry Thaw was and is a swindler and, not the least, a swindler of lesbian/gay history – one who catches us off guard, then slips away.

The point, then, cannot be to capture Thaw within or banish him from "our" history. To do so would be to impose upon him an identity composed by our own ethical choices; though they are opposite gestures, both capture and banishment replicate the logic of identity politics that Thaw escapes. Rather, the point must be to call that very logic into question without losing sight of Thaw's connection to the politics of sexuality.

A history of sexuality inflected with queer theory can grapple with such questions. The term "queer" undoes itself, refuses a set taxonomy or stable definition. Its politics emerge from the immorality and shame woven into the word itself, just as shame is felt in the body down to one's very sinews and bones. As a political weapon, the word itself has been queered from the wholly approbative and insulting to the celebrated and deployed, a "sly and ironic weapon."[33] If it can be an identity at all, it is a doubled identity: the shamed and the transformative (mis)appropriation of that shame.[34] Yet more aptly, the word is an adjective or verb, not a noun; it is strange or making strange, of questionable character or the performing of that questionable character.

Although one can claim queerness as an identity emerging out of a specific politics, can narrate the stories of other queers, can join Queer Nation, and so on, nothing in the term itself *prescribes* the content of that identity; in fact the term is defined by its very instability, its excess. Indeed, "queer identity" is in itself paradoxical because queerness is dependent upon fracturing the very notion of identity, including a monolithic and unproblematized lesbian/gay identity. Identity instead is envisioned as variable, provisional, constructed; queerness signals the fluidity and contingency of deviance, a broad category of outlawry that is defined in relation to the "normal" in any specific historical moment, rather than a positive identity in itself. Similarly, although one can celebrate queerness or queering just as one can celebrate lesbian/gay identity, nothing in the term *requires* celebration for the politics of queerness to be effective. In other words, queer history can queer the celebratory politics of lesbian/gay history; out of that queering can come a hard-boiled history, one with no *necessary* moral center, posing new questions and revealing different sexual practices in the name of exploding compulsory heterosexuality.[35]

To that extent, perhaps such a history might better be termed a "queered" history so as to underscore its processual or adjectival nature, a mode of reasoning that stands in relation to sexuality much as "feminist" stands to "woman." So envisioned, a queered history can keep in view the paradoxes and complexities, indeed the historical specificity of sexual practices, so as to reveal contestation within categories of sexual identity even as it promotes antihomophobic inquiry. As such, a queered history takes instability and scandal as its subjects. It can thus accommodate the outlawry of Harry Thaw because it does not require a stable, self-conscious homosexual identity as its political foundation; it only requires a refusal to respect the laws of compulsory heterosexuality. Thus, the self-consciousness embedded in queered history is not necessarily the self-consciousness of the historical subject,[36] but that of the historian interested in tracing the history of sexual outlawry as a way to critique homophobia and compulsory heterosexuality.[37]

Of what might queered histories consist, beyond biographies of sexual outlaws? To the extent that "queerness" escapes the logic of identity, queered histories might be histories of sexual practices that stand in an oblique relation to the "normal" or "natural." More generally, queered history might be conceived as a history of scandal and its consequences: a history of rumor; a history of blackmail; a history of lust and its particular inscriptions in medico-legal discourses; a history of excess and its masquerades. In Harry Thaw's case, for example, one might inquire into how the overdetermined nature of his public obsession with masculine honor and moral propriety functions as a particular kind of masquerade for the sexual outlaw's private vices. One might examine society scandal sheets to explore the circulation and effect of rumors on subsequent legal interpretations of Thaw's character. One might explore the repression of sexuality in contemporaneous accounts of Thaw's sadism (the excerpts from Nesbit's book, for example, allude to, but ultimately elide, the sexual content of Thaw's attacks). Or one might trace the relationship between constructions of sexual excess and constructions of insanity as they intersect in the notion of perversion. And from a confluence of these kinds of inquiries might flow the ultimate in queered historical projects: critical histories of heterosexuality.

Fundamentally, doing queered history is a scandalous project in itself. Queering history means acknowledging that the processes of history are unstable, the search for exemplary historical subjects always incomplete. It requires on our part a constant re-engagement, a constant questioning of our own assumptions about the "proper" subject of history. As Butler has suggested,

> If the term "queer" is to be a site of collective contestation, a point of departure for a set of historical reflections and future imaginings, it will have to remain that which is, in the present, never fully owned, but always and only redeployed, twisted, queered from prior usage and in the direction of urgent and expanding political purposes. . . .[38]

Moreover, doing queered history may require engagement with unsavory characters who, like Harry Thaw, have an attenuated but identifiable relationship with a critique of compulsory heterosexuality. Even if Thaw cannot be conceived as a gay man, historians, by calling attention to the way Thaw's sexual practices disrupt, undermine, and unmask the overdetermined love-triangle narrative promoted by this trial (and others more recent), can denaturalize and desta-

bilize public representations of compulsory heterosexuality.[39]

This historical gesture can further an anti-homophobic politics by revealing the constructed nature of heterosexuality even in the absence of lesbian/gay subjectivity. If, as Eve Sedgwick says, "queer" is a word that cannot be sanitized[40] – at least to the extent that it suggests a process of doing history, an antihomophobic mode of inquiry – then those who do queered history can locate such disruptions in the hegemony of heterosexuality only by guarding against the impulse to colonize or overinvest in our subjects, to celebrate or denigrate them without exploring their potential for reinventing and rewriting the history of sexuality. Queerness is about making the given seem strange. It is not necessarily content to be celebrated, for to be celebrated is to be identified, and to be identified is to be stabilized, to lose the nimble stance of critique.

Notes

This essay has benefitted tremendously from the thoughtful readings of Anne Herrmann, Austin Sarat, Lawrence Douglas, Nasser Hussain, and Karen Merrill.

1 This last dimension of their relationship is legendary. Nesbit became known as "the girl in the red velvet swing" after testifying at Thaw's trial that, during their first meeting, White sat her in a red velvet swing hung from a high ceiling, then pushed her higher and higher until her feet pierced a paper parasol suspended above. The scene is made a metaphor for their sexual passion in the 1955 film *The Girl in the Red Velvet Swing*, for which Nesbit worked as a consultant.

2 Nesbit wrote (possibly with the help of ghost-writers) two autobiographies, *The Story of My Life* (1914) and *Prodigal Days: The Untold Story* (1934). Both should be read as highly partial accounts of Nesbit's life, written as attempts to regain the respectability she lost after testifying at Thaw's trials. I cite them not as historically accurate accounts of events, but as texts to be read for their lay characterizations of sexual practices and identities.

3 Nesbit, *Prodigal Days*, 279. See also articles in *New York Times* (3–16 July 1919).

4 Ibid., 289.

5   In both, however, normative heterosexuality is reinforced by substitution, as Nesbit slyly suggests that she herself is the proper sexual referent in each case. The Gump boy resembles her (and she has in fact also been the object of Thaw's sadism) and is made a sexual object only because Thaw's madness has progressed to the point of inversion; Jackie, who *should* in fact be having the affair with her (given her reputation for beauty), can only be made a joke, a comical substitute for a woman who, by virtue of his identity, foils the "real" man in the scene, Nesbit's husband Clifford.

6   "Pansy" was a term used in the 1920s and 1930s to describe an effeminate man, "inverted" in his gender role (and thus sexuality). See George Chauncey, *Gay New York* (New York: Basic Books, 1994), 15.

7   For this important recuperative gesture, see (among many) Martin Duberman, Martha Vicinus, and George Chauncey, Jr., eds., *Hidden From History: Reclaiming the Gay and Lesbian Past* (New York: Meridian, 1990); Jonathan Ned Katz, *Gay American History: Lesbians and Gay Men in the U.S.A.*, rev. ed. (New York: Meridian, 1992); John D'Emilio, *Sexual Politics, Sexual Communities: The Making of a Homosexual Minority in the United States, 1940–1970* (Chicago: University of Chicago Press, 1983); Lillian Faderman, *Odd Girls and Twilight Lovers: A History of Lesbian Life in Twentieth-Century America* (New York: Columbia University Press, 1991); Chauncey, *Gay New York*.

8   For a brilliant and creative example of this search for gay ancestors, see Neil Bartlett, *Who Was that Man? A Present for Mr. Oscar Wilde* (London: Serpent's Tail, 1988); see also Chauncey, *Gay New York*.

9   Judith Butler, *Gender Trouble: Feminism and the Subversion of Identity* (New York: Routledge, 1990), vii.

10 At the same time, however much one might put stable identities into question, they remain crucial in the production of knowledge about past and current configurations of sexuality. To say that identity cannot be stabilized does not mean that it does not exist or have force in the world. I am reminded of a foray into a local bookstore, one well-versed in post-structuralist theory and (recently) spatially organized accordingly. Hoping to find recent books on abortion, I searched in vain for the store's section on "women" or "gender." It had been erased, I was told; I might look under law, or sociology, or sexuality (which meant "queer" or "spectacular," not "traditional" reproductive history).

"Women" having been recently exploded as a stable category of analysis (quite rightly in my view), I was left bookless.

11 See, for example, Frederick L. Collins, *Glamorous Sinners* (New York: Ray Long & Richard R. Smith, Inc., 1932); Paul R. Baker, *Stanny: The Gilded Life of Stanford White* (New York: The Free Press, 1989).

12 During Thaw's first trial, the prosecution introduced an affidavit signed by Nesbit alleging the facts of this attack. *New York Times* (16 March 1907), 2:2. Although Nesbit repudiated the substance of the affidavit during the trial, her later reclamation of the incident seems believable in light of other allegations against Thaw and his use of a horsewhip in subsequent legal proceedings. In addition to the Gump incident, see, for example, *Estardus v. Thaw*, 245 N.Y.S. 781 (1930).

13 Nesbit, *Prodigal Days*, 110–12.

14 Ibid., 286, 113.

15 See Collins, *Glamorous Sinners*, 237.

16 Nesbit, *Prodigal Days*, 111.

17 Feminism is of course quite capable of a recuperative stance itself, as lesbian/gay history is capable of a critical one in other contexts.

18 For an extended analysis of this problematic, see Eve Kosofsky Sedgwick, *Epistemology of the Closet* (Berkeley: University of California Press, 1990), 27–35.

19 Randolph Trumbach, "The Birth of the Queen: Sodomy and the Emergence of Gender Equality in Modern Culture, 1660–1750," in Duberman, Vicinus, and Chauncey, Jr., eds., *Hidden from History*, 131.

20 See Foucault: "Underneath the libertine, the pervert . . . on friendly terms with delinquents and akin to madmen." Michel Foucault, *The History of Sexuality, Volume 1: An Introduction* (New York: Vintage, 1980), 39–40.

21 On this distinction see Jeffrey Weeks, "Inverts, Perverts, and Mary-Annes: Male Prostitution and the Regulation of Homosexuality in England in the Nineteenth and Early Twentieth Centuries," in Duberman, Vicinus, and Chauncey, Jr., eds., *Hidden From History*, 205.

22 Nesbit, *Prodigal Days*, 112, 306.

23 Thaw was excessive in most aspects of his life. He once, for example, gave a dinner for over 100 women (no other men were present) over which he spent $500 a plate and $700 on jewelry for each woman. He would throw violent tantrums in the finest restaurants, drink several bottles of champagne in a sitting, send lavish anonymous gifts to chorus girls.

24 Quoted in Jonathan Ned Katz, *Gay American History*, 63.

25 Thaw apparently called White a "moral pervert" while trying to convince Anthony Comstock, the famous anti-smut activist, to investigate White and others. See Baker, *Stanny*, 351.

26 After being declared sane in 1915, for example, Thaw returned home to Pittsburgh and was met by a cheering crowd of over 1,000. *New York Times* (20 July 1915), 1:4.

27 Condensed from *The Oxford English Dictionary*, 2nd ed., v. XII (Oxford: Clarendon Press, 1989), 1014–15. This most recent edition adds a new definition: "Of a person (usu. a man): homosexual."

28 Butler, *Gender Trouble*, 92.

29 Judith Butler, "Sexual Inversions," in Domna Stanton, ed., *Discourses of Sexuality: From Aristotle to AIDS* (Ann Arbor: University of Michigan Press, 1992), 357.

30 Jennifer Terry, "Theorizing Deviant Historiography," *differences* 3:2 (1991): 55–74.

31 Ibid., 56.

32 Ibid., 59.

33 Anonymous Queers, "Queers Read This," in William B. Rubenstein, ed., *Lesbians, Gay Men, and the Law* (New York: New Press, 1993), 47.

34 On shame as constitutive of performing a (non-essential) queer identity, see Eve Kosofsky Sedgwick, "Queer Performativity: Henry James's *The Art of the Novel*," *GLQ* 1:1 (1993).

35 "Queer" as it is classically defined does not require this kind of anti-homophobic analysis; thus a "queer history" so defined could encom-
pass non-normative heterosexual practices. Nevertheless, "queer historians" of the present moment generally are allied with a confrontational lesbian/gay politics (though some might refuse the label of "gay male" or "lesbian"); to the extent that "queer" retains those current meanings, a queer history will incorporate them into its historiographic frame.

36 Although one could do a history of self-named queers as historical subjects; see Chauncey, *Gay New York*, esp. chap. 4, "The Forging of Queer Identities and the Emergence of Heterosexuality in Middle-Class Culture."

37 To that extent, queer history is akin to feminist history in that it is defined by the critical stance of the historian rather than the object of study.

38 Judith Butler, "Critically Queer," *GLQ* 1:1 (1993): 19.

39 In this respect one might ask of the O. J. Simpson case, who was Ronald Goldman, anyway? As the couple's third term, why has he been erased from public discourse about this double murder? Do his handsome looks, his earring, his "friendship but no more" with Nicole Brown Simpson make of him a narrative cipher in the story of heterosexuality gone wrong? Even if he were "straight," can he be read as a queer presence in this drama, a destabilizing force in an otherwise normative sexual narrative?

40 Quoted in Alisa Solomon, "Identity Crisis: Queer Politics in the Age of Possibilities," *Village Voice* (30 June 1992): 29.

2

Hermaphrodites with Attitude
Mapping the Emergence of Intersex Political Activism

Cheryl Chase

The insistence on two clearly distinguished sexes has calamitous personal consequences for the many individuals who arrive in the world with sexual anatomy that fails to be easily distinguished as male or female. Such individuals are labeled "intersexuals" or "hermaphrodites" by modern medical discourse.[1] About one in a hundred births exhibits some anomaly in sex differentiation,[2] and about one in two thousand is different enough to render problematic the question "Is it a boy or a girl?"[3] Since the early 1960s, nearly every major city in the United States has had a hospital with a standing team of medical experts who intervene in these cases to assign – through drastic surgical means – a male or female status to intersex infants. The fact that this system for preserving the boundaries of the categories male and female has existed for so long without drawing criticism or scrutiny from any quarter indicates the extreme discomfort that sexual ambiguity excites in our culture. Pediatric genital surgeries literalize what might otherwise be considered a theoretical operation: the attempted production of normatively sexed bodies and gendered subjects through constitutive acts of violence. Over the last few years, however, intersex people have begun to politicize intersex identities, thus transforming intensely personal experiences of violation into collective opposition to the medical regulation of

bodies that queer the foundations of heteronormative identifications and desires.

Hermaphrodites: Medical Authority and Cultural Invisibility

Many people familiar with the ideas that gender is a phenomenon not adequately described by male/female dimorphism and that the interpretation of physical sex differences is culturally constructed remain surprised to learn just how variable sexual anatomy is.[4] Though the male/female binary is constructed as natural and presumed to be immutable, the phenomenon of intersexuality offers clear evidence to the contrary and furnishes an opportunity to deploy "nature" strategically to disrupt heteronormative systems of sex, gender, and sexuality. The concept of bodily sex, in popular usage, refers to multiple components including karyotype (organization of sex chromosomes), gonadal differentiation (e.g., ovarian or testicular), genital morphology, configuration of internal reproductive organs, and pubertal sex characteristics such as breasts and facial hair. Because these characteristics are expected to be concordant in each individual – either all male or all female – an observer, once having attributed male or female sex to a particular individual, assumes the values of other unobserved characteristics.[5]

Because medicine intervenes quickly in intersex births to change the infant's body, the

Editors' note: The original subtitle was "An Emergence of Intersex Political Activism."

phenomenon of intersexuality is today largely unknown outside specialized medical practices. General public awareness of intersex bodies slowly vanished in modern Western European societies as medicine gradually appropriated to itself the authority to interpret – and eventually manage – the category which had previously been widely known as "hermaphroditism." Victorian medical taxonomy began to efface hermaphroditism as a legitimated status by establishing mixed gonadal histology as a necessary criterion for "true" hermaphroditism. By this criterion, both ovarian and testicular tissue types had to be present. Given the limitations of Victorian surgery and anesthesia, such confirmation was impossible in a living patient. All other anomalies were reclassified as "pseudohermaphroditisms" masking a "true sex" determined by the gonads.[6]

With advances in anesthesia, surgery, embryology, and endocrinology, however, twentieth-century medicine moved from merely labeling intersexed bodies to the far more invasive practice of "fixing" them to conform with a diagnosed true sex. The techniques and protocols for physically transforming intersexed bodies were developed primarily at Johns Hopkins University in Baltimore during the 1920s and 1930s under the guidance of urologist Hugh Hampton Young. "Only during the last few years," Young enthused in the preface to his pioneering textbook, *Genital Abnormalities,* "have we begun to get somewhere near the explanation of the marvels of anatomic abnormality that may be portrayed by these amazing individuals. But the surgery of the hermaphrodite has remained a terra incognita." The "sad state of these unfortunates" prompted Young to devise "a great variety of surgical procedures" by which he attempted to normalize their bodily appearances to the greatest extents possible.[7]

Quite a few of Young's patients resisted his efforts. One, a "'snappy' young negro woman with a good figure" and a large clitoris, had married a man but found her passion only with women. She refused "to be made into a man" because removal of her vagina would mean the loss of her "meal ticket," namely, her husband.[8] By the 1950s, the principle of rapid postnatal detection and intervention for intersex infants had been developed at Johns Hopkins with the stated goal of completing surgery early enough so that the child would have no memory of it.[9] One wonders whether the insistence on early intervention was not at least partly motivated by the resistance offered by adult intersexuals to normalization through surgery. Frightened parents of ambiguously sexed infants were much more open to suggestions of normalizing surgery, while the infants themselves could of course offer no resistance whatever. Most of the theoretical foundations justifying these interventions are attributable to psychologist John Money, a sex researcher invited to Johns Hopkins by Lawson Wilkins, the founder of pediatric endocrinology.[10] Wilkins's numerous students subsequently carried these protocols to hospitals throughout the United States and abroad.[11] Suzanne Kessler notes that today Wilkins and Money's protocols enjoy a "consensus of approval rarely encountered in science."[12]

In keeping with the Johns Hopkins model, the birth of an intersex infant today is deemed a "psychosocial emergency" that propels a multidisciplinary team of intersex specialists into action. Significantly, they are surgeons and endocrinologists rather than psychologists, bioethicists, representatives from intersex peer support organizations, or parents of intersex children. The team examines the infant and chooses either male or female as a "sex of assignment," then informs the parents that this is the child's "true sex." Medical technology, including surgery and hormones, is then used to make the child's body conform as closely as possible to that sex.

The sort of deviation from sex norms exhibited by intersexuals is so highly stigmatized that the likely prospect of emotional harm due to social rejection of the intersexual provides physicians with their most compelling argument to justify medically unnecessary surgical interventions. Intersex status is considered to be so incompatible with emotional health that misrepresentation, concealment of facts, and outright lying (both to parents and later to the intersex person) are unabashedly advocated in professional medical literature.[13] Rather, the systematic hushing up of the fact of intersex births and the use of violent techniques to normalize intersex bodies have caused profound emotional and physical harm to intersexuals and their families.

The harm begins when the birth is treated as a medical crisis, and the consequences of that initial treatment ripple out ever afterward. The impact of this treatment is so devastating that until just a few years ago, people whose lives have been touched by intersexuality maintained silence about their ordeal. As recently as 1993, no one publicly disputed surgeon Milton Edgerton when he wrote that in forty years of clitoral surgery on intersexuals, "not one has complained of loss of sensation, *even when the entire clitoris was removed*."[14]

The tragic irony is that, while intersexual anatomy occasionally indicates an underlying medical problem such as adrenal malfunction, ambiguous genitals are in and of themselves neither painful nor harmful to health. Surgery is essentially a destructive process. It can remove and to a limited extent relocate tissue, but it cannot create new structures. This technical limitation, taken together with the framing of the feminine as a condition of lack, leads physicians to assign 90 percent of anatomically ambiguous infants as female by excising genital tissue. Members of the Johns Hopkins intersex team have justified female assignment by saying, "You can make a hole, but you can't build a pole."[15] Positively heroic efforts shore up a tenuous masculine status for the remaining 10 percent assigned male, who are subjected to multiple operations – twenty-two in one case[16] – with the goal of straightening the penis and constructing a urethra to enable standing urinary posture. For some, the surgeries end only when the child grows old enough to resist.[17]

Children assigned to the female sex are subjected to surgery that removes the troubling hypertrophic clitoris (the same tissue that would have been a troubling micropenis if the child had been assigned male). Through the 1960s, feminizing pediatric genital surgery was openly labeled "clitorectomy" and was compared favorably to the African practices that have been the recent focus of such intense scrutiny. As three Harvard surgeons noted, "Evidence that the clitoris is not essential for normal coitus may be gained from certain sociological data. For instance, it is the custom of a number of African tribes to excise the clitoris and other parts of the external genitals. Yet normal sexual function is observed in these females."[18] A modified opera-

tion that removes most of the clitoris and relocates a bit of the tip is variously (and euphemistically) called clitoroplasty, clitoral reduction, or clitoral recession and is described as a "simple cosmetic procedure" to differentiate it from the now infamous clitorectomy. However, the operation is far from benign. Here is a slightly simplified summary (in my own words) of the surgical technique – recommended by Johns Hopkins surgeons Oesterling, Gearhart, and Jeffs – that is representative of the operation:

> They make an incision around the phallus, at the corona, then dissect the skin away from its underside. Next they dissect the skin away from the dorsal side and remove as much of the corpora, or erectile bodies, as necessary to create an "appropriate size clitoris." Next, stitches are placed from the pubic area along both sides of the entire length of what remains of the phallus; when these stitches are tightened, it folds up like pleats in a skirt, and recesses into a concealed position behind the mons pubis. If the result is still "too large," the glans is further reduced by cutting away a pie-shaped wedge.[19]

For most intersexuals, this sort of arcane, dehumanized medical description, illustrated with close-ups of genital surgery and naked children with blacked-out eyes, is the only available version of *Our Bodies, Ourselves*. We as a culture have relinquished to medicine the authority to police the boundaries of male and female, leaving intersexuals to recover as best they can, alone and silent, from violent normalization.

My Career as a Hermaphrodite: Renegotiating Cultural Meanings

I was born with ambiguous genitals. A doctor specializing in intersexuality deliberated for three days – sedating my mother each time she asked what was wrong with her baby – before concluding that I was male, with a micropenis, complete hypospadias, undescended testes, and a strange extra opening behind the urethra. A male birth certificate was completed for me, and my parents began raising me as a boy. When I was a year and a half old my parents consulted a different set of experts, who admitted me to a hospital for "sex determination." "Determine" is a remarkably apt word in this context, meaning both "to ascertain by investigation" and "to cause to come to a resolution." It perfectly describes the two-stage process whereby science produces through a series of masked operations what it claims merely to observe. Doctors told my parents that a thorough medical investigation would be necessary to determine (in the first sense of that word) what my "true sex" was. They judged my genital appendage to be inadequate as a penis, too short to mark masculine status effectively or to penetrate females. As a female, however, I would be penetrable and potentially fertile. My anatomy having been relabeled as vagina, urethra, labia, and outsized clitoris, my sex was determined (in the second sense) by amputating my genital appendage. Following doctors' orders, my parents then changed my name, combed their house to eliminate all traces of my existence as a boy (photographs, birthday cards, etc.), changed my birth certificate, moved to a different town, instructed extended family members no longer to refer to me as a boy, and never told anyone else – including me – just what had happened. My intersexuality and change of sex were the family's dirty little secrets.

At age eight, I was returned to the hospital for abdominal surgery that trimmed away the testicular portion of my gonads, each of which was partly ovarian and partly testicular in character. No explanation was given to me then for the long hospital stay or the abdominal surgery, nor for the regular hospital visits afterward, in which doctors photographed my genitals and inserted fingers and instruments into my vagina and anus. These visits ceased as soon as I began to menstruate. At the time of the sex change, doctors had assured my parents that their once son/now daughter would grow into a woman who could have a normal sex life and babies. With the confirmation of menstruation, my parents apparently concluded that that prediction had been borne out and their ordeal was behind them. For me, the worst part of the nightmare was just beginning.

As an adolescent, I became aware that I had no clitoris or inner labia and was unable to orgasm. By the end of my teens, I began to do research in medical libraries, trying to discover what might have happened to me. When I finally determined to obtain my medical records, it took me three years to overcome the obstruction of the doctors whom I asked for help. When I did obtain them, a scant three pages, I first learned that I was a "true hermaphrodite" who had been my parents' son for a year and a half and who bore a name unfamiliar to me. The records also documented my clitorectomy. This was the middle 1970s, when I was in my early twenties. I had come to identify myself as lesbian, at a time when lesbianism and a biologically based gender essentialism were virtually synonymous: men were rapists who caused war and environmental destruction; women were good and would heal the earth; lesbians were a superior form of being uncontaminated by "men's energy." In such a world, how could I tell anyone that I had actually possessed the dreaded "phallus"? I was no longer a woman in my own eyes but rather a monstrous and mythical creature. Because my hermaphroditism and long-buried boyhood were the history behind the clitorectomy, I could never speak openly about that or my consequent inability to orgasm. I was so traumatized by discovering the circumstances that produced my embodiment that I could not speak of these matters with anyone.

Nearly fifteen years later, I suffered an emotional meltdown. In the eyes of the world, I was a highly successful businesswoman, a principal in an international high tech company. To myself, I was a freak, incapable of loving or being loved, filled with shame about my status as a hermaphrodite and about my sexual dysfunction. Unable to make peace with myself, I finally sought help from a psychotherapist, who reacted to each revelation about my history and predicament with some version of "no, it's not" or "so what?" I would say, "I'm not really a woman," and she would say, "Of course you are. You look female." I would say, "My complete withdrawal from sexuality has destroyed every relationship I've ever entered." She would say "Everybody has their ups and downs." I tried another therapist and met with a similar response. Increasingly desperate, I confided my story to several friends, who shrank away in embarrassed silence. I was in emotional agony, feeling utterly alone, seeing no possible way out. I decided to kill myself.

Confronting suicide as a real possibility proved to be my personal epiphany. I fantasized killing myself quite messily and dramatically in the office of the surgeon who had cut off my clitoris, forcibly confronting him with the horror he had imposed on my life. But in acknowledging the desire to put my pain to some use, not to utterly waste my life, I turned a crucial corner, finding a way to direct my rage productively out into the world rather than destructively at myself. I had no conceptual framework for developing a more positive self-consciousness. I knew only that I felt mutilated, not fully human, but that I was determined to heal. I struggled for weeks in emotional chaos, unable to eat or sleep or work. I could not accept my image of a hermaphroditic body any more than I could accept the butchered one the surgeons left me with. Thoughts of myself as a Frankenstein's monster patchwork alternated with longings for escape by death, only to be followed by outrage, anger, and a determination to survive. I could not accept that it was just or right or good to treat any person as I had been treated – my sex changed, my genitals cut up, my experience silenced and rendered invisible. I bore a private hell within me, wretchedly alone in my condition without even my tormentors for company. Finally, I began to envision myself standing in a driving storm but with clear skies and a rainbow visible in the distance. I was still in agony, but I was beginning to see the painful process in which I was caught up in terms of revitalization and rebirth, a means of investing my life with a new sense of authenticity that possessed vast potentials for further transformation. Since then, I have seen this experience of movement through pain to personal empowerment described by other intersex and transsexual activists.[20]

I slowly developed a newly politicized and critically aware form of self-understanding. I had been the kind of lesbian who at times had a girlfriend but who had never really participated in the life of a lesbian community. I felt almost completely isolated from gay politics, feminism, and queer and gender theory. I did possess the rudimentary knowledge that the gay rights movement had gathered momentum only when it could effectively deny that homosexuality was sick or inferior and assert to the contrary that

"gay is good." As impossible as it then seemed, I pledged similarly to affirm that "intersex is good," that the body I was born with was not diseased, only different. I vowed to embrace the sense of being "not a woman" that I initially had been so terrified to discover.

I began searching for community and consequently moved to San Francisco in the fall of 1992, based entirely on my vague notion that people living in the "queer mecca" would have the most conceptually sophisticated, socially tolerant, and politically astute analysis of sexed and gendered embodiment. I found what I was looking for in part because my arrival in the Bay Area corresponded with the rather sudden emergence of an energetic transgender political movement. Transgender Nation (TN) had developed out of Queer Nation, a post-gay/lesbian group that sought to transcend identity politics. TN's actions garnered media attention – especially when members were arrested during a "zap" of the American Psychiatric Association's annual convention when they protested the psychiatric labeling of transsexuality as mental illness. Transsexual performance artist Kate Bornstein was introducing transgender issues in an entertaining way to the San Francisco gay/lesbian community and beyond. Female-to-male [FTM] issues had achieved a new level of visibility due in large part to efforts made by Lou Sullivan, a gay FTM activist who had died an untimely death from HIV-related illnesses in 1991. And in the wake of her underground best-selling novel, *Stone Butch Blues*, Leslie Feinberg's manifesto *Transgender Liberation; A Movement Whose Time Has Come* was finding a substantial audience, linking transgender social justice to a broader progressive political agenda for the first time.[21] At the same time, a vigorous new wave of gender scholarship had emerged in the academy.[22] In this context, intersex activist and theoretician Morgan Holmes could analyze her own clitorectomy for her master's thesis and have it taken seriously as academic work.[23] Openly transsexual scholars, including Susan Stryker and Sandy Stone, were visible in responsible academic positions at major universities. Stone's "'Empire' Strikes Back: A Posttranssexual Manifesto" refigured open, visible transsexuals not as gender conformists propping up a system of rigid, binary sex but as "a set of embodied texts whose potential for productive disruption of structured sexualities and spectra of desire has yet to be explored."[24]

Into this heady atmosphere, I brought my own experience. Introduced by Bornstein to other gender activists, I explored with them the cultural politics of intersexuality, which to me represented yet another new configuration of bodies, identities, desires, and sexualities from which to confront the violently normativizing aspects of the dominant sex/gender system. In the fall of 1993, TN pioneer Anne Ogborn invited me to participate in a weekend retreat called the New Woman Conference, where postoperative transsexual women shared their stories, their griefs and joys, and enjoyed the freedom to swim or sunbathe in the nude with others who had surgically changed genitals. I saw that participants returned home in a state of euphoria, and I determined to bring that same sort of healing experience to intersex people.

Birth of an Intersex Movement: Opposition and Allies

Upon moving to San Francisco, I started telling my story indiscriminately to everyone I met. Over the course of a year, simply by speaking openly within my own social circles, I learned of six other intersexuals – including two who had been fortunate enough to escape medical attention. I realized that intersexuality, rather than being extremely rare, must be relatively common. I decided to create a support network. In the summer of 1993, I produced some pamphlets, obtained a post office box, and began to publicize the Intersex Society of North America (ISNA) through small notices in the media. Before long, I was receiving several letters per week from intersexuals throughout the United States and Canada and occasionally some from Europe. While the details varied, the letters gave a remarkably coherent picture of the emotional consequences of medical intervention. Morgan Holmes: "All the things my body might have grown to do, all the possibilities, went down the hall with my amputated clitoris to the pathology department. The rest of me went to the re-

covery room – I'm still recovering." Angela Moreno: "I am horrified by what has been done to me and by the conspiracy of silence and lies. I am filled with grief and rage, but also relief finally to believe that maybe I am not the only one." Thomas: "I pray that I will have the means to repay, in some measure, the American Urological Association for all that it has done for my benefit. I am having some trouble, though, in connecting the timing mechanism to the fuse."

ISNA's most immediate goal has been to create a community of intersex people who could provide peer support to deal with shame, stigma, grief, and rage as well as with practical issues such as how to obtain old medical records or locate a sympathetic psychotherapist or endocrinologist. To that end, I cooperated with journalists whom I judged capable of reporting widely and responsibly on our efforts, listed ISNA with self-help and referral clearinghouses, and established a presence on the Internet (http://www.isna.org). ISNA now connects hundreds of intersexuals across North America, Europe, Australia, and New Zealand. It has also begun sponsoring an annual intersex retreat, the first of which took place in 1996 and which moved participants every bit as profoundly as the New Woman Conference had moved me in 1993.

ISNA's longer-term and more fundamental goal, however, is to change the way intersex infants are treated. We advocate that surgery not be performed on ambiguous genitals unless there is a medical reason (such as blocked or painful urination), and that parents be given the conceptual tools and emotional support to accept their children's physical differences. While it is fascinating to think about the potential development of new genders or subject positions grounded in forms of embodiment that fall outside the familiar male/female dichotomy, we recognize that the two-sex/gender model is currently hegemonic and therefore advocate that children be raised either as boys or girls, according to which designation seems most likely to offer the child the greatest future sense of comfort. Advocating gender assignment without resorting to normalizing surgery is a radical position given that it requires the willful disruption of the assumed concordance between body shape and gender category. However, this is the only position that prevents irreversible physical damage to the intersex person's body, that respects the intersex person's agency regarding his/her own flesh, and that recognizes genital sensation and erotic functioning to be at least as important as reproductive capacity. If an intersex child or adult decides to change gender or to undergo surgical or hormonal alteration of his/her body, that decision should also be fully respected and facilitated. The key point is that intersex subjects should not be violated for the comfort and convenience of others.

One part of reaching ISNA's long-term goal has been to document the emotional and physical carnage resulting from medical interventions. As a rapidly growing literature makes abundantly clear (see the bibliography on our website, http://www.isna.org/bigbib.html), the medical management of intersexuality has changed little in the forty years since my first surgery. Kessler expresses surprise that "in spite of the thousands of genital operations performed every year, there are no meta-analyses from within the medical community on levels of success."[25] They do not know whether postsurgical intersexuals are "silent and happy or silent and unhappy."[26] There is no research effort to improve erotic functioning for adult intersexuals whose genitals have been altered, nor are there psychotherapists specializing in working with adult intersex clients trying to heal from the trauma of medical intervention. To provide a counterpoint to the mountains of medical literature that neglect intersex experience and to begin compiling an ethnographic account of that experience, ISNA's *Hermaphrodites with Attitude* newsletter has developed into a forum for intersexuals to tell their own stories. We have sent complimentary copies of the newsletter filled with searing personal narratives to academics, writers, journalists, minority rights organizations, and medical practitioners – to anybody we thought might make a difference in our campaign to change the way intersex bodies are managed.

ISNA's presence has begun to generate effects. It has helped politicize the growing number of intersex organizations, as well as intersex identities themselves. When I first began organizing ISNA, I met leaders of the Turner's Syndrome Society, the oldest known support group focusing on atypical sexual differentiation, founded in 1987. Turner's Syndrome is defined by an XO genetic karyotype that results in a female body morphology with nonfunctioning ovaries, extremely short stature, and a variety of other physical differences described in the medical literature with such stigmatizing labels as "web-necked" and "fish-mouthed." Each of these women told me what a profound, life-changing experience it had been simply to meet another person like herself. I was inspired by their accomplishments (they are a national organization serving thousands of members), but I wanted ISNA to have a different focus. I was less willing to think of intersexuality as a pathology or disability, more interested in challenging its medicalization entirely, and more interested still in politicizing a pan-intersexual identity across the divisions of particular etiologies in order to destabilize more effectively the hetero-normative assumptions underlying the violence directed at our bodies.

When I established ISNA in 1993, no such politicized groups existed. In the United Kingdom in 1988, the mother of a girl with androgen-insensitivity syndrome (AIS, which produces genetic males with female genital morphologies) formed the AIS Support Group. The group, which initially lobbied for increased medical attention (better surgical techniques for producing greater vaginal depth, more research into the osteoporosis that often attends AIS), now has chapters in five countries. Another group, K. S. and Associates, was formed in 1989 by the mother of a boy with Klinefelter's Syndrome and today serves over one thousand families. Klinefelter's is characterized by the presence of one or more additional X chromosomes, which produce bodies with fairly masculine external genitals, above-average height, and somewhat gangly limbs. At puberty, people with K. S. often experience pelvic broadening and the development of breasts. K. S. and Associates continues to be dominated by parents, is highly medical in orientation, and has resisted attempts by adult Klinefelter's Syndrome men to discuss gender identity or sexual orientation issues related to their intersex condition.

Since ISNA has been on the scene, other groups with a more resistant stance *vis-à-vis* the medical establishment have begun to appear. In 1995, a mother who refused medical pressure for female assignment for her intersex child formed the Ambiguous Genitalia Support Network, which introduces parents of intersexuals to each other and encourages the development of pen-pal support relationships. In 1996, another mother who had rejected medical pressure to assign her intersex infant as a female by removing his penis formed the Hermaphrodite Education and Listening Post (HELP) to provide peer support and medical information. Neither of these parent-oriented groups, however, frames its work in overtly political terms. Still, political analysis and action of the sort advocated by ISNA has not been without effect on the more narrowly defined service-oriented or parent-dominated groups. The AIS Support Group, now more representative of both adults and parents, noted in a recent newsletter,

> Our first impression of ISNA was that they were perhaps a bit too angry and militant to gain the support of the medical profession. However, we have to say that, having read [political analyses of intersexuality by ISNA, Kessler, Fausto-Sterling, and Holmes], we feel that the feminist concepts relating to the patriarchal treatment of intersexuality are extremely interesting and do make a lot of sense. After all, the lives of intersexed people are stigmatized by the cultural disapproval of their genital appearance, [which need not] affect their experience as sexual human beings.[27]

Other more militant groups have now begun to pop up. In 1994, German intersexuals formed both the Workgroup on Violence in Pediatrics and Gynecology and the Genital Mutilation Survivors' Support Network, and Hijra Nippon now represents activist intersexuals in Japan.

Outside the rather small community of intersex organizations, ISNA's work has generated a complex patchwork of alliances and oppositions. Queer activists, especially transgender activists, have provided encouragement, advice, and logistical support to the intersex movement. The direct action group Transsexual Menace helped an ad hoc group of militant intersexuals calling

themselves Hermaphrodites with Attitude plan and carry out a picket of the 1996 annual meeting of the American Academy of Pediatrics in Boston – the first recorded instance of intersex public protest in modern history.[28] ISNA was also invited to join GenderPAC, a recently formed national consortium of transgender organizations that lobbies against discrimination based on atypical expressions of gender or embodiment. More mainstream gay and lesbian political organizations such as the National Gay and Lesbian Task Force have also been willing to include intersex concerns as part of their political agendas. Transgender and lesbian/gay groups have been supportive of intersex political activism largely because they see similarities in the medicalization of these various identities as a form of social control and (especially for transsexuals) empathize with our struggle to assert agency within a medical discourse that works to efface the ability to exercise informed consent about what happens to one's own body.

Gay/lesbian caucuses and special interest groups within professional medical associations have been especially receptive to ISNA's agenda. One physician on the Internet discussion group glb-medical wrote:

> The effect of Cheryl Chase's postings – admittedly, after the shock wore off – was to make me realize that THOSE WHO HAVE BEEN TREATED might very well think [they had not been well served by medical intervention]. This matters a lot. As a gay man, and simply as a person, I have struggled for much of my adult life to find my own natural self, to disentangle the confusions caused by others' presumptions about how I am/should be. But, thankfully, their decisions were not surgically imposed on me!

Queer psychiatrists, starting with Bill Byne at New York's Mount Sinai Hospital have been quick to support ISNA, in part because the psychological principles underlying the current intersex treatment protocols are manifestly unsound. They seem almost willfully designed to exacerbate rather than ameliorate already difficult emotional issues arising from sexual difference. Some of these psychiatrists see the surgical and endocrinological domination of a problem that even surgeons and endocrinologists acknowledge to be psychosocial rather than biomedical as an unjustified invasion of their area of professional competence.

ISNA has deliberately cultivated a network of nonintersexed advocates who command a measure of social legitimacy and can speak in contexts where uninterpreted intersex voices will not be heard. Because there is a strong impulse to discount what intersexuals have to say about intersexuality, sympathetic representation has been welcome – especially in helping intersexuals reframe intersexuality in nonmedical terms. Some gender theory scholars, feminist critics of science, medical historians, and anthropologists have been quick to understand and support intersex activism. Years before ISNA came into existence, feminist biologist and science studies scholar Anne Fausto-Sterling had written about intersexuality in relation to intellectually suspect scientific practices that perpetuate masculinist constructs of gender, and she became an early ISNA ally.[29] Likewise, social psychologist Suzanne Kessler had written a brilliant ethnography of surgeons who specialize in treating intersexuals. After speaking with several "products" of their practice, she, too, became a strong supporter of intersex activism.[30] Historian of science Alice Dreger, whose work focuses not only on hermaphroditism but on other forms of potentially benign atypical embodiment that become subject to destructively normalizing medical interventions (conjoined twins, for example), has been especially supportive. Fausto-Sterling, Kessler, and Dreger will each shortly publish works that analyze the medical treatment of intersexuality as being culturally motivated and criticize it as harmful to its ostensible patients.[31]

Allies who help contest the medicalization of intersexuality are especially important because ISNA has found it almost entirely fruitless to attempt direct, nonconfrontational interactions with the medical specialists who themselves determine policy on the treatment of intersex infants and who actually carry out the surgeries. Joycelyn Elders, the Clinton administration's first surgeon general, is a pediatric endocrinologist with many years of experience managing intersex infants but, in spite of a generally feminist approach to health care and frequent overtures from ISNA, she has been dismissive of the concerns of intersexuals themselves.[32] Another pediatrician remarked in an Internet discussion on intersexuality: "I think this whole issue is preposterous. . . . To suggest that [medical decisions about the treatment of intersex conditions] are somehow cruel or arbitrary is insulting, ignorant and misguided. . . . To spread the claims that [ISNA] is making is just plain wrong, and I hope that this [on-line group of doctors and scientists] will not blindly accept them." Yet another participant in that same chat asked what was for him obviously a rhetorical question: "Who is the enemy? I really don't think it's the medical establishment. Since when did we establish the male/female hegemony?" While a surgeon quoted in a *New York Times* article on ISNA summarily dismissed us as "zealots,"[33] there is considerable anecdotal information supplied by ISNA sympathizers that professional meetings in the fields of pediatrics, urology, genital plastic surgery, and endocrinology are buzzing with anxious and defensive discussions of intersex activism. In response to the Hermaphrodites with Attitude protests at the American Academy of Pediatrics meeting, that organization felt compelled to issue the following statement to the press: "The Academy is deeply concerned about the emotional, cognitive, and body image development of intersexuals, and believes that successful early genital surgery minimizes these issues." Further protests were planned for 1997.

The roots of resistance to the truth claims of intersexuals run deep in the medical establishment. Not only does ISNA critique the normativist biases couched within most scientific practice, it advocates a treatment protocol for intersex infants that disrupts conventional understandings of the relationship between bodies and genders. But on a level more personally threatening to medical practitioners, ISNA's position implies that they have – unwittingly at best, through willful denial at worst – spent their careers inflicting a profound harm from which their patients will never fully recover. ISNA's position threatens to destroy the assumptions motivating an entire medical subspecialty, thus jeopardizing the ability to perform what many surgeons find to be technically difficult and fascinating work. Melissa Hendricks notes that Dr. Gearhart is known to colleagues as a surgical "artist" who can "carve a large phallus down into a clitoris" with consummate skill.[34] More than one ISNA member has discovered that surgeons actually operated on their genitals at no charge. The medical establishment's fascination with its own power to change sex and its drive to rescue parents from their intersex children are so strong that heroic interventions are delivered without regard to the capitalist model that ordinarily governs medical services.

Given such deep and mutually reinforcing reasons for opposing ISNA's position, it is hardly surprising that medical intersex specialists have, for the most part, turned a deaf ear toward us. The lone exception as of April 1997 is urologist Justine Schober. After watching a videotape of the 1996 ISNA retreat and receiving other input from HELP and the AIS Support Group, she suggests in a new textbook on pediatric surgery that while technology has advanced to the point that "our needs [as surgeons] and the needs of parents to have a presentable child can be satisfied," it is time to acknowledge that problems exist that "we as surgeons . . . cannot address. Success in psychosocial adjustment is the true goal of sexual assignment and genitoplasty. . . . Surgery makes parents and doctors comfortable, but counseling makes people comfortable too, and is not irreversible."[35]

While ISNA will continue to approach the medical establishment for dialogue (and continue supporting protests outside the closed doors when doctors refuse to talk), perhaps the most important aspect of our current activities is the struggle to change public perceptions. By using the mass media, the Internet, and our growing network of allies and sympathizers to make the general public aware of the frequency of intersexuality and of the intense suffering that medical treatment has caused, we seek to create an environment in which many parents of intersex children will have already heard about the intersex movement when their child is born. Such informed parents we hope will be better able to resist medical pressure for unnecessary genital surgery and secrecy and to find their way to a peer-support group and counseling rather than to a surgical theater.

First-World Feminism, African Clitorectomy, and Intersex Genital Mutilation

We must first locate and challenge our own position as rigorously as we challenge that of others.

Salem Mekuria, "Female Genital Mutilation in Africa"

Traditional African practices that remove the clitoris and other parts of female genitals have lately been a target of intense media coverage and feminist activism in the United States and other industrialized Western societies. The euphemism *female circumcision* largely has been supplanted by the politicized term *female genital mutilation* (FGM). Analogous operations performed on intersexuals in the United States have not been the focus of similar attention – indeed, attempts to link the two forms of genital cutting have met with multiform resistance. Examining how first-world feminists and mainstream media treat traditional African practices and comparing that treatment with their responses to intersex genital mutilation (IGM) in North America exposes some of the complex interactions between ideologies of race, gender, colonialism, and science that effectively silence and render invisible intersex experience in first-world contexts. Cutting intersex genitals becomes yet another hidden mechanism for imposing normalcy upon unruly flesh, a means of containing the potential anarchy of desires and identifications within oppressive heteronormative structures.

In 1994, the *New England Journal of Medicine* paired an article on the physical harm resulting from African genital surgery with an editorial denouncing clitorectomy as a violation of human rights but declined to run a reply drafted by University of California at Berkeley medical anthropologist Lawrence Cohen and two ISNA members detailing the harm caused by medicalized American clitorectomies.[36] In response to growing media attention, Congress passed the Federal Prohibition of Female Genital Mutilation Act in October 1996, but the act specifically exempted from prohibition medicalized clitorectomies of the sort performed to "correct" intersex bodies. The bill's principal author, former Congresswoman Patricia Schroeder, received and ignored many letters from ISNA members and Brown University professor of medical science Anne Fausto-Sterling asking her to recast the bill's language. The *Boston Globe's* syndicated columnist Ellen Goodman is one of the few journalists covering African FGM to respond to ISNA. "I must admit I was not aware of this situation," she wrote to me in 1994. "I admire your courage." She continued, however, regularly to discuss African FGM in her column without mentioning similar American practices. One of her October 1995 columns on FGM was promisingly titled, "We Don't Want to Believe It Happens Here," but it discussed only immigrants to the United States from third-world countries who performed clitorectomies on their daughters in keeping with the practices of their native cultures.

While clitorectomized African immigrant women doing anti-FGM activism in the United States have been receptive to the claims made by intersex opponents to medicalized clitorectomies and are in dialogue with us, first-world feminists and organizations working on African FGM have totally ignored us. To my knowledge, only two of the many anti-FGM groups contacted have responded to repeated overtures from intersex activists. Fran Hosken, who since 1982 has regularly published a catalogue of statistics on female genital mutilation worldwide, wrote me a terse note saying that "we are not concerned with biological exceptions."[37] Forward International, another anti-FGM organization, replied to an inquiry from German intersexual Heike Spreitzer that her letter was "most interesting" but that they could not help because their work focuses only on "female genital mutilation that is performed as a harmful cultural or traditional practice on young girls." As Forward International's reply to Spreitzer demonstrates, many first-world anti-FGM activists seemingly consider Africans to have "harmful cultural or traditional practices," while we in the modern industrialized West presumably have something better. We have science, which is linked to the metanarratives of enlightenment, progress, and truth. Genital cutting is

condoned to the extent that it supports these cultural self-conceptions.

Robin Morgan and Gloria Steinem set the tone for subsequent first-world feminist analyses of FGM with their pathbreaking article in the March 1980 issue of *Ms.* magazine, "The International Crime of Genital Mutilation."[38] A disclaimer warns, "These words are painful to read. They describe facts of life as far away as our most fearful imagination – and as close as any denial of women's sexual freedom." For *Ms.* readers, whom the editors imagine are more likely to experience the pain of genital mutilation between the covers of their magazine than between their thighs, clitorectomy is presented as a fact of foreign life whose principal relevance to their readership is that it exemplifies a loss of "freedom," that most cherished possession of the liberal Western subject. The article features a photograph of an African girl with her legs held open by the arm of an unseen woman to her right. To her left is the disembodied hand of the midwife, holding the razor blade with which she has just performed a ritual clitorectomy. The girl's face – mouth open, eyes bulging – is a mask of pain. In more than fifteen years of coverage, Western images of African practices have changed little. "Americans made a horrifying discovery this year," *Life* soberly informed its readers in January 1997 while showing a two-page photo spread of a Kenyan girl held from behind as unseen hands cut her genitals.[39] The 1996 Pulitzer Prize for feature photography went to yet another portrayal of a Kenyan clitorectomy.[40] And in the wake of Fauziya Kassindja's successful bid for asylum in the United States after fleeing clitorectomy in Togo, the number of FGM images available from her country has skyrocketed.[41]

These representations all manifest a profound othering of African clitorectomy that contributes to the silence surrounding similar medicalized practices in the industrialized West. "Their" genital cutting is barbaric ritual; "ours" is scientific. Theirs disfigures; ours normalizes the deviant. The colonialist implications of these representations of genital cutting are even more glaringly obvious when images of intersex surgeries are juxtaposed with images of African FGM. Medical books describing how to perform clitoral surgery on white North

American intersex children are almost always illustrated with extreme genital close-ups, disconnecting the genitals not only from the individual intersexed person but from the body itself. Full-body shots always have the eyes blacked out. Why is it considered necessary to black out the eyes of clitorectomized American girls – thus preserving a shred of their privacy and helping ward off the viewer's identification with the abject image – but not the eyes of the clitorectomized African girls in the pages of American magazines?[42]

First-world feminist discourse locates clitorectomy not only "elsewhere," in Africa, but also "elsewhen" in time. A recent *Atlantic Monthly* article on African clitorectomy asserted that the "American medical profession stopped performing clitoridectomies decades ago," and the magazine has since declined to publish a contradictory letter to the editor from ISNA.[43] Academic publications are as prone to this attitude as the popular press. In the recent *Deviant Bodies* anthology, visual artist Susan Jahoda's "Theatres of Madness" juxtaposes nineteenth- and twentieth-century material depicting "the conceptual interdependence of sexuality, reproduction, family life, and 'female disorders.'"[44] To represent twentieth-century medical clitorectomy practices, Jahoda quotes a July 1980 letter written to *Ms.* magazine in response to Morgan and Steinem. The letter writer, a nurse's aide in a geriatric home, said she had been puzzled by the strange scars she saw on the genitals of five of the forty women in her care: "Then I read your article. . . . My God! Why? Who decided to deny them orgasm? Who made them go through such a procedure? I want to know. Was it fashionable? Or was it to correct 'a condition'? I'd like to know what this so-called civilized country used as its criteria for such a procedure. And how widespread is it here in the United States?"[45] While Jahoda's selection of this letter does raise the issue of medicalized American clitorectomies, it safely locates the genital cutting in the past, as something experienced a long time ago by women now in their later stages of life.

Significantly, Jahoda literally passed over an excellent opportunity to comment on the continuing practice of clitorectomy in the contemporary United States. Two months earlier, in the April 1980 issue of *Ms.*, feminist biologists Ruth Hubbard and Patricia Farnes also replied to Morgan and Steinem:

> We want to draw the attention of your readers to the practice of clitoridectomy not only in the Third Word . . . but right here in the United States, where it is used as part of a procedure to "repair" by "plastic surgery" so-called genital ambiguities. Few people realize that this procedure has routinely involved removal of the entire clitoris and its nerve supply – in other words, total clitoridectomy. . . . In a lengthy article, [Johns Hopkins intersex expert John] Money and two colleagues write . . . that "a three-year old girl about to be clitoridectomized . . . should be well informed that *the doctors will make her look like all other girls and women*" (our emphasis), which is not unlike what North African girls are often told about their clitoridectomies. . . . But to date, neither Money nor his critics have investigated the effect of clitoridectomies on the girls' development. Yet one would surely expect this to affect their psychosexual development and their feelings of identity as young women.[46]

While Farnes and Hubbard's prescient feminist exposé of medicalized clitorectomies in the contemporary United States sank without a trace, there has been an explosion of work that keeps "domestic" clitorectomy at a safe distance. Such conceptualizations of clitorectomy's geographical and temporal cultural remoteness allow first-world feminist outrage to be diverted into potentially colonialist meddling in the social affairs of others while hampering work for social justice at home.[47]

Feminism represents itself as being interested in unmasking the silence that surrounds violence against women. Most medical intersex management is another form of violence based on a sexist devaluing of female pain and female sexuality. Doctors consider the prospect of growing up as a boy with a small penis to be a worse alternative than growing up as a girl sans clitoris and ovaries; they gender intersex bodies accordingly and cut them up to make the assigned genders support cultural norms of embodiment. These medical interventions transform many transgressive bodies into ones that can be labeled safely as women and subjected to the many forms of social control with which women must contend. Why then have most first-world feminists met intersexuals with a blank stare?

Intersexuals have had such difficulty generating mainstream feminist support not only because of the racist and colonialist frameworks that situate clitorectomy as a practice foreign to proper subjects within the first world but also because intersexuality undermines the stability of the category "woman" that undergirds much of first-world feminist discourse. We call into question the assumed relation between genders and bodies and demonstrate how some bodies do not fit easily into male/female dichotomies. We embody viscerally the truth of Judith Butler's dictum that "sex," the concept that accomplishes the materialization and naturalization of power-laden, culturally constructed differences, has really been "gender all along."[48] By refusing to remain silenced, we queer the foundations upon which depend not only the medical management of bodies but also widely shared feminist assumptions of properly embodied feminine subjectivity. To the extent that we are not normatively female or normatively women, we are not considered the proper subjects of feminist concern.

As unwilling subjects of science and improper subjects of feminism, politicized intersex activists have deep stakes in allying with and participating in the sorts of poststructuralist cultural work that exposes the foundational assumptions about personhood shared by the dominant society, conventional feminism, and many other identity-based oppositional social movements. We have a stake, too, in the efforts of gender queens to carve out livable social spaces for reconfigured forms of embodiment, identity, and desire. In 1990, Suzanne Kessler noted that "the possibilities for real societal transformations would be unlimited" if physicians and scientists specializing in the management of gender could recognize that "finally, and always, people construct gender as well as the social systems that are grounded in gender-based concepts. . . . Accepting genital ambiguity as a natural option would require that physicians also acknowledge that genital ambiguity is 'corrected' not because it is threatening to the infant's life but because it is threatening to the infant's culture."[49] At that time, intersexuals had not yet been heard from, and there was little reason to think that physicians or other members of their culture would ever reflect on the meaning or effect of what they were doing. The advent of an activist intersex opposition changes everything.

Notes

My appreciation goes to Susan Stryker for her extensive contributions to the structure and substance of this essay.

1 Claude J. Migeon, Gary D. Berkovitz, and Terry R. Brown, "Sexual Differentiation and Ambiguity," in *Wilkins: The Diagnosis and Theatment of Endocrine Disorders in Childhood and Adolescence,* ed. Michael S. Kappy, Robert M. Blizzard, and Claude J. Migeon (Springfield, Ill.: Charles C. Thomas, 1994), 573–715.

2 Lalitha Raman-Wilms et al., "Fetal Genital Effects of First-Trimester Sex Hormone Exposure: A Meta-Analysis," *Obstetrics and Gynecology* 85 (1995): 141–8.

3 Anne Fausto-Sterling, *Sexing the Body: Gender Politics and the Construction of Sexuality* (New York: Basic Books, 2000).

4 Judith Butler, *Gender Trouble: Feminism and the Subversion of Identity* (New York: Routledge, 1990); Thomas Laqueur, *Making Sex: Body and Gender from the Greeks to Freud* (Cambridge, Mass.: Harvard University Press, 1990).

5 Suzanne Kessler and Wendy McKenna, *Gender: An Ethnomethodological Approach* (New York: John Wiley and Sons, 1978).

6 Alice Domurat Dreger, "Doubtful Sex: Cases and Concepts of Hermaphroditism in France and Britain, 1868–1915," (Ph.D. diss., Indiana University, 1995); Alice Domurat Dreger, "Doubtful Sex: The Fate of the Hermaphrodite in Victorian Medicine' *Victorian Studies* (spring 1995): 336–70; Alice Domurat Dreger, "Hermaphrodites in Love: The Truth of the Gonads," *Science and Homosexualities,* ed. Vernon Rosario (New York: Routledge, 1997), 46–66; Alice Domurat Dreger, "Doctors Containing Hermaphrodites: The Victorian Legacy," *Chrysalis: The Journal of Transgressive Gender Identities* (fall 1997): 15–22.

7 Hugh Hampton Young, *Genital Abnormalities, Hermaphroditism, and Related Adrenal Diseases* (Baltimore: Williams and Wilkins, 1937), xxxix–xl.

8   Ibid., 139–42.

9   Howard W. Jones Jr. and William Wallace Scott, *Hermaphroditism, Genital Anomalies, and Related Endocrine Disorders* (Baltimore: Williams and Wilkins, 1958), 269.

10 John Money, Joan G. Hampson, and John L. Hampson, "An Examination of Some Basic Sexual Concepts: The Evidence of Human Hermaphroditism," *Bulletin of the Johns Hopkins Hospital* 97 (1955): 301–19; John Money, Joan C. Hampson, and John L. Hampson, "Hermaphroditism: Recommendations Concerning Assignment of Sex, Change of Sex, and Psychologic Management," *Bulletin of Johns Hopkins Hospital* 97 (1955): 284–300; John Money, *Venuses Penuses* (Buffalo: Prometheus, 1986).

11 Robert M. Blizzard, "Lawson Wilkins," in Kappy et al., *Wilkins*, xi–xiv.

12 Suzanne Kessler, "The Medical Construction of Gender: Case Management of Intersexual Infants," *Signs: Journal of Women in Culture and Society* 16 (1990): 3–26.

13 J. Dewhurst and D. B. Grant, "Intersex Problems," *Archives of Disease in Childhood* 59 (1984): 1191–4; Anita Natarajan, "Medical Ethics and Truth-Telling in the Case of Androgen Insensitivity Syndrome," *Canadian Medical Association Journal* 154 (1996): 568–70; Tom Mazur, "Ambiguous Genitalia: Detection and Counseling," *Pediatric Nursing* (1983): 417–22; F. M. E. Slijper et al., "Neonates with Abnormal Genital Development Assigned the Female Sex: Parent Counseling," *Journal of Sex Education and Therapy* 20 (1994): 9–17.

14 Milton T. Edgerton, "Discussion: Clitoroplasty for Clitoromegaly due to Adrenogenital Syndrome without Loss of Sensitivity (by Nobuyuki Sagehashi)," *Plastic and Reconstructive Surgery* 91 (1993): 956.

15 Melissa Hendricks, "Is It a Boy or a Girl?" *Johns Hopkins Magazine,* November 1993, 10–16.

16 John F. Stecker et al., "Hypospadias Cripples," *Urologic Clinics of North America: Symposium on Hypospadias* 8 (1981): 539–44.

17 Jeff McClintock, "Growing Up in the Surgical Maelstrom," *Chrysalis: The Journal of Transgressive Gender Identities* (fall 1997): 53–4.

18 Robert E. Gross, Judson Randolph, and John F. Crigler, "Clitorectomy for Sexual Abnormalities: Indications and Technique," *Surgery* 59 (1966): 300–8.

19 Joseph E. Oesterling, John P. Gearhart, and Robert D. Jeffs, "A Unified Approach to Early Reconstructive Surgery of the Child with Ambiguous Genitalia," *Journal of Urology* 138 (1987): 1079–84.

20 Kira Triea, "The Awakening," *Hermaphrodites with Attitude* (winter 1994): 1; Susan Stryker, "My Words to Victor Frankenstein above the Village of Chamounix: Performing Transgender Rage," *GLQ* 1 (1994): 237–54.

21 Leslie Feinberg, *Stone Butch Blues* (Ithaca, NY: Firebrand, 1993); Leslie Feinberg, *Transgender Liberation: A Movement Whose Time Has Come* (New York: World View Forum, 1992).

22 See, for example, Judith Butler, *Bodies That Matter: On the Discursive Limits of "Sex"* (New York: Routledge, 1993); Butler, *Gender Trouble*; Laqueur, *Making Sex*; and Julia Epstein and Kristina Straub, eds., *Body Guards: The Cultural Politics of Gender Ambiguity* (New York: Routledge, 1991).

23 Morgan Holmes, "Medical Politics and Cultural Imperatives: Intersexuality Beyond Pathology and Erasure" (master's thesis, York University, Toronto, 1994).

24 Sandy Stone, "The *Empire* Strikes Back: A Posttranssexual Manifesto," in Epstein and Straub, *Body Guards,* 280–304, quotation on 296.

25 Suzanne Kessler, *Lessons from the Intersexed* (New Brunswick, NJ: Rutgers University Press, 1998).

26 Robert Jeffs, quoted in Ellen Barry, "United States of Ambiguity," Boston *Phoenix,* 22 November 1996, 6–8, quotation on 6.

27 AIS Support Group, "Letter to America," *ALIAS* (spring 1996): 3–4.

28 Barry, "United States of Ambiguity," 7.

29 Anne Fausto-Sterling, "The Five Sexes: Why Male and Female Are Not Enough," *The Sciences* 33, no. 2 (March/April 1993): 20–5; Anne Fausto-Sterling, *Myths of Gender: Biological Theories about Women and Men,* 2d ed. (New York: Basic Books, 1985), 134–41.

30 Kessler, "The Medical Construction of Gender"; Suzanne Kessler, "Meanings of Genital Variability," *Chrysalis: The Journal of Transgressive Gender Identities* (fall 1997): 33–8.

31 Anne Fausto-Sterling, *Sexing the Body*; Kessler, "Meanings of Genital Vaniability"; Alice Domurat Dreger, *Hermaphrodites and the Medical Invention of Sex* (Cambridge, Mass.: Harvard University Press, 1998).

32 "Dr. Elders' Medical History," *New Yorker,* 26 September 1994: 45–6; Joycelyn Elders and David Chanoff, *From Sharecropper's Daughter to Surgeon General of the United States of America* (New York: William Morrow, 1996).

33 Natalie Angier, "Intersexual Healing: An Anomaly Finds a Group," *New York Times,* 4 February 1996, E14.

34 Hendricks, "Is It a Boy or a Girl?" 10.

35 Justine M. Schober, "Long Term Outcomes of Feminizing Genitoplasty for Intersex' in *Pediatric Surgery and Urology: Long Term Outcomes*, ed. Pierre Mouriquant (Philadelphia: W. B. Saunders, 1998).

36 Patricia Schroeder, "Female Genital Mutilation," *New England Journal of Medicine* 331 (1994): 739–40; Nahid Toubia, "Female Circumcision as a Public Health Issue," *New England Journal of Medicine* 331 (1994): 712–16.

37 Fran P. Hosken, *The Hosken Report: Genital/Sexual Mutilation of Females*, 4th ed. (Lexington, Mass.: WIN News, 1994).

38 Robin Morgan and Gloria Steinem, "The International Crime of Genital Mutilation," *Ms.*, March 1980, 65–7ff.

39 Mariella Furrer, "Ritual Agony," *Life*, January 1997, 38–9.

40 Pulitzer Prize Board, "Feature Photography: Stephanie Welsh," 1996. Available online at http://www.pulitzer.org/winners/1996/winnes/works/feature-photography/.

41 Celia Dugger, "U.S. Grants Asylum to Woman Fleeing Genital Mutilation Rite," *New York Times*, 14 June 1996, A1; Celia Dugger, "New Law Bans Genital Cutting in the United States," *New York Times*, 12 October 1996, 1; Furrer, "Ritual Agony?

42 Dugger, "U.S. Grants Asylum"; Salem Mekuria, "Female Genital Mutilation in Africa: Some African Views," *Association of Concerned African Scholars Bulletin* (winter/spring 1995): 2–6.

43 Linda Burstyn, "Female Circumcision Comes to America," *Atlantic Monthly*, October 1995, 28–35.

44 Susan Jahoda, "Theatres of Madness," *Deviant Bodies*, ed. Jennifer Terry and Jacqueline Urla (Bloomington: Indiana University Press, 1995), 251–76.

45 Letter the editor, *Ms.*, July 1980, 12.

46 Ruth Hubbard and Patrica Farnes, letter to the editor, *Ms.*, April 1980, 9–10,

47 Seble Dawit and Salem Mekuria, "The West Just Doesn't Get It," *New York Times*, 7 December 1993, A27.

48 Butler, *Gender Trouble*, 8.

49 Kessler, "Medical Construction of Gender," 25.

3

Contested Membership
Black Gay Identities and the Politics of AIDS

Cathy J. Cohen

It has been fairly recently that scholars in the social sciences have begun to recognize that the concept of group identity in its essentialist core is in crisis. Influenced by postmodern and deconstructive discourse, historical analyses focusing on marginal groups, and a new emphasis on identity in social-movement theories, researchers are beginning to understand that the idea of group identity that many of us now employ is markedly different than the conception of a stable, static, and homogenous group previously assumed in the social sciences.[1] Just as most scholars have finally become accustomed to including in their analyses simple conceptions of identity coded in binary form (i.e. white/black; man/woman), we now face the realization that identities of difference (race, class, gender, sexuality) are themselves fragmented, contested, and, of course, socially constructed. . . .

While previously, most of the work on the social construction of group identity came from scholars in the humanities, researchers in the social sciences, especially those of us interested in the topics of race, gender, class, and sexuality, must find ways to incorporate such insight into our analyses. Moreover, we are being challenged by a rapidly expanding understanding of group identity to not only recognize and examine the socially constructed character of group identity, but also to investigate the stratification found in groups and the implications of such fragmentation on attempts at group mobilization and political action.[2] Thus, beyond examining the ways in which dominant groups and institutions change or alter their imposed definitions of marginal groups within different historical contexts, we must also understand how marginal group members define and redefine themselves, setting their own standards for "full group membership."[3]

This chapter takes up the topic of indigenous constructions of group membership and its impact on the political attitudes and mobilization of marginal group members. In particular, I am interested in how the concept of "blackness," as it is defined and refined within black communities, is used to demarcate the boundaries of group membership. As a second point of examination, I want to know how these indigenous definitions of blackness influence, shape, and lend legitimation to the political attitudes and behavior of community leaders and members.

Indigenous definitions of blackness, while of course building on dominant ideas or definitions of who *is* black, employ a more expansive, but at the same time often less inclusive, understanding of black group identity. They center not merely on easily identifiable biologically rooted characteristics, but also use moralistic and character evaluations to appraise membership. Individuals employ a "calculus" of indigenous membership which can include an assessment of personal or moral worth, such as an individual's contribution to the community, their adherence to community norms and values, or their faith-fulness to perceived, rewritten, or in some cases newly created African traditions. Thus, indige-nously constructed definitions of black group identity seek to redefine and empower blackness to the outside world by policing the boundaries of what can be represented to the dominant public as "true blackness." And it is through the process of *public policing*, where the judg-ments, evaluations and condemnations of recognized leaders and institutions of black communities are communicated to their con-stituencies, that the full membership of certain segments of black communities are contested and challenged.

Let me be clear that examples of the indige-nous construction of blackness and contests over such definitions abound in our everyday interactions. Whether it be the challenge to the authenticity of those black students who choose not to sit at "the black table" in the cafeteria or the looks of contempt or concern encountered by black group members seen walking with their white mates, informal or "hidden transcripts" of blackness guide interactions in black communi-ties, as they undoubtedly do in all communities.[4] However, in most cases full-scale contestation is not the norm in black communities. Instead, those whose position in the community is chal-lenged exist silenced and regulated for years. Only when the "subgroup" experiencing ostra-cization or *secondary marginalization* has alter-native means of securing resources, such as an external network of support, will the full battle over inclusion be fought.[5] Thus, in most cases those individuals deemed to be on the outside of "acceptable blackness" – either because of their addiction, their sexual relationships, their gender, their financial status, their relationship with/or dependency on the state, etc. – are left with two choices: either find ways to conform to "community standards" or be left on the margins where individual families and friends are expected to take care of their needs. . . .

As stated earlier, the objective of this analy-sis is not only to understand the processes through which indigenous constructions of group membership come about, but also to explore how these definitions impact on the behavior, in particular the political behavior, of marginal group members. To this end, I have chosen to center this analysis on the black community's response to the AIDS epidemic. Specifically, I will explore how indigenous con-tests over black gay male identity have framed and influenced black communities' conception of and response to AIDS.[6]

Throughout this chapter I use examples and quotes from community leaders located in black churches, electoral politics, activist organiza-tions, and the academy to examine the re-lationship between indigenous definitions of blackness, a public black gay identity, and the political response to AIDS in black communi-ties. Has the emergence of a public, empowered black gay identity, perceived and defined by many community leaders, activists, and members as standing outside the bounds of gen-erally recognized standards of blackness, been used by these leaders to justify their lack of an aggressive response to this disease? Do commu-nity leaders interpret a public black gay identity as a direct threat to the acceptability or "cultural capital" gained by some in black communities, in particular by the black middle class? In the minds of indigenous leaders and activists, does embracing or owning AIDS as a disease signifi-cantly impacting on members of black commu-nities also mean owning or finally acknowledging that sexual contact and intimate relationships between men is something found in, and inher-ently a part of, black communities?[7]

My central claim is that contestation over identity, in this case indigenous racial identity, has tangible effects, influencing the distribution of resources, services, access, and legitimacy within communities. In the case of AIDS, without the support of established leaders and organizations in black communities, under-funded community-based education programs encounter limited success, facilitating the con-tinued infection and death of black men, women, and children. Further, in the absence of political pressure from leaders, organizations, activists, and mobilized members of the black community the federal government is allowed to continue its shameful dealings, neglecting to provide the full resources needed to effectively fight this disease in black communities. Thus, those failing to meet indigenous standards of blackness find their life chances threatened not only by dominant institutions or groups, but also

Cathy J. Cohen

by their lack of access to indigenous resources and support. Therefore, scholars who profess to be concerned with the conditions of marginal group members face the monumental challenge of recognizing and examining the process of indigenous group definition without reifying the group as an essentialist and exclusionary category.

Furthermore, the importance of disputes over community membership and the importance of groups should not be understood only at an abstract, theoretical level where discussions of identity, authenticity, and essentialism are often held. This examination of the intersection of AIDS, black gay identity, and indigenous constructions of "blackness" provides us with an empirical example of the importance of group membership and group resources for marginal group members, as well as the dangers of identity politics. In this case we must be concerned with politics that only recognize and respond to the needs of those segments of black communities judged by our leaders to meet indigenous standards of group membership. This issue is of critical importance because it represents what I believe to be one of the more pressing political challenges currently facing marginal communities in the twenty-first century, namely how to maintain and rebuild a principled and politically effective group unity. How do marginal communities, still struggling for access and power from dominant institutions and groups, maintain some pseudo-unified political base in the face of increasing demands to recognize and incorporate the needs and issues of members who previously were silenced and made invisible with regards to structuring the politics of the community? How do marginal communities make central those who are the most vulnerable, and often most stigmatized members of the community, when many of the previous gains of marginal group members have been made through a strategy of minimizing the public appearance of difference between the values, behavior, and attitudes of marginal and dominant group members? How do we build a truly radical, liberating politics that does not recreate hierarchies, norms, and standards of acceptability rooted in dominant systems of power? These are the questions that frame this analysis. . . .

Emergence of a Visible Black Gay Identity

The perceived existence of a unifying group identity cannot be overstated when trying to explain the structured politics of black communities. Systems of oppression from slavery to redemption, to legal and informal Jim Crow segregation, and other more recent forms of segregation and deprivation have dictated that most African Americans share a history and current existence framed by oppression and marginalization. However, even as a unifier, blackness, or what qualifies as indigenously constructed blackness, has always been mediated or contested by other identities that group members hold. And at no time did both the primacy and the fragility of a unified group identity become more evident than in the liberation politics and social movements of the late 1960s and early 1970s. Whether it be civil-rights institutions, black liberation organizations or even electoral campaigns of black candidates, one primary identity – "blackness" – was understood to be the underlying factor joining all these struggles. Each organization espoused in their own way a commitment to the liberation of black people and anything thought to detract from this goal was dismissed and in some cases denounced. However, the uniformity of such a political worldview can also be challenged during this period.

During the 1960s and 1970s the black community experienced increasing stratification. Whether that stratification was based in the deindustrialization experienced in urban centers or the politicized nature of the times, which helped to promote consciousness of members' multiple identities, a segregated and seemingly unified black community had to deal openly with fragmentation. All across the country we witnessed the beginning of extreme bifurcation in black communities, with an expanding middle class and an expanding segment of poor black people. However, beyond economic segmentation, other identities or social locations became visible in defining the lived experience of black people. In black communities, as well as in the political groups of the time, individuals increasingly began to recognize and acknowledge the multiplicity of identities upon which their

48

oppression was based. Unfortunately, it was the inability of many of the race-based organizations to recognize and act on perceived tears in "unity" that led in part to the dismantling of many of these organizations.[8] However, it was also in this changing environment that the visibility of lesbian and gay people, including black lesbian and gay people, began to take shape in the community.

It is important to recognize that black gay men and lesbians have always existed and worked in black communities, but these individuals had largely been made invisible, silent contributors to the community.[9] When faced with the devastation of racism, the cost of silence and invisibility seemed a willing payment from lesbian and gay community members for the support, caring, and protection of members of the black community and, more importantly, the support and acceptance of immediate family members. bell hooks in her book *Talking Back* discusses the dilemma that many black lesbians and gay men confronted:

> The gay people we knew did not live in separate subcultures, not in the small, segregated black community where work was difficult to find, where many of us were poor. Poverty was important; it created a social context in which structures of dependence were important for everyday survival. Sheer economic necessity and fierce white racism, as well as the joy of being there with the black folks known and loved, compelled many gay blacks to live close to home and family. That meant however that gay people created a way to live out sexual preferences within the boundaries of circumstances that were rarely ideal no matter how affirming.[10]

Thus, if one was willing not to "flaunt" their sexual orientation in front of family members and neighbors (although many would secretly suspect that you were "that way") the primarily verbal abuse – like taunts of "faggot" and "bulldyke" – was generally kept to a minimum. Again, I do not want to minimize the importance of even such conditional support on the part of family, friends, and community. The prospect of facing continuous residential, occupational, and social exclusion as a manifestation of widespread racism, even in primarily white lesbian and gay

communities, underscores the importance of some feelings of safety and familiarity. These were the feelings of support bought by our silence.

However, the willingness and ability of black lesbians and gay men to remain quiet and invisible has radically changed. These changes have resulted in part from many of the factors which have spurred new identities as well as politicized identities of old. One major factor has been the proliferation of liberation and social movements demanding access and control for groups long pushed out of dominant society. Cornel West speaks of this situation when he argues that,

> During the late '50s, '60s and early '70s in the USA, these decolonized sensibilities fanned and fueled the Civil Rights and Black Power movements, as well as the student anti-war, feminist, gray, brown, gay, and lesbian movements. In this period we witnessed the shattering of male WASP cultural homogeneity and the collapse of the short-lived liberal consensus.[11]

Closely connected to involvement and association with organized social movements was the more formal establishment of an institutionalized, socially connected, and in many cases monetarily secure gay community in many of the nation's urban centers. These "ghettos" provided a space in which ideas of rights and political strategies of empowerment could be generated and discussed. These enclaves, as well as other dominant institutions such as universities, were integral in creating space for the exploration of independence away from local communities and families.[12]

In conjunction with the continued development of gay enclaves was the emergence of an outspoken and brave black lesbian and gay leadership who openly claimed and wrote about their sexuality (Audre Lorde, Cheryl Clarke, Barbara Smith, Pat Parker, Joseph Beam, Essex Hemphill . . .). These individuals were intent on creating new cultural voices. When they were denied the right to speak openly through traditional avenues in black communities these cultural leaders found and created new avenues to affirm their presence and connection to black communities. Publications like *This Bridge*

Called My Back, Home Girls, Brother to Brother, In the Life, and more recently videos such as *Tongues Untied* all sought to detail from various perspectives the struggle to consistently mesh one's black and gay identities.[13] All of these factors helped create an environment in which the silence that had structured the lives of many black lesbian and gay men seemed unacceptable.

The conditions listed above, however, did not lead to a massive coming-out process in black communities. In fact, the level of silence among black lesbian and gay men is still an immediate and pressing concern for those organizing in the community today. However, the environment that developed through the 1960s and 1970s created a situation in which some black women and men choose to identify publicly as black *and* gay. The choice, or in many cases the perceived need, to embrace publicly a black gay male or black lesbian identity undoubtedly escalated with the emergence of AIDS, an issue which demands either recognition and empowerment or death. Thus, after spending years affirming themselves, building consciousness, and contributing to black communities that had too often refused to embrace their particular needs, gay brothers and lesbian sisters faced an issue, in the case of AIDS, that threatened to kill black gays and lesbians as well as generally wreak havoc throughout black communities if we did not speak out and demand recognition. . . .

Two of the earliest national conferences on AIDS in People of Color communities were organized by lesbians and gay men. The Third World Advisory Task Force, a primarily gay group out of San Francisco, organized a western regional conference in the early part of 1986.[14] The National Coalition of Black Lesbians and Gays, a progressive national membership organization structured around local chapters, organized the "National Conference on AIDS in the Black Community" in Washington DC in 1986. This conference, which was co-sponsored by the National Minority AIDS Council and the National Conference of Black Mayors, was funded in part from a grant from the United States Public Health Service.[15] Further, black gay men across the country, from Washington DC to New York to Oakland to San Francisco to Los Angeles were instrumental in helping to establish some of the first AIDS service organi-

zations explicitly identifying minority communities as their target population. Additionally, black gay organizations such as Gay Men of African Descent (GMAD) of New York City have been and continue to be essential in educational efforts seeking to reach large numbers of black men.[16]

A number of factors were helpful in laying the groundwork for the response from black gay men and lesbians. The information this group received from white gay activists was extremely helpful. The realization that some black gay men and lesbians also possessed limited access and economic privilege was useful in developing contacts and pooling resources. Further, the personal experiences of loss which brought together and raised the awareness of black lesbians and gay men were undoubtedly instrumental in motivating some response. Finally, "out" black gays and lesbians were in the position of being less vulnerable to the moral judgments of traditional institutions in the black community. Because of their public identity as a black lesbian or gay man these individuals stood ready to challenge the marginalizing ideology associated with AIDS. Thus, as they attempted to speak to the entire black community about the dangers of this growing epidemic, the silence and invisibility which had once been a part of the survival contract of black lesbians and gay men could no longer exist if lives were to be saved.

AIDS and Policing Black Sexuality

. . . [I]n the face of substantial and increasing devastation being visited upon the black community through the AIDS epidemic, one might reasonably expect members or at least leaders of black communities to actively mobilize community support around demands for more resources, attention, and action in response to this disease. However, the evidence suggests that the response from black community leaders and activists has been much less public, confrontational, collective, and consistent than the statistics might dictate. Further, any cursory comparative examination of the political response emanating from predominately white lesbian and gay activists to this disease suggests that black organizations and institutions have been less active around this crisis. Over the years, members of gay and lesbian communities have found old and new ways to make officials, institutions, and at times the general public answer some of their demands.[17] Gay activists have developed sophisticated political tactics to respond to the indifference and hostility that the government and other institutions display toward People with AIDS. Rallies, sit-ins, lobbying, private meetings, civil disobedience, "phone zaps," few things seem too far out-of-bounds to make people listen and respond. And while the gay community has mounted a coordinated effort of traditional politics and public collective action to the AIDS epidemic, the response in the black community has been much less pervasive, public, and effective. Again, through the work of primarily black gay activists, important conferences and forums have been sponsored to educate members of black communities on the dangers of AIDS. Organizations like the Minority Task Force on AIDS and the Black Leadership Commission on AIDS have been established to provide services and develop educational programs for members of black communities. National leaders have even on occasion made mention of AIDS in their speeches to black constituents. However, generally there has been no substantial and sustained mobilization around this crisis in African-American communities. There have been few, if any, rallies, sit-ins, or petitions in black communities to bring attention to the devastation created by AIDS. There has been no sustained lobbying effort on the part of national black organizations like the NAACP or the Urban League. Instead, many in the black community continue to see AIDS as a horrible disease, believing that we should extend sympathy and compassion to its "victims," but claim no ownership as a community. AIDS is generally not understood as an internal political crisis that necessitates the mobilization of black communities. Even when AIDS is seen as a conspiracy against black communities, by the government or some other entity, no mobilization accompanies such suspicion.[18] For most in black communities, AIDS is still a disease of individuals, usually "irresponsible, immoral, and deviant" individuals, some of whom happen to be black.

Quite often, when trying to explain the response to AIDS in black communities, authors retreat to the familiar and substantively important list of barriers preventing a more active response from community leaders and organizations. Regularly topping this list is the claim that because black communities have fewer resources than most other groups they cannot be expected to respond to AIDS in a manner similar to "privileged" lesbians and gay men. And while there is truth to the claim that most black people operate with limited access to resources, this explanation is based on a very narrow conception of resources and a very limited understanding of the history of the black community. Most of the cities hardest hit by this disease (New York, Los Angeles, Washington DC, Detroit, Chicago, Atlanta) have been or are currently headed by black mayors. Thus, while black individuals suffer from limited resources, black elected officials control, or at least have significant input into, decisions about how resources will be allocated in their cities. Further, while individuals in the black community still suffer from marginalization and oppression, organizations like the NAACP, the SCLC, and the Urban League have been able to gain access to national agencies and policy debates. Thus the claim that black people have fewer resources than other groups, while accurate at the individual level, does not appropriately account for the institutional resources controlled or accessed by black elected officials and traditional organizations.

A second explanation that is sometimes offered focuses on the numerous crises plaguing black communities. Proponents of this view argue that members of the black community suffer from so many ailments and structural difficulties, such as sickle-cell anemia, high blood pressure, sugar diabetes, homelessness, persistent poverty, drugs, crime, discrimination . . . that no one should expect community leaders to turn over their political agenda to the issue of AIDS. Again, this position has merit, for in fact we know that black communities do suffer disproportionately from most social, medical, economic, and political ills. It is, however, specifically because of the inordinate amount of suffering found in black communities that we might expect more attention to this disease.

Because AIDS touches on, or is related to, so many other issues facing, in particular poor black communities – healthcare, poverty, drug use, homelessness, etc. – we might reasonably expect black leaders to "use" the devastation of this disease to develop and reinforce an understanding of the enormity of the crisis facing black communities. Rarely does an issue so readily embody the life and death choices facing a community and rarely is an issue so neglected by the leadership of that community.

Still others have suggested that, along with the lack of resources and the encompassing social problems of the black community, there exist numerous other issues which discourage black communities from taking any active ownership regarding this epidemic. For example, the portrayal of AIDS as a disease of white gay men in dominant media sources as well as in many community papers communicates that this epidemic does not threaten and need not interest the majority of black people. Further, the fact that when coverage around AIDS and black communities is provided it often continues the historical practice of framing or associating black people/Africa with disease (i.e. discussion of the origin of AIDS in Africa) helps reinforce a look-the-other-way attitude by indigenous leaders and organizations.[19] Again while both of these factors clearly play a part in understanding the community's response, I contend they still leave vacant a central component in this puzzle over black communities' lack of mobilization around AIDS.

Recently, scholars who study AIDS and black communities have begun to point to the issue of homophobia in the black community as the missing piece in our puzzle.[20] In this context their concern is not just with homophobia among individuals, but more importantly with the homophobia located and rooted in indigenous institutions like the black church, fraternal and social organizations, as well as some national political organizations. Different variants of this argument suggest that it is the black community's homophobia that significantly structures its response, or lack thereof, to AIDS in black communities.[21]

While we must pay attention to homophobia in the black community as one source of disinformation about AIDS, I do not believe that the concept or explanation of homophobia adequately captures the complexity of sexuality, in particular lesbian and gay sexuality, in black communities. This is not to say that homophobia, as a general process of socialization that we all endure, is not a part of black communities. However, homophobia as the fear or even hatred of gay and lesbian people does not represent the intricate role that sexuality has played in defining "blackness" throughout the years. Sexuality, or what has been defined by the dominant society as the abnormal sexuality of both black men and women – with men being oversexed and in search of white women, while black women were and are represented as promiscuous baby producers when they are not the direct and indirect property of white men – has been used historically and currently in this country to support and justify the marginal and exploited position of black people.

Scholars such as Takaki, Steinberg, Davis, Lewis, and Omi and Winant have all attempted, through various approaches, to detail the ways in which dominant groups, often with state sanctioning, have defined and redefined racial classification for their benefit and profit.[22] Whether it be the one-drop rule, one's maternal racial lineage, simplistic evaluations of skin color, or some other combination of biological, cultural, or behavioral attributes, ideas of who is to be classified as black have had a long and varied history in this country. However, beyond the mere designation of who belongs in a particular group, dominant groups have also engaged in the process of defining racial group meaning. Those characteristics or stereotypes propagated as representing the "essence" of black people have been constructed and informed by particular historical needs. Ideas about the laziness, inferiority, and in particular the sexual or abnormal sexual activity of black people have been advanced to justify any number of economic, political, and social arrangements.

This systematic degradation, stereotyping, and stigmatization of black Americans has all but dictated that attempts at incorporation, integration, and assimilation on the part of black people generally include some degree of proving ourselves to be "just as nice as those white folks." Thus, leaders, organizations, and institutions have consistently attempted to redefine and indigenously construct a new public image or understanding of what blackness would mean. This process of reconstructing or [im]proving blackness involves not only a reliance on the self-regulation of individual black people, but also includes significant "indigenous policing" of black people. Consistently, in the writings of black academics we hear reference to the role of the black middle class as examples and regulators of appropriate behavior for the black masses. Drake and Cayton, in their 1945 classic *Black Metropolis*, discuss the attitude of the black upper class toward the behavior of black lower classes.

> The attitude of the upper class toward the lower is ambivalent. As people whose standards of behavior approximate those of the white middle class, the members of Bronzeville's upper class resent the tendency of outsiders to "judge us all by what ignorant Negroes do." They emphasize their *differentness*. . . . The whole orientation of the Negro upper class thus becomes one of trying to speed up the process by which the lower class can be transformed from a poverty-stricken group, isolated from the general stream of American life, into a counterpart of middle-class America. [emphasis from original text][23]

Regulation of the black masses was often pursued not only by individuals, but also by an extensive network of community groups and organizations. James R. Grossman details how the Urban League in conjunction with black and white institutions worked to help black migrants "adjust" to urban standards of behavior.

> The Urban League and the *Defender*, assisted by the YMCA, the larger churches, and a corps of volunteers, fashioned a variety of initiatives designed to help – and pressure – the new comers to adjust not only to industrial work, but to urban life, northern racial patterns, and behavior that would enhance the reputation of blacks in the larger (white) community . . . The Urban League, through such activities as "Stranger Meetings," leafleting, and door-to-door visits, advised newcomers on their duties as citizens: cleanliness, sobriety, thrift, efficiency, and respectable, restrained behavior in public places . . . Under the tutelage of the respectable citizens of black Chicago, migrants were to become urbanized northernized, and indistinguishable from others of their race. At the very least, they would learn to be as inconspicuous as possible.[24]

It is important to remember that a substantial amount of indigenous policing focused on what would be represented publicly as the sexual behavior of black people. Community leaders and organizations, fighting for equal rights, equal access, and full recognition as citizens, struggled to "clean up" the image of sexuality in black communities. . . .

I want to be clear that contests or opposition to the public representation of black gay male sexuality in particular and non-normative sexuality in general is significantly motivated by a genuine threat to the cultural capital acquired by some in black communities, where cultural capital symbolizes the acceptance, access, and privilege of primarily black middle- and upper-class people.[25] Thus, for many black leaders and activists, visible/public black homosexuality is understood to threaten that "cultural capital" acquired by both assimilation and protest. From such a perspective the policing or regulation of black gay and lesbian behavior/visibility is seen as the responsibility not only of dominant institutions, but also leaders of indigenous institutions who can claim that they are protecting the image and progress of "the race/community." And it is through the fulfillment of these communal duties that internal ideas and definitions of blackness, thought to help with the task of regulation, emerge. These definitions set the rules that to be a "good" or "true" black person you must adhere to some religious standards of appropriate sexual behavior. To be a true black man is antithetical to being gay, for part of your duty as a black man is to produce "little black warriors in the interest of the Black nation." The rules continue suggesting that to be gay is to be a pawn of a white genocidal plot, intent on destroying the black community. To be gay is to want to be white anyway, since we all know that there is no tradition of homosexuality in our African history. Thus, to be gay is to stand outside the norms, values, and practices of the community, putting your "true" blackness into question. . . .

We can now understand why homophobia, as a simple makeshift explanation to represent the complexity of sexuality in black communities, is inadequate. Instead, to analyze black communities' response to AIDS we must address a whole set of issues including dominant representations of black sexuality, how these ideas/stereotypes have been used against black communities, and the perceived need to regulate black sexuality through indigenous definitions of blackness. From this starting point we may be better able to understand, although never accept, the range of opposition black gay men encounter as stemming not only from people's repudiation of the idea of sex between men, but also from the use of sexuality by dominant groups to stigmatize and marginalize further a community already under siege.

Again, it is important to note that what is at stake here is the question of membership, full empowered membership in black communities. Thus, visibility, access to indigenous resources, participation and acknowledgement in the structuring of black political agendas all are put into question when one's blackness is contested. And undoubtedly, there exist many factors that contribute to the black community's response to AIDS, including a real deficiency in community resources as well as a real mistrust of government-sponsored information on health care and disease in black communities.[26] However, I believe that a significant part of the explanation for the lack of forceful action around AIDS is directly tied to ideas and definitions of "black identity" put forth by indigenous leaders, institutions and organizations. These definitions of "blackness" stand in direct contrast to the images and ideas associated with those living with AIDS or HIV (Human Immunodeficiency Virus) in black communities. In particular, these indigenous constructions of "blackness" define behavior linked to the transmission of HIV as immoral and an embarrassment, threatening to the status and survival of community members.

Having laid out this argument concerning the contestation of black gay identity and its impact on political responses to AIDS in black communities, it is important to provide, even briefly, a concrete example of the way an indigenous institution such as the black church defines and responds to the needs of black gay men in the era of AIDS. I will also try to highlight a few of the ways black gay men have responded to the secondary marginalization they have experienced through black churches. Again, I use the church merely as an illustration of the process of marginalization and identity contestation in which numerous indigenous institutions engage.

"The Black Church"

Activists and scholars often have focused on the activity of the black church to understand and explain the political behavior of members of the black community, since traditionally the church has been perceived as the glue and motor of the community. If any activity was to touch every segment of the community it was believed that such efforts must be based in the black church. The work of Aldon Morris linking the black church to the civil-rights movement is a classic example of the role the black church is thought to play in struggles for liberation and rights.[27] However, even prior to the civil-rights movement the black church was used to build movements of freedom. It was the black church that acted as meeting space, school, healthcare facility, and distributor of food from slavery to Reconstruction, through the years of northern migration and the decades of Jim Crow segregation. In her article on the new social role of black churches Hollie I. West comments, "African American churches have traditionally served as a refuge from a hostile white world, beehives of both social and political activity.[28]

However, with the advent of AIDS, drug epidemics, and the increasing poverty and stratification of black communities, some organizers and activists are beginning to question the central authority given to the church. West suggests in her article that AIDS is a problem that pulls the church in two directions. "Some clergymen privately acknowledge the dilemma. They recognize the need to confront AIDS and drugs, but conservative factions in their congregations discourage involvement."[29] It has been a conservative ideology, based on strict norms of "moral" behavior, that has often framed the church's response to many of the controversial social issues facing black communities. Gail

Walker briefly delineates the contradictory nature of the black church:

The dual – and contradictory – legacy of the African-American church is that it has been among the most important instruments of African-American liberation and at the same time one of the most conservative institutions in the African-American community.[30]

The position of the black church on the issue of homosexuality has seemed fairly straightforward, but in fact it has both public and private dimensions. Holding with the teaching of most organized religions, members of black churches assert that homosexual behavior is immoral and in direct contrast to the word of God. Black ministers have consistently spoken out and preached against the immorality and threat posed to the community by gays and lesbians. Recently, black ministers from numerous denominations in Cleveland, Ohio organized in opposition to federal legislation to include gay men and lesbians under the protection of the 1964 Civil Rights Bill. These ministers, representing themselves as "true leaders" of the black church, wrote in the local black newspaper, the *Call and Post*:

We as members and representatives of African American protestant congregations reaffirm our identity as THE BLACK CHURCH. . . .
We view HOMOSEXUALITY (including bisexual, as well as gay or lesbian sexual activity) as a lifestyle that is contrary to the teaching of the Bible. Such sexual activity and involvement is contrary to the pattern established during creation. Homosexual behavior in the Bible is forbidden and described as unnatural and perverted. . . .
Our attitude toward any individuals that are involved in/with a HOMOSEXUAL LIFESTYLE is expressed through tolerance and compassion. The church's mission is to bring about RESTORATION . . .[31]

However, at the same time that condemnation of gay and lesbian sexual behavior is a staple of the black church, it is also a well-known fact that black gay men, in particular, can be found in prominent positions throughout the church. Thus, black gay men involved in the activities of black churches are faced with a familiar dilemma: they have the choice of being quietly accepted as they sing in the church choir, teach Sunday school, and in some cases even preach from the pulpit, or they can be expelled from the church for participating in blasphemous behavior. Nowhere in this choice does the idea of inclusion as fully recognized and empowered members exist. Thus, according to religious doctrine, black lesbian and gay members of the community are to be embraced and taken care of in a time of need. However, their gay identity places them outside the indigenously constructed boundaries of both Christian and black identification as recognized by the church.

AIDS activists argue that a moral framework rooted in middle-class values of assimilation and dominant ideas of Christianity has been used to justify the church's moral condemnation of black gay men and injection drug users. And it is this same moral framework that structures the church's understanding and reaction to AIDS in the black community. Nowhere recently has this principle of silent acceptance and care at the expense of a public denunciation been more evident than in struggles around the church's response to AIDS in black communities. It has been the contradictory nature of church actions and rhetoric that continues to frustrate many AIDS activists who looked to it initially for a swift, compassionate, and empowering response. Activists and those providing services claim that the church did little to nothing early in the epidemic to deal with this impending crisis for black communities. Further, when members of the church elite finally did mobilize, it was with negative judgments and pity. Dr. Marjorie Hill, former Director of New York City's Office of Lesbians and Gay Concerns under Mayor David Dinkins, explains that the church's history of activism is muted with regards to AIDS because of its insistence on denying public recognition of lesbian and gay community members.

Historically, activism in the black community has come from the church. However, the reluctance of the church to respond to AIDS means they are not following the mission of Christ. . . . The church has not dealt with the issue of homosexuality. Many have Gays who sing in the choir and play the organ and that is fine until they need the church's help and recognition. . . . Denial only works for so long, the reality of gay men and women will eventually have to be dealt with.[32]

There are others who argue that the church is making progress. For their part, church members point to the numerous AIDS ministries that have been established to deal with AIDS in black communities. They highlight what seems like revolutionary strides in the ability of black ministers to even mention AIDS from the pulpit. And while black lesbian and gay leaders commend those who engage in efforts to identify comfortable ways for black ministers and congregations to deal with the devastation of AIDS in their communities, they still contend that there remains an absence of full recognition of the rights and lives of those infected with this disease. The saying "love the sinner, hate the sin," is paramount in understanding the limited response of black clergy. Gay men are to be loved and taken care of when they are sick, but their loving relationships are not to be recognized nor respected. Most individuals affected by this disease can tell at least one story of going to a funeral of a gay man and never having their gay identity recognized as well as never hearing the word AIDS mentioned. Family members and ministers are all too willing to grieve the loss of a son or church member, without ever acknowledging the total identity of that son. Lost to AIDS is not only the son loved so dearly, but the totality of his life which included lovers and gay friends who also grieve for that loss.

It is important that we not lose sight of the fundamental obstacle to the church's whole hearted response to AIDS, and that is its adherence or reliance on a strict middle-class Christian code, which holds that behavior that transmits the virus is immoral, sinful, and just as importantly for the argument presented here, costly to the community's status and standing. Thus, until church leaders are ready to discuss issues of sexuality, drug use, and homosexuality in an inclusive discourse, their ability to serve the entire community as well as confront, instead of replicate, dominant ideologies will be severely inhibited. Rev. James Forbes of Riverside Church in New York City has been one of the few black clergy who has openly called on the church to open up its dialogue concerning AIDS. In a keynote address at the 1991 Harlem Week of Prayer, Rev. Forbes declared that until the black church deals with fundamental issues such as sexuality in an inclusive and accepting manner, it will never be able to deal adequately with the AIDS epidemic in the black community.

While ministers like Rev. Forbes preach the need for the church to reevaluate its stance on fundamental judgments of human sexuality, others believe that we may have seen the church move about as far as its going to go. Except for those exceptional congregations committed to a liberation theology, the provision of services for those with AIDS may be the extent of the church's response, because for many clergy there is no way to reconcile behavior that can lead to the transmission of the virus to the doctrine of the Christian church. Rev. Calvin Butts of Absynnian Baptist Church in Harlem explains,

> The response of the church is getting better. At one time the church didn't respond and when the church did respond it was negative. Ministers thought that a negative response was in keeping with the thinking that AIDS was transmitted by homosexual transmission, drugs, you know. But as more thoughtful clergy became involved issues of compassion entered the discussion and we used Jesus' refuge in the house of lepers as an example. People became more sympathetic when people close to the church were affected. Also the work of BLCA [Black Leadership Commission on AIDS] brought clergy together to work on our response. Unfortunately, there are still quite a few who see it as God's retribution.[33]

However, in an environment where their identity is contested and their full rights and connection with black communities is negated, many black lesbian and gay leaders are actively developing ways to ignore the dictates and challenge the power of the church, especially as it affects AIDS organizing. One such strategy has focused on black gay and lesbian leaders as well as AIDS activists identifying other ways to do effective work in the community without the help of the church. There are those who suggest that it does not matter whether the church responds because the church no longer touches those parts of the community most at risk for this disease. Colin Robinson, former staff member at Gay Men's Health Crisis (GMHC) and currently executive director of the organization Gay Men of African Descent (GMAD) explains that "the church is still hooked on sin, but compromised by sin. They will take care of you when you get sick, but they won't talk about it and that is no way to provide effective education."[34] George Bellinger, Jr., a member of GMAD and former Education Director of the Minority Task Force on AIDS in New York, suggests that "we put too much status in the church. They aren't connected to the affected populations and they bring with them all kinds of middle-class values.[35]

Others in the community have gone beyond developing AIDS education strategies to focus directly on challenging the teaching of the church about homosexuality, especially as black gay identities are offered as a contrast to the indigenous constructed image of "good black Christian folk." These individuals seek out leaders inside the community, like Rev. James Forbes, who have publicly challenged the representations of more conservative clergy. These activists seek a leadership that will embrace the idea of an empowered black lesbian and gay community. In the absence of these individuals, black gay activists have taken up the task of building their own religious institutions in cities like New York, San Francisco, and Los Angeles, that will put forth a different interpretation of biblical scripture.

All of these oppositional strategies contest the stigma of a black gay identity as constructed by the black church. Black gay activists understand that to engage the black community on the issue of AIDS as well as lesbian and gay rights they must contest and challenge the church's declaration and labeling of gay and lesbian lifestyles as immoral. Further, black lesbian and gay activists must take on the task of redefining themselves as integral, connected, and contributing members of the community, so as to access the community support we most desperately need.

Conclusion: A Few Last Comments

The goal of this chapter was to explore, in some concrete fashion, the contested nature of iden-tity within marginal communities. For far too long we have let assumptions of a stable, homogeneous group direct our attention to a framework of analysis that focuses on struggles between dominant and marginal groups. Left largely unexplored by social scientists are the internal struggles within marginal communities threatening to severely change the basis and direction of group politics. Throughout this paper I have attempted to explore how identities are constructed and contested and how in this case such disputes influenced the politics of AIDS in black communities.

Central to this entire discussion has been the idea that group identity, or at least the way many of us conceptualize it, has changed over the years. We can no longer work from an essentialist position, in which all marginal people, in particular all black people, are assumed to have the same standing within their communities. Instead, we must pay attention to the battles for full inclusion waged within these communities, because these battles provide important signals to the future political direction of the community. In the case of AIDS, it is fairly clear that the vulnerable status and contested identities of those most often associated with this disease in the black community, injection drug users and gay men, severely impacts on the community's response to the epidemic. And while indigenous institutions and leaders have increasingly demonstrated a willingness to fight political battles over AIDS funding and discrimination, there have been few attempts by these same leaders to redefine the community's battle against AIDS as a political fight for the empowerment of the most marginal sectors of the community.

However, the battle around AIDS, and who has full access to the resources and consciousness of the community does not stand alone. Similar battles are being waged around other issues, such as the "underclass." Those on the outside, those designated as "less than, secondary, bad, or culturally deviant," are developing new ways to challenge politically a cohesive group unity that rejects their claims at representation and in many cases ignores their needs. These individuals, like the black gay men discussed in this paper, can no longer afford to support a leadership that is content to have them seen, in some cases blamed, but not heard.

Thus, if there is one larger implication of this work that needs further investigation, it is how marginal groups facing increasing stratification and multiple social identities will adjust to build a somewhat unified identity for the pursuit of political struggles. The importance of groups in our political system cannot be denied. In a pluralistic political system access is usually based on the grouping of individuals with some shared interest, with these individuals pooling resources and influence to impact policy decisions. The role of collective mobilization becomes especially important for marginal groups with a history of being denied access to dominant political structures. These marginal groups often find themselves excluded and defined out of the political process. Thus, African Americans grouped together by the socially constructed category of race have found their political access restricted. Only through coming together to redefine their marginal identity into a new identity which both unifies and empowers the multiple segments of the community could any political battles hope to be won. . . .

Notes

1 For discussions of postmodern and deconstructive approaches see e.g. Sylvia Walby, "Post-Post-Modernism? Theorizing Social Complexity," *Destabilizing Theory: Contemporary Feminist Debates*, M. Barrett and A. Phillips (eds) (Stanford, Calif.: Stanford University Press, 1992), 31–52; Jane Flax, "Postmodernism and Gender Relations in Feminist Theory," *Feminism/Postmodernism*, L. J. Nicholson (ed.) (New York: Routledge, 1990), 39–62; and Steven Seidman, "Identity and Politics in a "Postmodern" Gay Culture: Some Historical and Conceptual Notes," *Fear of a Queer Planet: Queer Politics and Social Theory*, M. Warner (ed.) (Minneapolis: University of Minnesota Press, 1993), 105–42.

2 See e.g. Iris Marion Young, "The Ideal of Community and the Politics of Difference," *Feminism/Postmodernism*, L. Nicholson (ed.) (New York: Routledge, 1990), (30), 300–23; Shane Phelan, "(Be)Coming Out: Lesbian Identity and Politics," *Signs*, 19 (30), spring 1994: 765–90; Kimberle Crenshaw, "Demarginalizing the Inter-

section of Race and Sex: A Black Feminist Critique of Antidiscrimination Doctrine Feminist Theory and Antiracist Politics," *University of Chicago Legal Forum*, 1989, pp. 139–67; Lisa Lowe, "Heterogeneity, Hybridity, Multiplicity: Marking Asian American Differences," *Diaspora*, 1 (1), spring 1991: 24–44.

3 See e.g. Maria Lugones, "Purity, Impurity, and Separation," *Signs: Journal of Women in Culture and Society*, 19 (2), 1994: 458–79; and E. Frances White, "Africa on my Mind: Gender Counter Discourse and African-American Nationalism," *Journal of Women's History*, 2 (1), spring 1990: 73–97.

4 James C. Scott, *Domination and the Arts of Resistance: The Hidden Transcript* (New Haven: Yale University Press, 1990).

5 For a full discussion of the process of secondary marginalization see Cathy J. Cohen, "Power, Resistance and the Construction of Crisis: Marginalized Communities Respond to AIDS," unpublished manuscript, Dept. of Political Science, Yale University, 1993, pp. 72–5.

6 While several different segments of the black community have been associated with AIDS, I focus this inquiry on the struggle around black gay male identity because it seems most illustrative of the ways in which contests over indigenously defined identities can impact on the politics of marginal communities.

7 I should be clear that any number of organizations or leaders have constructed ways to "deal" with AIDS without directly confronting or embracing those stigmatized segments of black communities associated with this disease. Thus, you are much more likely to find "leaders" talking about the innocent children and women who are the victims of this disease in black communities than the gay men and intravenous drug users who suffer disproportionately in our communities.

8 See e.g. Cheryl Clarke, "The Failure to Transform: Homophobia in the Black Community," *Home Girls: A Black Feminist Anthology*, B. Smith (ed.) (New York: Kitchen Table: Women of Color Press, 1983), 197–208. I would caution the reader, however, not to discount the role that state-sponsored repression also played in leading to the destruction of many of these groups. It is now a well-documented fact that the FBI through the counterintelligence program (COINTELPRO) helped destroy many liberation groups, such as the Black Panther Party.

9 See Eric Garber, "A Spectacle in Color: The Lesbian and Gay Subculture of Jazz Age Harlem," in *Hidden from History: Reclaiming the*

Gay and Lesbian Past, M. Duberman, M. Vicinus and G. Chauncey, Jr. (eds) (New York: Meridian Books, 1990), 318–31; Jonathan Ned Katz, *Gay American History: Lesbians and Gay Men in the USA* (New York: Meridian Books, 1992).

10 bell hooks, *Talking Back: Thinking Feminist, Thinking Black* (Boston: South End Press, 1989), 120–21.

11 Cornel West, "The New Cultural Politics of Difference," in *Out There: Marginalization and Contemporary Cultures*, R. Ferguson, M. Gever, T. T. Minh-ha and C. West (eds) (Cambridge: The MIT Press, 1990), 25.

12 John D'Emilio. *Sexual Politics, Sexual Communities: The Making of a Homosexual Minority in the United States, 1940–1970* (Chicago: University of Chicago Press, 1983).

13 Cherríe Moraga and Gloria Anzaldúa (eds), *This Bridge Called My Back: Writings by Radical Women of Color* (Latham, New York: Kitchen Table: Women of Color Press, 1981); Barbara Smith (ed.), *Home Girls: A Black Feminist Anthology* (Latham, New York: Kitchen Table: Women of Color Press, 1983); Esse Hemphill (ed.), *Brother to Brother: New Writings by Black Gay Men* (Boston: Alyson Publications, Inc., 1991); Joseph Beam (ed.), *In The Life: A Black Gay Anthology* (Boston: Alyson Publications, Inc., 1986).

14 Ernest Quimby and Samuel R. Friedman, *Social Problems*, 36 (4), Oct. 1989.

15 Guy Weston, "AIDS in the Black Community," *BLACK/OUT*, 1 (2), fall 1986: 13–15.

16 There are conflicting views on the effectiveness of GMAD during the AIDS crisis. Some argue that in a crisis of this proportion GMAD should be a leader in this fight, holding programs whenever possible. Other GMAD members suggest, however, that there are more dimensions to the lives of black gay men than just the threat of AIDS. Thus it is the responsibility of GMAD to provide a supportive environment in which black gay men can dialogue and work on the opportunities and obstacles that structure their lives.

    While this debate will probably not be settled any time soon, I still believe, every time I see 75 black gay men at one of their meetings, that this is an example of the success of struggle. An example that needs work and adjustment, but a success still the same.

17 Undoubtedly, the organization most recognized as contributing to the organization of people in lesbian and gay communities is ACT UP (AIDS Coalition To Unleash Power). See e.g. Josh Gamson, "Silence, Death, and the Invisible Enemy: AIDS Activism and Social Movement 'Newness,'" in *Social Problems*, 36 (4) (Oct. 1989): 351–67.

18 Responses to a question from the 1993–1994 National Black Politics Study on the origin of AIDS found that nearly one-quarter (22 per cent) of African-American respondents agreed with the statement that "AIDS is a disease that is a result of an anti-black conspiracy."

19 Renee Sabatier, *Blaming Others: Prejudice, Race and Worldwide AIDS* (Washington: The Panos Institute, 1988); Cindy Patton *Inventing AIDS* (New York: Routledge, 1990).

20 Harlon L. Dalton, "AIDS in Blackface," *The AIDS Reader: Social, Political and Ethical Issues*, N. F. McKenzie (ed.) (New York: Meridan, 1991), 122–43; Evelynn Hammonds, "Race, Sex, AIDS: The Construction of 'Other,'" *Radical America*, 20 (6), 1987: 328–40; Phillip Brian Harper, "Eloquence and Epitaph: Black Nationalism and the Homophobic Impulse in Responses to the Death of Max Robinson," *The Lesbian and Gay Studies Reader*, H. Abelove, M. A. Barable, and D. M. Halperin (eds) (New York: Routledge, 1993), 159–75.

21 Now, before engaging in any discussion of homophobia in the black community these authors, as I myself do, make their obligatory claim that while we can talk about homophobia in the black community, this is not done to suggest that the black community is 'more' homophobic than any other community, in particular white "communities." In fact, there is a reasonable argument that marginal groups, either because of an understanding of the outsider position or a lack of power to enforce their prejudices, have been more inclusive and accepting of lesbian and gay members *relative to* other groups rooted in dominant society.

22 See Ronald Takaki, *Strangers From a Different Shore: A History of Asian Americans* (New York: Penguin, 1990); Stephen Steinberg, *The Ethnic Myth: Race, Ethnicity, and Class in America* (Boston: Beacon Press, 1989); F. James Davis, *Who is Black? One Nation's Definition* (University Park, Penn.: The Pennsylvania State University Press, 1991); Earl Lewis, "Race, The State, and Social Construction: The Multiple Meanings of Race in the Twentieth Century," 1994, unpublished manuscript; Omi and Winant, *Racial Formation*.

23 St Clair Drake and Horace R. Cayton, *Black Metropolis: A Study of Negro Life in a Northern City* (Chicago: University of Chicago Press, 1993), 563.

24 James R. Grossman, *Land of Hope: Chicago, Black Southerners, and the Great Migration*

(Chicago: University of Chicago Press, 1989), 145–6.

25 Pierre Bourdieu, "The Forms of Capital," in *Handbook of Theory and Research for the Sociology of Education*, J. G. Richardson (ed.) (New York: Greenword Press, 1986), 241–58.

26 We need only remember the Tuskegee Syphilis Experiment to understand where such mistrust is rooted. See James H. Jones, *Bad Blood: The Tuskegee Syphilis Experiment – A Tragedy of Race and Medicine* (New York: The Free Press, 1981); David McBride, *From TB to AIDS: Epidemics Among Urban Blacks Since 1900* (Albany: State University of New York Press, 1991); Evelynn Hammonds, "Race, Sex, AIDS: The Construction of Other," *Radical America*, 20 (6), 1987: 28–36.

27 Aldon D. Morris, *The Origins of the Civil Rights Movement: Black Communities Organizing for Change* (New York: The Free Press, 1984).

28 Hollie I. West, "Down from the Clouds: Black Churches Battle Earthly Problems," *Emerge*, May 1990: 51.

29 West, "The New Cultural Politics," 21.

30 Gail Walker, "'Oh Freedom': Liberation and the African-American Church," *Guardian*, Feb. 26, 1992, p. 10.

31 Rev. C. Jay Matthews, "The Black Church Position Statement on Homosexuality," *Call and Post*, June 10, 1993, p. 5c.

32 Interview with Dr. Marjorie Hill.

33 Interview with Rev. Calvin Butts.

34 Interview with Colin Robinson.

35 Interview with George Bellinger, Jr.

4

Leatherdyke Boys and Their Daddies
How to Have Sex Without Women or Men

C. Jacob Hale

There are times in life when the question of knowing if one can think differently
than one thinks, and perceive differently than one sees, is absolutely necessary
if one is to go on looking and reflecting at all.

Michel Foucault, *The Use of Pleasure*

Contemporary queer theory sees gender as a regulatory construct, a site of shifting power relations. Although queer theorists have made many claims about the power of queerly gendered bodies and performativities to disrupt enforced normative sex/gender systems, theory lags far behind community discourses here. In sexual-minority communities, such as queer leather communities, there are rich and subtly nuanced discourses of gendered pleasure, practice, desire, and subjectivity. These community discourses sometimes reflect rich and subtly nuanced embodiments of gender that resist and exceed any simple categorization into *female, male, woman, man,* and thus into *homosexual, bisexual,* or *heterosexual.*[1] Further, queer theory has tended to neglect "the implications of an enforced sex/gender system for people who live outside it," as Ki Namaste has argued with regard to queer theory's erasure of transgendered subjectivity.[2] When transgendered subjects participate in minority communities organized around radical sexual practice, new and theoretically interesting configurations of sex, gender, and sexuality arise. In this paper, I will theorize the genderings of US leatherdyke boys and their

leatherdyke daddies. I am especially concerned to explore how leatherdyke genderplay functions as a means for gender interrogation, solidification, resistance, destabilization, and reconfiguration. From this investigation, I will draw some tentative conclusions about multiple gender statuses already available in the United States.

First, I need to address briefly my qualifications to write on this topic and my subject position in relation to leatherdyke communities and practices. My birth certificate bears witness that when I was born, I was diagnosed "female" and given a heavily gendered feminine name. I was raised girl-to-woman, with a fairly unambiguous female body until I began injections of exogenous testosterone on 19 May 1995. For most of my adult life, I lived as a bisexual woman whose primary sexual relationships were with heterosexual men. In 1991 I "came out" as a lesbian, and two years later I began exploring SM and participating in leatherdyke friendship circles and community structures, primarily in Los Angeles. In 1995 I began transitioning female-to-male (ftm), leatherdyke-to-leatherfag.[3] I retain strong ties with a number of Los Angeles leatherdykes and continue to participate in some leatherdyke community public events, such as serving as a VIP boy for the 1997 Ms. Fallen Angels Contest, although I do not attend women-only play parties even when invited. Since I have not undertaken research even approximating careful ethnography, any generalizations must be tentative. Furthermore, it is crucial to note that not only are uses of leatherdyke genderplay as ftm transitioning technologies different for different ftms, but that many ftms have never participated in leatherdyke or other lesbian practices or communities at all.

From an external-to-leatherdyke-culture point of view, and as a first approximation that I will complicate later, "leatherdyke boys" are adult lesbian (dyke) females who embody a specific range of masculinities intelligible within queer leather (SM) communities; their "daddies" may be butch leatherdykes or, less frequently, gay leathermen. This delineation is, of course, vague insofar as it replicates the haziness of the boundaries between the categories *female, lesbian, dyke, queer, leather*, and *butch*. In this paper, I restrict my focus to leatherdyke boys and their leatherdyke daddies, leaving aside investigations of how gender works in interactions between leatherdyke boys and their gay leathermen daddies.

Leatherdyke boys perform masculinity in a wide range of ways. Playing as a boy does not necessitate age-play; status as a boy may simply indicate a masculine bottom status – submissive or masochistic or both – different from that of a slave. However, in my experience age-play is more common in leatherdyke boy–daddy settings than it is in gay male ones. When boy–daddy age-play occurs, play ages may bear no relation to the legal ages of the players; daddy may be younger than her boy, according to their birth certificates. Leatherdyke boys may have specific play ages, or may locate themselves vaguely as young children or as teenagers; some leatherdyke boys are little boys, some are big boys. Leatherdyke boys may relate to their daddies in loving, respectful, and attentive manners, or they may be bratty, rebellious, withdrawn, or distant. They may signal their status as boys with age- and gender-specific clothing – such as a Boy Scout shirt, schoolboys' short pants, a Catholic schoolboy uniform, school sports uniforms, or youthful hip hop styles that

are at odds with more traditional leather-community styles – or clothing may give no clues as to their status as boys. Clothing is very likely, however, to indicate their statuses as SM bottoms and as butches. Clothing may also vaguely indicate levels of SM experience and, in more precise ways, interest in particular sexual activities. In short, the range of masculinities open for leatherdyke boys' performativities is at least as wide as that open to young males, though it is inflected both through lesbian community butch styles and through leather-community means of signaling bottom status and interest in specific sexual activities.

Since leatherdyke boys' masculine performativities often occur in contexts separate from interactions with workmates, family (as defined by law), neighbors, and other friends and acquaintances outside of SM contexts, they are less bounded by cultural constructions of masculinity, which are inflected by such vectors of power as race, ethnicity, class, sexual orientation, or occupation, than the performativities of young males. For example, an upper-middle-class professional woman can become a sixteen-year-old headbanger rockerdude with a change of clothing and attitude.

Gayle Rubin has argued that "there are more ways to be butch" than "there are ways for men to be masculine," since "when women appropriate masculine styles the element of travesty produces new significance and meaning."[4] Rubin's point extends even further when applied to leatherdyke masculinities as enacted in leatherdyke play spaces: when leatherdyke boys' masculine performativities occur in conjunction with fairly unambiguous female embodiments in settings, such as play parties, where heavily gender-coded bodily zones are visible, their performativities are less bounded by cultural regulations of masculinity than young males' are.[5]

This is not to suggest that leatherdyke boys' masculine performativities are unregulated in leatherdyke contexts. Gender performativity, just as any other form of performativity, must occur within social constraints to be intelligible; it must be intelligible if it is to be efficacious; and if it is not efficacious it cannot succeed as performative. Further, wider lesbian community anxieties about masculinity, manhood, and maleness circulate throughout leatherdyke communities. These anxieties become especially acute in determining the boundaries of the category *woman* for admittance to women-only sexual spaces, due to a felt need to protect women's sexual safety in sexual spaces. Transsexuals – male-to-female (mtf) and, more recently, female-to-male – have become the major threat to the apparent purity of this boundary. Indeed, other than disputes about whether or not male-to-female transsexuals – with or without surgical alterations of their genitals – may attend the Michigan Womyn's Music Festival, the most anxiety-fraught and vociferous struggles around political boundaries of the category *woman* in lesbian communities have been disputes about how to define *woman* for purposes of admittance to leatherdyke play parties. Although most organizations that host such parties are geographically local, these disputes have been international, because people travel to attend parties out of their geographical regions and because of community discussions in publications such as the now-defunct leatherdyke magazine *Venus Infers* and on-line. Such disputes may reflect different local play-party traditions that shape policy. For example, as the predominantly separatist Seattle leatherdyke community involved in organizing Powersurge attempted to create an event that would draw national attendance and yet enforce their local separatist traditions and policies, they ran into friction with leatherdykes from other regions, such as San Francisco, with deliberately non-separatist traditions and policies.[6]

In these disputes, anxieties centered around both male embodiment and masculine behaviors. Usually, however, when unclothed embodiment is unambiguously female, a much wider range of masculine behaviors are tolerated than when embodiment is partially male. As Gayle Rubin has observed, "Obnoxious behavior that would be tolerated in a butch will often be considered intolerable in an FTM."[7] While a butch with a fairly unambiguous female body may be called up short for behaving badly, her behavior will not likely be attributed to her sex/gender status, embodiment, self-identifications, or history. In contrast, if an mtf or an ftm engages in the same behaviors, these behaviors are more likely to be labeled "male" and to be attributed to sex/gender history, identification, or embodi-

ment. Further, the person engaging in such behaviors may be banned from attending future play parties and exiled from leatherdyke communities and friendship circles, and causal attributions of objectionable behaviors to sex/gender may be cited as justificatory grounds for changing definitional policies to exclude other mtfs or ftms in the future.

Play party invitations, instruction in SM techniques, inclusion in community organizations and friendship circles, and access to sex/play partners are powerful means for leatherdyke community regulation of leatherdyke conduct, perhaps more so than are their analogs within broader lesbian communities. Despite these regulatory mechanisms, masculine gender performativities, in conjunction with female embodiment, are given a wider range of expression within leatherdyke contexts than in many other lesbian or dyke settings.

Leatherdyke boy–daddy play sometimes functions as a means of gender exploration, solidification, resistance, destabilization, and reconfiguration. This can be illustrated by examining some of the ways in which boy or daddy play within leatherdyke contexts can facilitate female-to-male transitioning paths. In this section, I will rely on my own personal experiences as a leatherdyke boy and the experiences of Spencer Bergstedt as a leatherdyke daddy prior to his transition.

There are at least three ways in which leatherdyke boy or daddy play can function to consolidate a leatherdyke boy's or daddy's self-identification as male or as a man. One, which is not exemplified by either Bergstedt or myself, is through a conception of submission, especially to pain, as the most masculine SM position, especially when the person to whom one submits is also masculine. A second is that which Bergstedt described to me in an interview on 9 August 1995: leatherdyke daddy play enabled him to explore his masculine dominance more thoroughly than he could in other areas of his life. A third is through exploration of masculine boyhoods or periods of adolescence that were missing from our lives as we developed pubescent female bodies – bodies that were supposed to end our lives as tomboys and signal the beginnings of womanhood. I will illustrate this by recounting some of my own personal experiences.

While still identifying as a dyke, Bergstedt served as International Ms. Leather 1994.[8] He currently sits on the executive board of the National Leather Association, holding the same position he did prior to transition. An attorney practicing in Seattle, Bergstedt has served on the boards of numerous other community organizations, including the Seattle City Commission on Lesbians and Gays. Active in transgender community work as well, Bergstedt was the treasurer for the Second Annual FTM Conference of the Americas in Seattle in August 1996 and is family law director of the International Conference on Transgender Law and Employment Project (ICTLEP). A topman who identifies as heterosexual, at the time of our interview Bergstedt had a significant other and was a "daddy with nine leatherkids" with whom he did not play at all. He describes himself as a "Daddy's daddy," someone to whom other daddies, including very experienced gay topmen, turn to for daddying, especially for advice about problems in their lives. Bergstedt characterized his daddying as providing "stable, nurturing male energy."

Bergstedt described SM as "a resource or a means of learning more about myself and growing more spiritually." Later in our interview, "tool" was the word he used. Bergstedt said that SM play has "little to do with sexual pleasure" for him; he is not sexual with most of the people he plays with and views SM play as more of a "spiritual exercise" through which he learns "who I am." Through leatherplay itself, Bergstedt was able to explore his masculinity and his dominance. He is well aware that dominance can be feminine and did not simply equate masculinity with dominance. Instead, he said that SM allowed him to explore "masculine ways of being dominant" to a greater extent than he could in other areas of his life. In SM, he said, "I could really *live* that." He illustrated the contrast with other areas of his life by recounting experiences he had while serving on the Seattle City Commission on Lesbians and Gays during a time when he identified as a dyke: "A number of the women who were on the commission at the time objected to my leadership style as being too male and too dominant and not processing enough, . . . too goal-oriented, whereas the men had very little problem with me at all." When I asked him whether the women on the commis-

sion raised similar objections to the leadership styles of the men, he answered, "No, just me." Bergstedt said that the message he was getting in this experience was that "the way that I was expressing my dominance and my personality was inappropriate for the gender role that those people perceived me to be in." In SM play, Bergstedt could "really live" his masculinity through exploring his masculine dominance. This was enabled by the "reinforcement and acceptance" he found for his expressions of masculine dominance in leather community circles, though Bergstedt's leather community participation, both before his transition and now, has been more extensive in pansexual and gay male circles than in leatherdyke ones. He asserts that, "to a person," all of the leatherfolk he knows have been supportive of his transition. Participating in SM has allowed him to form a chosen leather family, a family which is "tolerant of difference and change," thus giving him a safe and supportive environment for self-exploration.

In 1993, I identified as a lesbian and had for two years. For many years, I had not done solosex because the fantasies that came unbidden into my head scared me. I stayed away from reading books about male adolescence because I was frightened and ashamed by the arousal I experienced in response to scenes in which adolescent boys were punished. As I moved further into lesbian communities, my boy-identification strengthened, and I began exploring queer SM community events and literature. Eventually, I started seeing a young post-punk SM dyke whom I met at a Ron Athey performance. Within a few weeks, I started wearing more boyish clothes and jockey shorts, and I gave myself a boy name: first "Alex" and then "Jake." My play age quickly settled in at fourteen years of age. Scenes with this dyke, when she played daddy to my boy, centered on punishments in which invented junior high school locker-room sexual high jinks among boys and basketball played elaborate roles. That is, we engaged in fairly extensive psychological play, sometimes dissolving into giggles when our scripts got stuck. After she and I stopped seeing each other, I ran a personal ad for a dyke daddy in the *Lesbian News*, a free Los Angeles monthly. This time I found someone with many years of leather experience who treated me as "boy" and "son" most of the time we were together. Daddying, for this one, was about love, support, nurturance, and guidance, about helping and teaching, more than it was about punishment. I began to be introduced to other people as "Jake" in settings other than leatherdyke play parties, trying out different styles of masculine self-presentation and behavior, acquiring a leather family, and extending my queer leather community connections and participation. During this time, pronoun usage varied somewhat randomly: either feminine or masculine pronouns were used to refer to Daddy, to Daddy's best butch buddy who became my uncle, and to me.[9] My discomfort with hearing feminine pronouns used to refer to myself solidified here.[10]

Bergstedt's stories and mine are quite different, and we construct our stories quite differently. For him, SM as gender technology allowed him to explore, more fully than he could in other areas of his life, "who I really am," as he put it. For me, SM as gender technology allowed me to experiment with masculinities as part of a process of self-construction in which I became more masculine, in embodiment, in self-presentation, and in identification.[11] In my self-conception, who I "really" am is a matter of social/cultural facts about my categorical locations; there is facticity here, but it is not natural or essential and is continually changing as culturally available categories change and as I change relative to them. Yet there are some common themes to Bergstedt's story and mine: themes of explorations of masculinities, and of the reinforcement and acceptance we found in our leather worlds.

Leatherplay can create, so to speak, a culture of two, composed of those two people who are playing together. When I was a boy with my dyke daddy, in that culture of two I was a boy. I was not an adult woman playing a boy's role or playing a boy, nor was I an adult woman doing boy in some other way. Daddy's participation was necessary for me to be a boy with her. I was a boy with her by engaging in a gender performativity that made sense to both of us as a *boy's* gender performativity. Importing the words Bergstedt chose to speak of himself, Daddy gave me "reinforcement and acceptance" for being a boy. In this culture of two, informed and structured by leatherdyke community gender codes, my communication of a masculine gender identification was legible to

someone else, despite my female body. I needed to know that my gender identification could be enacted legibly to at least one other person for it to be convincing enough to me that it could transform from a self-identification fully contained within my fantasy structure to a self-identification with a broader social sphere of enactment. Daddy, of course, could not have read my gender performativity as a boy's gender performativity if there had not been culturally available constructs of *boy* into which she could fit it. For my performativity as boy to be legible to Daddy, I had to cite gender codes she understood as a boy's, though I was not limited to only those boyish codes she had already encountered. Indeed, there were times when I blew it, when what I said or did was way off the boy mark; sometimes these were painful moments, other times they were pleasantly amusing, and some other times they shifted our interaction into one between two adult butches. Los Angeles's leatherdyke community, particularly as it intersected with Los Angeles's gay male leather community and hip hop youth cultures, provided those cultural constructs of *boy* through which my gender performativity was intelligible as that of a leatherdyke boy at first, then as that of a leatherboy as I moved further into the leathermen's world and as my self-presentation became more masculine. Extending the realm of my gender performativities as boy, or man, beyond situations in which Daddy and I were the only people present opened up new possibilities of gender performativity into which I could fit as a boy or as a man; circumscribed those possible performativities in other ways; and extended the realms in which I could create a masculine self, or masculine selves, in relational gendered communications/communications of gender. Relationality of gender, I think, becomes clear in both Bergstedt's story and mine.

Another aspect of SM as gender technology, which did not come out clearly in my interview with Bergstedt, perhaps because I did not think to ask him about it then, is that leatherdyke genderplay enables a phenomenon sometimes called "retooling" or "recoding" our bodies in transcommunity discourse. Sexual interactions, along with public restrooms and medical settings, are some of the sites at which dominant cultural connections between genitals and gender are the tightest, so many transpeople must remap the sexualized zones of our bodies if we are to be sexually active. Through leatherdyke SM practice, I was able to disrupt the dominant cultural meanings of my genitals and to reconfigure those meanings. There was already precedence for such deterritorialization and reterritorialization in the leatherdyke communities in which I participated. SM practices that decouple genital sexuality from bodily pleasures provide the backdrop for such phenomena of remapping.[12] One such phenomenon is that inanimate objects – dildoes – sometimes take on some of the phenomenological characteristics of erogenous body parts. So, when Powersurge defined a woman as someone who could slam her dick into a drawer without hurting it, a common response among some butch leatherdykes and some ftms was to say that it sure would hurt if their dicks got slammed into a drawer; a dildo may not be a dick only in the conception, it may be a dick phenomenologically as well. Furthermore, sometimes leatherdykes resignify sexed bodily zones. Among some leatherdyke faggots, an important desideratum is to keep masculinity as seamless as possible during scenes, and gay leathermen's masculinities often provide the paradigms of masculinity here. Thus, if the body part a leatherdyke daddy is fisting is that which a physician would unequivocally deem a "vagina," it may be resignified so that its use for erotic pleasure is consistent with male masculinity. It may become a "hole," "fuckhole," "manhole," "boyhole," "asshole," or "butthole," and a leatherdyke boy pleading, "Please, Daddy, fuck my butt!" may be asking daddy to fuck the same orifice into which a physician would insert a speculum to perform a pap smear. Of course, this resignification may prove painful if this boy's daddy does not understand it. For some ftms who used to be leatherdykes, our abilities to rechart our bodies – I would even say to change our embodiments without changing our bodies, that is, to change the personal and social meanings of our sexualized bodies – began in the queer resignifying practices available to us in leatherdyke cultures. If we invent novel, idiosyncratic reconfigurations, there is an already-given precedence for male reconfigurations of our bodies, which enables our novel reconfigurations to emerge into the realm of efficacious performativity and social production.

Yet some ftms who used to be leatherdykes may have found, as I did, that there were limits to our abilities to reconstitute the sexualized social spaces of our bodies. Some of these limits are constituted personally in that we cannot ourselves reconfigure the social meanings of certain bodily zones, and others may be externally imposed in that we cannot manage to communicate our attempts at idiosyncratic rechartings in ways that others are able and willing to read. Leatherdyke practice may help us discern those aspects of our embodied subjectivities that are susceptible to our own agency, and those parts of our bodies that we must change if we are to live in our own skins.

Is a leatherdyke daddy a woman or a man? Is a leatherdyke boy a woman or a man or a boy? These questions, I think, are badly misguided: they presuppose overly simplistic understandings of how gender categories work, and in so doing they reinscribe the hegemonic stranglehold of the dominant sex/gender/sexuality system. Elsewhere I have argued that the dominant cultural category *woman* in the contemporary United States is not defined in terms of necessary or sufficient conditions, but rather in terms of thirteen criteria none of which is necessary nor sufficient for membership in that category. The notion that there is one characteristic – usually, though not always, understood as genital – sharply differentiating women from men is part of an oppressive sex/gender/sexuality system which Harold Garfinkel dubbed "the natural attitude toward gender" to indicate its status as a culturally constructed system to which we, as members of this culture, are held morally accountable for upholding and for which we are held morally accountable for upholding as fully natural. Careful analysis of leatherdyke boys' and daddies' performativities in light of both my earlier descriptive reconstruction of the category *woman* and Garfinkel's work on "the natural attitude" would show that, according to the dominant culture's principles, some leatherdyke daddies and boys are women, some are not, and that in many cases there is no fact of the matter. Furthermore, as I shall argue, such a question is culturally imperialistic in ways that foreground interesting contemporary gender formations within the United States.[13]

I take it as fairly noncontroversial that gender is culturally constructed and that leatherdyke communities constitute cultures that, though they are influenced by and may influence the dominant culture, are distinct if not autonomous from the dominant culture insofar as they produce cultural formations and structures different from those found in the dominant culture. Thus, we may legitimately consider "subcultures" as analytically separate from the dominant culture. Given this, we can see that a question that presupposes that a person has a unitary gender status across cultures with varying gender categories is conceptually misguided, even if some of the cultures in question are subcultures. Instead of speaking of a person's gender status, we might do well to speak of a person's gendered status in a given cultural location, at a given time, and for a given purpose.

In a short interlude, I would like to motivate this notion of multiple gendered statuses further by looking at a simpler case, one which does not involve different cultures, but one in which I, again, am my own example. Currently, I do not have a unitary sex/gender status under the law, even under the law in the state in which I was born and reside. My California driver's license bears the sex/gender designation "M," and my California birth certificate bears the sex/gender designation "F." This *apparent* discrepancy is due to the fact that different state laws and regulations govern change of sex/gender designation on these documents; while I have met the legal requirements to change that "F" to "M" on one, I have not met the legal requirements to make that change on the other and, further, have no particular need to change it. Indeed, my earlier use of "the law" was a setup, for there are multiple laws and regulations that define sex/gender status differently. Birth certificates and driver's licenses serve different state purposes. For example, one functions for medical record keeping (among many other purposes) in ways that the other does not. Thus, my sex/gender status is specific to state interests and purposes, and my sex/gender status is different relative to different state interests and purposes. Consequently, unitary sex/gender status is, in part, a juridical construction that falls apart on some transsexed (and intersexed) bodies. Unitariness of sex/gender status is a

juridical *fiction* in the strictest of senses; despite appearances to the contrary, there is absolutely no discrepancy between the gender/sex designations on my driver's license and my birth certificate.

In a broader sense, unitary sex/gender status is a culturally constructed fiction produced by the state, by medicine, by psychotherapy, and by other institutions and discursive structures. This construction of sex/gender status as unitary also breaks down on genderplaying leatherqueer bodies situated in "subcultures" with gender orchestrations different from dominant cultural constructs. From medical points of view, most leatherdyke boys and daddies are women; some male-to-female and female-to-male transsexual leatherdyke boys and daddies may count as men; and some leatherdyke boys and daddies may not have a unitary sex/gender status according to law or according to medicine if their sexed characteristics are not unambiguously female or male. This will vary from jurisdiction to jurisdiction, even from law to law within one jurisdiction, from medical specialty to medical specialty, and even from physician to physician within one medical specialty. From a broader cultural point of view, some nontranssexual, nonintersexual leatherdyke boys and daddies may not be easily classifiable if they do not clearly enough satisfy the defining criteria of the categories *woman* and *man*. Relative to leatherdyke cultural spaces, *woman* and *man* may be the most relevant gender categories, and the only two available in addition to neither, for purposes of deciding who gets to participate. These are not, however, the most relevant gender categories for other purposes, such as making sense of another person's behavior, determining how to interact with that person, or organizing sexual desire and sexual practice. For example, when my daddy goes to a women-only play party, probably the first thing she does is pay an admission fee and sign a release form. During this encounter, her operative sex/gender status is *woman*, since she must be a woman (however that is defined by the party organizers) to be admitted. Probably the next thing Daddy does is stow her toybag and hang up her leather jacket if it's a hot night, because Daddy likes to socialize a little and get into a party headspace before playing. During this time, her operative sex/gender status is *leatherdyke daddy,* for this is the category through which her interactions with others are organized, especially but not only those interactions in which eroticism is present. Once Daddy is in a scene with a butch faggot boy, once Daddy's dick has become a sensate dick in Daddy's phenomonological experience of his own embodiment and in Daddy's boy's phenomenological experience of Daddy's embodiment, Daddy may be simply a very butch gay male leather bear-daddy. Or something else entirely, depending on the specific content of the interactions between Daddy, Daddy's boy, and any other participants or observers. Thinking in terms of multiple, context-specific, and purpose-specific gendered statuses allows us to make better sense of this cultural phenomenon than does thinking in terms of (two or more) unitary sex/gender statuses.

The sense of multiple, context-specific, and purpose-specific sex/gender statuses I am urging is not simply one in which sex/gender varies from one cultural/historical location to another, nor even one in which individual persons may change their sex/gender statuses over the course of their lifetimes if they make comparably grand changes in themselves, such as those kinds of changes that transsexuals are expected to make. Nor is this the familiar point that gender identity is constructed in interaction with identities along other vectors of subjectivity and power. A very small amount of time elapses while Daddy walks from the entrance of the play party to stow her toybag, and she has not left one culture and entered another during that short walk, nor does she alter her body. Rather, the play party entrance is a spatial and discursive boundary between cultures, a boundary at which dominant cultural sex/gender categories operate for a specific purpose: to protect members of another, though not fully separate, culture from certain types of interference and violence. Once that boundary is passed, dominant cultural sex/gender categories are not entirely suspended, but they are superseded by another, incommensurable set of sex/gender categories. Furthermore, as I sit writing this I lack a unitary sex/gender status under California state law, although my historical and cultural location stays put. The type of multiplicity for which I am arguing is more profusely

multiple than that with which we have all become familiar.

One could claim, of course, that Daddy is a woman who is also a leatherdyke daddy, that being a leatherdyke daddy is one way to be a woman. However, this culturally imperialist claim misses the point that to insist that leatherdyke boys and their daddies are women, all the time, in all situations, and for all purposes, is to insist on ignoring the cultural situatedness – or, more accurately, the multiple cultural situatednesses – of leatherdyke gender performativities. Further, it is to insist on ignoring this in favor of upholding a patently oppressive hegemonic sex/gender/sexuality system that imposes the overarching categories *woman* and *man* at the expense of eliding the specificities of how sex/gender works in queer cultural discourses and practices. The decision about which of these views to accept is a *political* decision, a decision about whether or not the dominant culture's sex/gender discourse will be given discursive primacy over leatherdyke sex/gender discourse. One discourse is constituted and enforced by much greater power than the other, yet there is powerful agency in refusing to agree that one is entirely contained within its discursive structures. There is also power in the creative production of new, alternative gender formations.

When we consider the same leatherdyke boy or leatherdyke daddy in different cultural locations, such as competing for a leather title and working as attorney, we will likely be confronted with a fluidity of gender performativity, and perhaps of gender identification as well. Analytically replacing the notion of unitary gender status with that of multiple gendered statuses helps make sense of this sort of gender fluidity. Making this discursive change, however, does absolutely nothing to suggest that gender fluidity is more radical, subversive, transgressive, or disruptive than more stable gender performativities and identifications. Fluidity of gender performativity and identification is clearly not necessary to disrupt unitariness of sex/gender – as is shown by the examples of Daddy walking to stow her toybag and my current situation/s under California state law.

Wild gender multiplicity abounds, and we have some, though not unconstrained, agency within, and along, the soft, permeable edges of the multiple, overlapping boundaries of gender categories and incommensurable gender systems. Our urgent creative political work is not the proliferation of genders, nor are genders countable marks on one line or countable points within a flat, geometric space. Rather, we must familiarize ourselves and others with the multiplicity of genders already available in the curvatures of gendered spaces; we must develop further adept tactics – opened up by the purpose-relativity of gendered statuses – of naming and claiming multiply shifting, resistant sex/gender identifications; and we can use soft, permeable edges as sites for creative production of new, more just genderqueer discursive locations and structures for those of us who are thrust into black holes by location in any of the already given structures of sex/gender/ sexuality and who are dislocated from them all.

Notes

1   Personal ads in sexual-minority community publications sometimes confound readers who do not participate in the communities in which the publications are produced. For an analysis of one personal ad that illustrates my claims, see Jacob Hale, "Are Lesbians Women?" *Hypatia* 11 (spring 1996): 100–1.

2   Ki Namaste, " 'Tragic Misreadings': Queer Theory's Erasure of Transgender Subjectivity," in *Queer Studies: A Lesbian, Gay, Bisexual, and Transgender Anthology*, ed. Brett Beemyn and Mickey Eliason (New York: New York University Press, 1996), 183–206.

3   While this formulation accurately represents a limited slice of my self-identification when I began transition, it obscures the more complex self-identifications I have since formed in resistance to hegemonic constructions of transsexuality and to dominant manhood. For further investigation of the complexities of ftm self-identifications, see C. Jacob Hale, "Tracing a Ghostly Memory in My Throat: Reflections on Ftm Feminist Voice and Agency," in *Men Doing Feminism*, ed. Tom Digby (New York: Routledge, 1997).

4   Gayle Rubin, "Of Catamites and Kings: Reflections on Butch, Gender, and Boundaries," in *The Persistent Desire: A Femme–Butch Reader*, ed. Joan Nestle (Boston: Alyson, 1992), 469.

5   In addition to using *embodiment* with its more common meanings, I follow Steven G. Smith in thinking of embodiment as a process through which the community stipulates what counts as a male/female body, what life will be like in a male/female body in relation to other bodies, what norms (and latitudes) of character and conduct are associated with these bodies, and who is male and female. See Steven G. Smith, *Gender Thinking* (Philadelphia: Temple University Press, 1992), 91.

6   Tala Brandeis, "Dyke with a Dick," in *The Second Coming: A Leatherdyke Reader*, ed. Pat Califia and Robin Sweeney (Los Angeles: Alyson, 1996), 52–62; Pat Califia, "Who Is My Sister? Power-surge and the Limits of Our Community," *Venus Infers* 1.1 (n.d.): 4–7, 34–5; Michael M. Hernandez, "Boundaries: Gender and Transgenderism," in Califia and Sweeney, *Second Coming*, 63–70; Gayle Rubin, "The Outcasts: A Social History," in Califia and Sweeney, *Second Coming*, 339–46.

7   Gayle Rubin, "Catamites," 482 n. 29.

8   Anne Williams, "And the Winner Is . . . 1994 International Ms. Leather Is Anne C. S. Bergstedt," *Venus Infers* 2.1 (n.d.): 26–30.

9   My use of feminine pronouns to refer to leatherdyke boys and daddies in this article is an artificial and problematic means of communicating with readers who do not and have not participated in leatherdyke community circles.

10   For my former Daddy's perspective on some of these events, see Lee Lambert, "Daddy's Home! Raging Hormones," *Leather Journal* 76 (November 1995): 29.

11   This should not be misunderstood as invoking a butch–ftm masculinity continuum on which ftms are more masculine than butches. When I say that I became more masculine, I am describing changes I made during a specific time period and do not mean to suggest that I am more masculine now than I was then, nor that ftms are more masculine than butches. If anything, I am less masculine in some respects now than I was before exogenous testosterone, and I am certainly less masculine in some respects than a number of my butch friends. See Judith Halberstam, *Female Masculinity* (Durham, NC: Duke University Press, 1998); JordyJones, "Another View of F2M," *FTM Newsletter* 29 (January 1995): 14–15.

12   Bob Gallagher and Alexander Wilson, "Michel Foucault: An Interview: Sex, Power, and the Politics of Identity," *Advocate*, 7 August 1984, 26–30, 58; David M. Halperin, *Saint Foucault: Towards a Gay Hagiography* (New York: Oxford University Press, 1995), 85–91.

13 Kate Bornstein, *Gender Outlaw: On Men, Women and the Rest of Us* (New York: Routledge, 1994), 46–50; Joseph C. Finney, "Transsexuality and the Laws on Sexual Mores," in *Proceedings of the Second Interdisciplinary Symposium on Gender Dysphoria Syndrome*, ed. Donald R. Laub and Patrick Gandy (Stanford: Division of Reconstructive and Rehabilitation Surgery, Stanford University Medical Center, n.d.), 117–22; Harold Garfinkel, "Passing and the Managed Achievement of Sex Status in an 'Intersexed' Person, Part One," in *Studies in Ethnomethodology*, by Harold Garfinkel (Oxford: Polity, 1967), 116–85; Jacob Hale, "Are Lesbians Women?" *Hypatia* 11 (spring 1996): 94–121; John Heritage, *Garfinkel and Ethnomethodology* (Cambridge: Polity, 1984), 179–98; Suzanne J. Kessler, "The Medical Construction of Gender: Case Management of Intersexed Infants," in *Theorizing Feminism: Parallel Trends in the Humanities and the Social Sciences*, ed. Anne C. Herrmann and Abigail J. Stewart (Boulder, Colo.: Westview, 1994), 218–37; Suzanne J. Kessler and Wendy McKenna, *Gender: An Ethnomethodological Approach* (New York: John Wiley, 1978), 112–15.

Part II

The Cultural Construction of Gender and Sexuality

5

The Trials of Alice Mitchell
Sensationalism, Sexology,
and the Lesbian Subject in
Turn-of-the-Century America

Lisa Duggan

The years 1880 to 1920 were a crucible of change in gender and sexual relations in the United States. This long transition was neither even nor easy; it was deeply marked by conflict and tragedy as well as by erotic excitements. As Victorian certainties faded and the possibilities of the modern slowly materialized, new sexualities took shape and the modern desiring subject emerged.

Historians writing about this transition now generally agree that the modern lesbian was one such new desiring subject appearing at the turn of the century in Europe and Anglo-America.[1] They argue not that sexual relations or love between women were new then, but that the subjectivity this lesbian embodied was a radical innovation. She came to see herself as an erotic subject – as a woman whose desire for women was felt as a fundamental component of her sense of self, marking her as erotically different from most other women. As the period progressed, this new subjective sense of self interacted in a complex way with the emergence of public lesbian identities and communities.

The new lesbian relationships that formed in the midst of these changes significantly modified earlier forms of women's partnerships, which have been described by historians as falling within two broadly defined class-bound types – the romantic friendship in which bourgeois girls and women made passionate commitments to each other within a gender-segregated female world, and the "marriage" between a "female husband" who passed and worked as a man among workingmen and her "wife."[2] The historical picture of the transition from these earlier forms of relationship to modern lesbianism – the emergence of lesbian subjectivity into public visibility at the end of the nineteenth century – exists only in broad outline and mostly with respect to white women, both working class and bourgeois. The long historical process through which a new identity was constructed remains relatively obscure. At the heart of this obscurity lies the problematic relationship between the cultural representations (or texts) that historians use as sources and the living historical subjects who produced, consumed, and reproduced them.

The difficulty for historians is illustrated in the debate over the meaning of the figure of the "mannish lesbian" – a figure ubiquitous in published sources of many kinds by the early twentieth century (Newton 1989; Smith-Rosenberg 1989). Was this figure a distorted representation produced by antifeminist sexologists, intent on discrediting and stigmatizing the relationships of newly independent New Women? Or was the mannish lesbian in part a strategically deployed self-representation, used by some sexually active New Women to carve out a new identity? Underlying this debate are questions about the nature of the relationship between the representations of mannish lesbians in various texts and the subjectivities and identities of living women: Did hostile sexologists construct the mannish lesbian, or did she, in any meaningful way, construct herself?

Early in the nineteenth century, for instance, aristocratic British diarist Anne Lister represented herself as erotically interested in women exclusively and associated this interest with her appropriations of various aspects of masculinity (Lister [1791–1840] 1988). But women such as Lister were relatively isolated and did not form socially visible networks or forge connections linking their sexual subjectivity to public representations of lesbianism, as began to happen later in the century. Nonetheless, the manner in which they linked masculine traits, economic independence, and the erotic love of women drew on and reproduced tropes of sexual difference in combinations that presaged modern lesbian identities. The interrelations of their early representations with those of the first sexologists present historians with a polyvocal cultural dialogue not reducible to any single site of historical invention.

In these pages, I want to examine this complex dialogue in a new way. I want to look at the project of constructing identities as a historical process of contested narration, a process in which contrasting "stories" of the self and others – stories of difference – are told, appropriated, and retold as stories of location in the social world of structured inequalities. Looked at in this way, individual and collective subjectivities are interactively linked to representations (including self-representations) through historically and materially specific stories of identity. In illustration, I will show here how mass circulation newspapers fashioned stories out of living women's relationships, how sexologists then reappropriated those stories as "cases," and women themselves reworked them as "identities" in an extended battle over the meaning of women's erotic partnerships at the turn of the century. Out of this battle, the first publicly visible forms of modern lesbianism were born; as we shall see, it was a terrifyingly difficult birth.

Identity is defined in these pages as a narrative of a subject's location within social structure. As stories rather than mere labels, identities traverse the space between the social world and subjective experience, constituting a central organizing principle connecting self and world. Individual identities, usually multiple and often contradictory, structure and give meaning to personal experience. Collective identities – of gender, race, class, or nation – forge connections among individuals and provide links between past and present, becoming the basis for cultural representation and political action.

In an extended discussion of the problems facing feminists addressing such theoretical problems, Teresa de Lauretis modifies the post-structuralist rejection of the notion of unmediated experience by redefining experience "in the general sense of a process by which, for all social beings, subjectivity is constructed. Through that process one places oneself or is placed in social reality, and so perceives and comprehends as subjective (referring to, even originating in oneself) those relations – material, economic, and interpersonal – which are in fact social, and, in a larger perspective, historical" (1984, 159). I use the term *experience* in de Lauretis's sense. Identity, I argue, is the story or narrative structure that gives meaning to experience.

Stories of identity are never static, monolithic, or politically innocent. By situating people within shifting structures of social power and inequality, they become contested sources of authority and legitimation. This is especially true during moments of radical social transformation. Old stories assume new narrative meanings; new stories emerge, patched together from cultural fragments appropriated for new purposes.[3] Never created out of whole cloth, never uniquely individual, each narrative is a retelling, an act of social interaction, a positioned intervention in the shared, contested narratives of a given culture.[4]

"Lesbian" was just such a bitterly contested identity at the turn of the century, as new stories of lesbian life and experience developed at the changing nexus of gender identity and sexuality. The content of the identities "man" and "woman" shifted from their Victorian to their modern configurations, and the heterosexual/homosexual polarity emerged as a newly central preoccupation of gendered stories of identity.[5] Lesbianism in particular emerged as an issue in debates about female sexuality, aggression, economic independence, education, reform efforts, and feminism. Contests over the meanings of stories of lesbian identity expressed profound social anxiety over the boundary masculine/feminine itself. By tracing new stories of lesbian identity as they developed out of the earlier stories of romantic friends and female husbands and by examining how they were reworked and retold by different agents to different audiences for different and often conflicting social ends, we can observe the process of contested narration in motion.

One of the most sensational early accounts of a relationship perceived as of a new type was contained in the news reports of the 1892 murder of seventeen-year-old Freda Ward by nineteen-year-old Alice Mitchell in Memphis, Tennessee. Headlines nationwide announced that this was "A Very Unnatural Crime" in which the murderess claimed to have loved her victim so much that she killed her rather than live estranged from her. Though the murders of spouses and sweethearts – commonly called *love-murders* – were the frequent fare of sensational news, this one was treated as nearly incomprehensible and as unique on American soil. The *New York World*, for instance, reported that because of Alice Mitchell's act,

> a sober American community and an unimaginative American court must deal in matter-of-fact fashion with matters which have been discussed hitherto by French writers of fiction only. Gen. Luke E. Wright and Col. George Gantt, of Tennessee, find themselves compelled to do in open court the work that Balzac did in tracing to physical sources mental perversion. In the Criminal Court of Memphis, Shelby County, Adolphe Belot's *Mlle. [Giraud] Ma Femme* will be the only text-book at hand. Judge DuBose, of Tennessee, will have cited to him, as bearing on the case of an American girl, the creations of French writers whom he and all his associates have looked upon as perverted creatures, dealing with matters outside of real life, or at least outside of American life.
>
> In all the long history of crime and insanity there is no such case recorded. [1892]

Other such cases were in fact recorded. By 1892, there was a developing medical literature on same sex love and its relation to crime and insanity produced by American doctors who adapted the theories of Krafft-Ebing and other

Europeans. These doctors were captivated by Alice Mitchell's love-murder, which seemed a perfect illustration of their theories. Innumerable articles were published applying the new theories to this case, which was added in turn to later editions of Krafft-Ebing's *Psychopathia Sexualis* (1899, 550). By 1901 the first American edition of Havelock Ellis's *Sexual Inversion* stated that Alice Mitchell was "a typical invert of a very pronounced kind" and that "there have been numerous cases in America more recently" (1901, 121).

The story of Alice Mitchell's murder of Freda Ward persisted as a topic of newspaper sensationalism and of scientific sexology well into the twentieth century. The case also served as the partial basis for at least three works of fiction, a folk ballad that survived in oral tradition into the 1960s, and a proposed play for Sarah Bernhardt to be written by famed librettist Victorien Sardou (Bernhardt visited Mitchell in jail and kept a scrapbook on the case).[6]

Alice was not tried in criminal court for the murder. Instead, she appeared at a lunacy inquisition. The plan of the attorneys hired by her father was to have her declared "presently insane" and incompetent to stand trial, then confined to the state lunatic asylum as dangerous to the community. They brought physicians into the courtroom to testify as experts that Alice was insane. The prosecution countered that she was rational but vicious, degraded, and "fast."

To make their case, the defense attorneys constructed Alice's life as a case history and presented it to expert witnesses as the basis for their opinions. The case history read, in part, as follows:

HYPOTHETICAL CASE[7]

Alice was a nervous, excitable child, somewhat undersize. As she grew she did not manifest interest in those childish amusements and toys that girls are fond of.

When only 4 or 5 years old she spent much time at a swing in the yard of the family, in performing such feats upon it as skinning the cat and hanging by an arm or leg. She was fond of climbing, and expert at it.

She delighted in marbles and tops, in base ball and foot ball. . . . She spent much time with her brother Frank. . . . She preferred him and his sports to her sisters. He practiced with her at target shooting with a small rifle, to her great delight. She excelled this brother . . . at feats of activity. She was fond of horses. . . . To the family she seemed a regular tomboy.

. . . She disliked sewing and needle work. . . . To most persons, even her relatives, she seemed distant and indifferent. She was wholly without that fondness for boys that girls usually manifest.

She had no intimates or child sweethearts among the boys, and when approaching womanhood . . . she had no beaux and took no pleasure in the society of young men. She was regarded as mentally wrong by young men toward whom she had thus acted. . . .

For Fred Ward, a girl about her own age, she had an extraordinary fondness. . . . The attachment seemed to be mutual, but was far stronger in Alice Mitchell than in Fred.

They were very different in disposition. Fred was girl-like and took no pleasure in the boyish sports that Alice delighted in. Her instincts and amusements were feminine. She was tender and affectionate. Time strengthened the intimacy between them. They became lovers in the sense of that relation between persons of different sexes. . . .

In Feb. 1891, Alice proposed marriage. She repeated the offer in three separate letters. To each Fred replied, agreeing to become her wife. Alice wrote her upon the third promise that she would hold her to the engagement, and that she would kill her if she broke the promise. . . .

It was agreed that Alice should be known as Alvin J. Ward, so that Fred could still call her by pet name Allie, and Fred was to be known as Mrs. A. J. Ward. The particulars of formal marriage and elopement were agreed upon. Alice was to put on man's apparel, and have her hair trimmed by a barber like a man; was to get the license to marry, and Fred was to procure the Rev. . . . [or] a justice of the peace to marry them. The ceremony performed, they intended to leave for St. Louis. Alice was to continue to wear man's apparel, and meant to try and have a mustache, if it would please Fred. She was going out to work for Fred in men's clothes.

In the latter part of June, 1891, Ashley Roselle . . . began to pay court to Fred, who gave him one of her photographs. The watchful vigilance of Alice got track of this affair, and she remonstrated warmly with Fred, and charged her with deception and infidelity. Fred acknowledged she had done wrong, vowed unshaken fidelity to Alice, and promised never more to offend.

The scheme of marrying and eloping seemed almost ready for execution in the latter part of July. . . . By chance, Mrs. Volkmar, the married sister . . . with whom Fred was living, saw part of the correspondence of the girls, which disclosed the relations between them, and the plans to elope and marry. . . . An exciting scene ensued. Mrs. Volkmar wrote to Mrs. Mitchell, the mother of Alice, and at the same time wrote to Alice, returning the engagement ring, and other love tokens, and declaring that all intercourse between the girls must at once cease. . . .

The effect on Alice of the return of the engagement ring and the inhibition of all communication with Fred was almost crushing. She wept, passed sleepless nights, lost her appetite, frequently declined even to come to the table. . . .

. . . In her language she more than loved Fred. She took her life because she had told her she would, and because it was her duty to do it. The best thing would have been the marriage, the next best thing was to kill Fred. That would make sure that no one else could get her.

This account was, of course, a strategic construction, a case history designed to procure a particular medical opinion and a desired legal outcome. But unlike the medical case histories published in journals and texts, this one was corroborated by the testimony of witnesses and contested in court through cross-examination and the testimony of opposing witnesses. Family members and neighbors, as well as Alice herself, recounted their version of events, and Alice and Freda's letters were read aloud and printed in the papers. The newspaper reports of this hypothetical case, the testimony, and the trial summarized the many tellings and retellings of the story of love and murder from multiple points of view.

The relations of Alice and Freda emerged in these stories as a hybrid form developed from different class contexts. At first, their love was perceived as an ordinary, if excessive, schoolgirls' romantic friendship – in Memphis, such relations were called "chumming."[8] But their plans for cross-dressing and marriage pushed them beyond the bounds of that category. They had adopted a classic "passing" strategy – a strategy so rare among bourgeois white women that their plan was perceived as so radically inappropriate as to be insane. Though the local papers regularly noted cases of workingmen and farm laborers who turned out to be "passing" women, their lives and partnerships with other women were reported as simply eccentric or remarkable – not sexual, deviant, or insane. But at the trial, Alice's belief that she could marry Freda while disguised as "Alvin" was portrayed by her attorneys and their medical experts, and reported in the press, as a "morbid " or "imperative delusion" and a sign of sexual "perversion."

The descriptions of witnesses and experts at trial also reveal an emerging belief that Alice's plan to pass as Alvin was not merely a disguise but an expression of some deep and partially hidden truth – that Alice was masculine and that her masculinity and her desire for Freda were linked. For medical writers, this link was the basis for the construction of female sexual "inversion" (Chauncey 1982–3). But the link was also made by Alice before the interventions following the murder; it shaped her relations with Freda.

The "story" of Alice and Freda up to the time of the murder, as it was presented and reworked in the mass circulation press during 1892, was composed of three essential structural elements. First, the contrast drawn between Alice's "masculine" characteristics and Freda's "feminine" manner was universally agreed on – repeated not only by doctors but also by Alice's best friend Lillie, by the girls' school principal, and by neighbors. It also ran clearly through Alice's and Freda's published letters.

Second, conflict between Alice and Freda over the nature of their relationship was presented as the first and possibly the most important foundation for the later violence. Alice wanted Freda to commit herself totally to their love; Freda vacillated, making and breaking engagements with at least two young men. Alice was certain that she wanted to marry Freda and that she herself had no interest in men; Freda was full of doubt and treated Alice as one among several suitors. This conflict led Alice to threats of violence and a suicide attempt. The plan to elope was a sign of and a means to ensure Alice's ultimate success in securing the relationship and in ensuring that Freda would not betray Alice by marrying a man.

The third structural element of the story is conflict between the "engaged" couple and their female relatives. Although Freda's older sister and Alice's mother did not object to the intensity of their attachment or the continual displays of physical affection, nor even to their exchange of engagement rings, the plan to elope with Alice posing as Alvin led the older women to end all contact between the lovers. Male relatives and the world of male authority were not brought into the affair until after the murder; only then did Alice come into direct conflict with the male-dominated institutions of law and medicine.

Running through all three elements of the story are themes of cross-gender identification and cross-dressing. Though there was no evidence reported of any sexual contact between Alice and Freda (and both those who claimed they were "pure" and those who claimed they indulged in "unnatural practices" had ulterior motives), there were indications in the news accounts that they recognized, played with, and eroticized a masculine/feminine difference between them. In her most affectionate letters, Freda referred to Alice as "Alvin" and included lines such as "If you chew tobacco, love, I won't let you kiss me" (*Memphis Commercial* 1892e). In their conflict over the nature of their relationship, Alice used the plan to cross-dress and marry as a strategy to define their love as a serious commitment equivalent to any of Freda's potential connections to a man. In their conflict with female relatives, the gender-crossing and elopement plans were a red flag signaling that these young women had gone too far and that their relationship had to be viewed as dangerous and possibly sexual rather than as foolishly but harmlessly romantic.

Overall, the cumulative newspaper story of Alice and Freda constituted one version of a new narrative-in-formation – a cultural marker of the emergence of a partially cross-gender-identified lesbian and her separation from and conflict with the family-based female world of the nineteenth century and, in this version of the story, from the bourgeois values of sexual purity and motherhood. In this story, I interpret Alice's "masculinity" as a paradoxical strategy, moving her both away from and closer to a life with other women. Her cross-gender identification worked as an expression of difference from other women, as a rejection of the pastimes and the conventional family-based relations of the female world, and as a mark of her commitment to the lasting erotic love of women. As part of her conflict with Alice, Freda expressed another kind of ambivalence toward the world of women represented by her sisters; she was ultimately reintegrated into its conventions through obedience to female authority. Her attachment to Alice might have been an interlude in an otherwise traditionally feminine life. But Alice's wish to leave the female world and to escape its conventions was so profound and unshakable that its frustration led her to destroy Freda and eventually herself as well. Alice, committed to the Tennessee State Insane Asylum at Bolivar in 1892, died in 1898; her death was reported as due to tuberculosis, but in a later interview one of the attorneys involved in the case claimed that she had killed herself by jumping into the water tower (Coppock 1930).

This narrative-in-formation appeared in various permutations in newspapers throughout the period 1880–1920. But such narratives were not merely the lurid, sensational productions of prosperous white male editors and reporters. Though the newspaper stories did stress the element of violence for shock value, they were nonetheless based on the stories women told about their own relationships. The newspaper retellings, altered to fit the worldview and assumptions of reporters and editors and the expectations, fears, and fantasies of readers, were not free of the shaping influence of women like Alice Mitchell and of the story she told her family, lawyers, trial experts, and court. They were, that is, not simply impositions but appropriations.

The press coverage of the Mitchell–Ward murder in 1892 stimulated especially intense attention to many similar cases. Some were cast as memories of cases past (see, e.g., *Memphis Public Ledger* 1892a). Others were accounts of rumors, denied by the principals (such as *Memphis Commercial* 1892b). The story of Alice and Freda as it appeared in the mainstream daily press also had precursors in the disreputable crime and police papers of earlier decades (see, e.g., the *National Police Gazette* 1879). Some of these were picked up and circulated in the mainstream press and in the medical literature after the Mitchell–Ward murder. The newspaper stories that resulted varied somewhat, especially with regard to the class and racial contexts within which they were situated, but all shared one or more of the three structural elements of the Mitchell–Ward tale.

On February 11, 1892, for instance, the *Memphis Public Ledger* (1892b) appended to an article on the Mitchell–Ward case a short report headlined "The Case of Male Impersonator Marie Hindle, Who Beaued the Girls at Broome's Variety Theater. Almost a Parallel Case." It read:

Discussion of the Mitchell–Ward murder has brought to light a number of similar cases of abnormal affection existing between persons of the same sex, differing only in that they did not end in the death of one "lover" at the hands of the other. But there was a case of the kind located in Memphis, which narrowly missed being a prototype of that which is now engaging so much attention all over the country. It dates back nearly 23 years, but is still fresh in the memory of citizens who were familiar with the local life after dark of that period.

In 1869–70 the bright particular star of Broome's Variety Theater, on Jefferson Street, was Marie Hindle, a very attractive woman, who played male parts. Nature had especially fitted her for that line of the business. Her features and voice were masculine, and her tastes in accord with her physical peculiarities. Though by no means chary of accepting the admiration of the other sex, she cared nothing for men as such. Her inclination was altogether toward women, and she inspired in them a like feeling toward herself. It was remarked by the stage hands and those among the habitués who were admitted to the inner circle of the performers that Marie was a reigning beau among

78

the petticoat brigade, from the well-paid high kicker to the humblest "chair warmer."

Two of the former class were special favorites of hers. The girls were named Ione and Lizette, both pretty and clever and both madly in love with Marie. She distributed her favor with so much tact that each considered herself the queen bee in the Hindle hive, and neither had any eyes for the male creatures in their train when she was present. They were jealous of each other in a way, but Marie always managed to prevent active hostilities occurring between them. But the fires of rivalry were kindled and only needed occasion to break forth in flame.

The time came toward the close of the season when Marie had made ready to go on to New York to fill an engagement at the Bowery Theater. Ione and Lizette were wild with grief at the thought of parting from her, and would scarcely let her out of their sight. Naturally, each grudged the other a moment of their common idol's time, and jealousy gave place to hatred. When the day of separation came they were wrought up to a pitch that made them reckless of consequences. Both had laid on their war paint and got ready for action.

The night of Marie's departure found them in a state bordering on frenzy. Each had resolved to act as Marie's special escort from the Overton Hotel, where she was stopping, to the train that was to bear her away; and neither was aware of the other's intention. They chanced to meet at the ladies' entrance to the hotel. It was a match to the magazine. Instantly there came an explosion which attracted the attention of several men standing near, one of whom was Dick English, the river editor of the Appeal. He knew of the enmity existing between the two girls, and fearing lest they should do something desperate he ran toward them. By the time he reached the spot they had clinched and were struggling around in the alley. He kept on after them and reached them just as they pulled out knives and began carving each other. He seized them, and with the assistance of another man, who had followed him, succeeded in separating them and wresting their weapons from their hands, but not until both had received ugly slashes on the face and bosom. But for his timely arrival and prompt action there would have been murder done.

Marie Hindle repeated in New York the professional conquests of her Memphis career.

Again she became a successful rival of the gilded youth in the affections of the girls of the company and not a few among her audience. One of the latter she singled out for a favorite and they lived together up to the time of her death, which occurred not long ago. After this it was reported, and published in the papers, that she had actually married the girl.

"Mrs. Hindle" was interviewed by a New York paper soon after her partner passed away. She seemed overcome with grief at her loss and said that Marie had been "a dear, good husband."

This little story, both comic and contemptuous (and, of course, featuring male heroism), drew on and reframed various stock nineteenth-century narrative conventions. It was anything but "factual," and was full of gross errors as well as predictable distortions. Marie was actually Annie Hindle, the first male impersonator to make a name for herself on the American stage. (For a discussion of Annie Hindle's career, see Senelick [1982].) She did in fact marry a woman, Annie Ryan, with female impersonator Gilbert Saroney at her side. But it was Ryan who died in 1891. The story, both the apocryphal and the real, had little in common with the Mitchell–Ward case except for one important element – the masculine/feminine contrast between Hindle and her admirers, with only the manly Hindle believed to be inclined exclusively toward women in her affections. This difference was clearly eroticized, and the Variety Theater, on the very margins of respectability, provided a rare setting for its expression. Another 1892 article in a Lincoln, Nebraska entertainment paper, *Vanity Fair*, also linked the Mitchell–Ward case with the story of Hindle, getting more of the facts right and commenting that "it is a fact that this dashing singer was the recipient of as many 'mash' notes as ever went to a stage favorite of this country. Once she compared notes with H. J. Montague, that carelessly handsome actor at whose shrine so many silly women had worshipped; but Hindle's admirers outnumbered his, and they were all women, strange as it may seem" (1892).

The tragic conflicts that led to the Memphis murder never appeared in tales of Hindle's life and career (though she did have a brief and miserable marriage to the man who founded the Elks Lodge). Such good fortune was no doubt due to the theater's serving as an institution where collectivities of those with unconventional gender identifications and sexual lives could congregate relatively free from censure. For this reason Hindle's story also did not include isolation within the white bourgeois family, as did Alice Mitchell's. (Interestingly, both Alice and Freda were themselves "stage struck" and had fantasies of running off to join the theater.)

Another story published in the *Memphis Weekly Commercial* (1892) told a story of Addie Phillips, whose mother worried that her love for Minnie Hubbard would develop into a "Mitchell–Ward affair" and who was thrown into despair when Addie, after swearing never to marry a man, ran away from home and was found in a brothel. Male impersonation was associated in this era with the demimonde and geographically if not literally, with prostitution.[9] This story focused on young women from the barely respectable working class, at some social distance from Alice Mitchell's wealthy family. But the newspaper story drew many comparisons between them, finding some marked similarities across class lines and stressing the third element of the Mitchell–Ward "story" – the conflict between mother and daughter. The first element, the masculine/feminine contrast, was absent in this version, while the second element of conflict between the young women was only suggested: Addie was reported to have wished to marry Minnie, but when they ran away together, Minnie changed her mind and returned, to Addie's chagrin.

The mass circulation daily newspapers deliberately crossed class lines in their reporting as part and parcel of their marketing strategy – but the papers were controlled by local elites, and the stories of working-class life were (re)told from the elite perspective. The newspapers were explicitly racist, however. Comparisons across racial lines were much rarer and were laced with overt hostility or condescension. The *Memphis Commercial* (1892c) ran a series of stories under the heading "Similar Cases Recalled" on February 24, 1892, one of which follows:

Mobile, Ala. – Eleanora Richardson is now lying at her home in this city, between the borders of life and death from seven stab wounds, the most severe being through the lower rib. She will die. She is a handsome and well-formed mulatto, 17 years of age. Emma Williams, a black but comely woman of 23, is in jail, awaiting the results of the wounds she inflicted upon her friend. . . . The motive was a paroxysm of jealousy resulting from an unnatural passion similar to that case in Memphis, which has caused the world to wonder. The two women have been living in the same house for nearly a year. Eleanor says the past six months Emma Williams has been taking the most unusual interest in her. She has been showering caresses upon her daily and hourly, and though both were seen, the Williams girl went to work, and her wages supported and clothed her and the girl. If the Richardson girl spoke to a male acquaintance, the woman would upbraid her, and beg her not to allow any man to ever separate them. If any males called at the house the Williams woman would see them alone, invent excuses and resort to all artifices to prevent any interview with her companion. Last week Eleanora Richardson left the house where the Williams woman was and took up her residence with a married sister in another part of town. Her companion, wretched almost to the point of madness, yesterday afternoon was told by someone who knew of her unnatural infatuation, that Eleanora had left her because she was going to be married. This the Williams woman answered, "Never mind; I'll get her." She went immediately to the girl's house and . . . asked when . . . [she] was coming home. Her companion replied she would be back when her sister tired of her. Bursting into a fury of rage, the Williams woman said: "You are lying and trying to deceive me; you shall never marry that ———," and rushing upon her she drew the murderous knife from her stocking and attacked her, plunging the knife into her body repeatedly, saying with each stab "Oh, you darling." The girl's screams finally brought her sister's husband on the scene, and the furious woman was seized and disarmed, but not until she had inflicted wounds which the physicians declare dangerous and possibly fatal.

This tale deploys the second element of the Mitchell–Ward narrative, the conflict between the two women over the nature of the relationship. Few of the many stories in the newspapers during 1892 had all of the structural elements of the Alice and Freda case. All such elements were most likely to appear in stories about bourgeois white women and girls. Given that these narratives appeared in daily newspapers produced primarily by and for privileged white people, it is not surprising that most of them were "about" the gender and sexual disputes of this limited population. The stories of developing lesbian identity among working women and prostitutes or among African-American, Chicana, or Asian women were not entirely absent from the newspapers, but they were not developed at length there. Research into other sources of these narratives may show them to have been structured differently.

A typical account of love and conflict between young white bourgeois women appeared in a long article published in the *New York Sun* and reprinted in the *Memphis Commercial* (1892a) – a cautionary tale written by a girls' boarding school principal.

LIKE MISS MITCHELL

. . . When Blanche's parents brought her to our school and confided her to my care she had just passed her sixteenth birthday. She was of a vivacious disposition and of a will rather inclined to be imperious . . . Blanche was a very high-minded girl. Her ideals were all lofty. Though strangely ignorant of the real significance of love, courtship and marriage, she was very free with her criticisms of the attitude of men toward women. Her ideas on this subject were plainly derived from the literature of chivalry. . . .

Blanche lost no time in cultivating the friendship of Mary, the sweetest and most angelic of our flock. In disposition Mary was to Blanche as the soft spring rain is to the electricity which explodes and precipitates it to earth. She was of about the same age as Blanche, and equally innocent and ignorant. She seemed to yield with passive happiness to the new friendship held out to her. In a few weeks the individuality of Blanche seemed to have absorbed her individuality completely. They were constantly together, and both were supremely happy.

. . . Mary, like the ideal lady love, was softly and yieldingly affectionate. She leaned upon Blanche, looked up to her and trusted her as one whose strength and courage were wholly to be relied upon. Blanche on the other hand, exhibited the spirit, dash, and valor with the deferential devotion of the knight, the record of whose glorious career rested beneath her pillow. . . .

And when in a gayer mood I have seen her seize Mary unawares in the darkened hall or behind a door to steal a kiss, as is the fashion of more modern lovers. Neither made any attempt to conceal her infatuation from other pupils of the school, and as there were other cases of a similar kind, their behavior occasioned no particular comment. . . .

[Mary goes home to tend her sick mother and returns after several weeks, a changed girl.]

Mary had been playing a medley of gay dance music while Blanche stood regarding her gloomily from a corner of the room. Presently she approached the piano, and seizing Mary's hand to hers, exclaimed passionately: "Mary, Mary, don't you love me anymore?"

"Yes, my dicky bird – passionately," answered Mary gayily.

"But not as you used to," broke in the poor girl.

"Well, if you were a nice young man now, for instance," said Mary, smilingly, "the case would be –"

"Ah, you are false," broke in Blanche, wringing her hands. "You who promised to be true till death! What is it you have in that locket?" she demanded angrily. And while the rest of us looked on too astonished to move, Blanche snatched the gold ornament hanging at Mary's throat, opened it, and with a cry of rage dashed it on the floor. . . . A miniature photograph and a lock of dark hair were broken loose from their frame and lay on the carpet. Blanche stamped upon them and fled, weeping, to her room.

The photograph was that of a handsome, manly-looking young fellow, such as almost any girl might be pardoned for falling in love with. He was Mary's cousin, and it was their growing attachment for each other that had so long delayed Mary's return to school, after her mother had been pronounced convalescent.

Mary's compassion soon overcame her anger. She went to her friend's room and on the following day I noticed that their reconciliation seemed complete. But I was not at all pleased to see that Mary was again apparently under the influence of her irresistible girl friend. Day after day Blanche's attitude toward her grew more and more loverlike. They were constantly together. It was plain that the handsome dark-haired cousin was forgotten. . . . I noticed the sparkle of a little diamond on the third finger of Blanche's left hand.

"Why, what does this mean?" I asked.

"It means that we are engaged," said Blanche innocently. "I am so happy."

"Engaged!" To whom?" I demanded.

"Why, to my darling Mary, of course. To whom else?"

I glanced at Mary's left hand. The third finger bore the duplicate of Blanche's diamond. At first I was very much alarmed but gradually, as nothing further happened out of the ordinary, I concluded that my anxiety was groundless. . . .

In later years, when experience had burdened my knowledge of such matters, I would have acted on the warning which was now given in the actions of Blanche. She could not bear to have Mary out of her sight. . . .

[Blanche and Mary then make two attempted escapes from the school. On the first they are quickly caught, on the second they make it off the school grounds, leaving a note for the principal: "DEAR MISS LAGRANGE: It is useless for you to follow us. We have gone away, Mary and I, to be married, for we love each other, and have sworn never to be separated. Farewell, BLANCHE." But the girls are caught in the town and brought back.]

As Dr. Greene [from the town] came quite close, I saw beside him in his carriage the muffled-up figures of Blanche and Mary, while at their feet was the bundle which the eloping couple had taken with them. Mary was pale and frightened. Blanche was perfectly calm. Neither said a word.

When Dr. Greene drove back to the village he carried two telegrams. They were addressed to the parents of Blanche and Mary respectively, and urged their immediate presence at the school. Mary's parents arrived the next day, much alarmed. They agreed that it was best that Mary be taken home at once.

"Have you any objection to her cousin," I asked, "The manly-looking fellow with the dark hair?" They had not the slightest objection to him.

"Then," I said, "invite him to your house and Mary will be herself again in less than a week."

It was arranged that Mary's departure should be unknown to Blanche – at least, I supposed I had so arranged it. But the carriage had hardly passed the great gate when the sound of a pistol shot in the north dormitory created a panic in the house.

It was true. Poor Blanche had proven faithful to her ideal of lover, even to the extent of providing herself with the means of self-destruction. I had forgotten that her window commanded a view of the highway. She lay at full length on the floor. In one hand was the smoking pistol, and in the other a photograph of Mary.

The wound was not serious – the shock was even beneficial, for when Blanche was restored to consciousness after the lapse of several hours, she wept copiously, begged forgiveness for her rash act, and willingly accompanied her parents to her home. I learned afterward that a year of travel abroad not only restored her to a proper condition of mind, but supplied in the place of Mary a young gentleman who was in every way worthy of her, and to whom two years later she was happily married.

If the foregoing shall point a moral that will remain fixed in the memories of parents who read it, I am persuaded that they need never bewail such a misfortune as has plunged two Tennessee families into despair.

The narrative arrangement of this story suggests a clear motive – the principal is concerned to argue that schoolgirl friendships, even extremely intense ones, are not morbid or pathological as medical writers were beginning to argue, but simply based on ignorance and excessively romantic notions. Regulation of them could safely be left to vigilant female authority. She is therefore at considerable pains to portray the students as innocent of sexuality and to provide a suitably happy ending. It thus contrasts sharply with the more hostile, sensational newspaper stories, though it has all the elements of the masculine/feminine contrast, the conflict between the young women, and the conflict with female authority. This contrast shows how the narrative fragments could be recombined for a variety of purposes, as they continued to be over the next several decades.

During the 1890s, however, nearly all the newspaper stories had tragic endings. They were stories of struggle and failure; they ended with violence or loss. Only a very few, about women in exceptional circumstances like those of Annie Hindle, had happier endings. When successful partnerships between women were mentioned in the news columns, they almost always appeared in desexualized forms only. The suggestion of sexuality, however subtle or implicit, was generally paired with bloodletting.

This focus on violence was partly an artifact of the moralizing sensationalism of the press. The late-nineteenth century newspaper narratives of lesbian love featured violence as a boundary marker; murders or suicides served to abort the forward progress of the tale, signaling that such erotic love between women was not only tragic but ultimately hopeless. The selective nature of the reports made the exceptional cases of violent conflict among women seem characteristic of female sexual passion. The stories were thus structured to emphasize, ultimately, that no real love story was possible.

But the emphasis on conflict and violence in the newspaper stories must also have reflected the stories of overwhelming opposition and social isolation told by women whose erotic partnerships transgressed the boundaries of gender-appropriate, spiritual romantic friendship. Young women like Alice, Emma, and Blanche faced hostility and opposition not only from pathologizing sexologists and patriarchal social institutions but also from their closest female relatives and friends. In addition, they all struggled to establish a reciprocal love relationship with another woman who did not fully share their commitment to a life outside the traditional heterosexual family.

Such structural analysis of the newspaper narratives suggests that modern lesbian identity may have been constructed from an amalgam of elements drawn from the stories of romantic friendship and passing women. In 1892, Alice Mitchell did not present herself nor was she perceived as a "lesbian" – no such clear category yet existed. Rather, she combined her unremarkable story of schoolgirl "chumming" with a plan to cross-dress and marry Freda, and it was this combination and not either element by itself that signaled something new and incited opposition. It was Alice Mitchell's attempt to forge a new way of life – new in both material and social terms, a life outside the white bourgeois family and its hierarchical gender arrangements – that marked her as different and dangerous. Her love for other women was neither temporary nor complementary to heterosexual marriage; her appropriation of "masculinity" and her determination to marry Freda were not for the purpose of a temporary or superficial disguise but were the seeds of a new identity.

The relative powerlessness of lesbians (as of other marginalized groups) has been enforced historically by limiting their means of direct public self-representation, leaving lesbian historians few of women's own representations of their developing lesbian identities to use as sources. Instead, historians must make the most of mediated sources contaminated by hostility, like the turn-of-the-century newspaper narratives, by reading them "against the grain."[10] Not until the 1920s do we begin to have a body of self-representations, such as African-American blues songs outlining the exploits of masculine "bulldaggers" or The Well of Loneliness, Radclyffe Hall's widely circulated British novel featuring the "masculine" heroine Stephen Gordon.[11]

Both the hostile representations and the self-representations of lesbians at the turn of the century, however, suggest that for newly visible lesbians gender-crossing or cross-dressing became a term of address in several simultaneous dialogues. Through masculine identification they separated themselves from the family-based female world, defined their desire for other women as erotic, and declared their unyielding commitment to a new way of life. The feminine partners in developing lesbian relationships, from Freda Ward to *The Well*'s Mary, along with the feminine pairs joined in romantic friendships, were not perceived as lesbian until the mid-twentieth century and later.[12]

Analysis of the newspaper narratives discussed here also shows that turn-of-the-century sexologists, far from creating or producing new lesbian identities, drew their "cases" from women's own stories and newspaper retellings of them as well as from French fiction and pornography as "empirical" bases for their theories.[13] They did not initiate or control the social conversation from which lesbian identity developed but, rather, entered into it. Basing their descriptions on relationships like that of Alice and Freda, the sexologists took as their task the definition of *deviance*, the drawing of a line between acceptable romantic friends or simply eccentric passing women and intolerable lesbian lovers. In this they were not unique but, rather, like women such as Freda's sister who had drawn such a line in forbidding Freda any further contact with Alice. Sexologists' point of departure from all these other narratives of lesbian identity was their determination to interpret behaviors rooted in changing and contested social relations as biologically based and properly subject to medical regulation.

Sexologists decidedly did influence the conversations they entered. Many commentators have noted, for instance, the appropriation of medical language and biological assumptions in many lesbian self-representations, particularly in *The Well of Loneliness* (see Newton 1989; Smith-Rosenberg 1989). But in tracing the roots of Hall's narrative, it is equally important to note that *The Well* also shares the structure of the Mitchell–Ward newspaper stories – the masculine/feminine contrast, the conflict between the female partners, and the conflict with female authority (it is Stephen Gordon's mother who is most hostile to her, not her father). In Hall's version there is no violence, however – the conflict is experienced internally by Stephen Gordon, who releases the "normal" Mary rather than murdering her or killing

herself. This narrative structure, imbricated with the difficult, conflict-laden history of the emergence of lesbian identities in the twentieth century, may help explain the book's widespread, enduring popularity despite its medicalized portrait of "inversion."

Thus, we can look back now at the figure of the turn-of-the-century mannish lesbian and see her as at least a double-edged construction – a representation used by sexologists and others to attack the independence and achievements of New Women, yet at the same time a self-represented historical subject who was attacked (sometimes even by feminists) for what she embodied: her rejection of the feminine body and the maternal body for herself. Her self-presentation took her outside the boundaries of the female world; for her, feminine dress and gestures were unnatural. She therefore existed largely beyond the categories of thought that, wedded to a fixed dualistic view of gender, can comprehend her only as a dupe of pathologizing sexologists who accepted the overvaluation of the masculine or as simply male identified.[14] Yet her history also defies any attempt to represent her as simply a hero of lesbian resistance, as Alice Mitchell's story, with its horrific act of murder, clearly shows.

The emerging new narratives of lesbian identity shaped new ways of living for some women, as new material possibilities and social positions outside the kin-based family also came into being at the turn of the century. These narratives both reproduced aspects of conventional gender hierarchy and were subversive of them. They suggest that it is useful to relinquish the fixed opposition of oppression versus resistance and to modify our own often too simple historical tales of lesbian innocence, romance, or heroism. Lesbians do not come from outside culture, outside history, or outside class, race, and gender to raise the flag for a self-evident version of freedom, justice, and equality. Rather, lesbian resistance consists instead of our determination to dissent – to retell our culture's dominant stories with an eye to reorganizing its distribution of cultural and material resources. With these new stories we re-present and re-make the world from the interaction of our own points of view and those of others in an ongoing process of re-vision.

Notes

1 For overviews of this historical argument, see Weeks 1981, esp. "The Construction of Homosexuality," 96–121, and Foucault 1978. For a discussion of the emergence of the "lesbian" and "homosexual" in the American context, see Katz 1983, esp. "The Invention of the Homosexual, 1880–1950," 137–74, and D'Emilio and Freedman 1988, esp. "Toward a New Sexual Order, 1880–1930," 171–235.

2 For studies of romantic friendship, see Smith-Rosenberg 1975 and Faderman 1981. For discussions of "passing women," see Katz 1976 and San Francisco Lesbian and Gay History Project 1989.

3 These contests do not take place solely within various types of texts but are produced within and circulate through the material social world, both shaping and reflecting structured social antagonisms. For a particularly lucid discussion of this process, see Walkowitz 1989. Walkowitz stakes out a materialist grounding for her appropriation of poststructuralist theories of meaning production. See also Poovey 1988, where Poovey makes a specifically historical argument for the interdependence of material conditions and representations.

4 This notion somewhat parallels Judith Butler's metaphor of *performance*, or the set of repetitive practices through which identity is constituted (Butler 1990). My version of this argument was also influenced by Barbara Herrnstein Smith's interesting analysis of narrative construction as a purposeful act (Smith 1981).

5 For a provocative and influential argument placing the heterosexual/homosexual dyad at the center of cultural life in the modern West, see Sedgwick 1990.

6 Sensationalism: Coppock 1930. Sexology: Cauldwell 1950. Fiction: Hatch 1895; Freeman [1895] 1927; Carhart 1895. Ballad: Howard 1961. Bernhardt: *Memphis Appeal Avalanche* 1892.

7 The defense team's "hypothetical case" was reprinted in an article in the *Memphis Commercial* 1892d and in Sim 1892. Freda Ward was referred to throughout by her nickname, Fred.

8 For an account of this common phenomenon, also called "smashing," in a northern college setting, see Sahli 1979.

9 The proximity of theatrical and prostitution districts in England is discussed in Tracy Davis's fascinating study (1991). The theatre's role as a haven for the unconventional is also examined in McArthur 1984.

10 For an exploration of the possibilities for reading "against the grain" for the history of lesbians, see Terry 1991, which draws from the work of Gayatri Spivak and Michel Foucault to construct such a method.

11 On representations of "bulldaggers" in blues songs, see Carby 1990 and Garber 1989.

12 Research by Elizabeth Kennedy and Madeline Davis suggests that, even after World War II, this issue of whether "fems" were really "lesbians" was still open to dispute (Kennedy and Davis 1989).

13 I discuss at length this process of constructing a supposedly "empirical" basis for the typical lesbian case history of turn-of-the-century sexology in Duggan 1992, esp. in chap. 6, "Sapphic Slashers, or, the Scientific Construction of Lesbian Desire."

14 Such oversimple thought is represented in the work of Sheila Jeffreys, whose *The Spinster and Her Enemies: Feminism and Sexuality, 1880–1930* (1985) is structured as a stark melodrama with male villains and female victims and heroines appearing almost as cartoon characters. Jeffreys cannot conceive of the male-authored medical literature as any kind of resource for subversive appropriation but only as pure evil opposed to the pure good of woman's true nature. Paradoxically, such paradigms only end up reproducing the very gendered categories they are meant to attack.

References

Butler, Judith. 1990. *Gender Trouble: Feminism and the Subversion of Identity.* New York: Routledge.

Carby, Hazel. 1990. "It Jus' Be's Dat Way Sometime: The Sexual Politics of Women's Blues," In *Unequal Sisters: A Multicultural Reader in U.S. Women's History*, ed. Ellen DuBois and Vicki Ruiz, 238–49. New York: Routledge.

Carhart, J. W., M.D. 1895. *Norma Trist: A Story of the Inversion of the Sexes.* Austin, Tex.: Eugene von Boeckman.

Cauldwell, D. O., M.D. 1950. "Lesbian Love Murder." *Sexology* 16(12): 773–9.

Chauncey, George, Jr. 1982–83. "From Inversion to Homosexuality: Medicine and the Changing Conceptualization of Female Deviance." *Salmagundi* 58–9: 114–46.

Coppock, Paul. 1930. "Memphis' Strangest Love Murder Had All Girl Cast," *Memphis Commercial Appeal*, September 7, sec. 4, p. 5.

Davis, Tracy. 1991. *Actresses as Working Women: Their Social Identity in Victorian Culture.* London: Routledge.

de Lauretis, Teresa. 1984. *Alice Doesn't: Feminism, Semiotics, Cinema.* Bloomington: Indiana University Press.

D'Emilio, John, and Estelle Freedman. 1988. *Intimate Matters: A Social History of Sexuality in America.* New York: Harper & Row.

Duggan, Lisa. 1992. "The Trials of Alice Mitchell: Sexual Science and Sexual Identity in Turn of the Century America." Ph.D. dissertation, University of Pennsylvania.

Ellis, Havelock. 1901. *Sexual Inversion.* Philadelphia: F. A. Davis.

Faderman, Lillian. 1981. *Surpassing the Love of Men: Romantic Friendship and Love between Women from the Renaissance to the Present.* New York: Morrow.

Foucault, Michel. 1978. *The History of Sexuality, vol. 1: An Introduction,* trans. Robert Hurley. New York: Pantheon.

Freeman, Mary Wilkins. [1895] 1927. "The Long Arm." In *American Detective Stories,* ed. Carolyn Wells, 134–78. New York: Oxford University Press.

Garber, Eric. 1989. "A Spectacle in Color: The Lesbian and Gay Subculture of Jazz Age Harlem." In *Hidden from History: Reclaiming the Lesbian and Gay Past,* ed. Martin Duberman, Martha Vicinus, and George Chauncey, Jr., 318–31. New York: New American Library.

Hatch, Mary P. 1895. *The Strange Disappearance of Eugene Comstock.* New York: G. W. Dillingham.

Howard, Edwin. 1961. "Resurrected Ballad Recalls a Strange Memphis Killing." *Memphis Press Scimitar,* November 13.

Jeffreys, Sheila. 1985. *The Spinster and Her Enemies: Feminism and Sexuality, 1880–1930.* London: Pandora.

Katz, Jonathan Ned. 1976. *Gay American History: Lesbians and Gay Men in the U.S.A.* New York: Crowell.

———. 1983. *Gay/Lesbian Almanac: A New Documentary.* New York: Harper & Row.

Kennedy, Elizabeth, and Madeline Davis. 1989. "The Reproduction of Butch–Fem Roles: A Social Constructionist Approach." In *Passion and Power: Sexuality in History,* ed. Kathy Peiss and Christina Simmons, 241–56. Philadelphia: Temple University Press.

Krafft-Ebing, Richard von. 1899. *Psychopathia Sexualis, with Special Reference to Antipathic Sexual Instinct: A Medico-Forensic Study.* London: Rebman.

Lister, Anne. [1791–1840] 1988. *I Know My Own Heart: The Diaries of Anne Lister,* ed. Helena Whitbread. London: Virago.

McArthur, Benjamin. 1984. *Actors and American Culture, 1880–1920.* Philadelphia: Temple University Press.

Memphis Appeal Avalanche. 1892. "Bernhardt At The Jail: The Great Actress Wanted to See Miss Alice Mitchell." *Memphis Appeal Avalanche,* February 17, 4.

Memphis Commercial. 1892a. "Like Miss Mitchell . . . An Infatuation Which Existed Between Two School Girls." *Memphis Commercial,* February 14, 13.

———. 1892b. "Like the Memphis Case: Another Story Which Furnishes Rich Food for the Gossips." *Memphis Commercial,* February 19, 5.

———. 1892c. "Unfolded, Revelation of Facts Surrounding Freda Ward's Death. . . . Similar Cases Recalled." *Memphis Commercial,* February 24, 1–3.

———. 1892d. "Sane or Insane? Is She Cruel Murderess or Irresponsible Lunatic?" *Memphis Commercial,* July 19, 1.

———. 1892e. "Still in Doubt, Alice Mitchell's Sanity Not Yet Determined." *Memphis Commercial,* July 20, 1.

Memphis Public Ledger. 1892a. "United in Death: A Tragedy Almost Identical with that of Monday: A Girl's Love for a Girl: How It Caused a Murder and a Suicide Twenty Years Ago." *Memphis Public Ledger,* January 27, 1.

———. 1892b. "The Plea for Bail." *Memphis Public Ledger,* February 11, 2.

Memphis Weekly Commercial. 1892. "A Strange Affection, Addie Phillips Shows Traces of Alice Mitchell-Fondness, Another Case Partially Paralleling the Famous One." *Memphis Weekly Commercial,* March 23, 12.

National Police Gazette. 1879. "A Female Romeo: Her Terrible Love for a Chosen Friend of Her Own Sex Assumes a Passionate Character that Blazes into Jealousy of so Fierce a Quality that it Fires Her to the Sacrifice of the Object of Her Unnatural Passion: A Queer Psychological Study." *National Police Gazette,* June 7, 6.

Newton, Esther. 1989. "The Mythic Mannish Lesbian: Radclyffe Hall and the New Woman." In *Hidden from History: Reclaiming the Lesbian and Gay Past,* ed. Martin Duberman, Martha Vicinus, and George Chauncey, Jr., 281–93. New York: New American Library.

New York World. 1892. "Alice Mitchell's Crime." *New York World,* January 31, 6.

Poovey, Mary. 1988. *Uneven Developments: The Ideological Work of Gender in Mid-Victorian England.* Chicago: University of Chicago Press.

Sahli, Nancy. 1979. "Smashing: Women's Relationships before the Fall." *Chrysalis* 8:17–27.

San Francisco Lesbian and Gay History Project. 1989. "'She Even Chewed Tobacco': A Pictorial Narrative of Passing Women in America." In *Hidden from*

History: Reclaiming the Lesbian and Gay Past, ed. Martin Duberman, Martha Vicinus, and George Chauncey, Jr., 183–94. New York: New American Library.

Sedgwick, Eve Kosofsky. 1990. *Epistemology of the Closet.* Berkeley and Los Angeles: University of California Press.

Senelick, Laurence. 1982. "The Evolution of the Male Impersonator on the Nineteenth Century Stage." *Essays in Theatre* 1(1):31–46.

Sim, F. L., M.D. 1892. "Forensic Psychiatry: Alice Mitchell Adjudged Insane." *Memphis Medical Monthly* 12(8):377–428.

Smith, Barbara Herrnstein. 1981. "Narrative Versions, Narrative Theories." In *On Narrative*, ed. W. J. T. Mitchell, 209–32. Chicago: University of Chicago Press.

Smith-Rosenberg, Carroll. 1975. "The Female World of Love and Ritual: Relations between Women in Nineteenth-Century America." *Signs: Journal of Women in Culture and Society* 1(1):1–29.

——. 1989. "Discourses of Sexuality and Subjectivity: The New Woman, 1870–1936." In *Hidden from History: Reclaiming the Lesbian and Gay Past*, ed. Martin Duberman, Martha Vicinus, and George Chauncey, Jr., 264–80. New York: New American Library.

Terry, Jennifer. 1991. "Theorizing Deviant Historiography." *differences* 3(2):55–74.

Vanity Fair. 1892. "Marrying a Maiden! Can a Woman Legally Marry a Woman?" *Vanity Fair*, February 13, 1.

Walkowitz, Judith R. 1989. "Patrolling the Borders: Feminist Historiography and the New Historicism." *Radical History Review* 4:25–31.

Weeks, Jeffrey. 1981. *Sex, Politics and Society: The Regulation of Sexuality since 1800.* London: Longman.

6

The Returns of Cleopatra Jones

Jennifer DeVere Brody

Nostalgia can hide the discontinuities between the present and the past; it falsifies, turning the past into a safe, familiar place.

Anne Friedberg 1993, 188

What's Past is Prologue; but in black history it's also Precedent.

Ossie Davis 1990, foreword

The 1990s: a revival of products and pop-cultural icons from the 1970s is in full swing in the United States; platform shoes adorn fly feet; rapper Ice Cube sports an Afro; former President Jimmy Carter again makes headline news; Cher has a disco hit; blaxploitation queen Pam Grier graces the big screen. How have such artifacts from the polyester decade (allowing for the error of the idea of a historical era) reemerged and been recirculated in different communities? What could the renewed visibility and consumption of such phenomena mean to and for the continuing struggles of black feminists in the (post)black power era? Returning to an artifact from the 1970s, specifically the blaxploitation "heroine" Cleopatra Jones seen in the film *Cleopatra Jones* (1973) and its sequel *Cleopatra Jones and the Casino of Gold* (1975),[1] this essay poses possible answers to these questions and then attempts to expose problems relating to the practice of retroactive "queer" reading. In short, the goals of this essay are threefold: (1) to read the film character Cleopatra Jones as a figure of feminism compared to representations presented in both blaxploitation and neoblaxploitation films; (2) to

argue that queer appropriations are performative gestures of desire; and (3) to analyze the film *Casino of Gold* for its queer properties.

The article begins by reading *Cleopatra Jones and the casino of Gold* as "a piece of cultural ephemera from the black power era – [such as] hot combs, NuNile pomade, dashikis, Ron O'Neal as Superfly. . . . Like fellow African-American conceptualists who have used the conventions of museum display to work against official forms of popular memory – and forgetting – . . . [this reading belongs] to a generation who perceive earlier models of black political identity as 'past'" (Mercer 1994, 161). In the manner prescribed by the second epigraph, the film, read by black queer viewers as black history, can be both prologue to and precedent for examining representations of black women in the sense that the "same" object, the character Cleopatra Jones, represents what has always already been there – the differently read black subject.

Examining the returns of different returns and arguing that the yield (stopping point and cumulative product) depends on the field of desire – both the vintage and vantage from which one looks – this essay participates in the recent shift in cinema studies away from an emphasis on the psychoanalytic paradigm of the (straight) male gaze central to feminist film criticism of the 1970s and toward a 1990s cultural studies perspective that foregrounds the active role of the viewer in determining a film's or any other cultural product's meanings.[2] The rift between film studies and cultural studies has been characterized as centered on "the question of understand[ing] spectatorship as a product of textual address and meaning as being production-led [versus] understand[ing] spectatorship as a process of negotiation between product and consumer and meaning as consumption-led," as is the case with cultural studies (Wilton 1995, 145). Moving "beyond textual determinism to consider the politics of location" (Wilton, 1995, 146) opens up the theoretical possibility of seeing and reading the return of the character Cleopatra Jones in the sequel *Cleopatra Jones and the Casino of Gold* through a queer lens that (mis)identifies and desires the film's black heroine as queer.[3]

Returning to Cleopatra Jones

In the annals of Hollywood, Cleopatra Jones is anything but a conventional heroine. Jones is a karate-trained CIA special agent whose area of expertise is international drug trafficking. She occupies the paradoxical position of being both handmaiden to the black revolution and hired handgun for the US government. Most of all, however, she is a magnified and magnificent mahogany diva – especially as she was played by the 6'2" former model Tamara Dobson. Cleo's "feminist" image contrasts sharply with both past and recent filmic images of black women – particularly those produced by the exclusively male, Hollywood-sanctioned "Black pack" that includes acclaimed directors such as Spike Lee, Mario Van Peebles, Matty Rich, and John Singleton. The "New Boyz" films valorize the father and, as Mercer argues, "depend on gender polarization and the denigration of black women [at times calling to] excommunicate the black feminist . . . as either inauthentically black or as a manipulated fool whose

unflattering portrayals of [black masculinity] are said to collude with the white male power structure" (1992, 76). The so-called neoblaxploitation films of these directors (e.g., *Do the Right Thing*, *New Jack City*, *Boyz in the Hood*, or white-directed vehicles such as *Booty Call*) romantically reconstruct scenarios absent from many of the "original" blaxploitation films.[4] Unlike the current spate of neoblaxploitation films, several of the original blaxploitation films starred black women.

Among the most famous of these female-driven blaxploitation films are *Cleopatra Jones* (1973), *Coffy* (1973), *Friday Foster* (1975), and *Sheba Baby* (1975).[5] The genealogy of black heroines consisting of Cleo, Coffy, and Foxy Brown is just beginning to be revived for cultural consumption. Until very recently, black exploitation films produced by whites were unlikely candidates for critical reconsideration. Even at the moment of their release, the marginalization of female-driven blaxploitation films was not an uncommon phenomenon. Indeed, criticism, especially from the black intelligentsia, was concomitant with the release of these films. The fact that the films have been actively forgotten is in part a result of black intellectuals' increasing dissatisfaction with blaxploitation films and of black actresses' unwillingness to participate in such exploitative ventures.[6]

In a 1975 cover article in *Ms.* magazine, Jamaica Kincaid interviewed the so-called queen of blaxploitation, actress Pam Grier, who starred in many such films.[7] In the course of the article, Kincaid claims that Grier's films, notably *Coffy*, *Foxy Brown*, and *Friday Foster* "have never received critical notice because they were not meant to. They are mostly simplistic, sensational, violent, and technically faulty. But . . . the Pam Grier . . . vehicles have one . . . redeeming value – they are the only films to come out of Hollywood . . . to show us a woman who is independent, resourceful, self-confident, strong, and courageous. . . . They are also the only films to show us a woman who triumphs" (Kincaid 1975, 52). While this may have been true, Grier's characters triumphed only in the most limited way.

Generally speaking, Grier's films were "guilty" (a word used advisedly) of a kind of documentary realism or formulaic verisimilitude. Grier's characters almost always appear in closed interiors that suggest nineteenth-century domestic realism. The audience enters the "private" (and deprived) spaces of various houses in an inner-city neighborhood.[8] To emphasize Pam Grier's characters' confinement and their limitedness, they usually battle only one "bad guy" at a time. As exemplified by the films *Coffy* and *Foxy Brown*, Grier's vehicles work as women's revenge films in which an individual motivated by *personal* tragedy (loss of a family member) kills her opponents. This individual element in Grier's films marks her characters' crimes as specific – making them into mere personal vendettas – private matters that are not necessarily attacks on systemic oppression.[9] By contrast, Dobson's Cleo, especially in *Casino*, her second film, performs different roles and typically fends off throngs of fiends. The Cleopatra Jones films work more along the lines of (male) action films. The differences between the films need to be addressed because the visual images of Grier and Dobson mentioned below work against the reductive narratives that read their characters as essentially the same.

Several leading scholars and archivists of the blaxploitation genre mention the films in which the character Cleopatra Jones appeared under the rubric of the "blaxploitation shero" or, to use Donald Bogle's inaccurate term, "Macho Matriarch."[10] In so doing, these critics inevitably discuss Cleopatra Jones as part of a *group* of films that also includes at least four of Grier's films. The oblique references to Cleo in this critical context tend to gloss over her specificity, even though stills from the films seem to complicate her representation. . . .

Could we not follow Kobena Mercer's call for a "radical paradigm shift in black cultural politics requir[ing] that one see identification as a dynamic verb" (1994, 252)? Mercer's understanding of the complexity of identification underscores the fact that readers identify differently – that identity-based readings always involve disidentifications. Given that all action movies are in part fantasy projection, these films might recall the fantasies of power many black women desired. Such low-budget, mass-marketed films directed to a black urban audience need not "reflect" *a* reality. Realism or realistic representation may not even be required. Some critics believe that a focus on

"realism" and "positive" (and implicitly *black-made*) images counters the "negative" images of blackface performances and bald stereotypes that marked "black" performances in Hollywood; but, rather than rehearse the call for such "reality," one might make a plea for "reel-ism" – for reveling in the fantasy of filmic images that does not simply replicate an always already known "reality" but rather takes pains to read (as well as takes pleasure from reading) "realness" in queer phantasmatic terms.

Reading Back/Reading Lack: Toward a Black Queer Aesthetic

While most critics in the 1970s believed that *Cleopatra Jones and the Casino of Gold* failed both commercially and ideologically, a retrospective, retroactive reading reinterprets such "failure" and reproduces the film's character (in both senses of the term) as "queer." Through such performative acts of "rememory," to use Toni Morrison's term, one can enact a kind of "queer" appropriation of the film (1989, 32). The first epigraph of this essay claims nostalgia as a problem: it acknowledges that remembering Cleopatra Jones as a black queer figure requires forgetting the ultimate failure of the radical goals of black nationalism as practiced in the late 1960s and early 1970s, forgetting black women's multiple struggles for sexual equality, forgetting the class conflicts and homophobia of both the black and women's organizations that flourished during the period (Davis 1992, 317–24). In the 1990s United States, where there has been a resurgence in the production of black feminisms – from ad hoc coalitions such as African-American Women in Defense of Ourselves, to scholarly books, to the first national conference on black women in the academy – black feminists and feminisms can still face resistance. Angela Davis testifies to this problem of style over politics as well as to the marginalization of black feminism in the mid-1990s hypermasculine Million Man March moment in her essay "Afro Images: Politics, Fashion, and Nostalgia" (1994).

Davis critiques the commodification of her own image that appeared as a "docufashion" spread in an issue of *Vibe* magazine. In this fashion layout, the magazine's editors chose to replicate poses from Davis's police mug shots. Davis explains how such recontextualizations were not only absurd but also dangerous. She writes: "The way in which this document provided a historical pretext for something akin to a reign of terror for black women is effectively erased by its use as a prop for selling clothes and promoting seventies fashion nostalgia. What is also lost in this nostalgic surrogate for historical memory – in these 'arrested moments' to use John Berger's word – is the activist's involvement of vast numbers of black women in movements that are now represented with even greater masculinist contours than they actually exhibited at the time" (1994, 175). In short, Davis points out some of the pitfalls of recontextualizing such images. No doubt she would agree with Danae Clark's reading of "commodity lesbianism" (1995, 485). Clark explains that "style as resistance becomes commodifiable as chic when it leaves the political realm and enters the fashion world. This simultaneously diffuses the political edge of style. Resistant trends [such as wearing an Afro] become restyled as high-priced fashion" (1995, 494). These remarks are crucial to note because they contrast so clearly with the already-commodified, supposedly depoliticized film character Cleopatra Jones.

Borrowing and recontextualizing images from the past is part of the pleasure of queer reading. Although one can engage in the pleasures of pastiche and camp reading that allow one to imagine Cleopatra Jones as "queer," such musings, Clark argues, must be tempered with the awareness of the injury Davis claims as a result of *Vibe's* irreverent remembering that reduced her activism to a reading of her Afro. In contrast to such pleas for the truth-claims of History – for the way it really was – Stuart Hall argues that "identities should not be valued for their falsity/genuineness; but rather for the style in which they are imagined" (1989). This thesis, which draws on Benedict Anderson's notion of an imagined community, speaks to the attempt here to reimagine an image to suit one's desire for difference. While one might "buy" Cleo as a black queer (the ambiguity between being a black queer reader and having Cleo perform black queerness for one's own pleasure is deliberate), one need not own or rather understand her as such. In other words, one might come to see that "the desire to be like can itself be motivated and sustained by the desire to possess: being can be the most radical form of having" (Fuss 1995, 114). In this case, black queer and/or lesbian readers might see in/as Cleo a representation of their own identities and desires (assuming in theory that such a diverse category could cohere).

Considering Cleopatra Jones as a black queer character requires that one "see" this figure in a different light, as it were. Deliberately "emptied of its already ambivalent aura" (Mercer 1994, 161), the film sequel *Cleopatra Jones and the Casino of Gold* can serve as fodder for the desire of black queer consumers. This performative reading strategy has been deployed by black queer filmmakers Isaac Julien and Cheryl Dunye, whose nostalgic musings on "queer" figures (such as the historical Langston Hughes or an imaginary enigmatic "mammy") acknowledge that communities need to "invent" a past in order to (re)create communities of black queer readers in the present. "In this sense, queer visions of the past are equally visions for the future, making provisional statements about conditional, undecided, perhaps alternative worlds" (Bravmann 1997, 129). Both Julien's *Looking for Langston* (1989) and Dunye's *Watermelon Woman* (1996) claim such queer desire that paradoxically reproduces a history that never was. Their projects, like this one, acknowledge their own implicit projections while suggesting that the act of reading itself produces a queer product.[11] As Carole-Anne Tyler suggests, "the queer desire latent in [such] fantasies of the 'eyes of the homo' makes manifest one's own queer desire . . . [to see] a masquerade of heterosexuality . . . behind which is the enigma of desire that queers all identities, even queer ones. . . . Queer theory is a mandate to see such things; queer reading and writing demands that we attend to them, requiring in Hart and Phelan's words 'an allegiance to the radicality of unknowing who we are becoming'" (Tyler 1998, 185). In other words, what one sees is and is not what one gets.

As it happens, among the first to exhume Cleopatra Jones for the 1990s was the feminist (in word and deed) rap group Digable Planets, who reference Cleo in their 1992 hit track

"Rebirth of Slick (I'm Cool like That)."[12] At a 1993 conference on "queer" video, critic Alycee Lane presented a paper about *Cleopatra Jones*. It is mere coincidence that Queen Latifah's role as a black lesbian bank robber in F. Gary Gray's film *Set It Off* (1996) is named "Cleo"? Or that in Dunye's *Watermelon Woman* (1996) a character recommends renting the video *Cleopatra Jones?* Or that a 1998 invitation to the monthly Los Angeles lesbian dance party, Fuel, featured a Cleopatra Jones clone pointing a pistol while straddling a car and wearing a white fox fur stole? What can it mean that these feminists (and black lesbian feminists in particular) have revived Cleopatra Jones?[13] What do such readers take to be "familiar" about Cleo's character? How can they see her as a black queer figure? Perhaps the previous citations are nostalgic representations that express an impossible desire for what never was but what might always be when one can look through a queer lens. In order to (mis)recognize Cleo as a "queer" black heroine, these readers creatively have deformed and erased aspects of the film character's initial reception. In other words, the image of Cleopatra Jones can be "queered" only through a canny counterreading that privileges different desires that result from spatiotemporal distance.

All the Lesbians were White, All the Blacks were Straight, and Cleopatra Jones and Mi Ling Fong were Queer[14]

As filmed in *Casino*, Cleopatra Jones seems to challenge certain cinematic practices that have circumscribed the representation of black women on film that placed them primarily in purely domestic and domesticated spaces. Moreover, by crossing barriers between blackness (assumed to be heterosexual) and lesbian/queerness (assumed to be white), this reading of Cleo complicates categories and allows for different identifications. Lane claims that the success of *Cleopatra Jones* depended in part on Cleo's being "heterosexualized" and desirable (because not threatening) to a monolithic, adamantly *male* urban black community (1993). She observes that "part of [Cleo's] trueness or authenticity is the extent to which she can be inscribed within the community's ideo-

logical parameters" (1993, 8). Lane bases her reading on several scenes in the film in which black men observe Cleo without her knowledge, thereby making her the object of their desire and this "heterosexual" desire the lens through which she is seen. In her debut film, *Cleopatra Jones*, then, Cleo fit within the restricted ideological contours of a "straight" black male community. Although Cleo may have been "heterosexualized" in the first film, she is "queered" in the second.

In *Casino*, Cleo sets out to find her black American colleagues, Melvin and Marvin Johnson, "brothers" who have been kidnapped in a Hong Kong drug deal gone wrong. The film is an anticolonialist travel narrative in that Cleo is not there to conquer others but to reclaim lost cargo. Initially, the supposed bad guy is someone named Chen; it turns out, however, that Chen works for a heroin empire run by the villainous Bianca Jovan (played by Stella Stevens). Jovan is a stereotyped evil white lesbian who, like her casino, is known in the films as "The Dragon Lady." When the brothers Johnson are captured by Bianca's men, Cleo is sent by her boss, played by Norman Fell, to find them. Cleo's quest to find the Johnsons will lead her first to Mi Ling Fong (played by newcomer Tanny), another female undercover agent who has been asked to work with Cleo without the latter's knowledge, and finally to the island of Macau where the Dragon Lady reigns.

Cleo's rescue mission takes her beyond her home community to the "heart" of global capitalism. In leaving "home" to recover the stolen captives, the Johnson brothers, Cleo participates in a homosocial exchange between Cleo and Bianca in which the black men, whom she calls "hers" (they are "her" black brothers in the sense of the black nationalist discourse promoted at the time), are utterly ineffectual in the lair of the Dragon Lady. They are passive once they surrender to the Dragon Lady's possession, and rather than being raped, as female counterparts might have been, the black men are seduced. Pacified by being plied with pleasure in the form of Asian women "servants" and thus effectively disarmed, they become pawns between women. A scenario in which the heroes are distracted and detained by the trap of the sirens makes way for the introduction of a sister-heroine, who will not be distracted by love in the conventional sense, to come to the rescue. Thus, in the second film, it is black men who are endangered and Cleo who becomes their savior.

Although technically *Cleopatra Jones and the Casino of Gold* must certainly be classed as belonging to the tradition of "classical Hollywood cinema" that privileges realism, Cleo functions fantastically in this largely realist narrative. In short, Cleo appears to be "unreal" in *Casino* as she courageously careens through the congested streets of Hong Kong, creating chaos in open markets and on broad boardwalks. There is an ambivalent quality that emerges from reading Cleo's character in *Casino* – her cartoonish qualities and surrealness (which might actually make her a more appealing figure for queer theory to take up because her campiness highlights how her gender, race, and sexuality are being performed and stylized). The film begins with hyperelongated shots that distort the figures rather than "realize" them. This distortion reinforces the stylized violence that propels the film's major action scenes and highlights the manipulation of film technique in the construction of the character's identity.[15] Also, in the second film, Dobson did her own makeup – which is heavy (in both senses of the word). Cleo's outrageous outfits and her surreal, silvery eye shadow serve to illuminate her awareness of self-construction as a source of power. Drawing attention to her constructedness – to the many costumes she puts on and roles she plays – may even be a way of signifying the minstrel origins of American film from which no "black" representation can escape.[16] *Casino's* title song, "Playing with Fire," *questions* rather than confirms Cleo's identity through its lyrics, which warn Cleo that she is "playing with fire" and may lose herself in this new venture. Unlike the largely celebratory lyrics of *Shaft* (1971), for example, "Playing with Fire" is fraught with the dangers of Cleo's far-out, Far East mission.[17]

Despite garnering respectable returns at the box office, *Cleopatra Jones and the Casino of Gold* was dismissed by most critics on the grounds that the sequel did not live up to the original. Vincent Canby is just one of the critics who reads Cleo's venture to and adventure in Hong Kong as a diminished return. He argues that the shift in the mise-en-scène from "local"

(i.e., Watts in the first film) to "global" (i.e., Hong Kong in the second) is detrimental to Cleo's character. Most critics of the second film believe that Cleo lacks authority in Hong Kong, where she does not speak the native language and requires a native informant/local guide to aid her in her quest. And yet, by operating (granted, with assistance) outside a circumscribed community, she also broadens her jurisdiction. Hong Kong as a juncture for transnational capital in the age of globalization (not to mention the fact that the Fourth World Conference on Women was held in China in 1995) and Cleo's narrative, however contrived, at least suggest a reconsideration of the boundaries of blackness (and here one can think of the absolute circumscription and homogenization posited in the litany of contemporary black urban films produced by Hollywood). It is difficult to imagine a 1990s Hollywood film in which white men are marginalized, white women are demonized, and characters such as Cleopatra Jones and her Asian partner Mi Ling Fong dominate the screen.

Although ultimately the film upholds white heteropatriarchal values that call for the white femme fatale's destruction, its use of Cleo and Mi Ling to bring the Dragon Lady down is different from classic femme fatale plots.[18] Moreover, Mi Ling's position as Cleo's "third world" counterpart cancels stereotypes of the "oriental" third world woman as "more" gender-oppressed than her occidental sisters. Of course, one might also read this as a fantasy that women of color could count in oppressive systems – given the rhetoric of "positive" role models, these government agents deserve at least more than the scant and inaccurate attention they have received in reconsiderations of the blaxploitation genre.

Mi Ling is also important because, although the other Asian women in the film are eroticized and exoticized, she disrupts the fantasy that *all* Asian women are sexually available. Like Cleo, then, she stands out as an unusual figure in American iconography. This third world woman who has authority in her own, supposedly less civilized, country has not been seen in Hollywood. Mi Ling, as a secret agent operating in Hong Kong (a colonized city that she works both for and against), and Cleo occupy a rather similar position *vis-à-vis* their respective governing bodies. Showing them working together challenges narratives "that are centered in a vast space of micropractices and cultural forms . . . constituted and legitimated by men and/or in male-gendered terms" (Sassen 1998, 82). Moreover, the pair might be seen to enact an expanding vocabulary of political and erotic role playing where each plays the "Other."

Throughout *Casino of Gold*, Cleo periodically gestures, à la John Wayne, by thumping the broad brim of her fedora and speaking in a deep voice. This gestural masculinity underscores her ability to *act*, in both senses of the word. She is always seen strutting through the streets of Hong Kong in her curious collage of multicolored Georgio St. Angelo pantsuits and pigtails. During several shot-reverse-shot sequences, Cleo exchanges glances with Mi Ling – thus, the audience often sees things from their doubled perspective.

Early in the film, in a congested market, Mi Ling rushes to Cleo's rescue by jumping into the scene with a double kick. The next frame shows the two women back to back – hats juxtaposed, turning slowly, intimidating their opponents – as a gang of the Dragon Lady's goons closes in. This is just one of many shots in the film in which Cleo and Mi Ling are framed together. This sequence connects them so that they appear as one Janus-faced obverse/reverse figure. Their formal introduction follows this encounter. Cleo asks Mi Ling for her particulars after exclaiming, "Girl, when I looked up and saw you it was like money from home. Say, why did you follow me?" Mi Ling responds, "I wanted to see if you were as bad as you acted . . . and . . . I've seen worse!" They laugh in a flirtatious way. Cleo again expresses her gratitude to Mi Ling by stating, "I sure am glad that you were there to take care of business." There is a brief interlude where they meet a motorcycle technician, Davy Jones, whom Mi Ling introduces nonchalantly. He seems to function as a distraction in the scene for what is *not* occurring – that is, commerce between the opposite sexes. The women dismiss him quickly and proceed upstairs to an empty gym.

In the following scene, their flirtation takes the form of a mock duel where they show off for one another. Mi Ling repeats an often used phrase in the film, "One must always be ready for business." Throughout this film, this sentence serves as an introduction to scenes in which the line between (women's) business and pleasure is crossed. Along one wall of the gym, a row of mirrors revolves, revealing in the interstices a two-dimensional white cutout androgynous target with an enlarged red paper heart. Mi Ling, whose aim is perfect, throws first one dart then another – hitting the target squarely in the heart. Cleo is clearly impressed with this demonstration of skill. In response, she reaches into an open closet, pulls out a pistol, and shoots the same figure straight through the already darted heart. Cut to Mi Ling's face with her mouth and eyes open in astonishment. Like several other scenes in *Casino*, this one underscores that Mi Ling and Cleo are a formidable team that gets the job done . . . together. So too, the emphasis in this scene on "business" rather than romance might suggest that they are removed from conventional (heterosexual?) matters of the heart.

Mi Ling and Cleo alternate playing the Lone Ranger and Tonto – the film's running joke in terms of dialogue. Each is capable of taking care of herself, but together they cannot be beaten.[19] Unlike the "blackface" narratives of *Shaft* or *Superfly* that, like much black nationalist discourse, invert value systems, making black beautiful, the repartee and reversals within positions that Mi Ling and Cleo evince are more fluid. They seem to undercut the rigid and stable subjectivities of the Lone Ranger/Tonto – master/slave – binary. Also, unlike Pam Grier's role as Friday Foster, in which she plays a girl "Friday" consistently in a film of the same name, Cleo and Mi Ling alternate who is in the position of "Tonto/Friday." Thus, Mi Ling is not merely a "sidekick" to Cleo or vice versa.

In a reading of "same"-sex interracial relationships, B. Ruby Rich argues that, in some same-sex relationships, "Race occupies the place vacated by gender. The non-sameness of color, language, or culture is a marker of difference in relationships otherwise defined by the sameness of gender. Race is a constructed presence of same-gender couples, one which allows a sorting out of identities that can avoid both the essentialism of prescribed racial expectations and the artificiality of entirely self-constructed paradigms" (1993, 321). The difficulty with such a formulation is that race cannot be divorced from gender/sexuality as an analytic category. In thinking the category "race," one must implicitly think "sexuality." Thus, rather than grant Rich's intriguing reading, it is more important to try to write a counternarrative that emphasizes the interrelatedness of race and sexuality (disallowed by dominant discourses adhering to formulas of supremacist segregation). The problem here is that gender is always already imbricated with "race" and/or culture. Gender here cannot then be "the same."

Because *Casino* is a black action film from the era of blaxploitation, whiteness is not normative (Dyer 1992, 44–64). Indeed, one of the functions of the blaxploitation film is to render "whitey" bad (but never baaaaad!). To a certain extent, this representation subverts hegemonic representations of whiteness. Here it may be instructive to remember that blaxploitation films were marketed for and seen by predominantly black urban audiences.[20] These films were meant to rupture the idea that "white is right" at the same time that they simply ignored the good white suburban family, perhaps keeping that ideal whiteness unsullied by marginalizing it and keeping it offstage.

The representation of whiteness as "wrong" is rendered quite problematical through the inversion of "traditional" gender roles that convert *Casino*'s major white characters into a phallic white woman and a castrated white man. Original audiences perhaps were meant to read the main white characters, Norman Fell's ineffectual Stanley and Stella Stevens's rakish Dragon Lady, as examples of the pathologized effeminate man and masculine woman. There could then be a clear contrast by which the colored characters in the film could be read as "nonpathological." The fact that in 1974 the American Psychological Association deleted homosexuality from its official roster of mental diseases provides a coincidental parallel for the shift in reading the second Cleopatra Jones film as "queer." Such changes effect retroactive readings of *Casino* by lending it more readily to queer appropriations and interpretations because such pronouncements not only would have been in the public arena, but also retrospectively they convey a kind of authority to thinking about changes in the construction of sexual differences.

At the end of the civil rights era, feminism was coded as white, and the homophobic and often erroneous conflation of feminists and lesbians was evoked continually in a range of discourses – hegemonic and counterhegemonic alike. As in the first Cleopatra Jones film, the presence of an evil white lesbian – Bianca Jovan in the second film – cuts two ways. On the one hand, her proximity provides the viewer with a clear manifestation of lesbianism that separates Cleo from this "taint." On the other hand, Cleo's partnership with Mi Ling makes the "threat" of lesbianism seem less contained. Bianca's evilness is marked further by the fact that she is an adoptive, incestuous, and unnatural mother who murders her daughter and does not reflect what Hart terms "white heteropatriarchy." Hart discusses the way in which lesbians, who in a Western (straight male) imaginary are white, come to be conflated with single black women – all of whom mock the importance of white fathers in their refusal to reproduce "white heteropatriarchy." *Casino* dramatizes an analogy Hart claims links the (straight) single black woman with the (white) lesbian; however, since Hart's analysis is based on "mainstream" film, as a blaxploitation film, *Casino* complicates this analogy.

Wearing ornate swashbuckler "drag" and wielding an enormous sword, Bianca takes over a ship in the first scene. She next appears in her private rooms, a sequestered, surreal setting from which she rules her heroin empire and runs her casino. Stevens's character, who can perform the essential gestures of white femininity (evidenced in her polite hostess routine), is reminiscent of the many hyperfeminine femme fatales of classic Hollywood film noir. Yet as a drug trafficker and casino operator, Bianca circulates as opposed to being circulated – a taboo for women (Rubin 1975, 157–210). Bianca's ruthlessness is epitomized by the scene near the end of the film in which she drives a stake through her daughter's tongue because the girl had spoken on behalf of the Johnsons, whom Bianca believes are her rivals. In the film's only explicit sex scene, Bianca is seen amidst a group of naked Asian women rubbing oil on each other and moaning. Just before this "orgy" is interrupted, Bianca kisses her adopted "daughter" on the mouth. This gesture underscores the fact that her whiteness is colonizing, imperial, and individual. In contrast, *Casino* denies any overt sexual behavior for colored heroines. Their sexuality seems to be marked only by innuendo and gesture.

Although Cleo delivers innuendo-patched lines in the first film, she always is tied to a straight black male milieu that deters more overt queer associations. Unlike the first film, *Casino* offers no such ties. In the penultimate scene of *Casino*, Cleo brings Mi Ling as her date to the Dragon Lady's Casino. Dashingly dressed in sequined finery, the two enter the casino together. They ogle each other as much as they are ogled by the crowd of middle American and Chinese businessmen. Cleo asks Mi Ling, "What's your pleasure?" Mi Ling answers, "I'd like to be someplace else!" Cleo's bravado in this scene is sublime. She bets on roulette – "always on the black baby" – as Mi Ling exclaims, "I hope you have someone to leave all that money to." Cleo replies, "Honey, the way I feel tonight, Muhammad Ali could have his hands full." Cut to a man fiddling with a cigar as thick and brown as his fingers, who blows a kiss to Cleo. She answers his gesture by stating, "Don't race your motor, baby; it's not leaving the garage."

When Cleo and Mi Ling spy their blonde nemesis, the Dragon Lady Bianca, standing in a gaudy green gown on the stairwell, Mi Ling comments to Cleo that Bianca "hardly looks the type to kick small dogs and children." By suggesting that things are not what they seem, this comment might also apply to the lovely ladies themselves. In the finale of *Casino*, Cleo appears in her most feminine garb to perform her most violent acts. Her sequined lingerie-inspired gown and matching sheer boudoir-cape are shed just before her climactic encounter with the Dragon Lady to reveal Cleo's statuesque figure in a bodysuit. For certainly it must be said that Cleo and Mi Ling hardly "look the type" to murder people and be karate-kicking, "queer" special agents. Indeed, they "look like" Bianca. Bianca, Cleo, and Mi Ling could each vie for the role of most glamorous femme fatale.[21] In the roulette wheel scene, Bianca looks knowingly at Mi Ling and Cleo and says, "What is this, *two* beautiful ladies . . . *unescorted?*" The pause and emphasis here are crucial to the line's meaning. The last word, as delivered by Stevens, drips with irony since it is clear that she assumes, perhaps correctly, that Cleo and Mi Ling are "together." This statement is highlighted by the explicitly

marked lesbian gaze of Bianca herself. Cleo's response to this suggestive quip is, "Well, my mother trusts me." Again, Cleo's retort is equivocal and supports the argument that although her "queerness" is not (because it cannot be) marked, certainly her heterosexuality is not recorded and therefore not "secured" (as it appeared to be in the first film). This encounter with the Dragon Lady concludes with Cleo winking at Mi Ling as the two touch elbows, adding more "evidence" that the ambivalence around Cleo's sexuality opens a space that can be filled with other narratives of desire.

Cleo's moves in *Casino* remove her from the authorized "true" straight male black nationalist community to the space of the untrue; they are not only temporal and ideological but also racial, sexual, geopolitical. The first version succeeded in part because the discourses of black power and (white) feminism were distinct; however, by 1975 they were beginning to be reformed by the increased visibility and articulation of black feminism. Whereas in 1973 Tamara Dobson could argue in a *New York Times* interview that "Cleopatra Jones is not a women's libber" – that black liberation was different from (white) women's liberation, by 1975 this was no longer applicable (Klemesrud 1973). If Cleo's character made sense earlier because she was avowedly a "race woman" (to use the black vernacular term) who worked against (white) feminism and for the singular benefit of black men, by the end of the blaxploitation era cultural productions had to be more disavowing of feminism because of the success of feminist discourse in the culture at large. Part of the perceived failure of *Casino* among black nationalists might have been the film's inability to disavow sufficiently the potential homoerotic tensions inherent in the scenes described above.

Indeed, in the two years between 1973, when *Cleopatra Jones* was released, and 1975, the release date of *Casino*, racial as well as sexual politics had changed.[22] Black feminist criticism had become a critical practice sanctioned by and produced in the academy, and so-called black feminist practice flourished. The explicit, self-named political movement known as "black feminism," whose existence was essentially inchoate in the early 1970s, began to be articulated clearly after 1972, as did an explicitly black lesbian feminism (Giddings 1984, 344). One of the earliest collections of black feminist writing was Toni Cade's *The Black Woman* (1970). In New York in 1973, the year of the first Cleo film, the National Black Feminist Organization was formed.[23] The year 1974 witnessed the momentous publication of black activist Angela Davis's autobiography. The "black lesbian feminist" Combahee River Collective began meeting in the Boston area in 1974 and published its famous statement in 1977. So, too, interethnic organizing among feminists of color during the 1970s resulted in the publication of several important collections such as *This Bridge Called My Back* (1981), edited by Cherríe Moraga and Gloria Anzaldúa. In short, "third world feminism" began to be enacted on multiple stages and in various sites (Mohanty et al. 1991).

Casino's team, composed of an Asian woman and a black woman, is difficult to imagine in the current cultural climate.[24] Feminists of color, a resolutely political term, may need to envision, if not enact, other alliances such as the one tentatively shown in *Casino*.[25] Although the partnership between Cleo and Mi Ling is utopic, it still gestures toward a possible political alliance. Though temporary, their relationship is effective. It may even be read as an allegorical model for "black" feminism. The ending of the film has Cleo depart on a plane bound for Los Angeles – she waves from the door of the plane like the ending of the interracial romance film *The Bodyguard* (1992), which itself quotes from the final shot of *Casablanca* (1942). Implicit in the final shot is Cleo's safe return.

Jump-cut
treatment for The Return of Cleopatra Jones
Los Angeles, 1999

Clcopatra Jones returns to the screen to wrangle with long-term mayor Richard Rearguard over the misdirection of funds for the still unfinished Rebuild South Central Los Angeles Project. Cleo teams up with her newly immigrated (post-1997 Hong Kong) former partner (did they stop in Hawaii and become life partners?) Mi Ling Fong. Mi Ling and Cleo, with the help of "Salsa and Chips," a women-of-color computer collective run by an agent with the code name "Supermaria," come up with a plan to simulate/stage an

earthquake that wipes out all of the corrupt power mongers in Los Angeles's 90210 zip code.[26] Having dismantled Propositions 187 and 209, they blast open the border where among the ruins they build a new queer Afro-Asiatic Aztlán.

And who should star in this *Return of Cleopatra Jones?* Given the logic of Hollywood, the only choice to recreate the role of Cleo would be transvestite "supermodel" RuPaul. The 6'7" singer has already appeared in sensational (and sensationalized) cameos in Spike Lee's *Crooklyn* (1994) and in Beeban Kidron's *To Wong Foo* (1995). Given the present fondness for such films, where it is quite clear that the best "woman" for the job is a "man," RuPaul is the only conceivable choice to revive the larger-than-life role of femme fatale Cleopatra Jones. So too, given the desire for depoliticized retrowear, RuPaul, who is a M.A.C. supermodel and whose autobiography *Lettin It All Hang Out* (1995) is a tract of conspicuous consumption showcasing cars, designer clothes, and numerous other purchasable items,[27] seems to be the perfect person to star in a film produced through Hollywood's profit-motive machine that is committed to the Disneyification of historical memory. But would casting RuPaul elide the "problem" and perhaps the power of women/feminism altogether? The answer would depend on the value one stakes in reading relationships between representation and the real. How should black (lesbian) feminists be represented?

Ironically, the increase in black feminist visibility and power (which are not the same, as Peggy Phelan reminds us) may have disadvantaged the return (especially in Hollywood) of Cleopatra Jones (1993, 6–11). Such a film could only succeed if the new version could, like the first film, continue to disavow an actual, activist black feminist agenda. Powerful black women such as Anita Hill, Angela Davis, Jocelyn Elders, and Lani Guinier thus far have not been allowed to stand their own ground without reprimands. Perhaps this is why, even in the 1970s, black actress Ellen Holly proclaimed, "Fantasy Shafts go down easily: *real* black performances do not" (1974). This comment works with black gay performance troupe Pomo Afro Homos' characterization of the 1990s as an era in which "Negro faggotry is in vogue, [but] black gay men are not." Still, it is important to reference the possibility that the problematic of queer representation offers. By resignifying the products of Western capitalism, queer readings can shift meanings – and make interventions into the representation of ethnicity, sexuality, and other differences even if such reappropriations are themselves subject to sale.[28]

The times are ripe for the return of Cleopatra Jones. Although this return is not likely to result in the discovery of another Tamara Dobson or a comparable black *female* superstar, perhaps – given the precedent of (im)possibility set by the previous queer readings – it need not. In retrospect, what remains to be answered is how black feminisms and queer theory might transform possibilities for black queer desire and black women both on and off the screen. Getting behind the camera, as well as in front of it, may be a start. Nevertheless, there is good reason to believe that the rise of RuPaul will collide with the return(s) of Cleopatra Jones. In closing, there is only one thing to do: quote the refrain of RuPaul's hit song "Supermodel" and say, "RuPaul, you better WORK!"

Notes

1   *Cleopatra Jones* (1973) starred Tamara Dobson and Shelley Winters. Released by Warner Brothers, the film, directed by Jack Starrett and produced by William Tennant, used a screenplay cowritten by black actor Max Julien, who created the title character in a novel. The film grossed $3.25 million in commercial release. The soundtrack sold more than 500,000 copies. Besides spawning the 1975 sequel *Casino of Gold* (directed by Chuck Bail, written and produced by William Tennant, starring Tamara Dobson and Stella Stevens and introducing Tanny), the first film may also have been the catalyst for the ABC television series *Get Christie Love!* that starred Teresa Graves as a black female officer for the Los Angeles Police Department. The series ran from 1974 to 1975. For more information about these, see Bogle 1988.
2   See Mulvey 1975; Stacey 1987; White 1991; and Wilton 1995.
3   See Haraway 1991. For a genealogy of the concept of "queerness," see Jagose 1996 and McRuer 1997. For more on queer and popular cultural readings of history, see Lipsitz 1990

and Bravmann 1997. Key texts in queer theory are Sedgwick 1990; Warner 1993; and Butler 1993.
4   For example, comedian Keenan Ivory Wayan's film *I'm Gonna Git You Sucka* (1988) – send-up of *Shaft* (1971), *Superfly* (1972), and other successful blaxploitation films (all titled after the main male characters) – ignored Cleopatra Jones along with the other popular blaxploitation "sheroes" while Spike Lee's release *Girl 6* (1996), scripted by Suzi Lori-Parks, conflates Cleo with Coffy in its citation of the blaxploitation heroine. For a black feminist critique of Lee's work with which I concur, see Lubiano 1991.
5   *Cleopatra Jones and the Casino of Gold* breaks many generic stereotypes such as the female buddy film, the interracial buddy film, the action genre, etc. I do not include an analysis that focuses on "genre" in this essay.
6   Indeed, in 1973 a distinguished group of black actresses including Cicely Tyson and Beah Richards convened to discredit the roles for black women in film available at the time. The conference, sponsored by the Afro-American Studies Program at Boston University, yielded heated discussion and criticized the blaxploitation genre of which these films were not always a part, since some feminists celebrated them for their "break" with even earlier blaxploitation films. For more information, see *Proceedings of a Symposium on Black Images in Films: Stereotyping and Self-Perception as Viewed by Black Actresses* 1973. It is also important to note that recent feminist film theory criticism has ignored the blaxploitation shero in part because the propensity to analogize categories of race and sexuality persists. For example, Annette Kuhn and Susannah Radstone's reference *Women in Film: An International Guide* (1991) contains entries for "black women," "feminist film," "lesbians," and "heroines," none of which mentions female blaxploitation stars. A notable exception to such omissions is Jane Gaines's 1990 essay, "White Women and Looking Relations: Race and Gender in Feminist Film Theory."
7   The smash hit by the infamous Zucker Brothers, *Kentucky Fried Movie* (1977), spoofed *Cleopatra Jones* in an advertisement for a film called, appropriately, "Cleopatra Schwartz" in which Cleo, married to a rabbi, changes costumes nearly ten times in the three-minute segment. It is beyond the scope of this essay to comment on the multiple significations parodied in this film except to say that perhaps it parodied the actual alliance between blacks and Jews in the struggle for civil rights in the 1960s.

8   In the final scene of the film, Coffy, a nurse who inexplicably turns violent after her sister becomes a dope addict, confronts her ex-lover, a corrupt black official on his way to the governorship. We see Coffy seated with her shotgun cocked in her lap – "talking" with her former beau, who tries to spin-doctor himself out of his predicament (in the previous scene he had sanctioned Coffy's murder). As he spews spurious rhetoric about helping the black community, she debates her options. Coffy, although wielding the (phallic) power, is an ambiguous figure. The fact that she has chosen to go undercover as a prostitute (and to go down on many a mafia mogul) does seem to undercut her authority. The final fadeout shot of Grier as Coffy walking alone on the beach (worthy of an Isley Brothers album cover) as the title track, which is nondiegetic, tries to give closure and meaning to the film. The theme song, "Coffy Is the Color," written by Roy Ayers, heralds her as the heroine of an authentic black community. The refrain is "You're a shining symbol/You're a new breed, a future seed / Revenge is a virtue / You stood like we all wish we could." This final track portrays Coffy as an avenging angel who acts out revenge fantasies of the black community. She has stood up for the solidified "true" and "real" interests of the community by eliminating the black betrayers (invariably also white collaborators) who have employed black revolutionary rhetoric for deviant and ultimately destructive ends.

9   Similarly, in the film *Original Gangstas* (1995), Grier plays an angry mother whose son is killed as a result of gang violence. The community of Gary, Indiana, decides to fight back. Like previous films, this film situates Grier's character firmly within the community's hyper-masculine contours (literally all the other stars are blaxploitation heroes such as Fred Williamson, who produced the film for Orion Pictures, Jim Brown, Ron O'Neal, and Richard Roundtree).

10 Bogle 1980. After a discussion of Grier and Dobson, where he says that *all* the characters "took men when they wanted," Bogle qualifies his statement to say that Dobson's Cleopatra Jones "was a living wonder to behold, but impossible to possess" (190).

11 Such retroactive reading depends on a particular mode of reception. Although in the 1990s blaxploitation festivals have become popular in major US cities, the most common access to such films today is through video rental. The relatively private mode of reception that home video screenings afford (e.g., they allow one to rewind the tape; details are often distorted in translation

from film to video) changes how these films are seen.

12 Digable Planets, *Reachin': A New Refutation of Time and Space*, Warner Brothers Records, 1992.

13 An exception to the focus on Cleopatra Jones by black lesbian spectators is provided by Etang Inyang's video *Baddass Supermama* (1996), which pays tribute to Pam Grier in an homage similar to the citations of Jones.

14 Here I rewrite the title of the anthology *All the Women Are White, All the Blacks Are Men, and Some of Us Are Brave: Black Women's Studies* (Hull, Bell-Scott, and Smith 1982).

15 Even if this distortion is a result of cinema-scope translation to video – of the use of anamorphic lenses – it still works with the idea of retroactive reading since the film has not been rereleased and is not readily available except on video. Interestingly, my introduction to Cleopatra Jones came through the stories of two people, both of whom grew up in East Africa, where blaxploitation films were screened as recently as the 1980s. Thus, this geopolitical "return" to the United States is another aspect of the film's disjunctive temporality and its (re)distribution between first and third worlds.

16 See Snead 1994.

17 Listen to the two-volume set *The Very Best of Black Movie Hits* released on the Virgin label in 1997. This collection contains the theme song to *Cleopatra Jones* but not to *Cleopatra Jones and the Casino of Gold*.

18 See Doane 1991.

19 This leads me to ask, "Does it take two women of color to defeat one white woman?" Here, I allude to the infamous scene in *King Kong* (1931) in which an entire village of African maidens is offered in exchange for a single blonde heroine.

20 For more on the marketing of blaxploitation films, see Guerrero 1993.

21 In the first film, Cleopatra Jones also battled a white lesbian. That figure, named "Mommy" and played by Shelley Winters, was a "big momma" butch who wore a leather jacket and carried a switchblade. Thus, the differences between Cleo and her lesbian adversary were drawn more starkly in the first film than in the second.

22 It should be remembered that during the 1970s, "Black women were excluded from beauty, from advertising, from magazines" ("Interview with Pam Grier" 1996, 42). Coincidentally, "super-model" Veronica Webb wrote a cover feature for *Essence* (Fall 1996) that commented on the current "taste" for blonde models in the fashion industry. Her article describes the cyclical nature of such "blackouts." While I am sympathetic

to such statements, I also always think of my students who tell me, "So . . . advertisers show us a dark-skinned model, she's still selling cigarettes and liquor."

23 For a history of these types of organizations, see Harris 1997.

24 I emphasize popular culture here because in other venues such as independent film, alternative theater, and academic journals there has been collaboration between these ethnic groups; however, there has been tension in those venues as well. Gayatri Spivak's reading of the black and Asian lesbians portrayed in Hanif Kureishi's film *Sammy and Rosie Get Laid* addresses this problem. An excerpt from Spivak's essay reads: "Interraciality is predominantly lesbian and the other side of white is a variety of blackness. . . . In the wake of the Los Angeles clash between African-Americans and Asian migrants in the Rodney King protest of 1992, it would be idle to deny that one of the facts of the migrant's or marginal's everyday that all must combat in crisis and after is the hostility between inner-city Blacks of Afro-Caribbean, African and Asian origin" (1994, 253).

25 As my colleague Traise Yamamoto reminded me, the phrase "women of color" is resolutely political. There is no "women of color" food, for example, that would allow us to see this as a cultural marker.

26 The play on "salsa and chips" and "supermaria" is taken from a performance by Betty Gonzalez-Nash at Highways Performance Space in Los Angeles. For more on women's roles in globalization being like "narratives of eviction," see Sassen 1998.

27 It is not surprising that at age twelve, RuPaul wanted to "be Cleopatra Jones." He lists the first *Cleopatra Jones* film as one of his fifteen favorite drag films (1995, 65).

28 Although Marxist-influenced critics claim that "of all the spheres of ideological regulation, the disruption of the aesthetic sphere offers the least material or social disorganisation in the lives of those who would alter the system," this essay acknowledges that there may also be power in representations (Taylor 1989, 99). Certainly members of the religious right who seek to dismantle the National Endowment for the Arts feel that images are ideological. See Taylor 1989.

References

Bogle, Donald. 1980. *Brown Sugar: Eighty Years of America's Black Female Superstars.* New York: Crown.

———. 1988. *Blacks in American Film and Television: An Illustrated Encyclopedia.* New York: Simon & Schuster.

Bravmann, Scott. 1997. *Queer Fictions of the Past: History, Culture and Difference.* Cambridge: Cambridge University Press.

Butler, Judith. 1993. *Bodies That Matter: On the Discursive Limits of "Sex."* New York and London: Routledge.

Cade, Toni. 1970. *The Black Woman: An Anthology.* New York: Signet.

Clark, Danae. 1995. "Commodity Lesbianism." In *Out in Culture: Gay, Lesbian, and Queer Essays on Popular Culture*, ed. Corey Creekmur and Alexander Doty, 484–500. Durham, N.C.: Duke University Press.

Combahee River Collective. 1977. "A Black Feminist Statement." In *Words of Fire: An Anthology of African American Feminist Thought*, ed. Beverly Guy-Sheftall, 231–40. New York: New Press.

Davis, Angela. 1992. "Black Nationalism: The Sixties and the Nineties." In *Black Popular Culture*, ed. Gina Dent, 317–24. New York: Dia Press.

———. 1994. "Afro Images: Politics, Fashion, and Nostalgia." In *Picturing Us: African American Identity in Photography*, ed. Deborah Willis, 170–9. New York: New Press.

Davis, Ossie. 1990. "Foreword." In *Black Magic: A Pictorial History of African-American Performing Arts*, ed. Langston Hughes and Milton Meltzer. New York: Shocken Press.

Doane, Mary Ann. 1991. *Femmes Fatales: Feminism, Film Theory Psychoanalysis.* New York: Routledge.

Dyer, Richard. 1992. *Only Entertainment.* New York: Routledge.

Friedberg, Anne. 1993. *Window Shopping: Cinema and the Postmodern.* Berkeley and Los Angeles: University of California Press.

Fuss, Diana. 1995. "Fashion and the Homospectatorial Look." In *Identities*, ed. Anthony Appiah and Henry Louis Gates. Chicago: University of Chicago Press.

Gaines, Jane. 1990. "White Women and Looking Relations: Race and Gender in Feminist Film Theory." In *Issues in Feminist Film Criticism*, ed. Patricia Erens, 75–92. Bloomington: Indiana University Press.

Giddings, Paula. 1984. *When and Where I Enter: The Impact of Black Women on Race and Sex in America.* New York: Bantam.

Guerrero, Ed. 1993. *Framing Blackness: The African American Image in Film.* Philadelphia: Temple University Press.

Hall, Stuart. 1989. "New Ethnicities." *Black Film, British Cinema.* ICA Documents 7. London: Institute of Contemporary Arts.

Haraway, Donna. 1991. *Simians, Cyborgs, and Women: The Reinvention of Nature*, New York: Routledge.

Harris, Miriam. 1997. "From Kennedy to Combahee: Black Feminist Activism from 1960–1980." Ph.D. dissertation, University of Minnesota.

Hart, Lynda. 1994. *Fatal Women: Lesbian Sexuality and the Mark of Aggression*. Princeton, N.J.: Princeton University Press.

Holly, Ellen. 1974. 'Where Are the Films about Real Black Men and Women?" *New York Times*, May 30.

Hull, Gloria T., Patricia Bell-Scott, and Barbara Smith, eds. 1982. *All the Women Are White, All the Blacks Are Men, but Some of Us Are Brave: Black Women's Studies*. Old Westbury, N.Y.: Feminist Press.

"Interview with Pam Grier." 1996. *Black Elegance*, Spring, 39–42.

Jagose, Annamarie. 1996. *Queer Theory: An Introduction*. New York: New York University Press.

Kincaid, Jamaica. 1975. "Pam Grier – the Mocha Mogul of Hollywood." *Ms.* 4(2):49–53.

Klemesrud, Judith. 1973. "Tamara Dobson: Not Superfly but Super Woman." *New York Times*, August 1.

Kuhn, Annette, and Susannah Radstone, eds. 1991. *Women in Film: An International Guide*. New York: Fawcett Columbine.

Lane, Alycee. 1993. "Sexuality and Urban Spaces in *Cleopatra Jones*." Paper presented at "Looking Out/Looking Over: A Conference on Lesbian and Gay Film," University of California, Davis.

Lipsitz, George. 1990. *Time Passages: Collective Memory and American Popular Culture*. Minneapolis: University of Minnesota Press.

Lubiano, Wahneema. 1991. "But Compared to What? Reading Realism, Representation, and Essentialism in *School Daze*, *Do the Right Thing*, and the Spike Lee Discourse." *Black American Literature Forum* 25(2):253–82.

Mercer, Kobena. 1992. "Endangered Species." *Art Forum* 30(Summer):73–8.

——. 1994. *Welcome to the Jungle: New Positions in Black Cultural Politics*. London: Routledge.

McRuer, Robert. 1997. *The Queer Renaissance*. New York: New York University Press.

Mohanty, Chandra, Mary Russo, and Lourdes Torres, eds. 1991. *Third World Women and the Politics of Feminism*. Bloomington: Indiana University Press.

Moraga, Cherríe, and Gloria Anzaldúa, eds. 1981. *This Bridge Called My Back: Writings by Radical Women of Color*. Latham, N.Y.: Kitchen Table.

Morrill, Cynthia. 1994. "Revamping the Gay Sensibility: Queer Camp and Dyke Noir." In *The Politics and Poetics of Camp*, ed. Moe Meyer. London: Routledge.

Morrison, Toni. 1989. "Unspeakable Things Unspoken." *Michigan Quarterly* 5,1 (Winter):1–34.

Mulvey, Laura. 1975. "Visual Pleasure and Narrative Cinema." In *Feminism and Film Theory*, ed. Constance Penley, 57–68. New York: Routledge.

Phelan, Peggy. 1993. *Unmarked: The Politics of Performance*. New York: Routledge.

Proceedings of a Symposium on Black Images in Films: Stereotyping and Self-Perception as Viewed by Black Actresses. 1973. Boston: Boston University Press.

Rich, B. Ruby. 1993. 'When Difference Is More than Skin Deep." In *Queer Looks*, ed. Martha Gever and Pratibha Parmar. New York: Routledge.

Rubin, Gayle. 1975. "The Traffic in Women: Notes on the Political Economy of Sex." In *Toward an Anthropology of Women*, ed. Ruth Reiter, 157–210. New York: Monthly Review Press.

RuPaul. 1995. *Lettin It All Hang Out: An Autobiography*. New York: Hyperion.

Sassen, Saskia. 1998. *Globalization and Its Discontents: Essays on the New Mobility of People and Money*. New York: New Press.

Sedgwick, Eve Kosofsky. 1990. *Epistemology of the Closet*. Berkeley and Los Angeles: University of California Press.

Snead, James. 1994. *White Screens/Black Images: Hollywood from the Dark Side*, ed. Colin MacCabe and Cornel West. New York: Routledge.

Spivak, Gayatri. 1994. *Outside in the Teaching Machine*. New York: Routledge.

Stacey, Jackie. 1987. "Desperately Seeking Difference." *Screen* 28(1):48–61.

Taylor, Clyde. 1989. "Black Cinema in the Post-Aesthetic Era." In *Questions of Third Cinema*, ed. Jim Pines and Paul Willemen, 177–99. London: British Film Institute.

Tyler, Carole-Anne. 1998. "Desiring Machines? Queer Re-Visions of Feminist Film Theory." In *Coming Out of Feminism*, ed. Mandy Merck, Naomi Seqal, and Elizabeth Wright, 153–94. London: Blackwell.

Warner, Michael, ed. 1993. *Fear of a Queer Planet: Queer Politics and Social Theory*. Minneapolis: University of Minnesota Press.

Webb, Veronica. 1996, "Black Models." *Essence*, Winter, 33.

White, Patricia. 1991. "Female Spectator, Lesbian Spectator: The Haunting." In *Inside/Out: Lesbian Theories, Gay Theories*, ed. Diana Fuss, 142–72. New York: Routledge.

Wilton, Tamsin, ed. 1995. *Immortal Invisible: Lesbians and the Moving Image*. London: Routledge.

7

(Male) Desire and (Female) Disgust
Reading *Hustler*

Laura Kipnis

Let's begin with two images. The first is of feminist author–poet Robin Morgan as she appears in the anti-pornography documentary *Not a Love Story*. Posed in her large book-lined living room, poet-husband Kenneth Pitchford at her side, she inveighs against a number of sexualities and sexual practices: masturbation – on the grounds that it promotes political quietism – as well as "superficial sex, kinky sex, appurtenances and [sex] toys" for benumbing "normal human sensuality." She then breaks into tears as she describes the experience of living in a society where pornographic media thrive.[1] The second image is the one conjured by a recent letter to *Hustler* magazine from E. C., a reader who introduces an account of an erotic experience involving a cruel-eyed, high-heeled dominatrix with this vivid vocational self-description: "One night, trudging home from work – I gut chickens, put their guts in a plastic bag and stuff them back in the chicken's asshole – I varied my routine by stopping at a small pub."[2] Let's say that these two images, however hyperbolically (the insistent tears, the insistent vulgarity), however inadvertently, offer an approach route toward a consideration of the relation between discourses on sexuality and the social division of labor, between sexual representation and class. On one side we have Morgan, laboring for the filmmakers and the audience as a feminist intellectual, who constructs, from a particular social locus, a normative theory of sexuality. And while "feminist intellectual" is not necessarily the

highest-paying job category, it's a markedly different class location – and one definitively up the social hierarchy – from that of E. C., whose work is of a character that tends to be relegated to the lower rungs within a social division of labor that categorizes jobs dealing with things that smell, or that for other reasons we prefer to hide from view – garbage, sewage, dirt, animal corpses – as of low status, both monetarily and socially. E. C.'s letter, carefully (certainly more carefully than Morgan) framing his sexuality in relation to his material circumstances and to actual conditions of production, is fairly typical of the discourse of *Hustler* – in its vulgarity, in its explicitness about "kinky" sex, and in its imbrication of sexuality and class. So as opposed to the set of norms Morgan attempts to put into circulation (a "normal human sensuality" far removed from E. C.'s night of bliss with his Mistress, who incidentally, "mans" herself with just the kind of appurtenances Morgan seems to be referring to), *Hustler* also offers a theory of sexuality – a "low theory." Like Morgan's radical feminism, it too offers an explicitly political and counterhegemonic analysis of power and the body; unlike Morgan it is also explicit about its own class location.

The feminist antiporn movement has achieved at least temporary hegemony over the terms in which debates on pornography take place: current discourses on porn on the left and within feminism are faced with the task of framing themselves in relation to a set of arguments now firmly established as discursive landmarks: pornography is defined as a discourse about male domination, is theorized as the determining instance in gender oppression – if not a direct cause of rape – and its pleasures, to the extent that pleasure is not simply conflated with misogyny, are confined to the male sphere of activity. "Prosex" feminists have developed arguments against these positions on a number of grounds, but invariably in response to the terms set by their opponents: those classed by the discourse as sexual deviants (or worse, as "not feminists") – S/M lesbians, women who enjoy porn – have countered on the basis of experience, often in first person, both asserting that women *do* "look" and arguing the compatibility of feminism and alternative sexual practices, while condemning antiporn forces for their universalizing abandon in claiming to speak for all women. There have been numerous arguments about the use and misuse of data from media-effects research by the antiporn movement and charges of misinterpretation and misrepresentation of data made by proporn feminists (as well as some of the researchers). On the gendered pleasure front, psychoanalytic feminists have argued that fantasy, identification, and pleasure don't necessarily immediately follow assigned gender: for instance, straight women may get turned on by gay male porn or may identify with the male in a heterosexual coupling. Others have protested the abrogation of hard-won sexual liberties implicit in any restrictions on sexual expression, further questioning the politics of the alliance of the antiporn movement and the radical Right.[3] Gayle Rubin has come closest to undermining the terms of the antiporn discourse itself: she points out, heretically, that feminism, a discourse whose object is the organization of gendered oppression, may in fact not be the most appropriate or adequate discourse to analyze sexuality, in relation to which it becomes "irrelevant and often misleading."[4] Rubin paves the way for a reexamination of received truths about porn: is pornography, in fact, so obviously and so simply a discourse about gender? Has feminism, in arrogating porn as its own privileged object, foreclosed on other questions? If feminism, as Rubin goes on, "lacks angles of vision which can encompass the social organization of

sexuality," it seems clear that at least one of these angles of vision is a theory of class, which has been routinely undertheorized and underdetermined within the antiporn movement in favor of a totalizing theory of misogyny. While class stratification and the economic and profit motives of those in the porn industry have been exhaustively covered, we have no theory of how class plays itself out in nuances of representation.

The extent of misogyny is so monumental as to be not only tragic, but banal in its omnipresence. It may appear as superficially more evident in the heightened and exaggerated realms of fantasy, pleasure, and projection – the world of pornography – but this is only a localized appearance, and one that may be operating under other codes than those of gender alone. So if the question of misogyny is momentarily displaced here to allow a consideration of questions of class, it isn't because one supersedes the other but because bringing issues of class into the porn debates may offer a way of breaking down the theoretical monolith of misogyny – and in a manner that doesn't involve jumping on the reassuring bandwagon of repression and policing the image world or the false catharsis of taking symptoms for causes. The recent tradition of cultural studies work on the body might pose some difficult questions for feminism (and thus might contribute to the kind of revamped critical discourse on sexuality that Rubin calls for): questions such as whether antiporn feminists, in abjuring questions of class in analyzing representation, are constructing (and attempting to enforce) a theory and politics of the body on the wrong side of struggles against bourgeois hegemony and are thus ultimately complicit in its enforcement. But at the same time, in taking on porn as an object, US cultural studies – or at least that tendency to locate resistance, agency, and micropolitical struggle just about everywhere in mass cultural reception – might have difficulty finding good news as it takes on the fixity of sexuality and power.

Hustler is probably the most reviled instance of mass-circulation porn, and at the same time one of the most explicitly class-antagonistic mass-circulation periodicals of any genre. Although it's been the tendency among writers on porn to lump it together into an unholy triad with *Penthouse* and *Playboy*, the other two top-circulating men's magazines, *Hustler* is a different beast in any number of respects, even in conventional men's magazine terms. *Hustler* set itself apart from its inception through its explicitness and its crusade *for* explicitness, accusing *Playboy* and *Penthouse* of hypocrisy, veiling the body, and basically not delivering the goods. The strategy paid off – *Hustler* captured a third of the men's market with its entrée into the field in 1974 by being the first to reveal pubic hair – with *Penthouse* swiftly following suit (in response to which a *Hustler* pictorial presented its model shaved),[5] then upping the explicitness ante and creating a publishing scandal by displaying a glimpse of pubic hair on its cover in July 1976 (this a typically *Hustler* commemoration of the Bicentennial: the model wore stars and stripes, although not enough of them). Throughout these early years *Hustler*'s pictorials persisted in showing more and more of the forbidden zone (the "pink" in *Hustler*-speak), with *Penthouse* struggling to keep up and *Playboy* – whose focus was always above the waist, anyway – keeping a discreet distance. *Hustler* then introduced penises, first limp ones, currently hefty erect-appearing ones, a sight verboten in traditional men's magazines, where the strict prohibition on the erect male sexual organ impels the question of what traumas it might provoke in the male viewer. *Hustler*, from its inception, made it its mission to disturb and unsettle its readers, both psychosexually and sociosexually, interrogating, as it were, the typical men's magazine codes and conventions of sexual representation: *Hustler*'s early pictorials included pregnant women, middle-aged women (horrified news commentaries referred to "geriatric pictorials"), overweight women, hermaphrodites, amputees, and, in a moment of true frisson for your typical heterosexual male, a photo spread of a preoperative transsexual, doubly well endowed. *Hustler* continued to provoke reader outrage with a 1975 interracial pictorial (black male, white female), which according to *Hustler* was protested by both the KKK and the NAACP. It's been known to picture explicit photo spreads on the consequences of venereal disease, the most graphic war carnage – none of these your typical, unproblematic turn-on.

Even more so than in its explicitness, *Hustler*'s difference from *Playboy* and *Penthouse* is in the sort of body it produces. Its pictorials, far more than other magazines, emphasize gaping orifices, as well as a consistent sharp focus on *other* orifices. *Hustler* sexuality is far from normative. It speaks openly of sexual preferences as "fetishes," and its letters and columns are full of the most specific and wide-ranging practices and sexualities, which don't appear to be hierarchized and many of which have little to do with the standard heterosexual telos of penetration. (Male–male sexuality is sometimes raised as a possibility, as well, along with the men's magazine standard woman–woman scenario.) The *Hustler* body is an unromanticized body – no Vaselined lenses or soft focus: this is neither the airbrushed top-heavy fantasy body of *Playboy* nor the ersatz opulence, the lingeried and sensitive crotch shots of *Penthouse*, transforming female genitals into objets d'art. It's a body, not a surface or a suntan: insistently material, defiantly vulgar, corporeal. In fact, the *Hustler* body is often a gaseous, fluid-emitting, *embarrassing* body, one continually defying the strictures of bourgeois manners and mores and instead governed by its lower intestinal tract – a body threatening to erupt at any moment. *Hustler*'s favorite joke is someone accidentally defecating in church.

Particularly in its cartoons, but also in its editorials and political humor, *Hustler* devotes itself to what tends to be called "grossness": an obsessive focus on the lower stratum, humor animated by a downward movement, representational techniques of exaggeration and inversion. *Hustler*'s bodily topography is straight out of Rabelais, as even a partial inventory of the subjects it finds of interest indicates: fat women, assholes, monstrous and gigantic sexual organs, body odors (the notorious Scratch 'n Sniff centerfold, which, due to "the limits of the technology," publisher Larry Flynt apologized, smelled definitively of lilacs), and anything that exudes from the body: piss, shit, semen, menstrual blood (particularly when it sullies a sanitary or public site), and, most especially, farts: farting in public, farting loudly, Barbara Bush farting, priests and nuns farting, politicians farting, the professional classes farting, the rich farting. . . .[6] Certainly a far remove from your sleek, overlaminated *Playboy/Penthouse* body. As *Newsweek* complained, "The contents of an average issue read like something Krafft-Ebing might have whispered to the Marquis de Sade . . . . *Hustler* is into erotic fantasies involving excrement, dismemberment, and the sexual longings of rodents. . . . [W]here other skin slicks are merely kinky, *Hustler* can be downright frightful. . . . The net effect is to transform the erotic into the emetic."[7]

It's not clear if what sets *Newsweek* to crabbing is that *Hustler* transgresses bourgeois mores of the proper or that *Hustler* violates men's magazine conventions of sexuality. On both fronts its discourse is transgressive – in fact on *every* front *Hustler* devotes itself to producing generalized transgression. Given that control over the body has long been associated with the bourgeois political project, with both the "ability and the right to control and dominate others,"[8] *Hustler*'s insistent and repetitious return to the iconography of the body out of control, rampantly transgressing bourgeois norms and sullying bourgeois property and proprieties, raises certain political questions. On the politics of such social transgressions, for example, Peter Stallybrass and Allon White, following Bakhtin, write of a transcoding between bodily and social topography, setting up a homology between the lower bodily stratum and the lower social classes – the reference to the body invariably being a reference to the social.[9]

Here perhaps is a clue to *Newsweek*'s pique, as well as a way to think about why it is that the repressive apparatuses of the dominant social order return so invariably to the body and to somatic symbols. (And I should say that I write this during the Cincinnati Mapplethorpe obscenity trial, so this tactic is excessively visible at this particular conjuncture.) It's not only because these bodily symbols "are the ultimate elements of social classification itself" but also because the transcoding between the body and the social sets up the aesthetic mechanisms through which the body is a privileged political trope of lower social classes, and through which bodily grossness operates as a critique of dominant ideology. The power of grossness is predicated on its opposition from *and to* high discourses, themselves prophylactic against the debasements of the low (the lower classes, ver-

nacular discourses, low culture, shit . . .). And it is dominant ideology itself that works to enforce and reproduce this opposition – whether in producing class differences, somatic symbols, or culture. The very highness of high culture is structured through the obsessive banishment of the low, and through the labor of suppressing the grotesque body (which is, in fact, simply the material body, gross as that can be) in favor of what Bakhtin calls "the classical body." This classical body – a refined, orifice-less, laminated surface – is homologous to the forms of official high culture that legitimate their authority by reference to the values – the highness – inherent in this classical body. According to low-theoretician Larry Flynt, "Tastelessness is a necessary tool in challenging preconceived notions in an uptight world where people are afraid to discuss their attitudes, prejudices and misconceptions." This is not so far from Bakhtin on Rabelais: "Things are tested and reevaluated in the dimensions of laughter, which has defeated fear and all gloomy seriousness. This is why the material bodily lower stratum is needed, for it gaily and simultaneously materializes and unburdens. It liberates objects from the snares of false seriousness, from illusions and sublimations inspired by fear."[10]

So in mapping social topography against bodily topography, it becomes apparent how the unsettling effects of grossness and erupting bodies condense all the unsettling effects (to those in power) of a class hierarchy tenuously held in place through symbolic (and less symbolic) policing of the threats posed by bodies, by lower classes, by angry mobs.

Bakhtin and others have noted that the invention of the classical body and the formation of this new bodily canon have their inception in the sixteenth-century rise of individualism and the attendant formation and consolidation of bourgeois subjectivity and bourgeois political hegemony, setting off, at the representational level, the struggle of grotesque and classical concepts.[11] A similar historical argument is made by Norbert Elias in his study *The Civilizing Process*, which traces the effects of this social process on the structure of individual affect. The invention of Bakhtin's classical body entails and is part of a social transformation within which thresholds of sensitivity and refinement in the individual psyche become heightened.[12] Initially this reform of affect takes place in the upper classes, within whom increasingly refined manners and habits – initially a mechanism of class distinction – are progressively restructuring standards of privacy, disgust, shame, and embarrassment. These affect-reforms are gradually, although incompletely, disseminated downward through the social hierarchy (and finally to other nations whose lack of "civilization" might reasonably necessitate colonial etiquette lessons). These new standards of delicacy and refinement become the very substance of bourgeois subjectivity: constraints that were originally socially generated gradually become reproduced in individuals as habits, reflexes, as the structure of the modern psyche. And as Elias reminds us, the foundational Freudian distinction between id and ego corresponds to historically specific demands placed on public behavior in which certain instinctual behaviors and impulses – primarily bodily ones like sex and elimination – are relegated to the private sphere, behind closed doors, or in the case of the most shameful and most socially prohibited drives and desires, warehoused as the contents of the unconscious.

So we can see, returning to our two opening images, how Morgan's tears, her sentiment, might be constructed *against* E. C.'s vulgarity, how her desire to distance herself from and if possible banish from existence the cause of her distress – the sexual expression of people unlike herself – has a sort of structural imperative: as Stallybrass and White put it, the bourgeois subject has "continuously defined and redefined itself through the exclusion of what it marked out as low – as dirty, repulsive, noisy, contaminating. . . . [The] very act of exclusion was constitutive of its identity."[13] So disgust has a long and complicated history, the context within which should be placed the increasingly strong tendency of the bourgeois to want to remove the distasteful from the sight of society (including, of course, dead animals, which might interest E. C. – as "people in the course of the civilizing process seek to suppress in themselves every characteristic they feel to be animal").[14] These gestures of disgust are crucial in the production of the bourgeois body, now so rigidly split into higher and lower stratum that tears will become the only publicly permissible display of bodily

fluid. So the bodies and bodily effluences start to stack up into neat oppositions: on the one side upper bodily productions, a heightened sense of delicacy, and the project of removing the distasteful from sight (and sight, of course, is at the top of the hierarchization of the senses central to bourgeois identity and rationality); and on the other hand, the lower body and *its* productions, the insistence on vulgarity and violations of the bourgeois body. To the extent that in Morgan's project, discourse and tears are devoted to concealing the counterbourgeois body from view by regulating its representation and reforming its pleasures into ones more consequent with refined sensibilities, they can be understood, at least in part, as the product of a centuries-long sociohistorical process, a process that has been a primary mechanism of class distinction, and one that has played an important role as an ongoing tool in class hegemony. So perhaps it becomes a bit more difficult to see feminist disgust in isolation, and disgust at pornography as strictly a gender issue, for any gesture of disgust is not without a history and not without a class character. And whatever else we may say about feminist arguments about the proper or improper representation of women s bodies – and I don't intend to imply that my discussion is exhaustive of the issue – bourgeois disgust, even as mobilized against a sense of violation and violence to the female body, is not without a function in relation to class hegemony, and is more than problematic in the context of what purports to be a radical social movement.

Perhaps this is the moment to say that a large part of what impels me to write this essay is my own disgust in reading *Hustler*. In fact, I have wanted to write this essay for several years, but every time I trudge out and buy the latest issue, open it, and begin to try to bring analytical powers to bear upon it, I'm just so disgusted that I give up, never quite sure whether this almost automatic response is one of feminist disgust or bourgeois disgust. Of course, whether as feminist, bourgeois, or academic, I and most likely you are what could be called *Hustler*'s implied target, rather than its implied reader. The discourse of *Hustler* is quite specifically *constructed against* not only the classical body, a bourgeois holdover of the aristocracy, but all the paraphernalia of petite-bourgeoisiehood, as well. At the most manifest level *Hustler* is simply against any form of social or intellectual pretension: it is against the pretensions (and the social power) of the professional classes – doctors, optometrists, dentists are favored targets – it is against liberals, and it is particularly cruel to academics who are invariably prissy and uptight. (An academic to his wife: "Eat your pussy? You forget, Gladys, I have a Ph.D.") It is against the power of government – which is by definition corrupt, as are elected officials, the permanent government, even foreign governments. Of course it is against the rich, particularly rich women; it is down on the Chicago Cubs; and it devotes many pages to the hypocrisy of organized religion – with a multiplication of jokes on the sexual instincts of the clergy, the sexual possibilities of the crucifixion, and the scam of the virgin birth, and as mentioned previously, the plethora of jokes involving farting /shitting/fucking in church and the bodily functions of nuns, priests, and ministers. In *Hustler* most forms of social power are fundamentally crooked and illegitimate.

These are just *Hustler*'s more manifest targets. Reading a bit deeper, its offenses provide a detailed road map of a cultural psyche. Its favored tactic is to zero in on a subject, an issue, that the bourgeois imagination prefers to be unknowing about, that a culture has founded itself upon suppressing and prohibits irreverent speech about – things we would call "tasteless" at best, or might even become physically revulsed by: the materiality of aborted fetuses,[15] where homeless people go to the bathroom, cancer, the proximity of sexual organs to those of elimination – any aspect of the material body, in fact. A case in point, one that again subjected *Hustler* to national outrage: its two cartoons about Betty Ford's mastectomy. If one can distance oneself from one's automatic indignation for a moment, *Hustler* might be seen as posing, through the strategy of transgression, an interesting metadiscursive question: which are the subjects that are taboo ones for even sick humor? Consider for a moment that while, for example, it was not uncommon, following the Challenger explosion, to hear the sickest jokes about scattered body parts, while jokes about amputees and paraplegics are not entirely unknown even on broadcast TV (and of course abound on the

pages of *Hustler*), while jokes about blindness are considered so benign that one involving Ray Charles features in a current "blind taste test" soda pop commercial, mastectomy is one subject that appears to be completely off limits as a humorous topic. But back to amputees for a moment, perhaps a better comparison: apparently a man without a limb is considered less tragic by the culture at large, less mutilated, and less of a cultural problem than a woman without a breast; a mastectomy more of a tragedy than the deaths of the seven astronauts. This, as I say, provides some clues into the deep structure of a cultural psyche – as does our outrage. After all, what *is* a woman without a breast in a culture that measures breasts as the measure of the woman? Not a fit subject for comment. It's a subject so veiled that it's not even available to the "working through" of the joke. (It is again a case where *Hustler* seems to be deconstructing the codes of the men's magazine: where *Playboy* creates a fetish of the breast – its raison d'être is, in fact, very much the cultural obsession with them – *Hustler* perversely points out that they are, after all, materially, merely tissue – another limb.)[16]

Hustler's uncanny knack for finding and attacking the jugular of a culture's sensitivity might more aptly be regarded as intellectual work on the order of the classic anthropological studies that translate a culture into a set of structural oppositions (obsession with the breast/prohibition of mastectomy jokes), laying bare the structure of its taboos and arcane superstitions. (Or do only "primitive" cultures have irrational taboos?) *Hustler*, in fact, performs a cultural mapping similar to that of anthropologist Mary Douglas, whose study *Purity and Danger* produces a very similar social blueprint.[17] The vast majority of *Hustler* humor seems to be animated by the desire to violate what Douglas describes as "pollution" taboos and rituals – these being a society's set of beliefs, rituals, and practices having to do with dirt, order, and hygiene (and by extension, the pornographic). As to the pleasure produced by such cultural violations as *Hustler*'s, Douglas cheerily informs us, "It is not always an unpleasant experience to confront ambiguity," and while it is clearly more tolerable in some areas than in others, "there is a whole gradient on which laughter, revulsion and shock belong at different points and intensities."[18]

The sense of both pleasure and danger that violation of pollution taboos can invoke is clearly dependent on the existence of symbolic codes, codes that are for the most part only semiconscious. Defilement can't be an isolated event, it can only engage our interest or provoke our anxiety to the extent that our ideas about such things are systematically ordered and that this ordering matters deeply – in our culture, in our subjectivity. As Freud notes, "Only jokes that have a purpose run the risk of meeting with people who do not want to listen to them."

Of course, a confrontation with ambiguity and violation can be profoundly displeasurable as well, as the many opponents of *Hustler* might attest. And for Freud this displeasure has to do with both gender and class. One of the most interesting things about Freud's discussion of jokes is the theory of humor and gender he elaborates in the course of his discussion of them, with class almost inadvertently intervening as a third term.[19] He first endeavors to produce a typology of jokes according to their gender effects. For example, in regard to excremental jokes (a staple of *Hustler* humor), Freud tells us that this is material *common to both sexes*, as both experience a common sense of shame surrounding bodily functions. And it's true that *Hustler*'s numerous jokes on the proximity of the sexual organs to elimination functions, the confusion of assholes and vaginas, turds and penises, shit and sex – for example, a couple fucking in a hospital room while someone in the next bed is getting an enema, and all get covered with shit – can't really be said to have a gender basis or target (unless, that is, we women put ourselves, more so than men, in the position of upholders of "good taste").

But obscene humor, whose purpose is to verbally expose sexual facts and relations, is, for Freud, a consequence of male and female sexual incommensurability, and the dirty joke is something like a seduction gone awry. The motive for (men's) dirty jokes is "in reality nothing more than women's incapacity to tolerate undisguised sexuality, an incapacity correspondingly increased with a rise in the educational and social level" (p. 101). Whereas both men and women are subject to sexual inhibition or repression, apparently upper-class women are the more seriously afflicted in the Freudian world, and dirty jokes thus function as a sign for both sexual difference ("smut is like an exposure of the sexually different person to whom it is directed. . . . [I]t compels the person who is assailed to imagine the part of the body or the procedure in question" [p. 98]) and class difference. So apparently, if it weren't for women's lack of sexual willingness and class refinement the joke would be not a joke, but a proposition: "If the woman's readiness emerges quickly the obscene speech has a short life; it yields at once to a sexual action," hypothesizes Freud (p. 99). While there are some fairly crude gender and class stereotypes in circulation here – the figure of the lusty barmaid standing in for the lower-class woman – it's also true that obscene jokes and pornographic images *are* only perceived by *some* women as an act of aggression against women. But these images and jokes are aggressive only insofar as they're capable of causing the woman discomfort, and they're capable of causing discomfort *only* insofar as there *are* differing levels of sexual inhibition between at least some men and some women. So Freud's view would seem to hold out: the obscene joke is directed originally toward women; it not only presupposes the presence of a woman, but presupposes also that women are sexually constituted differently from men, and upper classness or upper-class identification – as Morgan's discourse also indicates – exacerbates this difference.

But if there are differing levels of inhibition, displeasure, or interest between some men and some women (although *Hustler*'s readership is primarily male, it's not exclusively male), the origins of this pleasure/displeasure disjunction are also a site of controversy in the porn debates. For Freud it's part of the process of *differentiation* between the sexes, not originative – little girls are just as "interested" as little boys. Antiporn forces tend to reject a constructionist argument such as Freud's in favor of a description of female sexuality as inborn and biologically based – something akin to the "normal human sensuality" Morgan refers to.[20] Women's discomfiture at the dirty joke, from this vantage point, would appear to be twofold. There is the discomfort at the intended violation – at being assailed "with the part of the body or the procedure in question." But there is the further discomfort of being addressed as a subject of repression – as a subject with a history – and the rejection of porn can be seen as a defense erected against representations that mean to unsettle her in her subjectivity. In other words, there is, in pornography, a violation of the very *premise* of the "naturalness" of female sexuality and subjectivity, exacerbated by the social fact that not all women *do* experience male pornography in the same way. That "prosex" feminists, who tend to follow some version of a constructionist position on female sexuality, seem to feel less violated by porn is some indication that these questions of subjectivity are central to porn's address, misaddress, and violations. To the extent that pornography's discourse engages in setting up disturbances around questions of subjectivity and sexual difference – after all, what does *Hustler*-variety porn consist of but the male fantasy of women whose sexual desires are in concert with men's? – and that this fantasy of female compliance is perceived as doing violence to female subjectivity by some women but not others, the perception of this violence is, to a large degree, an issue of difference among women.[21] But the violence here is that of misaddress, of having one's desire misfigured as the male's desire. It is the violence of being absent from the scene. The differences between female spectators as to how this address or misaddress is perceived appears to be bound up with the degree to which a certain version of female sexuality is hypostatized as natural, versus a sense of mobility of sexuality (at least at the level of fantasy). But hypostatizing female sexuality and assigning it to all women involves universalizing a historically specific class position as well, not as something acquired and constructed through difference, privilege, and hierarchy, but as somehow inborn. Insisting that all women are violated by pornography insists that class or class identification doesn't figure as a difference among women, that "normal human sensuality" erases all difference between women.

For Freud, even the form of the joke is classed, with a focus on joke technique associated with higher social classes and education levels. In this light it's interesting to note how little *Hustler* actually engages in the technique of

the joke – even to find a pun is rare. But then as far as obscene humor, we're subject to glaring errors of judgment about the "goodness" of jokes insofar as we judge them on formal terms, according to Freud – the technique of these jokes is often "quite wretched, but they have immense success in provoking laughter." Particularly in regard to obscene jokes, we aren't "in a position to distinguish by our feelings what part of the pleasure arises from the sources of their technique and what part from those of their purpose. Thus, strictly speaking, we do not know what we are laughing at."[22] And so, too, with displeasure – it would seem we can't be entirely sure what we're *not* laughing at either, and this would be particularly true of both the bourgeois and the antipornography feminist, to the extent that both seem likely to displace or disavow pleasure or interest in smut, one in favor of technique – like disgust, a mechanism of class distinction – and the other against perceived violations against female subjectivity. So for both, the act of rejection takes on far more significance than the terrains of pleasure; for both, the nuances and micrologics of *displeasure* are defining practices.

Yet at the same time, there does seem to be an awful lot of interest in porn among both, albeit a negative sort of interest. It's something of a Freudian cliché that shame, disgust, and morality are reaction-formations to an original interest in what is not "clean." One defining characteristic of a classic reaction-formation is that the subject actually comes close to "satisfying the demands of the opposing instinct while actually engaged in the pursuit of the virtue which he affects," the classic example being the housewife obsessed with cleanliness who ends up "concentrating her whole existence on dust and dirt."[23] And it does seem to be the case that a crusader against porn will end up making pornography the center of her existence. Theorizing it as central to women's oppression means, in practical terms, devoting one's time to reading it, thinking about it, and talking about it. It also means simultaneously conferring this *interest*, this subject-effect, onto others – predicting tragic consequences arising from such dirty pursuits, unvaryingly dire and uniform effects, as if the will and individuality of consumers of porn are suddenly seized by some (projected) all-controlling force, a force that becomes – or already is – the substance of a monotonic male sexuality. Thusly summing up male sexuality, Andrea Dworkin writes: "Any violation of a woman's body can become sex for men; this is the essential truth of pornography."[24]

The belief in these sorts of essential truths seems close to what Mary Douglas calls "danger-beliefs" – "a strong language of mutual exhortation":

> At this level the laws of nature are dragged in to sanction the moral code: this kind of disease is caused by adultery, that by incest. . . . [T]he whole universe is harnessed to men's [sic] attempts to force one another into good citizenship. Thus we find that certain moral values are upheld and certain social rules defined by beliefs in dangerous contagion.[25]

And Douglas, like Freud, also speaks directly about the relation of gender to the "gradient" where laughter, revulsion, and shock collide: her discussion of danger beliefs opens onto questions of class and hierarchy, as well. For her, gender is something of a trope in the realm of purity rituals and pollution violations: it functions as a displacement from issues of social hierarchy.

> I believe that some pollutions are used as analogies for expressing a general view of the social order. For example, there are beliefs that each sex is a danger to the other through contact with sexual fluids. . . . Such patterns of sexual danger can be seen to express symmetry or hierarchy. It is implausible to interpret them as expressing something about the actual relation of the sexes. I suggest that many ideas about sexual dangers are better interpreted as symbols of the relation between parts of society, as mirroring designs of hierarchy or symmetry which apply in the larger social system.[26]

While men certainly do pose sexual danger to women, the content of pollution beliefs expresses that danger symbolically at best: it would be implausible to take the content of these beliefs literally. So while, for Douglas, gender is a trope for social hierarchy, a feminist might interpret the above passage to mean that *danger* is a trope for gender hierarchy. Douglas's obser-

vations on the series of displacements between defilement, danger, gender, and class puts an interesting cast on female displeasure in pornography in relation to class hierarchies and "the larger social system." It also sheds light on the relation between *Hustler*'s low-class tendentiousness and its production of bourgeois displeasure, and on how the feminist response to pornography might end up reinscribing the feminist into the position of enforcer of class distinctions.

Historically, female reformism aimed at bettering the position of women has often had an unfortunately conservative social thrust, as in, for example, the case of the temperance movement. The local interests of women in reforming male behavior can easily dovetail with the interests of capital in producing and reproducing an orderly, obedient, and sober workforce. In social history terms we might note that *Hustler* galumphs onto the social stage at the height of the feminist second wave, and while the usual way to phrase this relation would be the term "backlash," it can also be seen as a retort – even a political response – to feminist calls for reform of the male imagination. There's no doubt that *Hustler* sees itself as doing battle with feminists: ur-feminist Gloria Steinem makes frequent appearances in the pages of the magazine as an uptight and, predictably, upper-class bitch. It's fairly clear that from *Hustler*'s point of view, feminism is a class-based discourse. *Hustler*'s production of sexual differences are also the production of a form of class consciousness – to accede to feminist reforms would be to identify upward on the social hierarchy.

But any automatic assumptions about *Hustler*-variety porn aiding and abetting the entrenchment of male power might be put into question by actually reading the magazine. Whereas Freud's observations on dirty jokes are phallocentric in the precise sense of the word – phallic sexuality is made central – *Hustler* itself seems much less certain about the place of the phallus, much more wry and often troubled about male and female sexual incommensurability. On the one hand it offers the standard men's magazine fantasy babe – always ready, always horny, willing to do anything, and inexplicably attracted to the *Hustler* male. But just as often there is her flip side: the woman who is disgusted by the *Hustler* male's desires and sexuality, a superior, rejecting, often upper-class woman. It becomes clear how class resentment is modulated through resentment of what is seen as the power of women to humiliate and reject: "Beauty isn't everything, except to the bitch who's got it. You see her stalking the aisles of Cartier, stuffing her perfect face at exorbitant cuisineries, tooling her Jag along private-access coastline roads. . . ." This reeks of a sense of disenfranchisement rather than any sort of certainty about male power over women. The fantasy life here is animated by cultural disempowerment in relation to a sexual caste system and a social class system. The magazine is tinged with frustrated desire and rejection: *Hustler* gives vent to a vision of sex in which sex is an arena for failure and humiliation rather than domination and power. There are numerous ads addressed to male anxieties and sense of inadequacy: various sorts of penis enlargers ("Here is your chance to overcome the problems and insecurities of a penis that is too small. Gain self-confidence and your ability to satisfy women will skyrocket," reads a typical ad), penis extenders, and erection aids (Stay-Up, Sta-Hard).[27] One of the problems with most porn from even a pro-porn feminist point of view is that men seize the power and privilege to have public fantasies about women's bodies, to imagine and represent women's bodies without any risk, without any concomitant problematization of the male body – which is invariably produced as powerful and inviolable. But *Hustler* does put the male body at risk, representing and never completely alleviating male anxiety (and for what it's worth, there is a surprising amount of castration humor in *Hustler*, as well). Rejecting the sort of compensatory fantasy life mobilized by *Playboy* and *Penthouse*, in which all women are willing and all men are studs – as long as its readers fantasize and identify upward, with money, power, good looks, and consumer durables – *Hustler* pulls the window dressing off the market/exchange nature of sexual romance: the market in attractiveness, the exchange basis of male–female relations in capitalist patriarchy. Sexual exchange is a frequent subject of humor: women students are coerced into having sex with professors for grades; women are fooled into having sex by various ruses, lies, or barters, usually engineered

by males in power positions – bosses, doctors, and the like. All this is probably truer than not true, but problematic from the standpoint of male fantasy: power, money, and prestige are represented as essential to sexual success, but the magazine works to disparage and counter identification with these sorts of class attributes on every other front. The intersections of sex, gender, class, and power here are complex, contradictory, and political.

Much of *Hustler*'s humor *is*, in fact, manifestly political, and much of it would even get a warm welcome in Left-leaning circles, although its strategies of conveying those sentiments might give some pause. A 1989 satirical photo feature titled "Farewell to Reagan: Ronnie's Last Bash" demonstrates how the magazine's standard repertoire of aesthetic techniques – nudity, grossness, and offensiveness – can be directly translated into scathingly effective political language. It further shows how the pornographic idiom can work as a form of political speech that refuses to buy into the pompously serious and high-minded language in which official culture conducts its political discourse: *Hustler* refuses the language of high culture along with its political forms. The photo spread, laid out like a series of black-and-white surveillance photos, begins with this no-words-minced introduction:

It's been a great eight years – for the power elite, that is. You can bet Nancy planned long and hard how to celebrate Ron Reagan's successful term of filling special-interest coffers while fucking John Q. Citizen right up the yazoo. A radical tax plan that more than halved taxes for the rich while doubling the working man's load; detaxation of industries, who trickled down their windfalls into mergers, takeovers, and investments in foreign lands; crooked deals with enemies of U.S. allies in return for dirty money for right wing killers to reclaim former U.S. business territories overseas; more than 100 appointees who resigned in disgrace over ethics or outright criminal charges . . . are all the legacies of the Reagan years . . . and we'll still get whiffs of bullyboy Ed Meese's sexual intimidation policies for years to come, particularly with conservative whores posing as Supreme Court justices.[28]

The photos that follow are of an elaborately staged orgiastic White House farewell party as imagined by the *Hustler* editors, with the appropriate motley faces of the political elite photomontaged onto naked and seminaked bodies doing fairly obscene and polymorphously perverse things to each other. (The warning "Parody: Not to be taken seriously. Celebrity heads stripped onto our model's bodies" accompanies each and every photo – more about *Hustler*'s legal travails further on.) That more of the naked bodies are female and that many are in what could be described as a service relation to male bodies clearly opens up the possibility of a reading limited to its misogynistic tendencies. But what becomes problematic for such a singular reading is that within these parodic representations, this staging of the rituals of male hegemony also works in favor of an overtly counterhegemonic political treatise.

The style is something like a *Mad* magazine cartoon come to life with a multiplication of detail in every shot (the Ted Kennedy dartboard in one corner; in another, stickers that exhort "Invest in South Africa"; the plaque over Reagan's bed announcing "Joseph McCarthy slept here"). In the main room of the party, various half-naked women cavort, and Edwin Meese is glimpsed filching a candelabra. Reagan greets a hooded Ku Klux Klanner at the door, and a helpful caption translates the action: "Ron tells an embarrassed Jesse Helms it wasn't a come-as-you-are party," while in the background the corpse of Bill Casey watches benignly over the proceedings (his gaping mouth doubles as an ashtray), as does former press secretary James Brady – the victim of John Hinckley's attempted assassination and Reagan's no-gun-control policy – who, propped in a wheelchair, wears a sign bluntly announcing "Vegetable Dip" around his neck. In the next room Ollie North as a well-built male stripper gyrates on top of a table while a fawning Poindexter, Secord, and Weinberger gathered at his feet stuff dollar bills into his G-string holster in homoerotic reverie. In the next room Jerry Falwell is masturbating to a copy of *Hustler* concealed in the Bible, a bottle of Campari at his bedside and an "I love Mom" button pinned to his jacket (this a triumphant *Hustler* pouring salt on the wound – more on the Falwell Supreme

Court case later on). In another room "former Democrat and supreme skagbait Jeane Kirkpatrick demonstrates why she switched to the Republican Party," as, grinning and topless, we find her on the verge of anally penetrating a bespectacled George Bush with the dildo attached to her ammunition belt. A whiny Elliott Abrams, pants around his ankles and dick in hand, tries unsuccessfully to pay off a prostitute who won't have him; and a naked Pat Robertson, doggie style on the bed, is being disciplined by a naked angel with a cat-o'-nine-tails. And on the last page the invoice to the American citizens: $283,000,000.

While the antiestablishment politics of the photo spread are fairly clear, *Hustler* can also be maddeningly incoherent, all over what we usually think of as the political spectrum. Its incoherence, as well as its low-rent tendentiousness, can be laid at the door of publisher Larry Flynt as much as anywhere, as Flynt, in the early days of the magazine, maintained such iron control over the day-to-day operations that he had to approve even the pull quotes. Flynt is a man apparently both determined and destined to play out the content of his obsessions as psychodrama on our public stage; if he weren't so widely considered such a disgusting pariah, his life could probably supply the material for many epic dramas. The very public nature of Flynt's blazing trail through the civil and criminal justice system and his one-man campaign for the first amendment justify a brief descent into the murkiness of the biographical – not to make a case for singular authorship, but because Flynt himself has had a decisive historical and political impact in the realpolitik of state power. In the end it has been porn king Larry Flynt – not the left, not the avant garde – who has decisively expanded the perimeters of political speech.

Larry Flynt is very much of the class he appears to address; his story is that of a pornographic Horatio Alger. He was born in Magoffin County, Kentucky, in the Appalachias, the poorest county in America. The son of a pipe welder, he quit school in the eighth grade, joined the navy at fourteen with a forged birth certificate, got out, worked in a General Motors auto assembly plant, and turned $1,500 in savings into a chain of go-go bars in Ohio named the Hustler Clubs. The magazine originated as a two-page newsletter for the bars, and the rest was rags to riches: Flynt's income was as high as thirty million dollars a year when *Hustler* was at its peak circulation of over two million. (He then built himself a scale replica of the cabin he grew up in, in the basement of his mansion to remind him, he says, where he came from. The model is complete with chickenwire and hay and a three-foot lifelike statue of the chicken he claims to have lost his virginity to at age eight.)

Since the magazine's inception Flynt has spent much of his time in and out of the nation's courtrooms on various obscenity and libel charges, as well as an array of contempt charges and other bizarre legal entanglements – notably his somehow becoming entangled in the government's prosecution of automaker John DeLorean. All proceeded as normal (for Flynt) until his well-publicized 1978 conversion to evangelical Christianity at the hands of presidential sister Ruth Carter Stapleton. The two were pictured chastely hand in hand as Flynt announced plans to turn *Hustler* into a *religious* skin magazine and told a Pentecostal congregation in Houston (where he was attending the National Women's Conference), "I owe every woman in America an apology." Ironically, it was this religious conversion that led to the notorious *Hustler* cover of a woman being ground up in a meat grinder, which was, in fact, another sheepish and flat-footed attempt at apologia by Flynt. "We will no longer hang women up as pieces of meat" was actually the widely ignored caption to the photo. (Recall here Freud's observation on the sophistication of the joke form as a class trait.)[29]

In 1978, shortly after the religious conversion, during another of his obscenity trials in Lawrenceville, Georgia, Flynt was shot three times by an unknown person with a .44 Magnum. His spinal nerves were severed, leaving him paralyzed from the waist down and in constant pain. He became a recluse, barricading himself in his Bel Air mansion, surrounded by bodyguards. His wife, Althea, then twenty-seven, a former go-go dancer in the Hustler clubs, took over control of the corporation and the magazine, and returned the magazine to its former focus. Flynt became addicted to morphine and Dilaudid, finally detoxing to methadone. (He repudiated the religious con-

version after the shooting.) Now confined to a wheelchair, he continued to be hauled into court by the government for obscenity and in various civil suits. He was sued by *Penthouse* publisher Bob Guccione and a female *Penthouse* executive who claimed *Hustler* had libeled her by printing that she had contracted VD from Guccione. He was sued by author Jackie Collins after the magazine published nude photos it incorrectly identified as the nude author. He was fined ten thousand dollars a day – increased to twenty thousand dollars a day – when he refused to turn over to the feds tapes he claimed he possessed documenting a government frame of DeLorean. Flynt's public behavior was becoming increasingly bizarre. He appeared in court wearing an American flag as a diaper and was arrested. At another 1984 Los Angeles trial, described by a local paper as "legal surrealism," his own attorney asked for permission to gag his client and after an "obscene outburst," Flynt, like Black Panther Bobby Seale, was bound and gagged at his own trial.

The same year the FCC was forced to issue an opinion on Flynt's threat to force television stations to show his X-rated presidential campaign commercials. Flynt, whose compulsion it was to find loopholes in the nation's obscenity laws, vowed to use his presidential campaign to test those laws by insisting that TV stations show his campaign commercials featuring hard-core sex acts. (The equal time provision of Federal Communications Act prohibits censorship of any ad in which a candidate's voice or picture appears, while the US Criminal Code prohibits dissemination of obscene material.) He had begun to make it his one-man mission to exploit every loophole in the first amendment, as well. In 1986 a federal judge ruled that the US Postal Service could not constitutionally prohibit *Hustler* and Flynt from sending free copies of the magazine to members of Congress, a ruling stemming from Flynt's decision to mail them the magazine so they could be "well informed on all social issues and trends." Flynt's next appearance, ensconced in a gold-plated wheelchair, was at the $45 million federal libel suit brought by the Reverend Jerry Falwell over the notorious Campari ad parody, in which the head of the Moral Majority describes his "first time" as having occurred with his mother behind an outhouse. A Virginia jury dismissed the libel charge but awarded Falwell two hundred thousand dollars for intentional infliction of emotional distress. A federal district court upheld the verdict, but when it landed in the Rehnquist Supreme Court, the judgment was reversed by a unanimous Rehnquist-written decision that the Falwell parody was not reasonably believable, and thus fell into category of satire – an art form often "slashing and one-sided." This Supreme Court decision significantly extended the freedom of the press won in the 1964 *New York Times v. Sullivan* ruling (which mandated that libel could only be founded in cases of "reckless disregard"). It "handed the press one of its most significant legal triumphs in recent years," was "an endorsement of robust political debate," and ended the influx of "pseudolibel suits" by celebrities with hurt feelings, crowed the grateful national press, amid stories generally concluding that the existence of excrescences like *Hustler* is the price of freedom of the press.

Flynt and wife Althea had over the years elaborated various charges and conspiracy theories about the shooting, including charges of a CIA-sponsored plot (Flynt claimed to have been about to publish the names of JFK's assassins – conspiracy theories being another repeating feature of the *Hustler mentalité*). Further speculation about the shooting focused on the mob, magazine distribution wars, and even various disgruntled family members. The shooting was finally acknowledged by white supremacist Joseph Paul Franklin, currently serving two life sentences for racially motivated killings. No charges were ever brought in the Flynt shooting. That Flynt, who has been regularly accused of racism, should be shot by a white supremacist is only one of the many ironies of his story. In another – one that would seem absurd in the most hackneyed morality tale – this man who made millions on the fantasy of endlessly available fucking is now left impotent. And in 1982, after four years of constant and reportedly unbearable pain, the nerves leading to his legs were cauterized to stop all sensation – Flynt, who built an empire on offending bourgeois sensibilities with their horror of errant bodily functions, is now left with no bowel or urinary control.

Flynt, in his obsessional one-man war against state power's viselike grip on the body of its citizenry, seized as his matériel the very pornographic idioms from which he had constructed his *Hustler* empire. The exhibitionism, the desire to shock, the deployment of the body – these are the affronts that have made him the personification of evil to both the state and antiporn feminists. Yet willingly or not, Flynt's own body has been very much on the line, as well – the pornographer's body has borne the violence of the public and private enforcement of the norms of the bourgeois body. If *Hustler*'s development of the pornographic idiom as a political form seems – as with other new cultural political forms – incoherent to traditional readings based on traditional alliances and oppositions – right–left, misogynist–feminist – then it is those very political meanings that *Hustler* throws into question. It is *Hustler*'s political incoherence – in conventional terms – that makes it so available to counterhegemonic readings, to opening up new political alliances and strategies. And this is where I want to return to the issue of *Hustler*'s misogyny, another political category *Hustler* puts into question. Do I feel assaulted and affronted by *Hustler*'s images, as do so many other women? Yes. Is that a necessary and sufficient condition on which to base the charge of its misogyny? Given my own gender and class status, I'm not sure that I'm exactly in a position to trust my immediate response.

Take, for example, *Hustler*'s clearly strategic use of nudity. It is unmistakable from the "Reagan's Farewell Party" photo spread that *Hustler* uses nudity as a leveling device, a deflating technique following in a long tradition of political satire. And perhaps this is the subversive force behind another of *Hustler*'s scandals (or publishing coups, from its point of view), its notorious nude photo spread of Jackie Onassis, captured sunbathing on her Greek island, Skorpios. Was this simply another case of misogyny? The strategic uses of nudity we've seen elsewhere in the magazine might provoke a conceptual transition in thinking through the Onassis photos: from Onassis as unwilling sexual object to Onassis as political target. Given that nudity is used throughout the magazine as an offensive against the rich and powerful – Reagan, North, Falwell, Abrams, as well as

Kirkpatrick and, in another feature, Thatcher, all, unfortunately for the squeamish, through the magic of photomontage, nude – it would be difficult to argue that the nudity of Onassis functions strictly in relation to her sex, exploiting women's vulnerability as a class, or that its message can be reduced to a genericizing one like "you may be rich but you're just a cunt like any other cunt." Onassis's appearance on the pages of *Hustler* does raise questions of sex and gender insofar as we're willing to recognize what might be referred to as a sexual caste system, and the ways in which the imbrication of sex and caste makes it difficult to come to any easy moral conclusions about *Hustler*'s violation of Onassis and her right to control and restrict how her body is portrayed. As recent pulp biographies inform us, the Bouvier sisters, Jacqueline and Princess Lee, were more or less bred to take up positions as consorts of rich and powerful men, to, one could put it bluntly, professionally deploy their femininity. This is not so entirely dissimilar from *Hustler*'s quotidian and consenting models, who, while engaged in a similar activity, are confined to very different social sites – such sites as those pictured in a regular *Hustler* feature, "The Beaver Hunt," a gallery of snapshots of non-professional models sent in by readers.[30] Posed in paneled rec rooms, on plaid Sears sofas or chenille bedspreads, amid the kind of matching bedroom suites seen on late-night, easy-credit furniture ads, nude or in polyester lingerie, they are identified as secretaries, waitresses, housewives, nurses, bank tellers, cosmetology students, cashiers, factory workers, saleswomen, data processors, nurse's aides. Without generalizing from this insufficiency of data about any kind of *typical* class-based notions about the body and its appropriate display, we can simply ask, where are the doctors, lawyers, corporate executives, and college professors?[31] Or moving up the hierarchy, where are the socialites, the jet-setters, the wives of the chairmen of the board? Absent because of their fervent feminism? Or merely because they've struck a better deal? Simply placing the snapshots of Onassis in the place of the cashier, the secretary, and the waitress violates the rigid social distinctions of place and the hardened spatial boundaries (boundaries most often purchased precisely as protection from the

hordes) intrinsic to class hierarchy. These are precisely the distinctions that would make us code differently the deployment of femininity that achieves marriage to a billionaire shipping magnate and one that lands you a spot in this month's "Beaver Hunt." The political implications of the Onassis photo spread call for a more nuanced theory of misogyny than those currently in circulation. If any symbolic exposure or violation of *any* woman's body is automatically aggregated to the transhistorical misogyny machine that is the male imagination, it overlooks the fact that *all* women, simply by virtue of being women, are not necessarily political allies, that women can both symbolize and exercise class power and privilege, not to mention oppressive political power.

Feminist antipornography arguments attempt to reify the feminine as an inviolate moral high ground against pornographic male desires. While apotropaic against the reality of male violence, their reification of femininity also demonizes any position that dares to suggest that femininity is not an inherent virtue, an inborn condition, or in itself a moral position from which to speak – positions such as those held by prosex feminists, psychoanalytic theory, and the discourse of pornography itself. But foremost among the myriad political problems that the reification of femininity gives rise to is the contradiction of utilizing class disgust as its agent.[32] And a theory of representation that automatically conflates bodily representations with real women's bodies, and symbolic or staged sex or violence as equivalent to real sex or violence, clearly acts to restrict political expression and narrow the forms of political struggle by ignoring both differences between women and the class nature of feminist reformism. The fact that real violence against women is so pervasive as to be almost unlocalizable may lead us to want to localize it within something so easily at hand as representation, but the political consequences for feminism – to reduce it to another variety of bourgeois reformism – make this an insufficient tactic.

However, having said this, I must add that *Hustler* is certainly not politically unproblematic. If *Hustler* is counterhegemonic in its refusal of bourgeois proprieties, its transgressiveness has real limits. It is often only incoherent and

banal where it means to be alarming and confrontational. Its banality can be seen in its politics of race, an area where its refusal of polite
speech seems to have little countercultural force.
Hustler has been frequently accused of racism,
but *Hustler* basically just wants to offend –
anyone, of any race, any ethnic group. Not
content merely to offend the Right, it makes
doubly sure to offend liberal and left sensibilities, too; not content merely to taunt whites, it
hectors blacks. Its favored tactic in regard to race
is to simply reproduce the stupidest stereotype
it can think of – the subject of any *Hustler*
cartoon featuring blacks will invariably be
huge sexual organs that every woman lusts
after, or alternately, black watermelon-eating
lawbreakers.

Notes

1   For an interesting and far more extensive analysis of the politics of *Not a Love Story*, see B.
Ruby Rich, "Anti-Porn: Soft Issue, Hard World,"
in *Films for Women*, ed. Charlotte Brunsdon
(London: British Film Institute, 1986), pp.
31–43.

2   Several writers who have visited the *Hustler*
offices testify that to their surprise these letters
are sent by actual readers, and *Hustler* receives
well over a thousand letters a month. As to
whether this particular letter is genuine in its
authorship I have no way of knowing, so I'm
simply considering it as part of the overall
discourse of *Hustler*.

3   Central anti-antiporn texts are *Pleasure and
Danger*, ed. Carole S. Vance (Boston: Routledge
and Kegan Paul, 1984); *Caught Looking:
Feminism, Pornography and Censorship*, ed. Kate
Ellis et al. (Seattle: Real Comet Press, 1988);
Powers of Desire: The Politics of Sexuality, ed. Ann
Snitow, Christine Stansell, and Sharon Thomp-
son (New York: Monthly Review Press), espe-
cially section 6 on, "Current Controversies." Also
see Linda Williams, *Hard Core: Power, Pleasure
and the Frenzy of the Visible* (Berkeley: University
of California Press, 1989); and Andrew Ross,
"The Popularity of Pornography," *in No Respect:
Intellectuals and Popular Culture* (New York:
Routledge, 1989), pp. 171–208, for a thorough
summation of antipornography arguments.

4   Gayle Rubin, "Thinking Sex: Notes for a Radical
Theory of the Politics of Sexuality," in *Pleasure
and Danger*, ed. Vance, pp. 267–319.

5   This corresponds to Linda Williams's analysis of
pornography as a "machine of the visible"
devoted to intensifying the visibility of all
aspects of sexuality, but most particularly
to conducting detailed investigations of female
bodies (Williams, *Hard Core*, pp. 34–57).

6   See Mikhail Bakhtin, *Rabelais and His World*
(Bloomington: University of Indiana Press,
1984).

7   *Newsweek*, February 16, 1976, p. 69.

8   Leonore Davidoff, "Class and Gender in
Victorian England," *Feminist Studies* 5 (Spring
1979): 97.

9   Peter Stallybrass and Allon White, *The Politics
and Poetics of Transgression* (Ithaca, N.Y.: Cornell
University Press, 1986).

10   Bakhtin, *Rabelais*, p. 376.

11   Ibid., p. 320. See also Francis Barker, *The
Tremulous Private Body* (New York: Methuen,
1984).

12   Norbert Elias, *The History of Manners* (New
York: Urizen Books, 1978).

13   Stallybrass and White, *Politics and Poetics of
Transgression*, p. 191.

14   Elias, *History of Manners*, p. 120.

15   And there are ongoing attempts to regulate this
sort of imagery. In the current NEA controversies, a Republican representative plans to intro-
duce amendments that would prohibit funding of
art that depicts aborted fetuses, the *New York
Times* reports (October 10, 1990, p. 6). This
would seem to be something of a short-sighted
strategy, as the aborted fetus has been the favored
incendiary image of antiabortion forces, including antiabortion artists. See pp. 27–9.

16   Of course, the counterargument could be made
that such a cartoon really indicates the murderous
male desire to see a woman mutilated, and that the
cartoon thus stands in for the actual male desire to
do violence to women. This was the widespread
interpretation of the infamous *Hustler* "woman in
the meat grinder" cover, about which more later.
This sort of interpretation would hinge on essen-
tializing the male imagination and male sexuality
as, a priori, violent and murderous, and on a fairly
literal view of humor and representation, one that
envisions a straight leap from the image to the
social practice rather than the series of mediations
between the two I'm describing here.

17   Mary Douglas, *Purity and Danger: An Analysis of
the Concepts of Pollution and Taboo* (London:
Routledge, 1966).

18   Ibid., p. 37.

19   Sigmund Freud, *Jokes and Their Relation to the
Unconscious* (New York: Norton, 1963), p. 90.
Freud's observations on jokes, particularly on

obscene humor, might be extended to the entirety of *Hustler*, as so much of its discourse, even aside from its cartoons and humor, is couched in the joke form.

20 For an interesting deconstruction of the essentialism/antiessentialism debate, see Diana Fuss, *Essentially Speaking: Feminism, Nature and Difference* (New York: Routledge, 1989).

21 By violence here I mean specifically violence to subjectivity – the perception of violation. The vast majority of porn represents sex, not physical violence. The continual conflation of sexual pornography and nonconsensual physical violence is a roadblock to thinking through issues of porn – only abetted by a theorist like Andrea Dworkin, for whom *all* heterosexuality is violence. It's akin to trying to understand popular culture by starting from the premise that all popular culture is violence and ignoring all examples that don't fit the model.

22 Freud, *Jokes*, p. 102.

23 J. Laplanche and J. B. Pontalis, *The Language of Psychoanalysis* (New York: Norton, 1973), pp. 376–8.

24 Andrea Dworkin, *Intercourse* (New York: Macmillan, 1987), p. 138.

25 Douglas, *Purity and Danger*, p. 3.

26 Ibid., p. 3. Compare Douglas's comments on danger beliefs around sexual fluids to this passage by Andrea Dworkin: "[I]n literary pornography, to ejaculate is to *pollute* the woman" (her emphasis). Dworkin goes on to discuss, in a lengthy excursus on semen, the collaboration of women-hating women's magazines, which "sometimes recommend spreading semen on the face to enhance the complexion," and pornography, where ejaculation often occurs on the woman's body or face (see Linda Williams, pp. 93–119, on another reading of the "money shot") to accept semen and eroticize it. Her point seems to be that men prefer that semen be a violation of the woman by the man, as the only way they can get sexual pleasure is through violation. Thus semen is "driven into [the woman] to dirty her or make her more dirty or make her dirty by him." But at the same time semen has to be eroticized to get the woman to comply in her own violation (Andrea Dworkin, *Intercourse*, p. 187). In any case, that Dworkin sees contact with male "sexual fluids" as harmful to women seems clear, as does the relation of this pollution (Dworkin's word) danger to Douglas's analysis.

27 *Hustler*'s advertising consists almost entirely of ads for sex toys, sex aids, porn movies, and phone sex services, as the automobile makers, liquor companies, and manufacturers of other upscale items that constitute the financial backbone of *Playboy* and *Penthouse* refuse to hawk their wares in the pages of *Hustler*. In order to survive financially, *Hustler* began, among other enterprises, a successful and extensive magazine distribution company that includes among its periodicals the *New York Review of Books*.

28 "Farewell to Reagan: Ronnie's Last Bash," *Hustler*, February 1989, pp. 66–74.

29 The story of the cover was related by Paul Krassner, who worked for *Hustler* in 1978, in "Is This the Real Message of Pornography?" *Harper's*, November 1984, p. 35. Recall also that this cover was instrumental in the founding the following year of Women Against Pornography. The meat-grinder joke seems to encapsulate many of the aforementioned issues of class, humor, vulgarity, and gender.

30 Recently *Hustler*, after yet another legal entanglement, began threatening in its model release form to prosecute anyone who sent in a photo without the model's release. They now demand photocopies of two forms of ID for both age and identity purposes; they also stopped paying the photographer and began paying only the model (currently $250 and the promise of consideration for higher-paying photo spreads).

31 Throughout this essay, my intent has not been to associate a particular class with particular or typical standards of the body, but rather to discuss how *Hustler* opposes hegemonic, historically bourgeois conceptions of the body. Whether the *Hustler* bodily idiom represents a particular class or class fraction is not readily ascertainable without extensive audience studies of the sort difficult to carry out with a privatized form like porn magazines. The demographics that are available aren't current (since the magazine doesn't subsist on advertising, its demographics aren't made public, and *Hustler* is notoriously unwilling to release even circulation figures). The only readership demographics I've been able to find were published in *Mother Jones* magazine in 1976, and were made available to them because publisher Larry Flynt desired, for some reason, to add *Mother Jones* to his distribution roster. Jeffrey Klein writes: "Originally it was thought that *Hustler* appealed to a blue collar audience yet . . . demographics indicate that except for their gender (85 percent male), *Hustler* readers can't be so easily categorized. About 40 percent attended college; 23 percent are professionals; 59 percent have household incomes of $15,000 or more a year [about $29,000 in 1989 dollars], which is above the national mean, given the median reader age of 30." His analysis of these figures is that

"probably it's more accurate to say that *Hustler* appeals to what people would like to label a blue-collar urge, an urge most American men seem to share" (Jeffrey Klein, "Born Again Porn," *Mother Jones*, February/March 1978, p. 18).

32 For an analysis of the structuring contradictions in the discourse of Catharine MacKinnon, who, along with Dworkin, is the leading theorist of the antipornography movement, see William Beatty Warner, "Treating Me like an Object: Reading Catharine MacKinnon's Feminism," in *Feminism and Institutions: Dialogues on Feminist Theory*, ed. Linda Kauffman (Cambridge: Basil Blackwell, 1989), pp. 90–125.

Part III

Sexual Citizenship and the Nation-State

8

Perversity, Contamination, and the Dangers of Queer Domesticity

Nayan Shah

In the prevailing nineteenth-century ideology, respectable domesticity enabled the proper moral and biological cultivation of citizen-subjects necessary for American public life to flourish. The formation of respectable domesticity connected practices of individual health and sexuality to collective social well-being. Modern, healthy society was conceptualized as a series of heterosexual married couples and their children, who, as middle-class families, perpetuated the race and enriched the nation. Sexual and social practices by which individuals sought intimacy outside the reproductive marriage were identified as disruptive to the family and were perceived as a perversion, betrayal, and distortion of "the race" and of racially defined communities. At the turn of the century, reproductive sexual relations became more stringently scrutinized within marriage, and sexual practices outside of marriage were perceived as a threat. In this way, sexual activity either served or imperiled the racial order and national power.[1]

Nineteenth-century white politicians and social critics characterized Chinatown as an immoral bachelor society of dissolute men who frequented opium dens, gambling houses, and brothels. In this transient working-class world, Chinese single men lived herded together in bunkrooms, and the few Chinese women who had immigrated were considered to be prostitutes. Together their lives were considered contrary to respectable domesticity and capable of undermining American morality and family life.

Physicians believed that Chinatown's vice culture and leisure spaces fostered intimate relationships between Chinese and white people that accelerated the transmission of syphilis and leprosy to white Americans. These dreaded diseases galvanized physicians to scrutinize Chinatown's perverse spaces, deviant sexualities, and peculiar domestic arrangements for both the clues and causes of contamination.

In the historiography and sociology of nineteenth- and early-twentieth-century Chinese American experience, Chinese bachelor sexuality is represented as deviant because the presumed sexual relations of these men living in San Francisco were considered nonreproductive and nonconjugal. Most Chinese men in the United States were separated from their wives, who remained in Guangdong. The few Chinese women present were considered to exist in sexual slavery, either as concubines to polygamous merchants or as prostitutes serving Chinese and white men. Even sympathetic sociologists and historians have interpreted the behavior of Chinese men as evidence of sexual maladjustment under a discriminatory immigration system in the United States. This interpretation presumes that the social relations Chinese men and women did have were delinquent and deficient of normative aspirations.[2]

Contemporaneous white critics sustained and bolstered a particular norm of heterosexuality and respectable domesticity in their fears about the dangers of deviant sexualities and queer domesticity in Chinatown. Normative visions of domesticity were defined by the narratives and explanations of its perversion and destruction. By attending to the concerns and policies developed to contain the contaminating effect of the perverse Chinatown social relations on the white public, historians can also observe a plurality of queer domestic arrangements, from female-headed household networks to workers' bunkhouses and opium dens.[3]

At the turn of the century, normal or respectable domesticity became increasingly defined by a self-contained household that had at its center the married couple's pursuit of reproduction. The space and social relations of queer domesticity countered or transgressed these normative expectations. It included emotional relations between men and women that upset normative heterosexual marriage, as well as homosocial and homoerotic relations. In urban subcultures of the time there existed a variety of sexual, social, and gender relations that could not easily be slotted into the emerging binary of "heterosexual" and "homosexual" – categories that were invented and became popular in the late nineteenth century and twentieth century. Sexuality was not a fixed set of acts, behaviors, and identities but rather a set of formations that encompassed a variety of social relations and sites. Exploring deviant sexualities and queer domesticities allows us to conceive of alternatives that do not funnel all valued erotic and sensual relations into heterosexual marriage and reproduction.[4]

The perversity of Chinatown sociability threatened white society because it provided a constellation of options to respectable domesticity. The social and leisure spaces of Chinatown could lure white men and occasionally white women into a social world that presented a viable substitute to the expectations of an incipient middle-class society.

Public health officials, politicians, and travelogue writers emphasized figures of Chinese immorality and infection who imperiled white society. First was the mercenary prostitute who infected white boys and young men with syphilis. Second was the sensuous and depraved "Chinaman" who lured unwitting white men and women into opium dens. Third was the abject leper who represented the disintegration

of the body that would be the fate of American society after years of intimate contact and miscegenation with the Chinese. These stereotyped and mute figures of moral and physical peril served as ciphers for the insistent worries of white officials and physicians. The process of knowledge formation focused on the deviant sexuality of these figures, paying careful attention to their conduct, their bodies, and the perverse spaces they inhabited. This local production of deviant sexualities, queer domesticity, and perverse geography provided a schema of the dangers of Chinatown and Chinese residents to middle-class white society in San Francisco and beyond.

Prostitution and Syphilis

In the mid-nineteenth century, white politicians, missionaries, and physicians castigated Chinese female prostitution as a leading threat to the moral and social order. Female prostitution and concubinage supposedly demonstrated the Chinese male disregard for marriage and respectable womanhood. The charge that Chinese female prostitution was an "offense to public decency" accumulated a web of moral and medical meanings. Critics of Chinese immigration emphasized how Chinese women were kidnapped or sold into "sexual slavery" to prostitution procurement rings run by criminal syndicates called "tongs."[5] At first, when Chinese female prostitutes were perceived as providing sexual services exclusively to Chinese men, white critics viewed them as merely immoral. But once they were believed to solicit white males, their presence was considered even more dangerous. The moral condemnation intensified, as critics presented narratives of Chinese prostitutes as the cause of venereal disease and gender transgression. In the mid-1870s, physicians made ominous predictions about syphilis transmission from Chinese female prostitutes to white male clients and their families. Politicians quickly latched onto this catastrophic health scenario and, in their diatribes against Chinese immigration, reduced all Chinese women to the menacing stereotype of the syphilitic prostitute.[6] Although the medical threat was potent and pervasive, it did not eclipse the moral condemnation of Chinese prostitution in political discourse. Political critics freely combined both perils in their critiques of Chinatown society. The San Francisco supervisors Willard Farwell and John Kunkler characterized Chinese prostitution as "the most abject and satanic conception of human slavery" and the "source of contamination and hereditary diseases."[7]

Police and political knowledge about Chinese female prostitutes concentrated on their public visibility and danger to San Francisco's social order. Although women of many nationalities engaged in commercial sex, the activity of Chinese women came under careful scrutiny by white politicians, officials, and commentators.[8] As early as 1854, moral reform groups and the police singled out Chinese prostitutes for their visibility on major thoroughfares such as Dupont Street, which linked residential neighborhoods with the downtown commercial district. The police and moral reformers sharply criticized Chinese women who solicited out of open windows and doors on street level. Unlike streetwalking, which prevailed in East Coast cities as a dominant form of solicitation, many Chinese women worked out of "cribs," which were small rooms, often no larger than five feet by six feet, on street level. From these "filthy holes," women were most likely to solicit white males who worked in the downtown business district and traveled through Chinatown between work and home. The Chinese women who inhabited these street-level rooms were branded as prostitutes, irrespective of any other aspect of their lives or labor.

Police and politicians equated the presence of Chinese women in street-level rooms with sex solicitation. And, they confidently sought to fix the identity of these Chinese women as prostitutes. In this era, across the globe, the process of policing prostitution began with branding a permanent and inflexible identity on a woman who exchanged sex for money as one of a series of activities to acquire money for herself or her family. Knowledge of the activities of working-class women in public emphasized details and scenarios that heightened suspicions of sex solicitation. The variety of work that Chinese women did as seamstresses or piece-workers for manufacturers was dismissed in light of the conviction that the selling of sex was the only true activity of these women and the sole way of understanding their lives.[9]

In the mid-nineteenth century, police harassment decisively reshaped the urban geography and the social lives of women who were presumed to solicit sex.[10] From 1854 to 1865 the San Francisco police conducted aggressive campaigns to drive "crib prostitutes" away from the high-traffic thoroughfares of Jackson and Dupont Streets. The police chief demanded that the cribs be moved to the alleys and that screens be constructed to "hide the degradations and vice . . . from the view of the women and children who patronize the streetcars."[11] He encouraged the public health authorities to devise a plan to "herd" Chinese women to a distant location where they would "not offend public decency."[12] After the 1865 harassment campaign, which the police chief boasted drove hundreds of Chinese prostitutes from the city, brothel owners and police reached a settlement that pushed Chinese prostitution to side streets and alleys hidden from public traffic. The city council ordered that the "location and sanitary regulation of Chinese women" would fall under the jurisdiction of the city health officer.[13]

By the 1880s, Chinese prostitutes' cribs and brothels were located in the alleys between Jackson and Pacific Streets. According to the maps generated by the board of supervisors 1885 report on the condition of Chinatown, Sullivan's Alley, Bartlett Alley, and Stout Alley had the greatest concentration of Chinese prostitution. On the other side of Chinatown, white prostitutes served customers on Spofford Street west of Washington Street, on Waverly Place, Sacramento Street, and the alleys in between.[14] The intense harassment had made many women even more vulnerable. They required increased protection from the tong criminal syndicates to survive, and they could not access other forms of employment, such as sewing or piecework manufacturing without the assistance of tong middlemen. By branding women as prostitutes, the police and reformers limited their possibilities for work and made them far more identifiable for police harassment. For the white public, however, the removal of the cribs and brothels from public view heightened their distance from, and ironically, the danger they posed to, white marital domesticity. Secrecy and removal from view only amplified anxiety that immoral and wicked activity transpired outside of public oversight.

Visibility presented multiple dangers to the viewers, their relatives, the officials, and those under observation. In political rhetoric, the sight of immorality could "offend" the dependents of white male citizens – their wives and children. However, offending the moral sensibilities of respectable women and their children might also have unpleasant ricocheting effects for their male relatives. The visibility of prostitutes could readily inform married women of the variable sexual privileges exercised by men outside of marital domesticity. Although much of the opprobrium was leveled specifically at the female prostitutes, the thriving sex trade might convince married women to dispense with white male prerogatives of sexual independence and refuse to countenance sexual betrayals. On the other hand, the visibility of the women from the streets made them vulnerable to police harassment as well as available for remunerative encounters with clients. Official efforts to remove women from public view disguised the sexual register of public activity and made the transparency of these social transactions more difficult. Pushing illicit sexual activity to semi-public resorts and dens in the alleys and side streets made the activity less amenable to surveillance. The frustration galvanized investigators to redouble their efforts and develop new techniques of surveillance and new knowledge about that which politicians and police forced out of view.

The new techniques of surveying and census enumeration generated a system of knowledge that would fix the identity of the women in question and ensure accurate police surveillance. The urgency in targeting Chinese prostitutes, however, unleashed confusion in identifying the signs of prostitution and distinguishing a professional prostitute from other women. The motives, location, and conduct of Chinese women had to be deciphered and classified. In the 1850s and 1860s, police singled out women who were observed peering out their windows or standing outside a door, or who worked in small, first-floor rooms. Police presumed that in these rooms women allowed the frequent arrival and departure of seemingly anonymous men. These

women were interpreted to be crib prostitutes. However, there were also women who lived in more secluded, upper-story apartments who lavishly entertained regular clients, primarily Chinese merchants. These women were identified as courtesans who charged premium prices for the entertainment and companionship they provided.[15]

The social lore about these two distinctive types of Chinese female prostitution, however, was not readily amenable to census tabulation. US census enumerators in 1870 and 1880 faced the daunting task of classifying the inhabitants of Chinatown boarding-houses, in which an average of seventeen individuals lived, into groups that conformed either to definitions of family or of distinctive types of prostitution. Typical dwellings were inhabited by Chinese men and women of all ages. The 1870 US census used a definition of "family" developed in 1850: "In whatever circumstances, in whatever numbers, people living under one roof and provided for at a common table, there is a family in the meaning of the law." One enumerator, William Martin, faced with boardinghouses containing on average seventeen Chinese female and male residents would divide the inhabitants by gender. Martin often recognized two "families" in such a dwelling – one family of female "prostitutes" and the other of male "laborers." In his tabulations, he identified 90 percent of all Chinese females over the age of twelve as prostitutes. Another enumerator, Henry Bennett, an editor and federal pension agent who was sympathetic to Chinese immigration, counted in his ward a greater number of families per dwelling and recognized a variety of married couples, children, male boarders, and female bonded servants (mui tsai) as distinct families.[16] In his overall calculations, only 53 percent of Chinese females over the age of twelve were designated as prostitutes. The 1880 census guidelines recognized the necessity for more elastic definitions of family, particularly in the "tenement houses and flats of the great cities," and instructed enumerators to record "as many families . . . as there are separate tables." The schedules themselves demanded that enumerators identify marital status and family relationships among members of a "family" group. These changes resulted in a greater number of identified families in each dwelling and a decline in the number of female prostitutes.[17]

The fact that a variety of households and domestic arrangements existed was seized by city officials as definitive evidence that typical Chinatown domesticity contradicted the nuclear family ideal. The 1885 board of supervisors' investigation of Chinatown counted only 57 women who were "living [in] families" with merchant husbands and legitimate children. According to this report, many merchants had several wives or concubines to "minister to animal passions" rather than to procreate. At the other extreme, there were 567 "professional prostitutes" – some of whom raised children – 87 children were counted – as their "associates and perhaps protégés." The majority of women, over 760 living with 576 children, were "herded together with apparent indiscriminate parental relations, and no family classification." Their apartments, the investigators concluded, indicated that their lives existed in "a middle stratum between family life and prostitution, partaking in some measure of each." The complicated social relations between women and children in these houses frustrated white officials, who insisted on firm boundaries in family relationships. The surveyors observed that "prostitutes," women (who apparently were not professional prostitutes), and children "live in adjoining apartments and intermingle freely," which meant for the surveyors that prostitution did not result in pariah status in the Chinese community. The multiple roles of mothering and caretaking that several women undertook for a set of children made it impossible for the surveyors to mark "where the family relationship leaves off and prostitution begins."[18]

These versions of queer domesticity exposed the implicit expectations about gender roles, household numbers, and spatial arrangements in conventional domestic definitions of public and private. The surveyors' definition of domesticity was challenged in the attempts to single out a conjugal couple and their progeny. The investigators found it difficult to understand why caring and nurturance would develop between several women and children without clear kinship or maternal ties. They could not respect as a domestic option the cohabitation of several women and children without a man at the

helm, so they ridiculed a white woman who lived among a large number of Chinese women and children for "berating" the surveyors for "invading their citadel of domestic rights." The absence of a family composed of a male patriarch, a sole wife, and their children made the claim of "domestic rights" appear ludicrous to the surveyors. There was a clear limit to which persons could deploy the "privacy" of social relations of domesticity to shield themselves from state intrusion into sexual activities and social affinities. The multiple women and children living together did not produce a reassuring transparency of gender roles and social affiliations of intimacy for the surveyors. For the occupants, however, the living space could be shared by dozens of people and yet produce privacy and clear webs of care and attention.[19] Prostitution and concubinage cast suspicion on all domestic relations and allowed city officials to persistently violate domestic spaces not conforming to their norms. For white observers, Chinese houses seldom possessed domestic features of intimacy, gender roles, or rights of privacy that characterized the white middle-class domestic ideal.

The policing of prostitution shifted from being a local effort to being a much broader one, with national immigration restrictions on Chinese and Japanese women. On the state level, from 1870 to 1874 the California legislature criminalized the entry of "lewd and debauched" Asian women into California, which in practice meant the state threatened steamship companies with heavy fines for transporting unmarried women. When challenged in the state courts, the San Francisco district attorney argued that California had jurisdiction in intervening in immigration regulations in order to exclude "pestilential immorality" from its cities. The debate over jurisdiction led the federal courts to overturn California immigration restrictions. In 1875, however, the US Congress followed California's lead and passed the Page Law, which prohibited the immigration of Chinese, Japanese, and "Mongolian" women for the purpose of prostitution.[20]

The immigration bar was immediately raised at the borders to all women without husbands or fathers to claim them. The suspicion of prostitution made them uncommonly vulnerable to immediate deportation. These barriers to entry, coupled with police harassment, caused the Chinese female population in San Francisco to stagnate. Although, according to the census, the overall number of San Francisco Chinese nearly doubled, from 12,022 in 1870 to 21,745 in 1880, the population of Chinese women hovered at 2,000. The vitriolic political campaigns against Chinese prostitution made many women vigilant about being categorized as prostitutes, and the census figures for Chinese female prostitutes declined sharply: the proportion of "prostitutes" among all Chinese women shrank from 79 percent in 1870 to only 28 percent in 1880.[21]

Although police and politicians vilified and harassed Chinese female prostitutes, they readily deferred to medical authority in regulating the Chinese women's "loathsome contagion."[22] In 1871, when the San Francisco Board of Supervisors considered proposals for medical inspection of female prostitutes citywide, the local medical profession remained undecided, fearful of appearing to endorse the "safe" functioning of commercialized sex. Christian leaders deplored the regulation plan, which they perceived as condoning vice, and women's suffrage activists criticized the hypocrisy of the legislation, which singled out women for inspection and harassment but ignored their male clients. Like similar legislation proposed in other American cities, the San Francisco attempt at European-style military and colonial medical regulation went down in defeat.[23]

Although many physicians were ambivalent about regulating prostitution, some energetically developed knowledge about the effects of the Chinese prostitute on society. In the mid-1870s, at the height of the anti-Chinese political debate, physicians expressed fears about the spread of syphilis from Chinese prostitutes to the white population. During the California State Senate investigation of Chinese immigration in 1876, the senators questioned physicians about the prevalence of syphilis among Chinese prostitutes and the ramifications for white society.[24] The most famous testimony came from Dr. Hugh Huger Toland, a member of the San Francisco Board of Health and founder of Toland Medical College (which subsequently became the University of California Medical School). Dr. Toland reported that he had exam-

ined white "boys eight and ten years old" with venereal diseases contracted at "Chinese houses of prostitution." These boys neglected their condition and hid it from their parents. When Toland diagnosed the disease as syphilis, the boys enlisted his assistance to "conceal their condition from their parents." Toland estimated that "nine-tenths" of all syphilis cases in white boys and young men were attributable to Chinese prostitutes: "When these persons come to me I ask them where they got the disease, and they generally tell me that they have been with Chinawomen. They think diseases contracted from Chinawomen are harder to cure than those contracted elsewhere, so they tell me as a matter of self-protection. I am satisfied from my experience, that nearly all boys in town, who have venereal disease, contracted it in Chinatown. They have no difficulty there, for the prices are so low that they go whenever they please. The women do not care how old the boys are, whether five years old or more, as long as they have money."[25]

A discourse on race, prostitution, and medical cure was prefigured in Toland's account of his patients' testimony. According to Toland, the doctor–patient confessional relationship yielded the true source of the boys' afflictions. Out of a desire for a cure, patients eagerly accused Chinese women. The boys' candor stemmed from an already prevailing notion that "diseases contracted from Chinawomen are harder to cure." The circulation of such a belief suggested a developed system of associations between Chinese prostitution, disease, and medical cure. The boys' visits to Dr. Toland demonstrated a knowledge that Chinese prostitutes transmitted specific diseases, for which medical men like Toland had developed special cures. Toland's testimony quickly became the master narrative of the medical menace of Chinese female prostitutes. During the decades that followed, politicians, medical professionals, and popular writers repeatedly invoked Toland's observations of the extreme youth of the victims and the peculiarly virulent venereal disease.[26]

Toland dismissed the possibility of the boys having access to multiple sexual partners who were diverse in race or gender. In order to mark Chinese women as the white boys' exclusive sexual partners, Toland elaborated an economy of prostitution in San Francisco. In this economy, Chinese prostitutes were available to white boys because their services cost less than their white female competitors. Emphasizing pre-adolescent boys as the clientele of Chinese prostitutes heightened the depravity and danger of Chinese women. Toland brushed aside any notion of male responsibility in this economy and any hint that adult men frequented brothels. He reversed the power dynamic between Chinese female prostitutes and their white male customers by characterizing the women as powerful, manipulative, and mercenary. White men were framed as the passive victims of the Chinese women's sexual lure; Chinese women, then, would "syphilize" or "inoculate" the men, unilaterally acting upon them, depositing disease in white men's bodies. The perversity of sexual encounters with Chinese women was underscored by the women's active role and domination, reversing prevailing social expectations.[27]

Dr. J. Campbell Shorb, a fellow member of the Board of Health, inserted "white girls" into these circuits of infection. He argued that the "excessively cheap" prices charged by Chinese women gave "these boys an opportunity to gratify themselves at very slight cost." The boys, then, would take their "'windfall' and go among white girls and distribute these diseases very generously."[28] The Chinese female prostitute became the economic counterpart of the Chinese male laborer – both characterized by "excessively cheap labor." Like the "coolie" who appealed to capitalists with his low wages, but whose employment could result in the degradation of American democracy, the Chinese prostitute offered sexual services for a bargain price that would later haunt the client, his spouse, and his progeny with venereal infection.

The medical narration of syphilis remade the signs of the unhealthy body.[29] Syphilis was a "secret scourge" that could persist without visible manifestations and could be conveyed from generation to generation. As a covert disease that could be transmitted from one to another without the knowledge of the sick or of the infected, syphilis was unlike such epidemic diseases as cholera and smallpox, which had immediate, visible, and lethal effects. Dr. Mary Sawtelle, a local physician and editor of the

Medico-Literary Journal, dramatized the difference between the two diseases and their impact on the individual and society:

> Small-pox is nothing. Suppose a few hundred people are destroyed by it. We might as well frighten ourselves with ghost stories. It may kill its victims, but death comes kindly. It may contort his features into a hideous deformity, but it does not lap over from one generation to another; does not eat away at his flesh and crumble his bones to ashes, and still leave him among his fellows to destroy and contaminate everything he touches or breathes upon as syphilis does; and every ship from China brings hundreds of these syphilitic and leprous heathens. They sit in the streetcar beside our wives and daughters. They are a stench. Their mean stature, their ugly faces and their imbecile nastiness mirrors to us what syphilis will do for a nation.[30]

Sawtelle's descriptions of syphilis were marked by national and racial references that relentlessly implicated Chinese immigrants as the source of all infection. Chinese physical features and behavior became the indications of syphilitic conditions. The indications of disease were enfolded into the physical signs of racial difference – odor, size, facial features – and estimations of mental traits: intelligence, morality, and character. The grave danger of syphilis infection was its transmission through the contaminated but seemingly healthy carrier. Sawtelle determined that Chinese immigrants were not only the transmitters of disease but also the cause of disease and the signal of its presence – by virtue of the "stench."

Sawtelle's discourse on syphilis created nightmares of proximity between the diseased and the healthy. She ventriloquized the male citizens' fear of "our wives and daughters" sitting next to "syphilitic and leprous heathens" on the streetcar. By escalating the earlier fears of Christian reformers and the police regarding the Chinese prostitute being visible to white women and children from the streetcar, Sawtelle revealed that any spatial barrier on the streetcar itself had been eliminated. Her description of the heathen Chinese body suggested a body that was uncontainable and that released contagion and odor to those around it. Like the "grotesque body" that figured in European descriptions of the carnivalesque, Chinese people were never "closed off from either their social or ecosystemic context." The focus on orifices and openings opposed the norms of the bourgeois body, which was discretely ordered, bounded, and sanitized.[31]

The marking of race and disease on the body became even more striking in the medical indications of syphilis infection on the skin and in the body. Syphilis infection was considered a generic condition of the Chinese race. According to Sawtelle, as syphilis became situated in the body, "ulcers" ate away at internal organs. The disease would first consume "the flesh and then the bones" and "copper-colored blotches" would appear on the skin.[32] The coloring of the skin became synonymous for the endemic syphilis in the Chinese race. Sawtelle speculated that white Americans would possess "that copper colored syphilitic skin" after the race had degenerated to the Chinese "level."[33] Her commentary on the transformation of white skin folded the degenerative consequences of race-mixing into the disfiguration and destruction of the body.

Since syphilis infection was imagined as emblematic of the Chinese race, its transmission was not restricted to sexual contact with Chinese women. Chinese men, in their capacity as domestic servants, were just as liable to infect white families. Since women represented a tiny proportion of the Chinese population and lived physically restricted in Chinatown, the threat Chinese men could pose in disseminating disease was far more ominous. This possibility diverted attention from the presumed role of white males in conveying syphilis from Chinese prostitutes to white wives to children. Instead it focused suspicion on Chinese "houseboys." Sawtelle claimed that "half of the Chinese servants employed in the families of the wealthy" were "reeking with this venereal virus." She highlighted the intimate nature of the contact between Chinese servants and their white employers by noting that Chinese men served as "chambermaids, house servants and nurses for Caucasian babies. They mouth the pap bottle for our innocent little ones." She castigated wealthy white employers for replacing Irish women workers with Chinese workers: "Those who

think it economy to have their food cooked and their children nursed by this class of help may, when it is too late, find it an expensive luxury."[34] In Sawtelle's medical horror story, the Chinese domestic servant became a contradictory figure who was simultaneously responsible for household cleanliness and the devious transmission of venereal disease. By insinuating that syphilis was conveyed by oral contact with a baby's bottle, Sawtelle saddled Chinese servants and their lethal child care with the responsibility of syphilis transmission.

Chinese "houseboys" represented a gender inversion of household service that made questionable their intentions, their care, and their manliness. Chinese men's role in nursing babies gave a curious gender inflection to the widespread bourgeois worries of hiring female nursemaids in European metropolitan as well as colonial and slave societies throughout the globe. Nineteenth-century household manuals and medical guides warned of the moral and physical consequences for white bourgeois children in developing intimate relations with a socially subordinate surrogate mother. Nursemaids were often accused of transmitting disease to their charges through leaking orifices such as nipples, noses, and mouths. In San Francisco, similar concerns of contamination heightened suspicions about the presence and role of the Chinese houseboy.[35] Some publications warned mothers of the dangers of unsupervised "Chinamen" who tended white children, "particularly little girls." These warnings, insinuating that Chinese men might sexually molest white girls, in addition to the concerns about possible syphilis transmission while nursing babies, redoubled white fears of the health and sexual dangers of employing Chinese male servants.[36]

The purported syphilis infection of Chinese houseboys drew questions about their social and sexual activities when they returned to the dens and bunkhouses of Chinatown, as well as about their racial inheritance. Among white physicians and critics, there was little consensus as to how Chinese men were infected. On the one hand, Dr. Thomas Logan, secretary of the California State Board of Health, believed that there was "infrequent evidence of syphilitic disease" transmission between Chinese women and men. The peculiar "physiology" of the "Asiatic race," particularly the "epilatory condition of the genital organs" and the absence of facial hair, indicated the "absence of strong and enduring sexual appetite."[37] On the other hand were those who speculated that Chinese men had more perverse tastes in sexual partners. Thomas H. King, a San Francisco merchant who had lived in China for ten years and served in the US consulate in Hong Kong, reported that sexual activity between Chinese males was common on ships: "Sodomy is a habit. Sometimes thirty or forty boys leaving Hong Kong apparently in good health, before arriving here would be found to be afflicted about the *anus* with venereal diseases, and on questioning by the Chinese doctors to disclose what it was, they admitted that it was a common practice among them."[38] Locating disease on the body, even by nonmedical informants, emphasized the growing popularity and power of medical narratives of examining and mapping the body. Reports of sodomy offered by other San Francisco informants detailed variations that involved lurid descriptions of genital mutilation and bestiality.[39] Speculations of sodomy, however, were only entertained when questioning the syphilis infection of Chinese men. In considering the syphilis infection of white males, the avenues of transmission were limited to heterosexual sex with Chinese female prostitutes, ignoring any possibility of white males having "infectious" sex with other men. The narratives of Chinese male "degenerates" and "mercenary" Chinese female prostitutes placed both as a threat to white American married heterosexual couples and their families.[40]

Perverse Encounters in Opium Dens

Chinese servants were not alone in traveling between white homes and Chinatown opium dens. White men and occasionally white women also experienced the web of perverse social relations, ambiguous sexuality, and queer domesticity in the Chinatown opium dens. The semipublic resorts became legendary for seducing white tourists with the "gentle harmony of their weird social intercourse."[41] The organization of space and the practice of smoking opium generated the possibilities of sexual relations

and social intimacy across race and class lines. Opium smoking was considered to transpire in "every sleeping-room in Chinatown"; the white writers and physicians focused their scrutiny on the "public opium resorts" that supplied opium equipment and "sleeping bunks" for Chinese and white smokers alike. The opium dens were often small, subterranean rooms with shelves on all sides that accommodated a dozen bunks.[42] Health officials feared the role of opium dens in transmitting syphilis and leprosy between the Chinese and "white persons." Opium dens became the emblematic semipublic site of bizarre social communion, moral degradation, and vice. Together with brothels and gambling houses, the opium dens generated a sociability and atmosphere that was liable to destroy the "very morals, the manhood and the health" of white Americans.[43]

The common method of smoking opium encouraged a special intimacy. The bunks could accommodate a pair of opium smokers who would lie facing each other with their heads resting upon blocks of wood or tin cans. Between them would be a lamp and a pipe with a sixteen-inch bamboo stem connected to a ceramic bowl. The preparation for smoking opium was elaborate and required instruction. The smoker dipped a needle into a container of prepared opium and then held the needle above the lamp's flame, where the opium bubbled and swelled to several times its original size. Once it was properly "cooked," the opium was transferred to the pipe's bowl, where it was rolled into a small "pill." This pill was forced into a hole at the center of the bowl and heated. The pipe was tilted and held over the flame, and the smoker drew in the fumes.[44]

The investigators identified most of the smokers as Chinese men but were acutely aware of dens that catered to white men and women. Dr. H. H. Kane speculated that the first white American was introduced to opium smoking in 1868 in San Francisco, and that the habit proliferated rapidly among white gamblers, sporting men, and prostitutes. Kane naively ignored the fact that American merchants and sailors had ample opportunity to partake in opium consumption as participants in nineteenth-century trade with China. The consumption of opium became widespread in Asia because of the heavy commercial traffic of opium between British India and China, which was forced by the British military to accept narcotic commerce.[45]

The techniques of observation and documentation of the illicit activity in the opium dens shifted from the textual to the visual with the use of new photographic technology to depict the dens during police raids. Isaiah West Taber and Company, famous for pictorial tourist photographs of San Francisco and the scenic West Coast, produced a series of images of the Chinatown opium dens in the early 1890s. In style and captions, they were more comparable to twentieth-century journalistic photographs than either tourist shots or the pictorialist art photographs of the period. Taber and other photographers used a magnesium flash and a dramatic viewpoint shot that provided the "you-are-there" quality of the images. Practical photographic flash was invented in the 1880s, and Taber quickly adapted the use of a flashlight or magnesium flash gun to produce dramatic interior shots. The caption writer concocted the dramatic, surprise entrance into the opium den and emphasized the heroic flashlight photographer who shot the pictures while a detective guarded the door. The textual cues demanded that the viewer ignore the substantial time needed to set up the camera, focus in semidarkness, and light the flash powder. Technically, the photographer's overexposure of the foreground objects and the surprised expressions of the Chinese subjects emphasized the drama and speed of the shot.[46]

Although the photography depicted only Chinese subjects in opium dens, medical reportage and travelogues detailed the disturbing repercussion of cross-racial social liaisons in the dens. The bunks were occupied at all hours of "night and day" as smokers puffed and dozed. Dr. W. S. Whitwell witnessed "ten to a dozen half-dressed American men and women and young girls, and perhaps two or more Chinamen. . . . Cheek by cheek, jowl by jowl, American men and women and Chinamen are smoking and dreaming the hours away."[47] The journalist George Fitch anticipated that "when a man or woman falls under the bondage of opium, self-respect is lost." Their social inhibitions were lowered by opium smoking and they were vulnerable to moral turpitude and immoral sexuality.[48]

The drug catalyzed a peculiar social communion. The very idea of opium "joints" entailed the image of a convention or congress of smokers affiliated with each other, not by status, religious belief, or occupation but by a shared pleasure in the drug. The allure of the opium den was that it promised withdrawal from the agitation of ordinary life, but it also made the attention to social distinction irrelevant. Opium smoking disrupted the sense of refinement and taste that distinguished the respectable from the lower classes. The failure to recognize and sustain cultural markers of demeanor and association ran counter to the expectations of people of "good repute." As a social setting the dens permitted mingling without regard for the social distinction of either class or race, creating the fraternity and egalitarianism of vice that undermined the republic of virtue and status distinctions.[49]

Moreover, the spectacle of white women in opium dens horrified white male observers. Kane argued that "many females are so much excited sexually by the smoking of opium during the first few weeks [that] . . . many innocent and over-curious girls have thus been seduced." The San Francisco physician Winslow Anderson described the "sickening sight of young white girls from sixteen to twenty years of age lying half-undressed on the floor or couches, smoking with their 'lovers.'"[50] The opium habit resulted in the "downfall of girls and the debasement of married women." Addicted white women often prostituted themselves in exchange for the drug, often seeking Chinese opium den operators as their principal clients. The damage to white women's virtue was irreversible from the perspective of physicians and journalists. The women were dismissed as "disreputable" and "fallen" by their very presence in a semipublic lounge and considered lost to good society.[51]

The psychic and material danger to white men, however, preoccupied the attentions of physicians and travelogue writers. The travelogue writer B. E. Lloyd was fascinated by the opium den denizens he counted as "our own respectable sons and brothers, who move in good society, and are of 'good repute.'"[52] The social intimacy between races in opium dens presented ominous perils to respectable men. George Fitch reported seeing a "very fastidious" man, who had "acquired the opium habit, lying side by side with a dirty coolie, each taking alternative puffs at the same pipe."[53] However, unlike a white opium addict, the neophyte was far less sanguine about receiving a pipe from the lips of a Chinese man. Allen Williams, a freelance reporter, related his own first experience of visiting a Chinatown opium den in New York. Williams described his ease in resting his head on the "shirt bosom" of his opium-fiend companion, Frank, and his "involuntary shiver of horror" when Tun Gee, "a cadaverous China-man," climbed into the same bunk facing him. Although Williams attributed his discomfort to Tun Gee's resemblance to a "certain Chinese leper," he was assured by his white companion that Tun Gee was one of the "best natured Chinaman" and a thoroughly good cook" of opium. Lying in close proximity, with nothing to separate the reporter's face from the Chinese man except the opium smoking equipment, Tun Gee prepared the opium pipe for the two white men. Williams refused to take another draw of the pipe after Tun Gee smoked from the same pipe and prepared it for several other rounds for his companion, Frank. His narrative emphasized both the extent and the limits of "careless" physical intimacy in the opium den. The physical intimacy of a white man reposed on the "breast" of his white male companion and the close proximity of a Chinese opium cook were considered acts of bizarre but not disturbing intimacy. The prospect of actively sucking the same pipe as the Chinese cook, however, created intense revulsion and panic. Williams worried that "an opium pipe, when passed in short succession from lip to lip, must be a not infrequent conveyance of disease. An efficient ally it is in extending the sway of that arch-enemy to the bones and tissues, Syphilis." He suspected contagion not from the mouth of his white companion but rather from the Chinese cook with the "cadaverous visage."[54]

The revulsion at sharing the same pipe amplified speculations of "loathsome contagion" that could be passed unwittingly from one smoker to the next. Kane believed that an opium smoker was most likely to contract syphilis "from the pipe-stem," which was passed from "mouth to mouth a hundred times a day for months and years." He detailed several instances

of unsuspecting smokers contracting syphilis from the pipe, including a "respectable young man" who contracted a "syphilitic chancre of the lip."[55] Suspicions about the virulent disease's transit emphasized the danger in sharing the pipe, an instrument of both oral pleasure and contact. The panic of ingesting the residues of bodily fluids and of sucking a pipe shared by multiple, anonymous mouths emphasized the promiscuous orality of the experience. In the circuits of smoking, the anonymity of the mouths that sucked on the same pipe provided no occasion for the exclusive possession of the instrument of pleasure. The pipe, the residues of saliva, and the act of sucking focused on a shared fixation on the pipe itself and the other mouths that took pleasure from it. The queer relations produced here could be ascertained by following the relays of erotic fascination through the unregulated, semipublic space of opium dens.

Starting in 1875 San Francisco and California passed laws prohibiting opium smoking and aggressively closed down Chinatown opium joints, but consumption of smoking opium continued to increase. Opium resorts proliferated outside the boundaries of Chinatown, and an estimated forty-five thousand pounds of the drug were imported into San Francisco annually in the 1880s. The legal importation of smoking opium ceased in 1909.[56] The extensive police raids on opium dens in San Francisco drove the white smokers out of Chinatown, but many other resorts and "lay-outs" emerged in boardinghouses in the nearby South of Market and the central business districts. With the proliferation of opium resorts outside of Chinatown, one police officer feared the spread of opium smoking to "schoolboys and clerks who would never have gone into a Chinese den," and who instead were "learning to like the habit" in "respectable places."[57]

Although the process of affiliation that developed around smoking opium resembled the creation of consumer taste and culture, it was not seen as a productive capitalist activity. The addiction to opium resulted in lethargy, diminished productivity, and the waste of time and capacity. The idea of addiction was an extreme example of the cultivation of consumer taste, because consumption was unmanageable and unproductive to the accumulation of capital.[58] Physicians tried to understand opium's "tranquilizing" effects, in which hours could be spent in exploring "pleasing hallucinations bordering on sweet oblivion." Rather than falling asleep, the smoker experienced the "dreams of wakefulness" that could be enjoyed quietly and within the opium den, "free of the annoyances of daily life." Practitioners and even some physicians believed that if such an experience could be harnessed and managed, then it would provide a useful "luxury" if taken in moderation. Dr. Flemming Cadrow, who had practiced in Hong Kong, believed that smoking opium could be used to "stimulate the faculties, to awaken and sharpen them," if used sparingly. Dr. Carrow saw the value of such a stimulant for "gentlemen tired of business or a student weary from prolonged mental effort [who] retires to his opium couch, where after one or two whiffs at his pipe, he is rested and consoled and ready for his work again." But most physicians believed that the insatiable craving opium produced could not be managed, and once addicted one was obliged to "spend certain hours a day" smoking. The result was an overwhelming "fascination with indolence" and the disintegration of individual health: the addict's "appetite gives way to anorexia, nausea and dizziness, the muscular system degenerates and [the] smoker becomes pale, nervous and emaciated, and entirely unfit for his vocation."[59]

For aspiring bourgeois men, the requirements of earning a living were achieved only by constant vigilance against multiple temptations or against premature exhaustion. This tension sometimes drove people toward activities that promised surcease to these demands for self-discipline and self-denial. The stringent moral rectitude required of the respectable classes was the obverse of an urban landscape of saloons, red-light districts, dance halls, and opium dens. The lure of the opium den was understood in terms of the wasting of time and moral energy. The threat that opium smoking posed to the nation was viewed in terms of its capacity to vitiate the life of the youth and to compromise the vigor of the users whose productivity, biological and economic, would be lost to the nation.[60] While the saloon of the new European immigrant and white working class was characterized by disorder and boisterousness, the opium den was quiet and its "inmates" were subdued. The sociability of the dens created an intimacy far different from that in the saloons. In saloons, drinkers remained standing or sitting; in the dens, smokers lay side-by-side in the bunks. While the saloon seemed to have a corrosive effect upon a solid home-life, the opium den promoted an indiscriminate intimacy that could be construed as a substitute for the prized intimacy of the middle-class home. The opium den of the immigrant Chinese presented a substitute more ominous than the saloon of the immigrant European, since Chinese immigrant men were perceived as conspicuous in their lack of affiliation with nuclear families.

Leprosy and Cautionary Tales of Miscegenation

The alleged sexual transmission of disease intensified fears of race degeneration. In nineteenth-century theories of race degeneration, there were two avenues of danger. The first emphasized the deterioration of the individual body, which was emblematic of health of the collective race, and the second focused on the fact that cross-racial reproduction produced defective, hybrid progeny. Both these scenarios bolstered the movement for social and legal prohibitions against heterosexual alliances between races.

Miscegenation law sought to regulate heterosexual marriage within racial bounds and finessed the perpetuation of racial purity in procreation.[61] Nineteenth-century California law developed injunctions against specific race mixing in marriage. As early as 1850 the state prohibited marriages between "white persons" and "Negroes and Mulattoes."[62] Injunctions against marriages between the Chinese and whites developed after a referendum proposed at the 1878 California Constitutional Convention. A delegate to the convention, John F. Miller, speculated that the "lowest, most vile and degraded" of the white race were most likely to "amalgamate" with the Chinese, resulting in a "hybrid of the most despicable, a mongrel of the most detestable that has ever afflicted the earth."[63] The ominous, apocalyptic pronouncement adapted scientific discourses of racial "hybrids" to stoke fears of cross-racial marriage among white people.

In the mid-nineteenth century, ethnologists had developed experiments and theories about the mixing of human races, using analogies from the crossing of plant species. Scientists believed in the existence of pure and superior races that would be contaminated by the hybrid progeny, who would have diminished physical and intellectual capabilities. In 1862 Dr. Arthur Stout feared the infusion of "bad blood" from the inferior "Mongolian" race to the superior "Caucasian" race. Stout argued that mixed-race men were "inferior to the pure races" and made the "worst class of citizens."[64] Race degeneration held grave consequences for the fitness and health of progeny over generations, and the proliferation of "degenerate hybrids" would "poison" and "undermine" both national strength and economic prosperity.[65] Stout's conclusions became a facet of the public health debate in 1871. Logan feared the "evils" that would occur with "the intermixture of the races and the introduction of the habits and customs of a sensual and depraved people" in the midst of a white population. However, Logan believed that the "intelligence" of the white race would prevail and limit "any serious risk of race degradation."[66] Yet, the outcome of hybrids was always subject to change because of the possibility of beneficial crosses between the races, which had already justified the valued mixture of northern and western European "races" as constitutive of "American civilization." In this vein, Stout revised his findings and suggested the value to American civilization that would accrue "if a first-class Chinese woman and a first-class white man would marry," a considerable improvement over the intermarriage of white men to "Negro" women and Indian women.[67]

Despite Stout's confidence of the advantages of selective elite mixtures, in 1880 the California legislature prohibited the licensing of marriages between "Mongolians" and "white persons."[68] However, for twenty-five years, the legislature did not amend the marriage statute itself to forbid marriages between whites and Asians. In the last quarter of the nineteenth century, journalists, officials, and missionaries occasionally reported that in San Francisco there were marriages between white women and Chinese men, three to twenty of them, according to the different reports.[69] Although the marriages provoked derisive comment from white men, legislators were not eager to invalidate the marriages. In 1905 at the height of the anti-Japanese movement, the legislature finally sealed the breach between the license and marriage laws and invalidated all marriages between Asian and white spouses.[70]

Syphilis and leprosy and narratives of their cross-racial transmission became both the metaphor and the material threat that contaminated the middle-class nuclear families and transgressed the boundaries of race and nationality. The Chinese leper's "invasion" of the United States began in 1871, when San Francisco public health authorities diagnosed Hong Tong as a leper and sent him to the Smallpox Hospital, where all infectious disease patients were detained.[71] In five years, the Board of Health put a dozen Chinese lepers in indefinite quarantine. The pace of the public health incarceration of Chinese lepers fed the political hysteria about the disease. In testimony to a US congressional committee in 1876, local physicians, politicians, and labor leaders argued that leprosy in California was an "inherent" condition of the Chinese race, and its rampant spread in the United States was inevitable with continued Chinese immigration.[72] The medical theory that leprosy was an "essentially Chinese disease" necessitated the social and sexual isolation of Chinese lepers from the diseased of other races. Over time, health authorities proposed to remove Chinese lepers from the Smallpox Hospital. Plans to place consumptives and lepers together were defeated by assertions that, despite the economy of the plan, it was inconceivable to condone the mixing of the "Mongolian race" and the "Caucasian race."[73] The solution was to segregate patients by disease and race; for lepers this resulted in the construction of one shack for "white lepers" and another for "Chinese lepers" on the edge of the Smallpox Hospital's property.[74]

Political pressure to solve the Chinese leper problem mounted. At the height of congressional inquiry into Chinese immigration in August 1876, the San Francisco Board of Health approved the deportation of dozens of Chinese lepers to Hong Kong.[75] From 1871 to 1883, the Board of Health confined seventy-nine lepers in the Smallpox Hospital and deported forty-eight of that number. Public health officials had unequivocally identified leprosy as an alien disease. For Chinese immigrants the policy of deportation for leprosy narrowed the health standards for continued residence in the nation.[76]

The deportations also exacerbated suspicions that any Chinese immigrant could be infected with leprosy, which the Workingmen's Party leaders played upon in their anti-Chinese campaigns. In one particularly sadistic act of street theater, the Workingmen's Party sympathizers drove disfigured Chinese men, alleged lepers, around San Francisco to display the physical manifestations of the disease. The street theater of the medically grotesque provided instruction in the dreadful consequences of Chinese settlement.[77] In travelogues and political speeches, the body of the leper became a horrifying spectacle. The decay and disintegration of the leper's body were painstakingly detailed in the descriptions of "ulcerated hands," shedded "scales," "putrefying sores," and "blue limbs."[78] The "swollen and repulsive features" of the leper's body combined with the knowledge that lepers were doomed to a slow and painful death did not inspire compassion. The mystery of their disease and the possibility that their condition was communicable contributed to calls to confine and expel the "intensely revolting" leper from American society.[79] The leper was literally less than human, a perception that justified the removal of diagnosed lepers from everyday social relations.

Although most of the lepers incarcerated were Chinese, a small but significant number were white. The cases of white lepers renewed worries about the contagiousness of the disease. Popular reports circulated on both coasts of white men catching leprosy through intimate contact with the Chinese or through the consumption of cigars allegedly wrapped by Chinese lepers. In order to quell growing public hysteria about leprosy, public health officials claimed that leprosy was limited to the Chinese and transmitted only through inheritance.[80] However, a vocal minority in the California public health circles disagreed and argued that

sustained contact with a leper could also result in infection. The social-contact theorists argued that leprosy had been unknown in Hawaii before the Chinese immigrated there and disseminated the affliction to the Hawaiian natives.[81] Both the theories of inheritance and of social contact focused on racial origins. In the United States, the race of the leper depended on the dominant race of immigrant lepers in the region. So on the Pacific Coast, leprosy was "essentially a Chinese disease," but in the eastern and southern United States, leprosy was considered a Greek or Norwegian disease.[82]

Since heredity and sexual contact were considered the source of disease transmission, fears of leprosy mixed with fantasies of miscegenation and illicit intimacy. The moral taint produced by narcotic addiction and extramarital sexual relations was transmuted into physical contagion. In this economy of perversion and race degeneration, Chinese bodies were considered to be saturated with loathsome contagion that spilled into the white bodies with whom they shared intimate physical contact. At Board of Health inquiries and medical society discussions, physicians offered examples of young white boys becoming infected by "leprous Chinamen" who served them food or shared their beds. Other leprosy cases had an explicitly sexual origin, such as the instances of European sailors who had "illicit" intercourse with Chinese female prostitutes in China or Hawaii. In all these scenarios, Chinese women and men were conceived of as the original source of leprosy. Even when leprosy was attributed to native Hawaiians, the Chinese figured in as the original "inoculators."[83]

With the focus on intimate contact, leprosy easily became analogous to syphilis. The similarities between the two diseases, with their long incubation periods and disfiguring physical manifestations, led the health officer John Meares to conclude that "the so-called leprosy [that the Chinese] have here is simply the result of generations of syphilis, transmitted from one generation to another."[84] Nearly two decades later, Dr. Henry Brown examined lepers under city care and expected that lepers would also exhibit a syphilis infection. He too believed that the Chinese were the source of both diseases. In each case study, Brown relentlessly pursued any hint of sexual and social contact with the Chinese in order to ascertain how someone who was European, native Hawaiian, or American Indian had contracted leprosy.[85]

Social relations outside the hospitals and asylums, however, were far less amenable to medical regulation. Meares believed that in the domain of sexual relations, medical interests had to be served by the powers of moral persuasion and legal regulation. Public health officials emphasized the devastating health consequences of "illicit" interracial sexual relations and hoped that moral policing would prevent respectable whites from sexual relations with the Chinese. Meares feared that this moral policing could lose its power with the social rehabilitation of the Chinese and their entry into American society. Such a collapse would make the stigma of miscegenation less onerous, and in the course of years, Meares speculated, "marriage between the Chinese and people of all nationalities will become a more frequent occurrence."[86]

Meares could only hope that the identification of Chinese lepers as inhuman, the publicity announcing the removal of these "creatures" from society, and their eventual deportation would feed the social aversion necessary to keep the races apart. By equating leprosy's disfiguration, disintegration, and dehumanization of the body with Chineseness, medical discourse intensified notions of incommensurate racial difference. Meares recognized that differences based on language, custom, and living standards could be narrowed and overcome with instruction, time, and circumstances.[87] The presumption that all Chinese were potential lepers, however, made the diseased body the immutable racial difference. Meares employed the rhetorical exhibition of Chinese lepers as a kind of public instruction, similar to that used by the anti-Chinese labor activists, to isolate the Chinese population and to make their integration into American society impossible. For medical men like Meares and for the politicians they persuaded, the failure to contain social interactions held grave consequences. In their nightmares, the price of Chinese assimilation was nothing less than the transformation of the United States into a "nation of lepers."[88]

The medical, travelogue, and legal narratives concerning the transgression of racial boundaries were considered to be material and metaphorical symptoms of the unhealthy fluidity and dangerous freedom in the cities. The suspicions of moral degeneration, sexual perversion, and loathsome disease in the Chinatown opium dens, female-headed houses, and bunkhouses generated a sense of revulsion for the white reader. By contrasting the danger of Chinatown sociability, the white physicians, politicians, and journalists sought to tutor the conduct of wayward white males and inculcate habits of domestic discipline to promote compulsory heterosexual family life. For males of the respectable and aspiring classes, the habits of fastidious self-denial and the strict observance of social distinctions were expected to eliminate the desire for sensuous pleasures with, and the accompanying contaminating contact with, Chinese males and females. The medical and moral narratives characterized these spaces of cross-racial sociability and sexual ambiguity with revulsion and horror.

Heterosexual identity, marriage, and respectable domesticity made claims for privacy and demanded defined sexual and gender roles for men and women. In contrast, the queer domestic spaces and relations perceived to thrive in Chinatown could guarantee neither privacy nor rigid sexual and gender identities for the inhabitants. The intimate relations in the apartments of Chinese women and children, in the opium dens, and workers' bunkhouses generated alternative social possibilities and knowledge of social relations. In defending respectable domesticity and the intensity of their revulsion for queer domesticity, white physicians and critics left little space to explore these queer domestic arrangements on the terms of their own viability. We have but hints of the erotic, social, and ethical relations and their meanings for Chinese immigrant men, women, and children as they related to each other and to the non-Chinese women and men who joined them in the spaces of opium dens, bunkhouses, and apartments. We can recognize that, in the apartment households led by Chinese women, parenting and caretaking relations developed differently than in nuclear-family household models. Many unrelated women might share caretaking duties of children, and children might develop affection and draw on social guidance from a variety of adults. In the opium dens, social status, profession, and race might be irrelevant to comfort, harmony, and community among those men and women who congregated to smoke opium. Rather than feature exclusive couplings of intimacy, the opium dens encouraged an ethics of sharing pipes, beds, and bodily contact among strangers or informal acquaintances.

In the medical rhetoric on Chinese female prostitution and opium dens, syphilis infection was presumed to alarm and dissuade the presumably healthy from contact with the potentially diseased. However, the presence of persons with disease, even incurable conditions such as leprosy and syphilis, need not provoke aversion, fear, and the severing of social ties. For Drs. Meares, Sawtelle, Toland, and Kane, incurable disease conveyed presumably by sexual intimacy or heredity had to be avoided at all costs to ensure the health of the individual and the respectability of family and society. These doctors promoted a particular ethics of public health that expected the person with a dreaded disease to remove himself or herself from social contact or be forcibly ostracized for failure to comply. Their concern emphasized the vulnerability of white individuals who would be contaminated by Chinese bachelors or female prostitutes. As a result of the zeal to protect white men, women, and children from potential contamination, the diseases of syphilis and leprosy hung like racial status for Chinese immigrants, amplifying their pariah status and justifying an embargo of care, affection, and affiliation. The exclusive pursuit of health, privacy, and defined gender and sexual roles for some was paramount to the organization of respectable domesticity.

Neither the medical menace nor miscegenation law succeeded in dissuading men and women from intimate relations across racial lines, however. Illness or the fear of infection could not prevent white men from frequenting opium dens, or white families from hiring Chinese servants, or white women from living with Chinese women or Chinese men. These men and women, Chinese and white, developed different kinds of subjectivity, expressions of social affiliation, and participation in communities that were ignored and devalued by those eager to buttress their own ideas of respectable

domesticity. Since queer domesticity produced alternative environments and relations of intimacy and social ethics, it was perceived to be a formidable threat to the norms of respectable domesticity. In order to flourish, these queer communities did not need to be organized by marriage and heterosexual identity, by race or class status.[89]

Notes

1 Estelle Freedman and John D'Emilio, *Intimate Matters; A History of Sexuality in America* (New York; Harper and Row, 1998); Ann Laura Stoler, *Race and the Education of Desire* (Durham, NC: Duke University Press, 1996); Michel Foucault, *History of Sexuality, Vol. I: An Introduction* (New York: Vintage Books, 1990); Jeffrey Weeks, *Sex, Politics, and Society* (London: Longman, 1981); George L. Mosse, *Nationalism and Sexuality: Middle Class Morality and Sexual Norms in Modern Europe* (Madison: University of Wisconsin Press, 1985); Roddy Reid, *Families in Jeopardy: Regulating the Social Body in France, 1750–1910* (Palo Alto: Stanford University Press, 1993); Pierre Bourdieu, "On the Family as a Realized Category," *Theory, Culture, Society* 13, no. 3 (1996): 19–26.
2 Jennifer Ting, "Bachelor Society: Deviant Heterosexuality and Asian American Historiography," in *Privileging Positions: The Sites of Asian American Studies*, ed. Gary Okihiro et al. (Pullman: Washington State University Press, 1995), pp. 271–9; Richard Fung, "Burdens of Representation, Burdens of Responsibility," in *Constructing Masculinity*, ed. Maurice Berger et at. (London: Routledge, 1995), pp. 291–9; Susan L. Johnson, "Sharing Bed and Board: Cohabitation and Cultural Difference in Central Arizona Mining Towns, 1863–1873," in *Women's West*, ed. Susan Armitage and Elizabeth Jameson (Norman: University of Oklahoma Press, 1987).
3 I use "queer" as an analytical category to examine social formations, gender expressions, and special arrangements that counter and transgress the normal and conventional. See Michael Warner, *Fear of a Queer Planet; Queer Politics and Social Theory* (Minneapolis: University of Minnesota Press, 1993); Gayatri Gopinath, "Homo-Economics: Queer Sexualities in a Transnational Frame," in *Burning Down the House: Recycling Domesticity*, ed. Rosemary George (Boulder, Colo.: Westview Press, 1998), pp. 102–24; Chandan R. Reddy, "Homes, Houses, Non-

Identity: Paris is Burning," in *Burning Down the House: Recycling Domesticity*, ed. Rosemary George (Boulder, Colo.: Westview Press, 1998), pp. 355–79; Janet Jakobsen, "Queer Is? Queer Does?" *GLQ: A Journal of Lesbian and Gay Studies* 4, no. 4 (fall 1998): 511–36.

4 Freedman and D'Emilio, *Intimate Matters*; Jonathan Ned Katz, *The Invention of Heterosexuality* (New York: Penguin Books, 1995); George Chauncey, *Gay New York* (New York: Basic books, 1994); Kevin J. Mumford, *Interzones: Black/White Sex Districts in Chicago and New York in the Early Twentieth Century* (New York: Columbia University Press, 1997); Joanne Meyerowitz, *Women Adrift: Independent Wage Earners in Chicago, 1880–1930* (Chicago: University of Chicago, 1988); Chad Heap, "Slumming: The Politics of American Culture and Identity, 1910–1940" (Ph.D. diss., University of Chicago, 2000); Gayle Rubin, "Thinking Sex: Notes for a Radical Theory on the Politics of Sexuality," in *Pleasure and Danger: Exploring Female Sexuality*, ed. Carol Vance (Boston: Routledge and Kegan Paul, 1984), pp. 267–319; Audre Lorde, The Uses of the Erotic: the Erotic of Power," in *Sister Outsider: Essays and Speeches* (Trumansburg, NY: Crossing Press, 1984), pp. 53–9; Lauren Berlant and Michael Warner, "Sex in Public," *Critical Inquiry* 24, no. 2 (winter 1998): 547–66.

5 California Legislature, Special Committee on Chinese Immigration, *Chinese Immigration: Its Social, Moral, and Political Effect* (Sacramento, 1876); U.S. Congress, Senate, Report of the Joint Special Committee to Investigate Chinese Immigration, 44th Cong., 2nd sess., 1877, S. Rept. 689, p. 649; reprinted in Chinese Consolidated. Benevolent Association, *Memorial of the Six Chinese Companies Testimony of California's Leading Citizens before the Joint Special Congressional Committee* (San Francisco: Alta Print, December 8, 1877).

6 The notion of the syphilitic prostitute emerged as a persistent figure in debates over morality, health, and the social order in capitalist western Europe and North America. Sander Gilman, "AIDS and Syphilis; The Iconography of Disease," in *AIDS: Cultural Analysis, Cultural Activism*, ed. Douglas Crimp (Cambridge: MIT Press, 1998), pp. 87–107; Mary Spongberft, *Feminizing Venereal Disease; The Body of the Prostitute in Nineteenth-Century Medical Discourse* (New York: New York University Press, 1997).

7 Willard B. Farwell, *The Chinese at Home and Abroad, Together with the Report of the Special Committee of the Board of Supervisors of San Francisco on the Condition of the Chinese Quarter and the Chinese in San Francisco, July 1885* (San Francisco: Bancroft, 1885), p. 14. For a similar combination of sexual slavery and syphilis, see J. Marion Sims, "Address to the American Medical Association Annual Meeting," *Transactions of the American Medical Association* 27 (1876): 106.

8 Jacqueline Baker Burnhart, *The Fair but Frail: Prostitution in San Francisco, 1849–1900* (Reno: University of Nevada Press, 1986).

9 Judith Walkowitz, *Prostitution in Victorian Society: Women, Class, and the State* (New York: Cambridge University Press, 1980); Luise White, "Prostitution, Differentiation, and the World Economy: Nairobi, 1899–1939," in *Connecting Spheres; Women in the Western World, 1500 to the Present*, ed. Marilyn Boxer and Jean Quataert (New York: Oxford University Press, 1987); White, "Prostitution, Identity, and Class Consciousness during World War II," *Signs: Journal of Women in Culture and Society* 11, no. 2 (winter 1986): 255–73.

10 Timothy J. Gilfoyle, "The Urban Geography of Commercial Sex: Prostitution in New York City, 1790–1860," *Journal of Urban History* 13 (August 1987): 384–87; Neil Larry Shumsky and Larry M. Springer, "San Francisco's Zone of Prostitution, 1880–1934," *Journal of Historical Geography* 7, no. 1 (1981): 71–89: Neil Larry Shumsky, "Tacit Acceptance; Respectable Americans and Segregated Prostitution, 1870–1910," *Journal of Social History* 19 (summer 1986): 665–79.

11 San Francisco Common Council, *Ordinances and Joint Resolutions of the City of San Francisco* (San Francisco: Mason and Valentine, 1854); Frank H. Soule et al., *Annals of San Francisco and History of California* (1855; reprint, Palo Alto: Lewis Osborne, 1966), p. 550; San Francisco Board of Supervisors (hereafter SFBS), *San Francisco Municipal Report*, 1862–3, pp. 139–40; Brenda E. Pillors, "The Criminalization of Prostitution in the United States; The Case of San Francisco, 1854–1919" (Ph.D. diss., University of California at Berkeley, 1982), p. 96; Sucheng Chan, "The Exclusion of Chinese Women, 1870–1943" in *Entry Denied: Exclusion and the Chinese Community in America*, 1882–1943 ed. Sucheng Chan (Philadelphia: Temple University Press, 1991), p. 97.

12 SFBS. *San Francisco Municipal Report*, 1864–5, p. 139.

13 SFBS, *San Francisco Municipal Report*, 1865–6, pp. 124–6; Mary Ryan, *Women in Public: Between Banners and Ballots, 1825–1880* (Baltimore: Johns Hopkins University Press, 1990), pp.

110–11; S. Chan, "The Exclusion of Chinese Women," pp. 97–8; Barnhart, *The Fair but Frail*, pp. 49–50.

14 G. B. Densmore, *The Chinese in California: Description of Chinese Life in San Francisco. Their Habits, Morals, Manners* (San Francisco: Petit and Russ, 1880), p. 81; Farwell, *The Chinese at Home and Abroad*.

15 Densmore, *The Chinese in California*, p. 81; Benson Tong, *Unsubmissive Women: Chinese Prostitution in Nineteenth Century San Francisco* (Norman: University of Oklahoma Press, 1994).

16 For more on the mui tsai system of female bond-servants and the confusion with sexual slavery, see Judy Yung, *Unbound Feet: A Social History of Chinese Women in San Francisco* (Berkeley and Los Angeles: University of California Press, 1995); Maria Jaschok, *Concubines and Bondservants: A Social History* (London: Zed Books, 1988).

17 George Anthony Peffer, *If they Don't Bring Their Women; Chinese Female Immigration before Exclusion* (Urbana: University of Illinois Press, 1999), pp. 87–100. Peffer offers a detailed study of the substantial bureaucratic changes in census enumeration between the 1870 and 1880 censuses, as well as biographical background on the 1870 census enumerators, which deepens historical understanding of the political biases and bureaucratic constraints in developing a tabulation and identification of families and female prostitution in San Francisco. See also Carroll Wright and William C. Hunt, *History and Growth of the United States Census* (Washington D.C.: Government Printing Office, 1900), pp. 156–7, 167–71; Margo J. Anderson, *The American Census: A Social History* (New Haven: Yale University Press, 1988).

18 Farwell, *The Chinese at Home and Abroad*, pp. 8–9.

19 Ibid., p. 16.

20 Historians Sucheng Chan and George Peffer have determined that the Page law substantially limited the number of Chinese women who immigrated into the United States. S. Chan, "The Exclusion of Chinese Women," pp. 98–109; Peffer, "Forbidden Families; Emigration Experiences of Chinese Women under the Page Law, 1875–1882," *Journal of American Ethnic History* 6 (1986): 28–46.

21 Lucie Cheng Hirata, "Free, Indentured, Enslaved; Chinese Prostitutes in Nineteenth Century America," *Signs* 5 (autumn 1979): 3–29; S. Chan, 'The Exclusion of Chinese Women," p. 107; Tong, *Unsubmissive Women*.

22 SFBS, *San Francisco Municipal Report, 1859–60*, p. 42.

23 Mrs. C. M. Churchill, "The Social Evil: Which Do You Prefer?" broadside, BL; California State Board of Health (hereafter CSBH), *Biennial Report*, 1870–1, pp. 45, 48; Ryan, *Women in Public* pp. 124–5; James Boyd Jones, "A Tale of Two Cities: The Hidden Battle against Venereal Disease in Civil War Nashville and Memphis,' *Civil War History* 31, no. 3 (September 1985): 270–6; John C. Burnham, "Medical Inspection of Prostitutes in America in the Nineteenth Century: The St. Louis Experiment and Its Sequel," *Bulletin of the History of Medicine* 45, no. 3 (May–June 1971): 203–18.

24 At least eight individuals – doctors, clergymen, and police officers – were questioned by the California state senators on the relationship between Chinese prostitutes and the spread of syphilis, particularly to the population of white boys and young men. The testimony was printed in California Legislature Special Committee on Chinese Immigration, *Chinese Immigration;* see the testimony of Rev. Otis Gibson, p. 35; F. A. Gibbs, chairman of the Hospital Committee, p. 88; Dr. H. H. Toland, pp. 102–5; Dr. J. C. Shorb, pp. 106–8; David C. Woods, superintendent of the Industrial School, p. 113; James Duffy, Sacramento police officer, p. 125; James Coffey, Sacramento police officer, p. 126; and Matthew Kracher, former Sacramento chief of police, p. 131.

25 California Legislature, Special Committee on Chinese Immigration, *Chinese Immigration*, p. 103.

26 U.S. Congress, Senate, *Report of the Joint Special Committee*, p. 14; Farwell, *The Chinese at Home and Abroad*, pp. 12013; Workingmen's Party of California, Anti-Chinese Council, (WPC hereafter), *Chinatown Declared a Nuisance!* (San Francisco: Workingmen's Party of California, 1880), pp. 4–5; American Federation of Labor, *Some Reasons for Chinese Exclusion: Meat vs. Rice, American Manhood against Asiatic Coolieism. Which Shall Survive?* (Washington: American Federation of Labor, 1901), p. 28; Dr. M. P. Sawtelle, "The Foul Contagious Disease: A Phase of the Chinese Question," *Medico-Literary Journal* 1, no. 3 (November 1878): 8; Densmore, The Chinese in California, p. 81; Walter Raymond, *Horrors of the Mongolian Settlement*, pp. 55, 57; Charles Frederick Holder, "Chinese Slavery in America," *North American Review* 165 (September 1897): 288–94.

27 Sims, "Address to the American Medical Association Annual Meeting," p. 107.

28 California Legislature, Special Committee on

Chinese Immigration, *Chinese Immigration*, p. 107.

29 Thomas W. Laqueur, "Bodies, Details, and the Humanitarian Narrative," in *The New Cultural History*, ed. Lynn Hunt (Berkeley and Los Angeles: University of California Press) pp. 176–204; Gilman, "AIDS and Syphilis," pp. 87–107.

30 Dr. M. P. Sawtelle, "State Sanitation," *Medico-Literary Journal* (February 1880): 2–3.

31 Peter Stallybrass and Allon White, *The Politics and Poetics of Transgression*, (London: Methuen, 1986), p. 22.

32 Sawtelle, "The Foul Contagious Disease," p. 5.

33 Sawtelle, "State Sanitation," p. 3.

34 Sawtelle, "The Foul Contagious Disease," pp. 4–5; Sawtelle, "State Sanitation," pp. 2–3.

35 Stoler, *Race and the Education of Desire*, pp. 147–64; Napur Chaudhrui, "Memsahibs and Motherhood in Nineteenth Century Colonial India," *Victorian Studies* 31, no. 4 (1988): 517–36; Robert Schell, "Tender Ties: Women and the Slave Household, 1652–1834," in *The Societies of Southern Africa in the 19th and 20th Centuries*, University of London Institute of Commonwealth Studies no. 17 (London: University of London, 1992); Jim Swan, "Mater and Nannie: Two Mothers and the Discovery of the Oedipus Complex," *American Imago* 31, no. 1 (spring 1974): 1–64.

36 Sarah E. Henshaw, "Chinese Housekeepers and Chinese Servants," *Scribner's Monthly* 12 (1876): 736.

37 Thomas Logan, cited in CSBH, *Biennial Report*, 1870–1, p. 46.

38 Thomas King, cited in Canada, Royal Commission on Chinese Immigration, *Report of the Royal Commission on Chinese Immigration: Report and Evidence* (Ottawa: Royal Commission on Chinese Immigration, 1885), p. 194.

39 C. C. Cox and J. T. Tobin, cited in Canada, Royal Commission on Chinese Immigration, *Report of the Royal Commission on Chinese Immigration: Report and Evidence*, pp. 14, 228.

40 Elaine Kim, "Such Opposite Creatures: Men and Women in Asian American Literature," *Michigan Quarterly Review* 29, no. 1 (winter 1990): 68; Ting, "Bachelor Society."

41 H. H. Kane, *Opium Smoking in America and China: A Study of Its Prevalence and Effects, Immediate and Remote, on the Individual and the Nation* (New York: G. P. Putnam's Sons, 1882).

42 Opium dens were concentrated in the areas with a large number of houses with Chinese prostitutes, such as Bartlett Alley (2), Dunscombe

Alley (6), Jackson Street (6), and Dupont Street (3), as well as in zones of white prostitution on Spofford Alley, Washington Street, Waverly Place, and Sacramento Street. City officials identified in 1885 nearly thirty resorts, most of which accommodated fewer than fourteen bunks. Of these, five were on the first floor of buildings and the rest were in basements and subbasements. The investigators reported that all of the resorts were "filthy." Farwell, *The Chinese at Home and Abroad*, pp. 26–7.

43 WPC, *Chinatown Declared a Nuisance!* pp. 12–13.

44 W. S. Whitwell, "The Opium Habit," *Pacific Medical and Surgical Journal* (hereafter *PMSJ*) 30, no. 6 (June 1887): 321–38; David T. Courtright, *Dark Paradise: Opiate Addiction in America before 1940* (Cambridge: Harvard University Press, 1982); Kane, *Opium Smoking in America and China*.

45 Kane, *Opium Smoking in America and China*; Peter Ward Fay, *Opium War, 1840–1842* (New York: W. W. Norton, 1976).

46 Elizabeth Anne McCauley, "Taber and Company's Chinatown Photographs: A Study in Prejudice and Its Manifestations," *Bulletin of the University of New Mexico Art Museum*, no. 13 (1980–1): 12–13.

47 Whitwell, "The Opium Habit," p. 329; "The Opium Curse," *PMSJ* 35, no. 12 (December 1892): 745–6.

48 George H. Fitch, "A Night of Chinatown," *Cosmopolitan* 2, no. 6 (February 1887): 356.

49 Pierre Bourdieu, Distinction: *A Social Critique of the Judgement of Taste*, trans. Richard Nice (Cambridge, MA: Harvard University Press, 1984).

50 Kane, *Opium Smoking in America and China*, p. 8; Charles E. Terry and Mildred Pellens, *The Opium Problem* (New York: n.p., 1928), p. 73; Winslow Anderson, "The Opium Habit in San Francisco," *Medical Surgical Reporter 57* (1887): 784.

51 Kane, *Opium Smoking in America and China*, p. 14; Farwell, *The Chinese at Home and Abroad*, p. 15.

52 B. E. Lloyd, Lights and Shades in San Francisco (San Francisco: A. L. Bancroft and Co., 1876) pp. 261–2.

53 Fitch, "A Night in Chinatown," p. 356.

54 Allen S. Williams, *The Demon of the Orient and His Satellite Fiends of the Joint: Our Opium Smokers as They Are in Tartar Hells and American Pardises* (New York: Allen S. Williams, 1883), pp. 18–19. Williams relates a parallel tale later in the book about a *New York Times* reporter who has a similar experience of revulsion after

recognizing that the same pipe was shared by Chinese and white smokers.

55 Kane, *Opium Smoking in America and China*, p. 78.

56 Terry and Pellens, *The Opium Problem*, pp. 50, 74; William J. Courtney, *San Francisco Anti-Chinese Ordinances, 1850–1900* (San Francisco: Rand E. Research Associates, 1974), pp. 2–3.

57 *San Francisco Chronicle*, July 25, 1881, cited in Kane, *Opium Smoking in China and America*, pp. 10–14.

58 Curtis Marez, "The Other Addict: Reflections on Colonialism and Oscar Wilde's Opium Smoke Screen," *English Literary History* 64 (spring 1997): 257–87; Marez, "The Coquero in Freud: Psychoanalysis, Race, and International Economies of Distinction," *Cultural Critique* 26 (1994): 65–93.

59 "The Opium Curse," p. 745; Whitwell, "Opium Habit," pp. 334–6.

60 Farwell, *The Chinese at Home and Abroad*, p. 103.

61 In the United States, of the forty-one colonies and states that prohibited interracial marriage, twenty-two also prohibited some form of inter-racial sex. All miscegenation laws explicitly spec-ified an interdiction of marriage between whites and blacks; in addition, twelve states banned marriages between whites and American Indians; fourteen states barred marriages of whites with Chinese, Japanese, and Koreans; nine states banned marriages of whites with Malays (Filipinos); and seven outlawed the marriages of whites with either "Hindus" or "Asiatic Indians." Peggy Pascoe, "Miscegenation Law, Court Cases, and Ideologies of Race in Twentieth Century America," *Journal of American History* 83, no. 1 (June 1996): 44–69; Byron Curti Martyn, "Racism in the United States: A History of Miscegenation Legislation and Litigation" (Ph.D. diss., University of Southern California, 1979); Megumi Dick Osumi, "Asians and California's Anti-Miscegenation Laws," in *Asian and Pacific American Experiences: Women's Perspectives*, ed. Nobuya Tsuchida (Minneapolis: Asian Pacific American Learning Resource Center and General College, University of Minnesota, 1982), pp. 2–8; Peggy Pascoe, "Race, Gender, and Intercultural Relations: The Case of Interracial Marriage," *Frontiers* 12, no. 1 (1991): 5–18.

62 *Compiled Laws of California* (Garfielde and Snyder 1853), p. 175; *Civil Code of the State of California*, 1874, p. 30, and 1876, p. 594.

63 Constitutional Convention of California, *Debates and Proceedings of the Constitutional Convention of California*, 1878–79 (Sacramento, 1880), 1: 632.

64 Stout defined the "American people" either as the "Anglo-Saxon" race or the "Caucasian type." His typology of races included Caucasians, aboriginal Americans (sometimes referred to as American Indians, considered a variant of the Mongolian race), Mongolians (or sometimes Asiatics), and Negroes. Stout drew from racial taxonomy developed by Josiah Nott and George Gliddon in *Types of Mankind* (Philadelphia: Lippincott, 1854). He also cited the work of Samuel Morton, Alexander von Humboldt, and Louis Agassiz. Arthur B. Stout, *Chinese Immigration and the Physiological Causes of the Decay of a Nation* (San Francisco: Agnew & Deffebach, 1862), reprinted in CSBH, *Biennial Report*, 1870–1, pp. 58–63.

65 *CSBH, Biennial Report*, 1870–1, p. 63.

66 Ibid., p. 47.

67 A. B. Stout, cited in Canada, Royal Commission on Chinese Immigration, *Report of the Royal Commission on Chinese Immigration: Report and Evidence*, p. 317.

68 In 1880, section 5069 was amended to prohibit issuance of a marriage license to a white person wishing to marry a "Mongolian" (at this point, such a marriage was not actually illegal, however). In 1905, the marriage statute was amended to make all marriages between Mongo-lians and whites "illegal and void." In 1933 the category "Malays" was added in order to include Filipinos under the statute. *Cal. Stats. Code, Amendments*, 1933, ch. 41, sec. 1, p. 3; *Civil Code of the State of California*, 1883, article 2, para. 69; *Cal. Stats. Code*, 1905, ch. 414, para. 2, 554.

69 The following mentioned instances of white women marrying or cohabiting with Chinese men: The Reverend A. W. Loomis in 1876 counted five cases of Chinese men living with white women. In 1885 the board of supervisors reported ten cases of "white women living and cohabiting with Chinamen in the relation of wives or mistresses" and presented an inventory of street addresses of white women living with Chinese men. Augustus Ward Loomis, "Chinese in California," [articles and letters to H. H. Bancroft], 1876, in Hubert Howe Bancroft Col-lection, MSS C-E 158, BL; Farwell, *The Chinese at Home and Abroad*, pp. 15–16; Mary Coolidge, *Chinese Immigration* (New York: Henry Holt and Company, 1909), p. 441.

70 Miscegenation was invalidated by the California Supreme Court decision in *Perez v. Lippold* in 1948. The California legislature lacked the will to repeal the invalidated marriage code to conform with the jurisprudence until 1969 when the invalidated statutes were repealed. *Cal. Stats.*

Code, 1969, ch. 1608, para. 3, p. 3313; *California Civil Code, Annotated* (West 1982).

71 *The Workingman's Advocate*, October 9, 1869, October 11, 1873, and May 6, 1876, cited in Stuart Creighton Miller, *The Unwelcome Immigrant: The American Image of the Chinese, 1785–1788* (Berkeley and Los Angeles: University of California Press, 1969), p. 198; H. S. West, comp., *The Chinese Invasion, Revealing the Habits, Manners, and Customs of the Chinese, Political, Social, and Religious, on the Pacific Coast, Coming in Contact with the Free and Enlightened Citizens of America* (San Francisco: Bacon and Company, 1873), pp. 68–70, 107.

72 U.S. Congress, Senate, *Report of the Joint Special Committee*, pp. 131, 132, 180, 182, 199–201, 202–5, 1100.

73 "Abstract of the Proceedings of the Board," included in CSBH, *Biennial Report*, 1892–4, p. 7.

74 SFBH, *Annual Report*, 1907–8, p. 11.

75 After the deportation, public health officials believed the leprosy crisis had been solved, and for two years they denied the existence of any more Chinese lepers in the city. In October 1878, under mounting political pressure, the city admitted fifteen new leprosy cases to the Smallpox Hospital in a period of three weeks.

76 Letter to John J. Reichenbach, Chairman of the Hospital Committee of the Board of Supervisors, from Dr. John W. Foye, Resident Physician, City and County Small-pox Hospital [Twenty-sixth Street Smallpox Hospital], January 15, 1884, reprinted in Farwell, *The Chinese at Home and Abroad*, pp. 105–10; F. W. Hopkins, "Leprosy in Madeira and San Francisco – A Contrast," *Pacific Medical Journal* 38, no. 12 (December 1895): 743.

77 *New York Times*, September 28, 1878; Zachary Gussow, *Leprosy, Racism, and Public Health: Social Policy in Chronic Disease* Control (Boulder, Colo.: Westview Press, 1989), p. 128.

78 Lloyd, *Lights and Shades in San Francisco*, p. 264.

79 *Chinatown, San Francisco, California* (San Francisco: Bancroft Company 1893), p. 6.

80 Miller, *The Unwelcome Immigrant*, p. 164; SFBH, *Annual Report*, 1878–9, p. 6; SFBH, *Annual Report*, 1883–4, p. 6; U.S. Congress, Senate, *Report of the Joint Special Committee*, p. 204; Henry Gibbons Sr., "On the Danger of Pestilence in California," included in CSBH, *Biennial Report*, 1878–9, pp. 89–90, reprinted in PMSJ 22, no. 6 (November 1879): 253; "Leprosy in California," *New York Times*, July 20 1881, cited in Gussow, *Leprosy, Racism, and Public Health*, p. 128.

81 Dr. A. W. Saxe, "Hawaiian Leprosy," *Transactions of the Medical Society of the State of California* 14 (1883–4): 210–16; "Leprosy in Hawaii," OMT 4, no. 8 (August 1890): 441–5; Dr. L. F. Alvarez, "Leprosy in the Hawaiian Islands," *Pacific Medical Journal* 38, no. 1 (January 1895): 17–23; Dr. Winslow Anderson, "The Hawaiian Islanders and Leprosy," *Pacific Medical Journal* 39, no. 9 (September 1896): 551–8.

82 Society Proceedings – Sacramento Society for Medical Improvement, Annual Meeting, March 20, 1894," OMT 8, no. 5 (May 1894): 322–4; Letter to Reichenbach from Foye, reprinted in Farwell, *The Chinese at Home and Abroad*, pp. 105–10; F. B. Sutliff, "A Safe View Regarding the Contagion of Leprosy," OMT 9, no. 4 (April 1895): 194–8; Albert S. Ashmead, "Is Leprosy Contagious or Not?" *Pacific Medical Journal* 40, no. 12 (December 1897): 747; "Dermatology, Syphilis, and Venereal Disease," OMT 12, no. 2 (February 1908): 91–2 "Leprosy in the United States," *Pacific Medical Journal* 45, no. 8 (August 1902): 487–8.

83 "Society Proceedings – Sacramento Society for Medical Improvement, Annual Meeting, March 20, 1894," pp. 322–4; Sutliff, "A Safe View Regarding the Contagion of Leprosy," pp. 194–8.

84 Testimony of John Meares, in U.S. Congress, Senate, *Report of the Joint Special Committee*, cited in Canada, Royal Commission on Chinese Immigration, *Report of the Royal Commission on Chinese Immigration: Report and Evidence*, p. 198; and testimony of Fred Gibles, in U.S. Congress, Senate, *Report of the Joint Special Committee*, p. 203.

85 Henry R. Brown, "Summary of Leprosy Cases, February 16, 1894," included in SFBH, *Annual Report*, pp. 84–6, reprinted in *Pacific Medical Journal* 37, no. 10 (October 1894): 614–25.

86 *SFBH, Annual Report*, 1883–4, p. 6.

87 Ibid.

88 Farwell, *The Chinese at Home and Abroad*, p. 111.

89 Reddy, "Homes, Houses, Non-Identity," pp. 355–79; Gordon Brent Ingram, Anne-Marie Bouthillette, and Yolanda Ritter, eds., *Queers in Space: Communities, Public Places, Sites of Resistance* (Seattle: Bay Press, 1997), p. 10.

9

The Talk of the County
Revisiting Accusation, Murder, and Mississippi, 1895

John Howard

I have no memory of the events described below. Although they took place in and around my hometown, seventy-seven years before I was born, they were never told to me. And although, at the time, they commanded newspaper headlines from New Orleans to Memphis and became "the talk of the county," that talk somehow subsided.

. . .

"Collective memory ultimately is located not in sites but in individuals," Susan A. Crane writes. "All narratives, all sites, all texts remain objects until they are 'read' or referred to by individuals thinking historically."[1]

. . .

On Thursday, 15 August 1895, at the Rankin County Courthouse in Brandon, Mississippi, a jury convicted Dabney Marshall, Harry Coleman, and Robert Fox of murder. The next morning the "thoroughly famous trio" returned to the scene of the crime – the Brandon railroad station – where, one week prior, R. T. "Tip" Dinkins lay dead of gunshot wounds. Under guard, the three men boarded a westbound train and traveled twelve miles to the state capital of Jackson, also home of the state penitentiary.

In a banner headline story, "They Wear Stripes," Jackson's *Daily Clarion-Ledger* described the last leg of their trip – the principal event around which I organize this essay – in this way:

No potentate or military hero was ever accorded a more enthusiastic [or more hostile] reception on his return from foreign conquests than the people of Jackson gave the three young Vicksburgers who killed "Tip" Dinkins at Brandon last Friday morning. . . . When the train arrived at the State Street crossing several hundred men and boys were on hand eager to catch a glimpse.

Marshall was the first to appear. . . . [His] face was wreathed in a broad but sickly smile as he bowed to one or more old acquaintances in the howling, hissing mob that surrounded him. . . . Coleman, who is about as diminutive as Marshall, but not quite so effeminate, was with Marshall, in front; Fox was next, accompanied by Marshall's father, who had him by the arm; and with Sergeant Parker [of the state prison] bringing up the rear, the half mile walk to the penitentiary was begun.

Marshall and Coleman led the way, apparently unconcerned as to their surroundings and treating the now largely augmented and boisterous mob with silent contempt, but Fox wore a scared, frightened look as if he expected violence. . . . The platforms were crowded with relatives and friends and attorneys of the three once popular men.

Hundreds of people stood close up to every corner and lined the streets along which the sad procession moved at a rapid, business-like gait, the rear being brought up by a mob of other hundreds of men and boys, white and black, all scuffling for the vantage ground nearest the prisoners, pushing and jostling each other in their efforts to get a good look at them.

Old men, solid citizens of seventy-five years of age, were seen to run a block or two to catch up with or head off the procession that they might catch a glimpse of the distinguished arrivals. Offensive epithets, jibes, and jeers were heard on the sides, most of them being uttered for Marshall's express benefit, but he walked on to his destination, giving no intimation that he heard them. Buggies and carriages joined in the wild rush to the penitentiary and by the time the procession arrived there the streets were crowded with wheeled vehicles as well as a thousand or more or less curious people. The crowd did not stop at the gates, but rushed in with the prisoners, up the broad paved walk and into the hall leading to the ponderous iron doors.

Once on the inside, the three young men were treated as all new arrivals to that gloomy hostelrie are treated. They were taken in charge by Sergeant J. W. Lary, who took them to his office, stripped them, took their descriptions, [and] dressed them in regulation suits of stripes.

The men are numbered and described as follows on the prison register:

T. Dabney Marshall, No. 32 – Sentenced from Rankin County for life; crime murder; age 34, born Nov. 30, 1861; height 5 feet 5½ inches, weight 108 pounds; hair brown, eyes gray; occupation lawyer; does not use tobacco; health fairly good; native of Hinds County; no whiskers; has no wife; no children; both parents living; residence Vicksburg; habits of life good; education fair; near-sighted; wears glasses.

Robt. C. Fox, No. 28 – Sentenced from Rankin County for life; crime murder; age 26, born December 9, 1869; height 5 feet 10 inches, weight 160 pounds; occupation hardware clerk; smokes tobacco; health good; born in Hinds County; wears mustache; has no wife or children; both parents living; education fair; scar in center of forehead.

Harry H. Coleman, No. 33 – Sentenced from Rankin County for life; crime murder; age 23, born April 29, 1872; height 5 feet 7½ inches; weight 131 pounds; hair brown, eyes blue; occupation law student; smokes and chews; health good; native of Vicksburg; no wife or children; both parents living; habits of life good; no whiskers; education fair; first finger left hand missing.

The young men are trying hard to bear up under their misfortune, but it can be seen that their punishment is hard, all the fortitude of which they are possessed being required to nerve them to look the situation in the face. The future of Dinkins' slayers is dark indeed.[2]

Ironically, in the same issue of the newspaper, in an editorial entitled "Draw the Veil," the *Clarion-Ledger* encouraged its readers to forget the saga so dramatically told in its pages over the previous two weeks:

Is it not time to draw the veil upon their unfortunate lives and turn to things more pleasant? Let the doors that deprive the prisoners of their liberty shut off all peering eyes and gossipy tongues. Let them alone in their misfortune and misery.

These men come from good families, high minded, law-abiding people, and while they deserve no clemency, and will receive none, having committed a most foul murder, . . . they should not be pursued in their cells and tormented to appease the morbid appetite of the public.

These men have mothers whose heartstrings are now bursting with grief at the shame brought upon their families – tender-hearted old mothers who nursed them into life and prayed over them as they rocked them to sleep in babyhood days. For their sake, if for no other, let us draw the veil, and leave these misguided young men alone to their own gloomy thoughts.

After today, the *Clarion-Ledger* closes its columns to the Brandon tragedy.

Ironic, indeed, is this call to forgetting. For it was the *Clarion-Ledger*'s own "gossipy tongue" that set events in motion and ultimately led to the shooting on 9 August of Tip Dinkins. According to the *Vicksburg Evening Post*, Jackson's *Daily Clarion-Ledger* was as much to blame as were the three assailants.[3] Now Jackson editors urged Mississippians to forget. Such is the ebb and flow of queer spectacle and queer erasure.[4]

In 1895 the *Clarion-Ledger*'s "Around the City" column consisted of several one- or two-sentence observations of various sorts: political prognostications, traffic mishaps, news of visitors to the city and residents' travels outside the city, church affairs, public scandals, and gossip. The 3 August edition included the newspaper's first mention of Dabney Marshall, this not-so-veiled reference to the Vicksburg attorney and aspiring politician: "A sensational report is in circulation on the Warren County candidate for floater senator, which, if proven true, will doubtless cause him to retire from the race."

Marshall felt compelled to respond. His reply became the 5 August lead story, topping all national and international reporting. Under the headline, "Marshall Denies It," his letter to the editor was printed, apparently verbatim: "In your Saturday's issue you say there is a sensational rumor afloat concerning me, which if proven true will cause me to retire from the senatorial race. I hereby denounce the rumor as absolutely and utterly false in every particular. I have never done a low, mean, or disgraceful thing in my life. The people of the whole state will bear me out in this assertion."

What, precisely, was Marshall denying? What was "It" – the ambiguous referent of the newspaper headline – that Marshall stood accused of? The exact details can never be known. As the *Clarion-Ledger* later declared, "The charges made against T. Dabney Marshall by the man he afterwards killed will perhaps on account of their filthy and abhorrent nature never find their way into print." Indeed, it seems, they never did. But it is clear that one night in mid-July, Marshall and Dinkins had shared a hotel room in Raymond, a few miles southwest of Jackson. The next day Dinkins told two friends that Marshall behaved abominably. That is, Marshall apparently made a sexual overture. "Mr. Dinkins told this [unprintable story] in the strictest confidence," the *Clarion-Ledger* reported, "but it got out, as all such things generally do, and in a few days was the talk of the county."[5]

Also unknowable are the multiple forms the story surely took in its telling and retelling, after Dinkins's disclosure to his friends. It is likely that these initial accounts circulated mostly among a white elite to which both Dinkins and Marshall belonged. Heirs of the planter class, the two men had known agrarian life but chose the professions. When floods devastated Dinkins's Issaquena County plantation, he left the area to take control of a road machinery shop in Madison, subsequently headquartered in Jackson. Although Marshall was born on his father's seven-hundred-acre cotton plantation on the Big Black River, just inside Hinds County, he practiced law in the Warren County seat of Vicksburg, as did his uncle, state senator and former representative, T. A. Marshall. Both Tip Dinkins and Dabney Marshall were well connected politically and socially. In post-Reconstruction Mississippi, the white minority ruling class was so small and insular that Dinkins knew all of his assailants. In fact, he was related by marriage – through the first of his two wives – to Robert Fox.[6]

What did or did not happen between Marshall and Dinkins that night in Raymond and how it was or was not talked about in Mississippi became questions more of honor than of criminality.[7] Though an 1839 state statue prohibited "unnatural intercourse" and though seven men were incarcerated under the law as of 1880, more than in any other state, peer group standards proved of greatest concern in the Dinkins–Marshall incident.[8] Indeed, at first, some viewed Dinkins as the more culpable of the two men for having leveled the "nasty charges." Marshall, in turn, had every right, the *Clarion-Ledger* implied, to demand a retraction. Words, it seems, were more pertinent than acts. Dinkins, in referring to the incident, had spoken in (necessarily) unbecoming ways. The talk that resulted affronted community standards, even as it was perpetuated, in carefully chosen language, by the community and by its newspapers. Given that Dinkins would not recant – because, he said, the charges were true – Marshall was justified in killing him, at least early on. Had Marshall "defended his honor . . . when the charges were first made," community members reportedly felt, "his course would have been endorsed."[9]

Weeks passed, however, before Marshall and his colleagues confronted Dinkins in Brandon, where – they learned from his Jackson boardinghouse matron – he had made a sales call to the Rankin County Board of Supervisors. Worse still, Marshall did not call for a duel, an honorable resolution; rather, he ambushed Dinkins. Coleman and Fox acted not as seconds, but as participants in the surprise shooting at the train station. Combined, the three fired a "veritable fusillade" of bullets at Dinkins.[10] Such action seemingly confirmed Marshall's cowardice and compromised his masculinity. It further implicated his associates, whose marital status the prison attendant and the *Clarion-Ledger* would duly note as single.

During the week following the murder and leading up to the conviction, Marshall resigned as the Democratic Party nominee for state floater senator from Hinds and Warren Counties. Party officials proposed an investigation of the hotel incident. And Dinkins's brothers and friends insisted that were an inquiry ordered, Marshall would be "proven the most abject craven in the state." According to the prosecuting attorneys in the case at Brandon, "half a dozen witnesses" could verify (somehow without incriminating themselves) "that Marshall had been guilty of this [again, unspecified] revolting performance on previous occasions."[11]

But Marshall had his own formidable counsel. "A splendid and forcible orator," Anselm J. "Anse" McLaurin of Brandon had been nominated unanimously for governor by the 1,500 Democratic Party delegates assembled in Jackson the week before.[12] Politics and gossip had intermingled at the convention, as party news and the Marshall scandal shared the headlines. When McLaurin accepted the Marshall case, many questioned his decision. The *Memphis Scimitar* declared a conflict of interests. If McLaurin were unsuccessful at trial, the newspaper asserted, he could pardon the assailants once he assumed office. (Given the white Democratic stranglehold on state politics, the general election later that year was a mere formality.) McLaurin demurred. As the *Clarion-Ledger* paraphrased his disingenuous response, McLaurin saw himself as "a poor man [who] had just finished an expensive campaign. . . . [He] was not Governor yet," and he had a family to support.[13]

At trial, even the "foremost criminal lawyer in Mississippi," perhaps the state's most widely known political figure, could not save Dabney Marshall from conviction.[14] In Brandon, where "nothing else [was] talked about," public opinion was said to be "strong against Marshall and his friends" – purportedly "unanimous."[15] McLaurin did secure a plea bargain, however. By confessing to the shooting, the three would not hang. Rather, they would serve life sentences. The revered Methodist bishop Charles B. Galloway advised his cousins, the Dinkins

family, to consent to the agreement. Mrs. Dinkins in particular felt that her deceased son's cronies should not be executed. Thus ended "the Brandon tragedy" – what the *Clarion-Ledger* called "the most sensational case ever known in Mississippi."[16]

The *Daily Clarion-Ledger* not only reported these events. It also shaped the outcome and helped mold public attitudes toward Marshall, his rumored activities, and the murder of Dinkins. The culminating news story – the representation of the penitentiary procession – articulated possible courses of community retribution, such as mob violence, as well as potential means of viewing and delineating individuals of Marshall's type. Clearly awestruck at the masses, the reporter expected an assault on the lead prisoner, a fallen member of "the classes." Elitist contempt was registered on the faces of both Marshall and Coleman, the reporter suggested, whereas Fox seemingly understood the danger. Logically, the murder might have triggered a lynching, the paper maintained – thereby occluding the practice's racial contours while linking these sorts of white men to the worst of fates in Mississippi. That a lynching did not take place, the *Clarion-Ledger* wrongly predicted, attested to the legal profession's ascendancy and expediency and a concomitant end to extralegal executions in the state.[17] Fox's fear, though justified, clearly indicated a faintheartedness; the diminutive stature of both Marshall and Coleman spoke for itself. Their effeminacy – a term of great derision when employed by longtime *Clarion-Ledger* publisher R. H. Henry – marked the men as deviant.[18]

Today, historians of sexuality ordinarily point to the late nineteenth century as the advent of modern conceptions of homosexuality, as the emergence of an identity-based sexual being – the modern homosexual. In a mutually scripting relationship, this deviancy is said to have informed sexual normalcy, and thus the Western world simultaneously witnessed "the invention of heterosexuality."[19] That flowering of medical and legal discourses of sexuality could only partially reflect the realities of queer cultures in turn-of-the-century American cities, before the discourses and the remembrances of those cultures somehow withered into obscurity. Although scholar George Chauncey, in an important act of reclamation, skillfully outlines the workings of a "gay male world" in late-nineteenth- and early-twentieth-century New York City, he acknowledges but does not explain the fact that such worlds, since that time, have "been almost entirely forgotten in popular memory."[20] How can we account for this social amnesia? Is it possible to speak of a queer collective memory? If so, how did it fail us? Or did it? And who are among the "us" to which I refer? For whom are acts of reclamation important today?

Dabney Marshall may or may not have belonged to "a colony of male sex perverts [who] in every community of any size [were] usually known to each other and [were] likely to congregate together," as one scientist proclaimed in 1889.[21] Brandon, with roughly eight hundred residents; Jackson, with seven thousand; or even Vicksburg, with twice that in 1895, may or may not have harbored easily identifiable queer networks. As yet, traditional historical sources are of little help. Still, the Marshall incident and the subsequent talk of the county offer a useful window onto processes of remembering and forgetting homosexuality. Further, they point up the distinctive features of life in post-Reconstruction Mississippi that led to a multiplicity of queer memories, memories I seek to recover through history.

. . .

When I grew up in Brandon in the 1960s and 1970s, our town rapidly was becoming an interstate suburb of Jackson. Nonetheless, a small, white core of old, "established" families remained in old Brandon. My family lived a few houses away from the McLaurin family, descendants of Marshall's attorney, Anselm J. McLaurin, governor of Mississippi from 1896 to 1900. My father and "Mr. John" McLaurin were lifelong friends. John's son Anse was my attorney when I asked my wife for a divorce. During all that time, I never heard about the Brandon tragedy of 1895. Nor did I hear about it after I came out as gay.

Studies of memory necessarily chart multiple historical moments. Memory is about different times in conversation with each other. My time and, with greater emphasis, that of Marshall – as well as his remembered antecedents

– are among the concerns of this essay. Today's popular and scholarly impulse to connect contemporary lesbian and gay persons and politics to prior queer figures and events is problematic, presentist, and yet persistent. Many are invested in such connections. My autobiographical impulse to ancestry, as informed by feminist theory and performed via the recuperation of Marshall's historical specificity, engages this vital lesbian and gay historiographical preoccupation: subjectivity. Who are our subjects? Over this essay's chronological expanse alone, the century between Marshall's adulthood and mine, the very nature of queer subjectivity (inverts, uranians, hermaphrodites, perverts, homosexuals, transsexuals, lesbians, gays, intersexuals, transgender persons) has varied radically, proving unstable in ways that are markedly distinct from that of racial minorities, to name but one other means of categorization. The last "one hundred years of homosexuality," as David Halperin calls it, proves a vibrant period across which divergent queer identities, behaviors, and affinities have been forged.[22] Perceived ancestries are likely to be based in part on class and race – as, for example, I seem to share them with Marshall. Also, as I will argue, they are based on place.

. . .

"The importance of history to gay men and lesbians goes beyond the lessons to be learned from the events of the past to include the meanings generated through retellings of those events and the agency those meanings carry in the present," says theorist Scott Bravmann. "Lesbian and gay historical self-representations – queer fictions of the past – help construct, maintain, and contest identities – queer fictions of the present."[23]

. . .

How in 1895 could an aggressive newspaper, determined to boost sales, balance the medium's sensationalistic tendencies against the prevailing, Victorian penchant for propriety? Under such conditions, homosexuality was made "unmentionable."[24] And yet, as the Dabney Marshall case demonstrates, it was widely talked about. Further, it was written about – but, of course, in particular ways.

In the *Clarion-Ledger* and in other press accounts from the period, conventions of discourse around taboo sexuality were established, observed, and perpetually renegotiated. Memory played an important role. In none of its voluminous coverage – from the first "Around the City" rumormongering until the closing on the penitentiary procession – did the *Clarion-Ledger* give an explicit account of "what transpired" between Marshall and Dinkins that July evening in the Raymond hotel. In alluding to Marshall's "shame," the *Clarion-Ledger* had to rely on readers' recall and on cognitive processes of association.[25]

Scarcely three months prior to the Marshall sentencing, a world-renowned writer was convicted on several counts of "gross indecency" with "male persons" in London.[26] The *Clarion-Ledger* took up this readily available, international controversy, describing Marshall's alleged behavior as "a crime similar to the one for which Oscar Wilde is now serving a term in the English prison."[27] This referential idiom – a Victorian-era tendency to connote homosexuality only through reference to prior cases – is likewise evident in C. S. Clark's 1898 description of Toronto street boys' sexual interactions with men: "According to their reports . . . the crime that banished Lord Somerset from London society is committed."[28] Such rhetorical strategies kept prior episodes alive in popular memory; but they also obscured important differences between cases, such as disparities of age and class between the sex partners. Further details, such as the extent of consent, coercion, and payment for the sex act, also fell away.

Even the Wilde trials yielded press reports conspicuously silent regarding the writer's purported offense. Of the London coverage, Ed Cohen observes that "at no point did the newspapers describe or even explicitly refer to the sexual charges made against Wilde."[29] Jonathan Ned Katz notes a similar New York press "reticence concerning Wilde's exact crime." Thus if Marshall's disgrace was said to mirror that of Wilde, and yet Wilde's disgrace was never pinpointed in print, then a confusion resulted. The referential idiom, it seems, had no concrete referent. Wilde had transgressed, journalists ambiguously disclosed. "This ambiguity," Katz concludes, "either left readers quite in the dark about Wilde's transgression, or" – as is much more likely and as I shall explore later around the Dabney Marshall incident – it "forced them to use their imaginations to make sense of the reports."[30]

In addition to this international scandal used to describe the Marshall incident, there were local analogues as well, called up not only for their familiarity, but also for their power as cautionary tales. Marshall's actions were said to mirror those of a certain Mr. "Cowsert of YMCA fame [who] pleaded guilty and left his home in Natchez to suicide, it is reported, in Chicago." Likewise tragic – and worthy of a brief retelling here – was the case of "W. R. Sims . . . , fired out of the faculty at the State University."[31]

The Sims incident well illustrates the tensions between secrecy and disclosure, both individual and institutional, as it demonstrates varied understandings of queer desire in the American South before the turn of the twentieth century. In 1889, when William Rice Sims joined the University of Mississippi faculty in Oxford, he left behind a soiled reputation at Vanderbilt, his former employer. Somehow, news of his "vicious tendency" initially did not reach Oxford, as Chancellor Robert B. Fulton later lamented.[32] Six years passed before Sims was found out. In March 1895, under intense scrutiny, the professor of English and belles lettres confessed to having improper relations with young men from both the local community and the student body.

The matter was handled internally. Chancellor Fulton talked it over with the twelve members of the faculty. Then he relayed their deliberations in a letter to the executive committee of the Board of Trustees.

Sims, Fulton explained, was "suffering from perverted sexual mania." "Grave rumors in the community" seemed true. On the 233-student campus, Sims may have "improperly handled" 2 of the 204 males.[33] Fulton told the executive committee that although he was "fully aware of the abhorrence with which this vice is thought of, . . . it has a physical basis, either inherited or acquired." The chancellor adopted a medical rhetoric of diagnosis and consequently posited the only humane option: Sims needed "treatment as much as [any] man . . . suffering from any other mania." The faculty shared Fulton's "painful anxiety" but likewise wanted to support Sims. During their colleague's leave, other members of the faculty would teach his courses, though they "wish[ed] the salary to go to him." All agreed that this "quiet way of guarding the interests of the University" was best. They wanted to head off any "undue publicity." Fulton apologized to the committee members for having written "more freely than [otherwise] would be prudent . . . believing that you should know all the facts."[34]

By the time Sims reached Baltimore's Johns Hopkins University Hospital, however, the chancellor had learned of many more allegations against him, and Fulton's goodwill was exhausted. As he wrote to Sims, "I [desired] a quiet departure . . . in order that you might escape the violent treatment which a sudden exposure might have brought to you from this outraged community." Intellectual forbearance now waned: "I did not myself know of one half of the rumors in regard to your conduct circulating in the community [and] reach[ing] back to the first year of your connection with the University." Fulton hoped that "Divine Grace" would allow Sims to "turn your back on the past." Nonetheless, Fulton advised Sims, he should not return to the university.[35]

In a second letter to his superiors, this time to the entire Board of Trustees, Fulton recommended that they accept the resignation Sims initially "placed at my disposal," since "each day has brought some new revelation." Further, while reassuring them that the "evil . . . wrought with students" had been minimal, Fulton was impelled to explicate the nature of Sims's "awful condition." In language far more frank than that of the press, he made it clear: Sims had gratified "his sexual passions by handling the private parts of boys."[36] The chairman of the Board sent his approval of Fulton's recommendation, and on 3 June 1895 the Board voted to divide Sims's remaining salary among the three professors who had covered his classes.[37]

The "unfortunate Sims matter," though revealing relatively little about Sims's life or those of his partners, makes evident a range of beliefs regarding homosexuality. While some Oxford townspeople may have urged violent retaliation as in Jackson, the cooler heads of an educated elite ostensibly prevailed. Fulton took on the language of sexologists at the same time that he moralistically decried Sims's "vice,"

which could be overcome only with heavenly intervention. Despite these conflicting positions, one basic assumption underpinned all of the university correspondence and deliberation. The sharing of "expert" opinion allowed a candid discussion seemingly impossible in wider forums. University officials could ascertain with confidence Sims's condition and thus chart his fate. Although news would inevitably seep out and down to the community, to be recalled dimly in future scandals, university administrators deployed a policy of quiet containment, even as they bore the consequences of Vanderbilt's similar strategy.

Lisa Duggan, in her rigorous and compelling analysis of the trials of Alice Mitchell – a young Memphis resident who killed her lover, Freda Ward, in 1892 – points up lurid press "memories of cases past" strikingly comparable to recollections of Sims and others in the wake of the Dabney Marshall affair. The Mitchell trials, however, garnered national press coverage and sparked reports of "related" incidents as much as twenty-three years past involving women.[38] Interestingly, in reporting the 1895 Marshall affair, the *Clarion-Ledger* did not recall the geographically and temporally proximate Mitchell case. This silence may reflect polarized or perhaps disconnected notions of distinctively male perversions and what was increasingly referred to as lesbianism. In Mississippi, the summoning up of exclusively male case studies around the Marshall episode may bespeak more than a traditional press overrepresentation of a gendered, male public sphere. It also suggests that the panoply of sexual practices and personages outlined by legal and medical authorities may have resulted in only a sporadic linking of male and female homosexualities in the popular imagination.

Memory served to elucidate male persons seemingly akin to Marshall: the main characters of these commonplace narratives. But although these narratives, taken together, presumably would have suggested a collectivity of queer southerners – after all, lots of these sorts of stories circulated – dominant strategies of individualization and isolation fractured collectivity through marginalizing, criminalizing, and pathologizing discourses. For queer southerners who read or heard about or were somehow involved in these scandals, group identities may have cohered, but only against formidable odds. For example, once sent away to Johns Hopkins University Hospital, William Rice Sims could not return to Oxford; Fulton insisted that his remaining possessions be shipped to him.[39] Mr. Cowsert "of YMCA fame" suffered the mythical erasure – realized or not – of suicide, a fate repeatedly offered in these "related" narratives.[40] If Marshall and company were not themselves executed, legally or extralegally, they were shunted to the margins, to jail, reinforced by the *Clarion-Ledger*'s call to forgetting, the press insistence that their lives, once fully exploited for their media value, be wiped from the public record. (And yet, those press records remain for our latter-day inspection and, perhaps, identification.)

Late-nineteenth-century scandals of homosexuality and homoaffectionalism helped construct identities through a "historical process of contested narration," as Duggan terms it.[41] In this process, varied discourses carried unequal weight and power. Sims, Cowsert, and Marshall – as well as those southerners who harbored non-normative desires and thus felt some kinship with the accused – participated in public discussions infrequently and with limited discursive resources. Framed within an evermore professionalized cult of expertise, these men became the objects of study and investigation. They achieved agency and subjectivity only through a constant reworking of dominant conceptions proliferating in medical literature, case law, and mass media. To chart the ways in which these alternative subjectivities and notions were crafted, then disrupted over time, we must inventory a range of queer memories – especially the divergent memories transmitted from a single incident such as the Marshall case. Thereby, we begin to chronicle a contested lineage of queer desire.

. . .

Brandon. The Rankin County Courthouse square. The train station, no longer standing. The streets of Jackson. My interest in Dabney Marshall is invigorated by my personal experiences of, my queer experiences in, these places where – once upon a time, way back when – he also walked, talked, was talked about, and was

made to fashion his life. But any affiliation with Marshall on my part – or by anyone else – must necessarily be partial, tentative, gestural. His times were markedly different from my own; his circumstances were markedly different from those other turn-of-the-century southerners who, in some small, perhaps unspoken way, experienced an affinity with him. In tracking those affinities and differences, I must speculate about the myriad ways in which memories of Marshall were called up and closed off over time.

. . .

"When I find traces of his life, and of other lives," Neil Bartlett writes of another group of turn-of-the-century queer antecedents, "I'm not sure how to react, whether to celebrate or turn away, . . . angry, angry that all these stories have been forgotten. This 'evidence' raises important questions about our own attitude to our own history. Do we view it with dismay, since it is a record of sorrow, of powerlessness, a record of lives wrecked? Or is it possible to read even these texts, written as they were by journalists, policemen, and court clerks, with delight, as precious traces of dangerous, pleasurable, complicated gay lives?"[42]

. . .

If memories reside within individuals, as Susan A. Crane asserts, they also are anchored in physical space. Though sites may not readily give up the details of their past, human musings on the past often rely on restive, ungovernable associations of place. During and after the Marshall incident, material elements of the built environment would figure prominently in ruminations on it. But these elements would both affirm and challenge bedrock historical assumptions about homosexuality and space.

The ostensible emergence of the modern homosexual in Dabney Marshall's lifetime is linked in the historical literature to processes of industrialization and urbanization, most compellingly in John D'Emilio's influential essay, "Capitalism and Gay Identity."[43] Gay identity and community were dialectically shaped in the cities – spaces of anonymity and economic independence, seemingly free of so-called small-town values. Clearly, gayness and place have been linked in particular ways. But how might we frame queer identities and ancestries in other ways? that is, in other places? In a regionalist critique of an urban-focused American lesbian and gay history, I would like to assess queerness in the towns and small cities of the still agrarian South. Specific socioeconomic conditions there suggest specific place-based experiences of sexuality and memories thereof.

The early rumors about Dabney Marshall circulated among a privileged slice of Mississippi social and political life. That political life was all but foreclosed to the state's African American majority when Anselm J. McLaurin and other delegates to the 1890 constitutional convention disenfranchised black citizens and "formalized . . . white rule."[44] Even when the rumors were committed to print – in daily newspapers in Jackson, Vicksburg, Memphis, and New Orleans; in weeklies published at county seats throughout the state – relatively few learned of the Marshall affair in this way.[45] Rates of illiteracy were high in Mississippi, especially for African Americans. Although educated blacks published a number of newspapers during this period, we cannot know their views of the Marshall affair since no copies of the papers remain.[46]

To retrieve the varied reactions of a wide range of Mississippians, we might instead take a metaphorical walk along the same streets of the penitentiary procession, as so elaborately described by the *Clarion-Ledger*. For the march that the Marshall entourage undertook that sixteenth day of August 1895 not only occasioned a spectacle suited to the ideologies of official history, highlighted by an eventual ordering of chaos and the incarceration of the deviants. It also fostered thoughts, desires, and perhaps actions at odds with normative structures. The way those aberrant manifestations were carried forward in time through memory might be suggested if we undertake what Christine Boyer calls a "new memory walk" – if we retrace those steps and begin to imagine the multiple narratives *generated* by, the multiple memories subsequently *transmitted* about, the 1895 procession. In this way, we might craft "new maps that help us resist and subvert the all-too-programmed and enveloping messages" of both our culture today and theirs.[47] Most important, we thereby can begin to piece together more accurate histories of consciousness that account for diverse experiences of difference and dissent across space and time.

People filled the streets. Though it was as hot as any August day in Mississippi, the curious were out in force, aware – from newspaper accounts, by word of mouth – that Marshall, Coleman, and Fox had been convicted the day before and that the three would be arriving in Jackson that morning. Though this throng, as the *Clarion-Ledger* asserted, was largely male – a homosocial public realm with its attendant homosexual possibilities and anxieties – women, in boardinghouses, in shops and groceries, in any number of businesses, residences, and other establishments, likewise heard and witnessed the spectacle, through open windows and from front porches, if not on the frenetic sidewalks.[48]

From the train station on State Street, the penitentiary procession set out on foot along the railroad tracks, after the train, just one block west to President Street. Then it headed north. It proceeded into the city center on President, turning left at the Hinds County Courthouse, built by slaves in the 1840s, and walking another block. After it turned right onto Congress Street, the group came upon the city's principal artery.

Up the grade to the right, two blocks east, Capitol Street originated at the front door of the capitol building, clearly visible. An impressive neoclassical structure completed in 1838, it occupied the focal point around which the city had been platted, a symbol of civic pride.[49] But this intersection of Capitol and Congress Streets marked the intersection of not one, but two key visual axes in Jackson. While off to the right – just beyond the Chinese laundry and other storefronts – the capitol building was perched on the city's eastern edge with its back to the Pearl River, just perceptible in the distance ahead was the penitentiary, on downtown's northernmost boundary.[50] These two mammoth structures dominated sight lines and housed respectively the state's lawmakers and lawbreakers. The buildings functioned, in turn, to craft order and contain disorder. In a stark contrast exemplified in architecture, the ominous penitentiary beckoned to the procession, as the trek continued past the elegant capitol and fashionable Capitol Street, Jackson's main street.

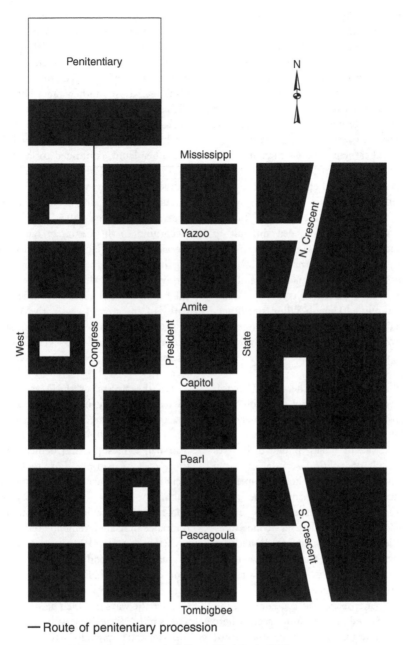

— Route of penitentiary procession

Downtown Jackson, Mississippi, 1895

Yet, as Ted Ownby writes of this period, "the Southern main street" itself harbored much disorder in the form of raucous, male-dominated activities: "The competitiveness, the drunkenness, the possibility of violence, and indiscriminate mixing of all sorts of men put emotions on edge." For black men and boys, in particular, the street was rife with discord. "The element of conflict that accompanied most main-street recreations, making them exciting for some and threatening for others, was sometimes particularly intense in the postbellum years as the races mixed in new ways."[51] In the shadows of the capitol building, where sinister Jim Crow provisions passed into law, black Mississippians gauged the threat of mob violence with added investment, especially as the Marshall gawkers grew more numerous and more boisterous. As African American men looked after young boys, they no doubt instilled a caution and wariness that imbued conceptions of the event.

We can only imagine how older men – black or white, Chinese or Choctaw – responded when inquisitive youngsters asked about the reasons for the crowd's enmity, the reasons for Marshall's predicament. Or how men and boys speculated among themselves, shared stories, conventional wisdom, and opinions. Was homosexuality the topic of their talk? If so, was it framed as an elite, white phenomenon? Such a conclusion would not have been difficult to reach. Homosexual scandals often were newsworthy only to the extent that they involved newsworthy figures, such as senatorial candidate Dabney Marshall, literary celebrity Oscar Wilde, and the like. Though Wilde and others were accused of running with a more dangerous, baser class of pervert, stories of those nonelite companions frequently receded from the headlines.

Further, as guardians of the official record, newspaper editors chose, by not reporting it, to forget or obscure ordinary aspects of queer life, the everyday queer experience. If queer sexuality became a part of broad, public discourses only as a result of political scandal or social trauma, then it surely became linked in memory to scandal and tragedy. Too, sensational, moralistic representations of homosexuality among the famous, the stuff of legend, conceivably enabled ordinary Mississippians to disassociate that morality and spectacle from their own queer actions or queer neighbors. Yes, Mississippians found evidence of difference in themselves, their friends, family members, and acquaintances in the small towns and rural farming areas where most lived – and, indeed, among the crowd vying for a glimpse of the accused. But Marshall and prior referenced figures of scandal probably dominated remembrances of queer sexuality, as a phenomenon shaped in contradistinction to official ideologies and punishments.

But even official voices clashed and popular opinions differed, as local loyalties shaped understandings of the Marshall incident. Whereas the *Clarion-Ledger* and the *New Orleans Times-Democrat* reported great initial

"excitement" in Brandon over the scandal, such that "nothing else [was] talked about," interest quickly faded, given that "all concerned" in the matter were out-of-towners, "comparative strangers."[52] Many Jacksonians sided with Dinkins, whose mother and siblings resided in the area. "The people of Jackson," the *Clarion-Ledger* asserted, were "very well satisfied" with the trial's outcome. Some elite Vicksburgers, on the other hand, continued to lay blame on the *Clarion-Ledger*. They sought to protect their native son Dabney Marshall, the scion of a distinguished family, and they looked down on the press antics in the smaller, younger capital city. According to the Cashman family's *Vicksburg Evening Post*, the Jackson journalists, by spreading innuendo, demonstrated both "intent and motive" to ruin Marshall.[53] His troubles were their fault. And in Vicksburg, at least, "the sympathy of the street [was] with Mr. Marshall in this deplorable affair."[54] From Rankin to Warren Counties, and no doubt even that day on the streets of Jackson, perceptions were tinged with localism.

On the streets, as the Marshall procession passed, the posturing of men and boys was enacted and situated in relation to varied displays of masculinity among the convicted. Marshall's physique and demeanor, as well as those of Coleman and Fox, took on an excess weightiness, because the referential idiom in the talk of the county – the signifying of nebulous, non-normative sexualities through aphoristic reference to related, remembered events – lacked a certain candor. Where spoken and written language failed, body language seemed to help. Not only the quality of Marshall's physical appearance ("diminutive" and "effeminate"), but also the ways in which he stepped ("lightly") and smiled ("sickly") were evaluated by the reporter and implied to be reflective or revelatory of Marshall's being. As Ed Cohen describes the related Wilde case, because "the newspapers could not offer any more concrete representation of the physical acts that were ostensibly at issue than a physical description of the actor who was legally determined to have performed them," Wild's body became a "metonym" or sign system. The London papers "continually capitalize[d] upon the . . . appearance of the male body" – much as the *Clarion-Ledger* reporter focused on Marshall's bearing and carriage – "as a descriptive trope that personalize[d] the . . . proceedings." Thus in London, as in Jackson, observers "contextually portray[ed] these patterns of 'indecent' relationship as inhering in the modes of embodiment attributed to the individuals in question."[55] Whereas Marshall attempted a queer act with Dinkins that ultimately was unknowable, Jacksonians evinced an insatiable need to know at least the form of a queer body, the telltale signs of deviancy.

Men and boys took measure of one another for any number of reasons. As the spectacle unfolded and as it was later described in innumerable conversations, individuals sized each other up. They took stock of one another, in part, to gauge affinity. In any grouping or especially in any mob, a central question arose: Are we all in accord? So too in one-on-one settings, one surely wondered of the other, Are you of the same mind as I? Do you, one might have asked, view this incident as I do? As Mississippians assessed one another around the time of the Marshall incident, the myriad reactions to it were sometimes borne out more clearly than at other times. In delicate verbal dances, queer Mississippians might have identified one another through this ritual of opinion and disclosure, as counterhegemonic or reverse discourses were cautiously elaborated. Since, for a time, Marshall was all that was talked about, that talk, at least occasionally, must have offered moments of queer alliance.

At the northwestern corner of Capitol and Congress, the marchers passed on the left the stately, two-story governor's mansion with rounded front portico and Corinthian columns – where Anselm J. McLaurin would soon take over residence from John M. Stone. Further north behind the mansion on Congress, also on the left, were Smith Park and the First Methodist Church, pastored by Charles Galloway. Humbler structures also lined the street, private homes from one to two-and-a-half stories, all with wide front porches likely filled with onlookers, as the procession reached its destination at the end of Congress.

Marshall's penitentiary march, then, amounted to a community spectacle, differently discerned by different observers. It represented a generative memory walk – creating a momentous occasion and locating it in relation to both the everyday and hallowed spaces of the city. The procession bound experiences and, subsequently, remembrances of the event in discrete, spatial dimensions. Later, perhaps years after the fact, as an individual walked or drove through Jackson, or passed through on a streetcar or train, involuntary memories could be triggered by the mundane physical attributes of one particular street corner where Marshall perhaps spoke back to the crowd, or another stretch of cobblestones where an elderly man ran to catch up. Thus, it was not only the consciously commissioned and constructed monuments – such as the Confederate war memorials erected in front of the courthouse in Rankin County and throughout the South at this time – but also the ordinariness of place that could summon up past traumas and prompt recollections, particularly for marginalized peoples engaged and invested in counterhegemonic readings of those events.

For many people, however, the perceptive possibilities of the spectacle were overdetermined. Reception and judgment operated too closely, almost simultaneously, in time and space. Critical evaluation of Marshall, his crime(s), his ilk, was foreshortened by a seemingly all-consuming masculinist stance at the moment, enacted on the streets, represented in the pages of the newspaper. So too the ways of remembering the event must have been limited by the restrictive means of writing and talking about it: the referential idiom, the derisive catcalls and epithets heard on the streets, and the other narrow discourses that prescribed and proscribed the talk of the county.

Individuals who witnessed the spectacle or read about Marshall in the newspaper presumably harbored *individual* memories for a time, maybe a generation, the duration of their lifetime. But, as Dolores Hayden surmises, "*social* memory relies on story-telling."[56] The Marshall affair would be lost to memory if the story were not recounted to others. Such recountings were discouraged, likely as they were to engage taboo subject matter and to implicate the teller for exhibiting too much interest. Retellings for any purpose other than ridicule, derision, or snide entertainment were undertaken with great care and delicacy. For this reason, the carrying forward of social memory in time clouded the circumstances of Marshall's existence. Far more than it revealed about Marshall or homosexuality, the Marshall spectacle imparted the protocols for engaging in the talk of the county. After Marshall was largely forgotten, memories of these strictures would persist. But, too, the landscape would persist, apt to elicit old and new place-bound memories.

The referential idiom, as I have called it, and its inherent instability of referent presumably would make difficult an event's cohesion in collective memory. The oblique language that marked this event and its protagonist as somehow queer seemingly would close off precision in recollection. But can memories be precise? When, if ever, are they? Might there be a liberatory potential in just such ambiguity? I speculate that it was the very ambiguity, allusion, and innuendo of these incidents that opened up an imaginative space for queer southerners, those who drew particular affinities to Marshall. The productive capacity of the ambiguous for queers allowed certain observers of this event and others who learned about it in the retelling to imagine alternative understandings and ways of life. Thoughts of Marshall, for some, allowed thoughts – and allegiances – of difference and dissent.

If the referential idiom rendered memories imprecise, it also destabilized the nature of the forbidden. What exactly was proscribed? Meanings were clouded as much by polite conventions of discourse as by the innate inability of muckrakers, politicians, or any other surveillant authority to fully ascertain the transgressive acts. The act of which Marshall was accused was, in effect, inscrutable. Thus in relating it, contemporary journalistic accounts, no less than my own history making here, inevitably engaged in conjecture and comparison.

Yes, Marshall was a murderer. This much we know. But his actions must be considered in the context of the violent society he inhabited. Tip Dinkins's allegations threatened Marshall's livelihood, his political career, his income, perhaps even his life. To level such charges meant to endanger another's very being. Often words were indeed more pertinent than acts, in that many transgressions could be overlooked as long as they were not talked about.

Many Mississippians shared Marshall's view that some "insults and wrongs . . . only can be washed away in blood."[57] For some, Marshall simply mishandled the killing. Marshall's revenge, however, should not be construed as a flat denial of the charges of homosexuality. His carefully crafted disavowal – he had never, he wrote, "done a low, mean, or disgraceful thing" – might well have signified a distancing from lurid depictions of queer sexuality, not queer sexuality itself. In a culture characterized by politesse and indirection, by scrupulous shading of language, Marshall conceivably meant to suggest that his *passions* were anything but disgraceful.

. . .

In the early 1990s, with a group of campus activists in Tuscaloosa, Alabama, I watched a film by Gregg Araki called *The Living End.*[58] In it, two gay men, on the road, try to outrun the law and HIV. In a pivotal scene, the gun-toting partner is met on a darkened street by a group of would-be gay bashers, men with rocks and clubs ready to do harm. The man shoots them. The audience cheered wildly.

. . .

"Fundamentally, doing queered history is a scandalous project in itself," writes legal scholar Martha Umphrey. "Queering history means acknowledging that the processes of history are unstable, the search for exemplary historical subjects always incomplete. It requires on our part a constant reengagement, a constant questioning of our own assumptions about the 'proper' subject of history. . . . Moreover, doing queered history may require engagement with unsavory characters who . . . have an attenuated but identifiable relationship with a critique of compulsory heterosexuality."[59]

. . .

Probably the most fundamental, tangible site of memory for the events of August 1895 was "that gloomy hostelrie" to which the murderer Dabney Marshall was confined, to which the unruly crowd accompanied him and his two accomplices. The penitentiary loomed large, a retro–Norman fortress with gatehouse, turrets, and twin towers, all topped with battlements. Situated prominently in the urban landscape, it was not simply a symbol of order and power, authority and control. It was, as well, a memory device, a potent reminder. The prison in our midst acknowledged the deviance in our midst.

And yet, only a few months after Marshall's incarceration, the prison population was relocated out of the city, to the countryside, to a work camp near Oakley in rural Hinds County. Formerly occupants of the capital city citadel, an ongoing spectacle for all to behold, the men were pushed to the margins, the hinterlands, to the site Marshall described as "a low swampy place."[60]

But Marshall had it well. Friends sent gifts of clothing and candy, and the captain at Oakley Convict Farm furnished him with "the nicest of meals."[61] Reflective of class as much as perceived gender role, Marshall received anything but the hard labor prescribed by the judge. ("Work in the field," Marshall confided to a friend, "would kill me.") Instead, he was given charge of the commissary. There, he was responsible for "the weighing out of all food eaten, the ordering of it when out, and the keeping of a record of the same."[62] He handled freight and mail, and during his breaks he tended his potted gardens along the building's gallery: wild violets, yellow jasmines, and petunias. Also during his free time at Oakley, Marshall wrote lengthy letters to friends and family members (letters filled with vivid descriptions that later proved useful to at least one historian of the penal system in Mississippi – a historian whose account of Marshall would suit my own inquiries into the past).[63]

Marshall endeared himself to inmates by offering legal advice, by helping them draw up petitions for the ever-elusive, all-coveted executive order: a pardon. Marshall too hoped for pardon. His father, from that very first day his son walked through the penitentiary gate, lobbied for reprieve. And in the end, Dabney Marshall proved both the *Clarion-Ledger* and the *Memphis Scimitar* wrong. The former assured its readers on that fifteenth day of August 1895 that Marshall "deserve[d] no clemency, and [would] receive none"; the latter insinuated that attorney-turned-governor Anselm J. McLaurin would surely breach ethics and free his client. It was rather the year after McLaurin left office, 1901, the year that the old penitentiary in Jackson was torn down to make way for a new capitol building – a domed structure bigger and more commanding than the one at the summit of Capitol Street, an expenditure McLaurin bitterly fought, an edifice Charles Galloway verbosely dedicated at the lavish opening ceremonies – that T. Dabney Marshall returned to Vicksburg the recipient of a full pardon.[64]

As the Jackson penitentiary was pulled down, replaced by a more magnificent monument to lawmaking and governance, some memories may have died with it. The criminal element, the outlaw, the queer in us all, edged ever further from sight, to the periphery, a geographic marginalization. Thieves and robbers, murderers and sodomites, were removed from the heavily trafficked public center, from the seat of political power. And yet such movement dispersed queer potentials, which as ever defied confinement to a single, visible urban space. Indeed, the public wanted more. On a spring day in 1896, Dabney Marshall noticed "quite a number of visitors at the camp" near Oakley – some "to see relatives," others just "seeking to feed a morbid curiosity with the sight of misfortune."[65] Marshall made a point to meet these visitors, the inquisitive, the curious, those who would not heed official calls to forgetting, those interested in learning more about Marshall and his kind.

I cannot help but wonder: Would Marshall find the latter-day curious, would he find me, you, us, as he found the visitors, "even more than usually bête and banal"? Aren't we, today's readers of the Marshall scandal, equally as engaged and implicated as his contemporaries in the production, maintenance, and perhaps reconstitution of normalcy and difference?

Indeed, I believe, we are. My unfolding of salacious details in this essay was intended to mirror and perform the voyeurism of the Marshall scandal, thereby implicating us all in the consistently sensationalized accounts and understandings of queer lives. Paradoxically, as we have seen, outlandish queer spectacle was often followed by prodigious attempts at queer erasure, both physically and discursively. Queer outlaws were exiled, sometimes killed; queer stories were renounced. Official calls to forgetting thus amounted to more than mechanisms of genteel conversation. They also were strategies of oppression. To declare particular individuals and events as unworthy of remembrance helped to assure their inferior status over time.

And yet the county did talk. The Brandon tragedy, while perpetuating notions of marginality, recirculated memories of prior queer figures. Their stories were again told – at least for a time. If the most elite of those figures such as Oscar Wilde would not be forgotten in the subsequent century, others such as William Sims and Dabney Marshall would be. Or so it seemed. How do historians prove that memories did not persist? How does anyone demonstrate any historical absence? Because I had never heard of Marshall; because I shared a certain lineage with him as a queer white Mississippian, indeed a Brandonian; because the elders and archivists I work with there likewise knew nothing of his story – I assumed it had been lost to queer collective memory. Perhaps it is no longer. We historians are beholden to the communities that support us. We must be made to answer when we declare, "I have no memory."

Notes

1 Susan A. Crane, "Writing the Individual Back into Collective Memory," *American Historical Review* 102 (December 1997): 1381. I would like to thank Novid Parsi for his generous assistance and incisive commentary throughout this project. Thanks also go to Fitz Brundage and Elizabeth Kennedy for their very helpful suggestions.
2 *Jackson Daily Clarion-Ledger* (hereafter *CL*), 16 August 1895. Several subsequent references to *Clarion-Ledger* reports are cited, along with the data of publication, in the text.
3 *CL*, 15 August 1895.
4 In this essay, I use *queer* to broadly signify not just homosexuality but sexual non-normativities of myriad types. As Donna Jo Smith well explains, "my use of the term *queer* is meant to circumvent the limitations to our historical projects effected by the narrow model of lesbian/gay identity that has been utilized in many U.S. histories to date, so that identities and behaviors such as 'bisexual' and 'transgendered' and desires as yet unmapped and perhaps 'unmappable' can be considered within my discussion." Smith, "Queering the South: Constructions of Southern/Queer Identity," in John Howard, ed., *Carryin' On in the Lesbian and Gay South* (New York: New York University Press, 1997), 383.
5 *CL*, 9, 15 August 1895.
6 For biographical data on Dinkins, I have relied on *CL*, 14 August 1895; on Marshall, *Biogra-*

phical and Historical Memoirs of Mississippi (Chicago: Goodspeed Publishing, 1891), 400–1, and T. Dabney Marshall Subject File, Mississippi Department of Archives and History, Jackson (hereafter MDAH). In re-creating the political and social worlds of the late-nineteenth-century South, I have relied on two landmark texts: Edward L. Ayers, *The Promise of the New South: Life after Reconstruction* (New York: Oxford University Press, 1992), and C. Vann Woodward, *Origins of the New South, 1877–1913* (Baton Rouge: Louisiana State University Press, 1951). Broad insights into constructions of sexuality are drawn from John D'Emilio and Estelle Freedman, *Intimate Matters: A History of Sexuality in America* (New York: Harper and Row, 1988).
7 The literature on honor and violence in the South is vast. Most useful for my purposes have been Edward L. Ayers, *Vengeance and Justice: Crime and Punishment in the Nineteenth-Century American South* (New York: Oxford University Press, 1984), and Bertram Wyatt-Brown, *Southern Honor: Ethics and Behavior in the Old South* (New York: Oxford University Press, 1982).
8 Jonathan Katz, *Gay American History: Lesbians and Gay Men in the U.S.A.* (New York: Thomas Y. Crowell, 1976), 37. This is a per capita calculation. Though seven men were likewise held in Tennessee, that state's larger population meant a lower incarceration rate.
9 *CL*, 9 August 1895.
10 Ibid. Sixteen bullets were found, nine in Dinkins's body. *CL*, 13 August 1895.
11 *CL*, 13, 15 August 1895.
12 *CL*, 7, 8 August 1895.
13 *CL*, 14 August 1895.
14 *CL*, 8 August 1895.
15 *CL*, 13, 14 August 1895.
16 *CL*, 15 August 1895.
17 Lynchings reached horrific proportions in Mississippi just before and after the turn of the twentieth century. "During the period from 1889 to 1945, the half century Roy Wilkins called the 'lynching era,' Mississippi accounted for 476, or nearly 13 percent, of the nation's 3,786 recorded lynchings." Of the 476 killed, only 24 were white. Neil R. McMillen, *Dark Journey: Black Mississippians in the Age of Jim Crow* (Urbana: University of Illinois Press, 1989), 229.
18 R. H. Henry, *Editors I Have Known: Since the Civil War* (New Orleans: E. S. Upton Printing, 1922), 301.
19 Jonathan Ned Katz, *The Invention of Heterosexuality* (New York: Dutton, 1995).

20 George Chauncey, *Gay New York: Gender, Urban Culture, and the Making of the Gay Male World, 1890–1940* (New York: Basic Books, 1994), 1.

21 G. Frank Lydstron, "Sexual Perversion, Satyriasis, and Nymphomania," *Medical and Surgical Reporter* 61 (1889): 254; Chauncey, *Gay New York*, 12 (quotation).

22 David M. Halperin, *One Hundred Years of Homosexuality and Other Essays on Greek Love* (New York: Routledge, 1990).

23 Scott Bravmann, *Queer Fictions of the Past: History, Culture, and Difference* (Cambridge: Cambridge University Press, 1997), 4.

24 *CL*, 15 August 1895.

25 *CL*, 9 August 1895.

26 Neil Bartlett, *Who Was That Man? A Present for Mr. Oscar Wilde* (London: Serpent's Tail, 1988), 159–60.

27 *CL*, 9 August 1895. Wilde's visit to the state in 1882 had elicited much comment from Mississippi journalists and other observers, particularly about his clothing and comportment. See Eileen Knott, William Warren Rogers, and Robert David Ward, "Oscar Wilde in Vicksburg, at Beauvoir, and Other Southern Stops," *Journal of Mississippi History* 59 (Fall 1997): 183–210.

28 Cited in Steven Maynard, "'Horrible Temptations': Sex, Men, and Working-Class Male Youth in Urban Ontario, 1890–1935," *Canadian Historical Review* 78 (June 1997): 191.

29 Ed Cohen, *Talk on the Wilde Side: Toward a Genealogy of a Discourse on Male Sexualities* (New York: Routledge, 1993), 4.

30 Jonathan Ned Katz, *Gay/Lesbian Almanac: A New Documentary* (New York: Carroll and Graf, 1983), 258–9.

31 *CL*, 15 August 1895. Allan Bérubé argues that in various parts of the United States, as early as the 1890s, "ordinary . . . bathhouses – and YMCAs – developed reputations as 'favorite spots' for men to have sex with each other. Word got out that a certain manager, masseur, employee, or police officer would look the other way when they were on duty, or that homosexuals were known to gather there at certain hours, usually in the afternoon or late at night." "The History of Gay Bathhouses," in Dangerous Bedfellows, eds., *Policing Public Sex: Queer Politics and the Future of AIDS Activism* (Boston: South End Press, 1996), 190. Also on queer uses of YMCA facilities, see John Donald Gustav-Wrathall, *'Take the Young Stranger by the Hand: Same-Sex Relations and the YMCA* (Chicago: University of Chicago Press, 1998).

32 R. B. Fulton to Donald McKenzie (each member of Board Trustees [*sic*]), 26 March 1895, Robert B. Fulton Collection, Archives and Special Collections, University of Mississippi, University (hereafter RBFC). I am grateful to Lisa K. Speer, acting curator of the Mississippi Collection, for her assistance in locating these documents.

33 On university demographics, I have consulted Dunbar Rowland, ed., *The Official and Statistical Register of the State of Mississippi, 1904* (Nashville: Brandon Printing, 1904), 267; also, *Historical and Current Catalogue of the University of Mississippi, Forty-Second Session, 1893–1894*. Of the two students allegedly involved with Sims, at least one seems to have been dismissed, though not expressly for this reason. In a letter that same month, Chancellor Fulton requested that a Crystal Springs, Miss., man "withdraw" his son from the university, given his poor academic performance: "You will see from his reports that his work is unsatisfactory except in the class in English," taught by Sims. "The members of the Faculty," Fulton added, "are convinced that he could do better work elsewhere." In a revealing final sentence, perhaps indicative of a policy of quiet containment, Fulton stated that "no censure is attached to the young man's moral character by the action which the Faculty has taken." R. B. Fulton to S. H. Aby, 16 March 1895, RBFC.

34 R. B. Fulton to Sir [members of the Executive Committee], 18 March 1895, RBFC.

35 R. B. Fulton to Dr. Wm. Rice Sims, 25 March 1895, RBFC.

36 R. B. Fulton to Donald McKenzie, 26 March 1895. Based on other references in the letters and given that university students were among them, the "boys" can be assumed to have been postadolescent. Nonetheless, this language eerily foreshadows a twentieth-century custom of conflating man–man adult consensual sex with man–boy coerced intercourse.

37 R. H. Thompson to Chancellor R. B. Fulton, 30 March 1895, RBFC; Motion of Mr. Thompson, Resolved, and Motion of Mr. Martin, Resolved, Board of Trustees Minutes, University of Mississippi, Archives and Special Collections, University of Mississippi, University.

38 Lisa Duggan, "The Trials of Alice Mitchell: Sensationalism, Sexology, and the Lesbian Subject in Turn-of-the-Century America," *Signs: Journal of Women in Culture and Society* 18 (Summer 1993): 791–814.

39 R. B. Fulton to Dr. Wm. Rice Sims, 25 March 1895, RBFC.

40 On homosexual suicide mythology and homosexual homicide mythology, see John Howard, *Men Like That: A Southern Queer History*

(Chicago: University of Chicago Press, 1999), chap. 5.

41 Duggan, "Trials of Alice Mitchell," 793.

42 Bartlett, *Who Was That Man?*, 129.

43 John D'Emilio, "Capitalism and Gay Identity," in Ann Snitow, Christine Stansell, and Sharon Thompson, eds., *Powers of Desire: The Politics of Sexuality* (New York: Monthly Review Press, 1983), 100–13. See also D'Emilio's groundbreaking monograph, *Sexual Politics, Sexual Communities: The Making of a Homosexual Minority in the United States, 1940–1970* (Chicago: University of Chicago Press, 1983).

44 McMillen, *Dark Journey*, 36.

45 In the *Vicksburg Evening Post*, e.g., see 9, 10, 12–17 September 1895. References to county weeklies' coverage of the events appear throughout the Jackson and Vicksburg press accounts. Copies of those papers are no longer extant.

46 Julius E. Thompson, *The Black Press in Mississippi, 1865–1985* (Gainesville: University Press of Florida, 1993), 8.

47 Christine M. Boyer, *The City of Collective Memory: Its Historical Imagery and Architectural Entertainments* (Cambridge: MIT Press, 1994), 29.

48 My re-creation and analysis here rely on readings of contemporaneous fire insurance maps. [Map of] *Jackson, Hinds Co., Mississippi* (New York: Sanborn-Perris Map Co., Ltd., 1895).

49 On state politics and city building during this period, I have relied on both John Bettersworth, *Mississippi: A History* (Austin, Tex: Steck Co., 1959), and James W. Loewen and Charles Sallis, eds., *Mississippi: Conflict and Change*, rev. ed. (New York: Pautheon, 1980).

50 On Mississippians of Chinese descent, see James W. Loewen, *The Mississippi Chinese: Between Black and White* (Cambridge: Harvard University Press, 1971).

51 Ted Ownby, *Subduing Satan: Religion, Recreation, and Manhood in the Rural South, 1865–1920* (Chapel Hill: University of North Carolina Press, 1990), 54–5.

52 *CL*, August 10, 13, 1895.

53 *CL*, August 15, 1895.

54 *Vicksburg Evening Post*, 9 August 1895.

55 Cohen, *Talk on the Wilde Side*, 190, 209.

56 Dolores Hayden, *The Power of Place: Urban Landscapes as Public History* (Cambridge: MIT Press, 1995), 46. Emphasis added. Hayden makes an interesting, related point in this work: "In the last forty years, civil rights marches in southern cities, women's marches to 'Take Back the Night' or win abortion rights, and Gay and Lesbian Pride parades in major cities have also established their participants in public space, as part of campaigns to achieve greater political representation. Historical changes in parades can reveal large social transformations, such as when a group is or is not too controversial to march, or when an entire parade is overtaken by commercial interests and every float becomes an advertisement" (pp. 38–9). The transformation from penitentiary procession to Lesbian and Gay Pride parades is significant, indeed.

57 T. Dabney Marshall to Miss Alice [Shannon], 10 September 1895, Crutcher-Shannon Papers, MDAH.

58 For the screenplay of this film, see Gregg Araki, *The Living End: An Irresponsible Movie; Totally F—ed Up: A Screenplay* (New York: Morrow, 1994).

59 Martha M. Umphrey, "The Trouble with Harry Thaw," *Radical History Review* 62 (Spring 1995): 20–1.

60 T. Dabney Marshall to Miss Alice Shannon, 7 May 1896, Crutcher-Shannon Papers, MDAH.

61 T. Dabney Marshall to Mother, 13 April 1896, Crutcher-Shannon Papers, MDAH.

62 Marshall to Shannon, 7 May 1896, ibid.

63 David M. Oshinsky, *"Worse than Slavery": Parchman Farm and the Ordeal of Jim Crow Justice* (New York: Free Press, 1996), 157–61.

64 Ibid., 159.

65 Marshall to Mother, 13 April 1896.

10

The Brandon Teena Archive

Judith Halberstam

The facts of the case: The tragic facts of the Brandon Teena case are as follows: on December 31, 1993 three young people were shot to death execution style in a town called Falls City in rural Nebraska. Ordinarily this story would have evoked only mild interest and a few questions about the specific brutalities of rural America; however, one of the three victims was a young white person who had been born a woman but who was living as a man and had been dating local girls. The other two victims, Brandon's friend Lisa Lambert and her friend Philip DeVine – a disabled African-American man – appeared to have been killed because they were in the wrong place at the wrong time (although this too is debatable). The murderers were two young local white men, John Lotter and Thomas Nissen. Lotter is on death row and Nissen turned evidence against Lotter in order to escape the death penalty. He is serving a life sentence.

Knowing One's Place

This essay is less concerned with the details of the Brandon Teena case, which are by now well known, and more preoccupied with the development, over a relatively short period of time, of a massive archive of representations of the events and experiences associated with the name "Brandon Teena." I will attempt to track the strange path of this event from the shadow lands of marginal queer rural life in Middle America to the glare of the spotlight in Hollywood. By now, the life and death of a young transgender man named Brandon Teena has been so thoroughly mythologized through novels, films, documentaries, plays and web sites that it offers a unique opportunity to analyze how and why certain stories, indeed certain lives, become representative beyond the subcultures that claim them.

I offer here an assortment of frameworks for understanding the symbolic weight of the narrative of Brandon Teena at this time: first we might consider the narrative of the life and desires of Brandon Teena as illuminative of transgender identities and histories in the twentieth century; second, we can examine the specificity of the rural setting for this narrative and use it to consider questions about the bias in queer studies towards narratives of urban sexual formations; third, the relay of race and class in this particular story of sex and violence brings up questions about the racial formation of whiteness and the defense of white manhood that leads in some sense to the murder of a so-called imposter. Finally, I want to examine the particular features of the narrative that make it both ready for and resistant to mainstreaming.

When I began thinking and writing about the Brandon Teena murders in 1996, I approached the material with the bewilderment of a typical urban queer who wanted to know why Brandon, but also his African-American friend Philip DeVine, did not pick up and leave Falls City as soon as they could and furthermore why they were there in the first place. Falls City, in all the literature, sounded like the last place in North America where one would want to try to pass as a man while dating local girls; it was also clearly not a good place to be one of the few people of color in town and dating a white woman. De-industrialization and the farming crises of the 1970s and 1980s had made this town, like so many other midwestern small towns, a place of poverty and neglect where jobs were hard to come by. For the young white men in town, minorities were to blame for this latest downward swing in their fortunes and certainly the federal government offered no real hope of retribution. Poverty and diminished job prospects in Nebraska in the late 1980s created the wicked brew of violence and boredom which animates so many feckless youth to acts of outrage.

Having read much of the material on Brandon Teena's short life and brutal murder and having viewed a documentary about the case, I quickly rationalized the whole episode as an inevitable case of a queer running afoul of the rednecks in a place one would not want to live in anyway. In the fall of 1996 I was invited up to Seattle to speak at a gay and lesbian film festival following the screening of the documentary, *The Brandon Teena Story* by Susan Muska and Greta Olafsdottir. I would be joined as a discussant by Seattle local transman and anthropologist Jason Cromwell and LA based Philosophy Professor and FTM (female-to-male transsexual) Jacob Hale. We conferred briefly before the panel and after sitting through the disturbing documentary, we went to the stage to engage the audience. The organizers of the conference seemed to assume that the documentary would spur a debate about whether we should understand Brandon as an FTM without access to sex reassignment surgery or as a transgender butch who had deliberately decided not to transition. My comments skimmed over this debate, which seemed beside the point to me, and went straight to the question of regionality, location, and rural existence. I commented that Nebraska was not simply anywhere in this tape but that the video makers had skillfully tried to situate the landscape as a character in this drama. The audience made noises of approval. Next I went on to the topic of life in small, mostly white, midwestern towns and I suggested that many of these places were the breeding grounds for cultures of hate and meanness that had both homophobic and racist dimensions. The audience was quiet. Too quiet.

The question-and-answer period began without controversy and a few people testified to the difficulties they had encountered as FTMs or as partners of FTMs. Others talked about the traumatic experience of watching the tape and coming so close to the horrific details of Brandon's murder. Then something strange happened. A harmless question came my way: "what do you think of the tape? Do you think it is good? Do you think the directors were at all condescending." While I did have some real problems with the tape and its representations of the people of Falls City, I felt that I had been invited to lead an even handed discussion of *The Brandon Teena Story* and so I shrugged off the implied criticism and said that I thought Muska and Olafsdottir had done some amazing interviews. The next question went a bit deeper: what did you think about the depiction in the tape of rural life and furthermore what do you mean by small towns in the heartland being "cultures of hate and meanness." I tried to explain that I was trying to describe the bigotry that resides in mostly white non-urban constituencies. Then it got ugly. A woman stood up and denounced my comments as insensitive to those people present who may have come from small towns and who, furthermore, very much wanted to return to a small town life and did not believe that the small town was an essentially racist or bigoted place. The audience broke out into spontaneous and sustained applause and then one person after the other stood up to testify that they too were from a small town or a rural background and that they too felt offended.

Apart from a bruised ego (it is no fun to have an audience give a standing ovation to someone who has just told you that you are full of it), I left Seattle unscathed but this experience followed me and forced me to reconsider what was at stake in the myth making that now surrounds the murder of Brandon Teena. This murder does not *only* pry open a Pandora's box of questions about transgender life in the late twentieth century, nor is it simply a lesson in the hard facts of transphobia; if properly handled, the Brandon Teena case represents an archive of material on urban versus rural queer life; small town versus big city hatreds and pleasures; race, class, sexuality and violence in spaces off to the side of what gets recognized in North America as queer life. This archive, furthermore, is not simply a collection of materials about Brandon himself – it is a wealth of information about his family, his girlfriends, his male friends, about Philip Devine and Lisa Lambert and about the urban reader.

The murder of Brandon Teena, like the murder of Matthew Shepherd some six years later, did in fact draw public attention to the peculiar vulnerabilities of queer youth (whether transgender or gay/lesbian) living in North America's heartland. In both cases, the victims became martyrs for urban queer activists fighting for lesbian, gay, bisexual and transgender rights, and in both cases the victims were mythologized in a huge and diverse array of media as extraordinary individuals who fell prey to the violent impulses of homophobic and transphobic middle-America masculinities. But, while it is tempting to use the materials produced in the aftermath of the killings of Brandon Teena and Matthew Shepherd to flesh out the details of the lives and deaths of the subjects, it makes more sense to my mind to collect the details, the stories, the facts and the fictions of the cases and create deep archives for future analysis about the many rural lives and desires that were implicated in the lives and deaths of these individuals. In the case of Brandon Teena, such an archive would contain vital information about racial and class constructions of identity and desire in rural areas and it would furthermore provide some details about the elaborate and complex desires of young women, here specifically the young women who were drawn to Brandon's incomplete and compelling manhood.

So, while in other work on this archive, I have examined the "politics of transgender biography" and considered the difficulties involved in telling stories about people who have created very specific life narratives, here, I want to lay out the geo-political ramifications of the murder of Brandon Teena by imagining a so-called "Brandon Teena Archive" made up of the insights and revelations allowed by a careful consideration of the many lives and social formations that Brandon's life and death sheds light upon. If we think of the murder of Brandon Teena as less of a personal tragedy and more as a symbolic event relating to queer and transgender lives everywhere, we can approach the geographical and class specificities of rural Nebraska. The execution of Brandon Teena, Lisa Lambert, and Philip DeVine was in fact like an earthquake or a five alarm fire: it damaged more than just the three who died and the two who killed, it actually devastated the whole town and brought a flood of reporters, cameras, and journalists into the area to pick through the debris and size up the import of the disaster. Amidst the flood of articles, news shows and talk shows that covered the case were two films, one an independent documentary and the other a feature film. Because these two films, more than any other representations of the case have determined what the legacy of the Brandon Teena murders will be, they bear close examination. Ultimately, I think there are more comprehensive narratives to tell about this case and more complicated uses to make of the archive than these two films allow, but in order to think about other ways of understanding the stories associated with Brandon Teena we have to see how they have been crystallized by Muska and Olafsdottir's documentary, *The Brandon Teena Story*, and Kimberly Peirce's Oscar winning feature, *Boys Don't Cry*. As we move from the independent video to a popular film, we can ask which narratives are emphasized? Which are lost altogether? Which narratives carry the case into mainstream attention and which parts of the story actually block wider transmission? What makes the violent death of one queer more important than the violent deaths of others? How does the death of the transgender man in this narrative eclipse the simultaneous murder of a disabled African-American man? What is the role of memorialization in the transition of the Brandon Teena story from obscurity to widespread notoriety and finally who is authorized to tell the story and why? But before we turn to a consideration of the representations of the case on film and video, I want to first contextualize the Nebraska murders in relation to work on rural queers.

Urban vs. Rural: The Lost Binary in Queer Studies

In her lyrical rendering of life in an "other" America, the coal camps and "hollers" of West Virginia, Kathleen Stewart explores at length the meaning of memory for those who live life in forgotten places of neglect and poverty, in what she calls the "space on the side of the road." In her ethnography, Stewart collects untidy narratives which disorganize the conventional forward motion of ethnographic telling and allow us insight into the particular pull exerted by small town life for even those subjects who are brutalized by it. One such narrative, for example, emerges when West Virginian Sylvie Hess recounts to Stewart a rambling recollection of a childhood experience in response to a question about why she could not make a life in the city. In order to explain the attraction of her dilapidated rural home town, Sylvie recalls her favorite animal from childhood, a cow called Susie, who followed her around throughout her day when she was a young child. One day, however, the cow was killed by some dogs who "ripped out her throat and tore her all to pieces . . ." Lingering for a moment over the brutal memory of her favorite cow "layin' there all tore up," Sylvie abruptly switches gears and comments: "But that place was sa perty!" Stewart comments: "Here, home is a vibrant space of intensity where things happened and left their mark. Home is sweet not despite the loss of her favorite sheep but because of it."[1] Stewart's insightful rendering of the seemingly contradictory impulses animating Sylvie's memory provides momentary access for the urban reader to the appeal of the small rural town for the working-class subjects who stay there and find beauty and peace in between the brutal realities of poverty, isolation, illness, and violence. For Stewart, the rural poor represent a forgotten minority in the American imagination and offer a fertile site for the ethnographic project of documenting difference.

In gay/lesbian and queer studies there has been very little attention paid to date to the specificities of rural queer lives. Indeed, most queer work on community, sexual identity, and gender roles has been based on and in urban populations and exhibits an active disinterest in the productive potential of non-metropolitan sexualities and genders and identities.[2] Most theories of homosexuality within the twentieth century assume that gay culture is rooted in cities, that it has a special relationship to urban life, and that, as Gayle Rubin comments in "Thinking Sex," erotic dissidents require urban space because in rural settings queers are easily identified and punished; this formulation of the difference between urban and rural environments, of course, implies that while rural communities invest heavily in all forms of social and sexual conformity, urban culture thrives upon social and sexual difference. In theory such a distinction makes a lot of sense but in practice we might find that rural environments nurture elaborate sexual cultures even while sustaining surface social and political conformity.

Rural and small town queer life is generally mythologized by urban queers, then, as sad and lonely or else rural queers might be thought of as "stuck" in a place that they would leave if they only could. Only recently has the rural/urban divide and binary begun to produce some interesting inquiries into life beyond the metropolitan center; in some recent work, the rural/urban binary reverberates in really productive ways with other defining binaries like traditional/modern, western/non-western, natural/cultural, modern/postmodern. The editors of one anthology of queer writings on sexual geographies, for example, suggest that rural or non-metropolitan sites have been elided within studies of sexuality and space which typically focus either on "sexualized metropolitan areas such as New York and Berlin or on differently sexualized, marginalized and colonized spaces including the Orient and Africa."[3] By comparison, they propose, "much less has been said about other liminal or in-between spaces including the small towns and rural parts of Europe, Australia and North America."[4] The volume as a whole points to the dominance of models of what David Bell terms helpfully "metrosexuality" and the concomitant representation of the rural as either essentially "hostile" or essentially "idyllic."[5]

The notion of "metrosexuality" as a cultural dominant in US theorizing about gay/lesbian lives also gives rise to the term "metronormativity." This term can map the normalizing power of one particular gay/lesbian narrative centered upon "coming out" and involving some form of "migration" either from a rural space to an urban space or from heterosexual life in the city to queer life in the city. According to this narrative, gay or lesbian subjectivity lies dormant within the body awaiting only the right set of circumstances in order to emerge. As Alan Sinfield points out however, this naturalized model of queer selfhood fails to reflect the constructedness of gay/lesbian identities within metropolitan contexts but also the construction of queer identity *as* metropolitan. Accordingly, formulaic accounts of rural sexual identity involve a story of coming to consciousness in relation to the discovery of materials or community in an urban setting. The rural queer, within this standardized narrative, emerges from the dark night of a traditional and closeted world and blooms in the sunshine of modern gay urban life. In reality, many rural queers yearn to leave the city and return to their small towns and many recount complicated stories of love, sex and community in their small town lives which belie the closet model. As John Howard comments in *Men Like That*, a study of gay men in rural Mississippi, the rural is made to function as a closet for urban sexualities in most accounts of rural queer migration. But in actual fact, the ubiquity of queer sexual practices for men at least in rural settings suggest that some other epistemology than the closet governs sexual mores in small towns and wide open rural areas.

Metronormativity, while it reveals the rural to be the devalued term in the urban/rural binary governing alternative US sexual identities, can also shed light on the strangely similar constructions of rural queer sexualities in the US and non-metropolitan sexualities in other parts of the world. For example, Alan Sinfield, in his illuminating essay on US sexual hegemonies, notes that the dominance of North American conceptions of gay identity circulate globally so that "the metropolitan gay model will be found in Johannesburg, Rio de Janeiro, and Delhi, as well as New York and London, in interaction with traditional local, non-metropolitan, models."[6] At the same time then we might expect that the non-metropolitan models also share certain characteristics cross-culturally less because of capitalist modalities like gay tourism, upon which the metropolitan model depends, and more because of the 166separation of these local sexualities from the so-called gay global model. Rural US queer sexualities then may in fact be more like the queer organizations of desire and identity among the queer Filipino men about whom Martin Manalansan writes and within the same sex sexual practices between women in Taiwan which anthropologist Antonia Chao studies. Like other non-metropolitan sex/gender systems, rural sexual practices and roles may be characterized by distinct gender roles, active/passive sexual positioning, passing practices, and like other non-metropolitan models they may exist in proximity to rather than in distinction from heterosexualities.

Some US based scholars have begun to research the meaning of rural queer lives but in general the most important work on rural queers seems to be coming from the UK. This might have something to do with the pervasiveness of postcolonial thought in the former center of empire. As I discuss in another chapter of this project, British masculinities and British metropolitan sexualities have been as radically altered by the colonial encounter as the formerly colonized peoples who now flock to England and change forever the meaning of Englishness. In the US however, rural populations are studied more often in relation to class or the formation known as "white trash" and only rarely is the plight of the rural poor linked to other subaltern populations around the world. There are of course good reasons for not simply lumping all rural populations into one large subaltern formation: as George Lipsitz has documented, even working-class whites in the US have a "possessive investment in whiteness" which situates them in often contradictory relations to power and dominant discourses.[7] White rural populations in the US, particularly in the Midwest, must in fact be thought about through the racial project of whiteness and through the historical construction of working class "whiteness" as a place of both privilege and oppression. Because of this complex construction we must avoid either romanticizing rural lives or demonizing them: rural queers in particular may participate in certain orders of bigotry (like racism or political conservatism) while being victimized and punished by others (like homophobia and sexism).

The Brandon Teena story brings to light at least three historiographical problems related to the topic of studying queer rural life: first, this narrative reveals how difficult transgender history has been to write in general, but also how there may be specific dimensions of transgender identity that are particular to a rural setting. Given that many gay, lesbian and transgender people who grow up in and live in small rural areas may not identify at all with these labels, the rural context allows for a very different array of acts, practices, performances and identifications. Second, the Brandon Teena story suggests that too often minority history hinges upon representative examples provided by the lives of a few extraordinary individuals. And so in relation to the complicated matrix of rural queer lives, we tend to rely on the story of a Brandon Teena or a Matthew Shepherd rather than finding out about the queer people who live quietly if not comfortably in isolated areas or small towns all across North America. Precisely because queer history has been so preoccupied with individuals, it has been harder to talk about class and race and it has seemed much more relevant to discuss gender variance and sexual practices. All too often, community models are offered only as a generalized model of many individuals rather than as a complex interactive model of space, embodiment, locality, and desire. The Brandon Teena archive, then, needs to be read less in terms of the history of one extraordinary person and more in terms of the constructions of community and self that it brings to light.

A final historigraphical problem has to do with finding accurate or productive narratives of queer life in rural areas. In truth, it is not always easy to fathom the contours of queer life in rural settings because, particularly in the case of gay men, queers from rural settings are not well represented in the literature that has been so much a hallmark of twentieth-century gay identity. Gay men and lesbians from rural settings tend not to be artists and writers in such great numbers and so most of the coming out stories that we read are written by people from cities or suburbs. As Eve K. Sedgwick's work has shown in compelling detail, the history of twentieth-century literature in an Anglo-American context has been indelibly marked and influenced by the contributions of white gay men; consequently, literature has been a very powerful vehicle for the production and consolidation of gay identity. But again, very little of this literature has anything at all to say about rural life and most of it ties homosexual encounters to the rhythms of the city. Just a quick glance at some of the most influential high culture texts of queer urban life would reveal gay guidebooks to Oscar Wilde's London, Jean Genet's Paris, Christopher Isherwood's Berlin, E. M. Forster's Florence, Thomas Mann's Venice, Edmund White's New York, John Rechy's LA, Allen Ginsberg's San Francisco, and so on.

Canonized literary production by Euro-American lesbian writers similarly focuses, although less obsessively, upon urban locations like Paris, London and New York, but in queer writing by women we do find some of the themes that we might also expect to find in accounts of rural queer life like stories of isolation and numerous passing narratives. While fictional narratives of queer rural life are quite hard to find, some ethnographic work and some oral histories did emerge in the 1990s. John Howard's *Men Like That* is an exemplary and unique history and ethnographic survey of the sexual practices and social mores of men who have sex with men in Southern Mississippi. Another notable collection of the oral histories of a group of midwestern gay men, all of whom grew up on farms, was compiled by Will Fellows.

If we return to the Brandon Teena story now we can see that it offers some material answers to questions about transgender history, community participation in a passing person's life and more importantly it provides counter narratives to the dominant stories of urban gay and lesbian and transsexual life. Brandon Teena clearly knew what was possible in Falls City, Nebraska and he seemed to know what limits might be imposed upon his passing performance. His migration was precisely the reverse of the usual move from country to city; indeed, he moved to the small geographically isolated town of Falls City from a large city, Lincoln, not in order to be a stranger with no history but because he had friends there. As Angelia R. Wilson comments, in an essay about "Gay and Lesbian Life in Rural America": "Unknown outsiders are never welcomed in small towns." And she continues: "The key to survival in a rural community is interdependence."[8] Brandon developed quite quickly a friendship network which included both his girlfriends and his killers but he seemed to take a certain comfort in being known and in knowing everyone in town. By moving to a small town and setting up life as a young man, furthermore, Brandon was operating within a long tradition of passing women in rural areas of North America.

Many urban gays, lesbians and transgender people responded to the murder of Brandon with a "what do you expect" attitude, as if brutality was an inevitable consequence of trying to pull off such a risky endeavor as passing for male in some godforsaken place. But what such a response ignores is the fact that Brandon had been passing for male with mixed success in Lincoln, Nebraska since his early teenage years; but it was when he left the city and made a reverse migration to the small town of Falls City, that he really pulled off a credible presentation as male. Obviously, the small town can accommodate some performances even as it is a dangerous place for others – for example, an exhibition of normative masculinity in a transgender man may go unnoticed while an overt and public demonstration of non-normative gendering may be severely and frequently punished. These urban responses also misunderstand completely the appeal of the small town to certain subjects. Like Sylvie Hess, the West Virginian who remembers the loss of a favorite animal and the beauty of the place of its death side by side, the rural queer may be attracted to the small town for precisely those reasons that make it seem uninhabitable to the urban queer. So, rather than trying to figure out whether Brandon was a stone butch, a self-hating lesbian or a transsexual man and then trying to argue about why he did not leave a small, homogenous and hostile environment for the safety in numbers offered by his more urban home, I want to grapple with precisely the appeal of the small town and how it gets represented in two films about the case: *The Brandon Teena Story* and *Boys Don't Cry*.

Going Mainstream

In *The Brandon Teena Story*, Susan Muska and Greta Olafsdottir attempt to place the narrative of Brandon's life and death firmly in the countryside of Nebraska. We see prolonged shots of the rolling Nebraska countryside, road signs welcoming the traveler to Nebraska's "good life," and scenes of everyday life and culture in small town America. The film makers make it clear that their relationship to Falls City and its communities is ironic and distanced; the camera peers voyeuristically at the demolition derby, the local line-dancing and karaoke bar, and at the lives of the people touched by the Brandon story. In a significant scene providing "local color," the camera pans the backs of local men watching a demolition derby; as the gaze sweeps over them, the men are rendered in slow motion as they turn and gaze back with hostile stares of non-recognition. Interactions between the camera and its subjects register the film makers as outsiders to the material realities of the rural Midwest, mark the objects of the gaze as literally haunted by an invisible camera, and finally these interactions place the viewer at a considerable distance from the actors on the screen. This distance both allows for the emergence of multiple versions of the Brandon Teena Story but also pins the narrative of violent homophobic and transphobic violence firmly to the landscape of white trash America and forces modes of strenuous disidentification between viewer and landscape.

The landscape of Nebraska then serves as a contested site upon which multiple narratives unfold, narratives indeed which refuse to collapse into simply one story, "the Brandon Teena story." Some viewers of *The Brandon Teena Story* have accused the film makers of an obvious class bias in their depictions of the people of Falls City; others have seen the film as an accurate depiction of the cultures of hate sometimes fostered in small, mostly white towns. Any attempt to come to terms with the resonances of Brandon's murder will ultimately have to grapple with both of these proposals. One way in which *The Brandon Teena Story* deploys and perpetuates a class bias in relation to the depiction of anti-queer violence is by depicting many of its interview subjects in uncritical ways as "white trash." In their introduction to an anthology titled *White Trash: Race and Class in America*, Matt Wray and Annalee Newitz define the term "white trash" as both a reference to "actually existing white people living in (often rural) poverty" but also a term designating "a set of stereotypes and myths related to the social behaviors, intelligence, prejudices, and gender roles of poor whites."[9] The editors offer a "local politics of place" to situate and combat and explain such stereotypes.

One way in which the *The Brandon Teena Story* is able to grapple with the lives beneath the stereotypes (of white trash, of gender impersonation) is by allowing some of the women whom Brandon dated to explain themselves and articulate their own extraordinary desires. In the media rush to uncover the motivations behind Brandon's depiction of himself as a man, most accounts of the case have overlooked the fact that Brandon was actively chosen over more conventionally male men by the women he dated despite the fact that there were few social rewards for doing so. One girlfriend after another in the tape characterize Brandon as a fantasy guy, a dream guy, a man who "knew how a woman wanted to be treated." Gina describes him as romantic and special and attentive, while Lana Tisdale describes him as "every woman's dream." Brandon, we might conclude, lived up to and even played into the romantic ideals that his girlfriends cultivated about masculinity. Brandon's self-presentation must be read, I believe, as a damaging critique of the white working-class masculinities around him; at the same time, however, his performance of courtly masculinity is a shrewd deployment of the middle-class and so-called respectable masculinities that represent an American romantic ideal of manhood. In the accounts that the women give of their relations with Brandon we understand that he not only deliberately offered them a treatment they could not expect from local boys, he also acknowledged the complexity of their self-understandings and desires.

In order to understand the kinds of masculinities with which Brandon may have been competing, we can turn to the representations of the murderers themselves. While some accounts of the Brandon Teena case have attempted to empathize with the men who murdered Brandon – John Lotter and Tom Nisser – by revealing their traumatic family histories and detailing their encounters with abuse, the video tries to encourage the men to give their own reasons for their brutality. The conversations with Nissen and Lotter are fascinating for the way they allow the men to cooly describe rape and murder scenes, and also because Latter in particular articulates an astute awareness of the violence of the culture into which he was raised. Nissen, however, shows little power of self-reflection; the tape represents him as ultimately far more reprehensible than his partner in crime. For one second in the video, the camera focuses upon a small tattoo on Nissen's arm but does not allow the viewer to identify it. In Aphrodite Jones's book on the Brandon Teena case, she provides information that situates this tattoo as a symbol of white supremacy politics. Tom Nissen we learn was involved off and on throughout his early life with a group called "White American Group for White America."[10] While Nissen's flirtation with brutally racist white supremacist groups need not surprise us it does nonetheless flesh out the particular nexus of hate that came to focus upon Brandon, Lisa Lambert, and Philip DeVine. Nowhere in the documentary, however, nor in media coverage of the case, does anyone link Nissen's racial politics with either the brutalization of Brandon or the execution of the African-American, Philip DeVine – indeed the latter is always constructed as a case of "wrong place, wrong time" but DeVine's situation needs to be explored in more detail. In *The Brandon Teena Story*, Philip's murder is given little airplay and none of his relatives or family appear in the tape.

Given the slow boil of the case of Brandon Teena, the gradual way in which it moved from an event with only local significance to a symbol of the distinctions and disjunctures between gay and lesbian communities and a newly visible transsexual/transgender community, most queer spectators did not have huge hopes for the feature film by Kimberly Peirce. So, when Hilary Swank stepped up to the stage to accept an Oscar in the year 2000 for her performance as Brandon in Peirce's film, the case of the young transgender man moved out of the shadows of the subculture and into the full glare of mainstream publicity. In the case of *Boys Don't Cry*, Kimberly Peirce did a fairly good job of keeping the viewer trained on the seriousness of Brandon's masculinity, the authenticity of his presentation as opposed to its elements of masquerade, but she was not so good at protecting other contradictory elements of the story.

Romance

In order for the film to play to larger audiences, it became less a tale of transformation and alternative gendering and more of a love story. In the production notes, we are told: "Peirce went on her odyssey to Falls City where she interviewed the real Lana Tisdale, Brandon's one true love." It is hard to credit this description of Lana Tisdale as Brandon's one true love given that the two only dated for a matter of weeks before the subsequent rape and murder of Brandon. They first started dating on December 12, 1993 and by the last day of the year, Brandon was dead. One of the producers of the film says of director Peirce: "What Kim realized is that the story of Brandon Teena wasn't so much about his tragic murder or the brutality he experienced at the end of his life, but about this remarkable love he had found, about finally finding someone who could accept him on his own terms." The producers and director also suggest that the film gets at the "emotional truth" of the film even though in the interviews they conducted with the real life characters, they felt that stories were constantly changing and even that people were lying to them. This notion of the "truth" of the story obscures the actual agenda of mainstreaming, within which contradictions are quickly erased through the organization of facts and fictions around a mythic tale of love and conquest.

We could look at one strange scene from the end of the film that invests heavily in the romantic narrative in which Brandon's shortcomings are redeemed by the love of a good woman. Brandon has just endured an incredibly brutal rape and assault within which he has been exposed to Lana as a woman. He sits in a shed behind his friend "Candace's" (Lisa Lambert) house. Lana comes to see him and a strange sex scene ensues. What we see here is in many ways an extension of the scene in which Brandon was de-pantsed; Lana calls him "pretty" and asks him what he was like as a girl. They both agree that his whole journey to manhood has been pretty weird and then they move to make love and Brandon allows Lana to remove his shirt and coat. While earlier Peirce created quite graphic depictions of sex between Brandon and Lana, now the camera in true romantic style cuts away as if to suggest that the couple are now making love as opposed to having sex. The scene raises a number of logistical and philosophical questions about the representation of the relationship between Brandon and Lana: First why would Brandon want to have sex within hours of a rape? Second, how does the film pull back from its previous commitment to his masculinity here by allowing his femaleness to become legible and significant to Lana's desire? Third, in what ways does this scene play against the earlier more "plastic" sex scenes in which Brandon used a dildo and wouldn't allow Lana to touch him? And, fourth, how are those scenes undone by this scene?

When asked in an interview about this scene, Peirce reverts to a very tired humanist narrative to explain this extraordinary scene and she says that after the rape, Brandon could not be either Brandon Teena or Teena Brandon and so he becomes truly "himself" and in that scene "receives love" for the first time as a human being. Peirce claims that Lana herself told her about this encounter and therefore it was true to life. In the context of the film however, which has made no such commitment to authenticity, the scene ties Brandon's humanity to a particular form of naked embodiment that ultimately requires him to be a woman.

Race

The second effect of mainstreaming then was the erasure of Philip DeVine the African American disabled man who was shot in the farmhouse along with Brandon and Lisa Lambert. As we noted in relation to Muska and Olafsdottir's documentary, DeVine received only scant treatment in this video despite the connections of at least one of the murderers to a white supremacist group. Now, in the feature film, the death of DeVine has been rendered completely irrelevant to the narrative that has been privileged. Peirce claimed that this subplot would have compli-

Judith Halberstam

cated her film and made the plot too cumbersome – but race is a narrative trajectory that is absolutely central to the meaning of the Brandon Teena murders and the Brandon Teena archive. DeVine was dating Lana Tisdale's sister Leslie and had a fight with her the night he showed up at Lisa Lambert's house in Humboldt County. His death was neither accidental nor an afterthought; his connection to Leslie Tisdale could be read as a similarly outrageous threat to the supremacy and privilege of white manhood that the murderers Lotter and Nissen rose to defend. By taking DeVine out of the narrative and by not even mentioning him in the original dedication of the film (To Brandon Teena and Lisa Lambert), the film makers have sacrificed the hard facts of racial hatred to a streamlined story of love, death, and gender impersonation in the heartland.

Conclusion

Ultimately, the Brandon Teena archive is not simply the true story of a young queer misfit in rural North America. It is also a necessarily incomplete and ever expanding record of how we select our heroes and how we commemorate our dead. James Baldwin, in his account of the 1979 Atlanta murders of black children, calls our attention to the function of streamlining in the awful vicinity of violent erasure. In *The Evidence of Things Unseen*, Baldwin writes: "The cowardice of this time and place – this era – is nowhere more clearly revealed than in the perpetual attempt to make the public and social disaster the result, or the issue of a single demented creature, or, perhaps, half a dozen such creatures, who have, quite incomprehensibly, gone off their rockers and must be murdered and locked up." The desire, in other words, the desperate desire, to make hate murders the work of crazies and to point to the US justice system as the remedy for unusual disturbances to the social order of things must be resisted in favor of political accounts of crime and punishment. In the end, we are not simply celebrating a Brandon Teena and denouncing a John Lotter or Thomas Nissen, nor should we be seeing love as the redemptive outcome to a tale of hate; the real work of the Brandon Teena archive must be to

provide a record of the complex interactions of race, class, gender and sexuality, which result in murder but whose origins lie in state authorized formations of racism, homophobia, and poverty. Justice in the end lies in the unravelling of the crime not simply in its solution, and when we cease to unravel we become collaborators. "The author of a crime," writes Baldwin, "is what he is . . . but he who collaborates is doomed forever in that unimaginable and yet very common condition which we weakly call hell." Come hell or Hollywood, the stories we collect in the Brandon Teena Archive must be about much more than one remarkable individual and the two cowards who killed him: these materials should stretch far beyond the usual stories of love and hate and the various narratives of accommodation which seem to be so comforting to US readers; this archive lends us precisely the kind of evidence for things unseen that Baldwin sought, and in the end, if we read it right, it may finally tell us a different story about late twentieth-century desire, race, and geography.

Notes

1 Kathleen Stewart, *A Space On The Side of the Road: Cultural Poetics in an "Other" America* (Princeton, NJ: Princeton University Press, 1996): 65.
2 Alan Sinfield usefully defines the "metropolitan" for use in queer studies. He remarks upon the interactive definitions of "metropolitan" and "non-metropolitan" and defines metropolitan sexualities as those that take place in "global centers of capital" and in "principal cities in a nation state." He qualifies this homogenizing notion of the metropolitan, however, by noting that "subordinated groups living at or near the centres of capital, and specifically non-white minorities, may be in some aspects non-metropolitan; a Filipino living in New York may share some ideas and attitudes with people living in the Phillippines." See Alan Sinfield, "The Production of Gay and the Return of Power" in *De-Centering Sexualities: Politics and Representations Beyond the Metropolis*, ed. Richard Phillips, Diane Watt, and David Shuttleton (London: Routledge, 2000): 21.
3 Richard Phillips et al., "Introduction," *De-Centering Sexualities: Politics and Representations Beyond the Metropolis*: 1.

2168

4 Ibid.: 1.

5 See David Bell's essay in *De-Centering Sexualities* on "Eroticizing the Rural": 83–101.

6 Sinfield, *De-Centering Sexualities*: 21.

7 George Lipsitz, *The Possessive Investment in Whiteness: How White People Profit from Identity Politics* (Philadelphia, PA: Temple University Press, 1998).

8 Angelia R. Wilson, "Getting Your Kicks on Route 66: Stories of Gay and Lesbian Life in Rural America, c. 1950's–1970's" in *De-Centering Sexualities*: 208.

9 Matt Wray and Annalee Newitz (eds.), *Whitetrash: Race and Class in America* (New York: Routledge, 1997).

10 See Aphrodite Jones, *All S/he Wanted* (New York: Pocket Books, 1996): 154.

11

Sex in Public

Lauren Berlant and Michael Warner

1 There Is Nothing More Public Than Privacy

A paper titled "Sex in Public" teases with the obscurity of its object and the twisted aim of its narrative. In this paper we will be talking not about the sex people already have clarity about, nor identities and acts, nor a wildness in need of derepression; but rather about sex as it is mediated by publics.[1] Some of these publics have an obvious relation to sex: pornographic cinema, phone sex, "adult" markets for print, lap dancing. Others are organized around sex, but not necessarily sex *acts* in the usual sense: queer zones and other worlds estranged from heterosexual culture, but also more tacit scenes of sexuality like official national culture, which depends on a notion of privacy to cloak its sexualization of national membership.

The aim of this paper is to describe what we want to promote as the radical aspirations of queer culture building: not just a safe zone for queer sex but the changed possibilities of identity, intelligibility, publics, culture, and sex that appear when the heterosexual couple is no longer the referent or the privileged example of sexual culture. Queer social practices like sex and theory try to unsettle the garbled but powerful norms supporting that privilege – including the project of normalization that has made heterosexuality hegemonic – as well as those material practices that, though not explicitly sexual, are implicated in the hierarchies of property and propriety that we will describe as heteronormative.[2] We open with two scenes of sex in public.

Scene 1

In 1993 *Time* magazine published a special issue about immigration called "The New Face of America."[3] The cover girl of this issue was morphed via computer from head shots representing a range of US immigrant groups: an amalgam of "Middle Eastern," "Italian," "African," "Vietnamese," "Anglo-Saxon," "Chinese," and "Hispanic" faces. The new face of America is supposed to represent what the modal citizen will look like when, in the year 2004, it is projected, there is no longer a white statistical majority in the United States. Naked, smiling, and just off-white, *Time*'s divine Frankenstein aims to organize hegemonic optimism about citizenship and the national future. *Time*'s theory is that by the twenty-first century interracial reproductive sex will have taken place in the United States on such a mass scale that racial difference itself will be finally replaced by a kind of family feeling based on blood relations. In the twenty-first century, *Time* imagines, hundreds of millions of hybrid faces will erase American racism altogether: the nation will become a happy racial monoculture made up of "one (mixed) blood."[4]

The publication of this special issue caused a brief flurry of interest but had no important effects; its very banality calls us to understand the technologies that produce its ordinariness. The fantasy banalized by the image is one that reverberates in the law and in the most intimate crevices of everyday life. Its explicit aim is to help its public process the threat to "normal" or "core" national culture that is currently phrased as "the problem of immigration."[5] But this crisis image of immigrants is also a *racial mirage* generated by a white-dominated society, supplying a specific phobia to organize its public so that a more substantial discussion of exploitation in the United States can be avoided and then remaindered to the part of collective memory sanctified not by nostalgia but by mass aversion. Let's call this the amnesia archive. The motto above the door is Memory Is the Amnesia You Like.

But more than exploitation and racism are forgotten in this whirl of projection and suppression. Central to the transfiguration of the immigrant into a nostalgic image to shore up core national culture and allay white fears of minoritization is something that cannot speak its name, though its signature is everywhere: national heterosexuality. National heterosexuality is the mechanism by which a core national culture can be imagined as a sanitized space of sentimental feeling and immaculate behavior, a space of pure citizenship. A familial model of society displaces the recognition of structural racism and other systemic inequalities. This is not entirely new: the family form has functioned as a mediator and metaphor of national existence in the United States since the eighteenth century.[6] We are arguing that its contemporary deployment increasingly supports the governmentality of the welfare state by separating the aspirations of national belonging from the critical culture of the public sphere and from political citizenship.[7] Immigration crises have also previously produced feminine icons that function as prostheses for the state – most famously, the Statue of Liberty, which symbolized seamless immigrant assimilation to the metaculature of the United States. In *Time*'s face it is not symbolic femininity but practical heterosexuality that guarantees the monocultural nation.

The nostalgic family values covenant of contemporary American politics stipulates a privatization of citizenship and sex in a number of ways. In law and political ideology, for example, the fetus and the child have been spectacularly elevated to the place of sanctified nationality. The state now sponsors stings and legislation to purify the internet on behalf of children. New welfare and tax "reforms" passed under the cooperation between the Contract with America and Clintonian familialism seek to increase the legal and economic privileges of married couples and parents. Vouchers and privatization rezone education as the domain of parents rather than citizens. Meanwhile, senators such as Ted Kennedy and Jesse Helms support amendments that refuse federal funds to organizations that "promote, disseminate, or produce materials that are obscene or that depict or describe, in a patently offensive way, sexual or excretory activities or organs, including but not limited to obscene depictions of sadomasochism, homo-eroticism, the sexual exploitation of children, or individuals engaged in sexual intercourse."[8] These developments, though distinct, are linked in the way they organize a hegemonic national public around sex. But because this sex public officially claims to act only in order to protect the zone of heterosexual privacy, the institutions of economic privilege and social reproduction informing its practices and organizing its ideal world are protected by the spectacular demonization of any represented sex.

Scene 2

In October 1995, the New York City Council passed a new zoning law by a forty-one to nine vote. The Zoning Text Amendment covers adult book and video stores, eating and drinking establishments, theaters, and other businesses. It allows these businesses only in certain areas zoned as nonresidential, most of which turn out to be on the waterfront. Within the new reserved districts, adult businesses are disallowed within five hundred feet of another adult establishment or within five hundred feet of a house of worship, school, or day-care center. They are limited to one per lot and in size to ten thousand square feet. Signs are limited in size, placement, and illumination. All other adult businesses are required to close within a year. Of the estimated 177 adult businesses in the city, all but 28 may have to close under this law. Enforcement of the bill is entrusted to building inspectors.

A court challenge against the bill was brought by a coalition that also fought it in the political process, formed by anticensorship groups such as the New York Civil Liberties Union (NYCLU), Feminists for Free Expression, People for the American Way, and the National Coalition Against Censorship as well as gay and lesbian organizations such as the Lambda Legal Defense Fund, the Empire State Pride Agenda, and the AIDS Prevention Action League. (An appeal was still pending as of July 1997.) These latter groups joined the anticensorship groups for a simple reason: the impact of rezoning on businesses catering to queers, especially to gay men, will be devastating. All five of the adult businesses on Christopher Street will be shut down, along with the principal venues where men meet men for sex. None of these businesses have been targets of local complaints. Gay men have come to take for granted the availability of explicit sexual materials, theaters, and clubs. That is how they have learned to find each other; to map a commonly accessible world; to construct the architecture of queer space in a homophobic environment; and, for the last fifteen years, to cultivate a collective ethos of safer sex. All of that is about to change. Now, gay men who want sexual materials or who want to meet other men for sex will have two choices: they can cathect the privatized virtual public of phone sex and the internet; or they can travel to small, inaccessible, little-trafficked, badly lit areas, remote from public transportation and from any residences, mostly on the waterfront, where heterosexual porn users will also be relocated and where the risk of violence will consequently be higher.[9] In either case, the result will be a sense of isolation and diminished expectations for queer life, as well as an attenuated capacity for political community. The nascent lesbian sexual culture, including the Clit Club and the only video rental club catering to lesbians, will also disappear. The impact of the sexual purification of New York will fall unequally on those who already have fewest publicly accessible resources.

2   Normativity and Sexual Culture

Heterosexuality is not a thing. We speak of heterosexual culture rather than heterosexuality because that culture never has more than a provisional unity.[10] It is neither a single Symbolic nor a single ideology nor a unified set of shared beliefs.[11] The conflicts between these strands are seldom more than dimly perceived in practice, where the givenness of male–female sexual relations is part of the ordinary rightness of the world, its fragility masked in shows of solemn rectitude. Such conflicts have also gone unrecognized in theory, partly because of the metacultural work of the very category of heterosexuality, which consolidates as *a sexuality* widely differing practices, norms, and institutions; and partly because the sciences of social knowledge are themselves so deeply anchored in the process of normalization to which Foucault attributes so much of modern sexuality.[12] Thus when we say that the contemporary United States is saturated by the project of constructing national heterosexuality, we do not mean that national heterosexuality is anything like a simple monoculture. Hegemonies are nothing if not elastic alliances, involving dispersed and contradictory strategies for self-maintenance and reproduction.

Heterosexual culture achieves much of its metacultural intelligibility through the ideologies and institutions of intimacy. We want to argue here that although the intimate relations of private personhood appear to be the realm of sexuality itself, allowing "sex in public" to appear like matter out of place, intimacy is itself publicly mediated, in several senses. First, its conventional spaces presuppose a structural differentiation of "personal life" from work, politics, and the public sphere.[13] Second, the normativity of heterosexual culture links intimacy only to the institutions of personal life, making them the privileged institutions of social reproduction, the accumulation and transfer of capital, and self-development. Third, by making sex seem irrelevant or merely personal, heteronormative conventions of intimacy block the building of nonnormative or explicit public sexual cultures. Finally, those conventions conjure a mirage: a home base of prepolitical humanity from which citizens are thought to come into political discourse and to which they are expected to return in the (always imaginary) future after political conflict. Intimate life is the endlessly cited *elsewhere* of political public discourse, a promised haven that distracts citizens from the unequal conditions of their political and economic lives, consoles them for the damaged humanity of mass society, and shames them for any divergence between their lives and the intimate sphere that is alleged to be simple personhood.

Ideologies and institutions of intimacy are increasingly offered as a vision of the good life for the destabilized and struggling citizenry of the United States, the only (fantasy) zone in which a future might be thought and willed, the only (imaginary) place where good citizens might be produced away from the confusing and unsettling distractions and contradictions of capitalism and politics. Indeed, one of the unforeseen paradoxes of national-capitalist privatization has been that citizens have been led through heterosexual culture to identify both themselves *and their politics* with privacy. In the official public, this involves making sex private; reintensifying blood as a psychic base for identification; replacing state mandates for social justice with a privatized ethics of responsibility, charity, atonement, and "values"; and enforcing boundaries between moral persons and economic ones.[14]

A complex cluster of sexual practices gets confused, in heterosexual culture, with the love plot of intimacy and familialism that signifies belonging to society in a deep and normal way. Community is imagined through scenes of intimacy, coupling, and kinship; a historical relation to futurity is restricted to generational narrative and reproduction.[15] A whole field of social relations becomes intelligible as heterosexuality, and this privatized sexual culture bestows on its sexual practices a tacit sense of rightness and normalcy. This sense of rightness – embedded in things and not just in sex – is what we call heteronormativity. Heteronormativity is more than ideology, or prejudice, or phobia against gays and lesbians; it is produced in almost every aspect of the forms and arrangements of social life: nationality, the state, and the law; commerce; medicine; and education; as well as in the conventions and affects of narrativity, romance, and other protected spaces of culture. It is hard to see these fields as heteronormative because the sexual culture straight people inhabit is so diffuse, a mix of languages they are just devel-

oping with premodern notions of sexuality so ancient that their material conditions feel hard-wired into personhood.

But intimacy has not always had the meaning it has for contemporary heteronormative culture. Along with Foucault and other historians, the classicist David Halperin, for example, has shown that in ancient Athens sex was a transitive act rather than a fundamental dimension of personhood or an expression of intimacy. The verb for having sex appears on a late antique list of things that are not done in regard to or through others: "namely, speaking, singing, dancing, fist-fighting, competing, hanging oneself, dying, being crucified, diving, finding a treasure, having sex, vomiting, moving one's bowels, sleeping, laughing, crying, talking to the gods, and the like."[16] Halperin points out that the inclusion of fucking on this list shows that sex is not here "knit up in a web of mutuality."[17] In contrast, modern heterosexuality is supposed to refer to relations of intimacy and identification with other persons, and sex acts are supposed to be the most intimate communication of them all.[18] The sex act shielded by the zone of privacy is the affectional nimbus that heterosexual culture protects and from which it abstracts its model of ethics, but this utopia of social belonging is also supported and extended by acts less commonly recognized as part of sexual culture: paying taxes, being disgusted, philandering, bequeathing, celebrating a holiday, investing for the future, teaching, disposing of a corpse, carrying wallet photos, buying economy size, being nepotistic, running for president, divorcing, or owning anything "His" and "Hers."

The elaboration of this list is a project for further study. Meanwhile, to make it and to laugh at it is not immediately to label any practice as oppressive, uncool, or definitive. We are describing a constellation of practices that everywhere disperses heterosexual privilege as a tacit but central organizing index of social membership. Exposing it inevitably produces what we have elsewhere called a "wrenching sense of recontextualization," as its subjects, even its gay and lesbian subjects, begin to piece together how it is that social and economic discourses, institutions, and practices that don't feel especially sexual or familial collaborate to produce as a social norm and ideal an extremely narrow context for living.[19] Heterosexual culture cannot recognize, validate, sustain, incorporate, or remember much of what people know and experience about the cruelty of normal culture even to the people who identify with it.

But that cruelty does not go unregistered. Intimacy, for example, has a whole public environment of therapeutic genres dedicated to witnessing the constant failure of heterosexual ideologies and institutions. Every day, in many countries now, people testify to their failure to sustain or be sustained by institutions of privacy on talk shows, in scandal journalism, even in the ordinary course of mainstream journalism addressed to middlebrow culture. We can learn a lot from these stories of love plots that have gone astray: about the ways quotidian violence is linked to complex pressures from money, racism, histories of sexual violence, cross-generational tensions. We can learn a lot from listening to the increasing demands on love to deliver the good life it promises. And we can learn from the extremely punitive responses that tend to emerge when people seem not to suffer enough for their transgressions and failures.

Maybe we would learn too much. Recently, the proliferation of evidence for heterosexuality's failings has produced a backlash against talk-show therapy. It has even brought William Bennett to the podium; but rather than confessing his transgressions or making a complaint about someone else's, we find him calling for boycotts and for the suppression of heterosexual therapy culture altogether. Recognition of heterosexuality's daily failures agitates him as much as queerness. "We've forgotten that civilization depends on keeping some of this stuff under wraps," he said. "This is a tropism toward the toilet."[20]

But does civilization need to cover its ass? Or does heterosexual culture actually secure itself through banalizing intimacy? Does belief that normal life is actually possible *require* amnesia and the ludicrous stereotyping of a bottom-feeding culture apparently inadequate to intimacy? On these shows no one ever blames the ideology and institutions of heterosexuality. Every day, even the talk-show hosts are newly astonished to find that people who are committed to hetero intimacy are nevertheless unhappy.

After all is said and done, the prospects and promises of heterosexual culture still represent the optimism for optimism, a hope to which people apparently have already pledged their consent – at least in public.

Recently, Biddy Martin has written that some queer social theorists have produced a reductive and pseudoradical antinormativity by actively repudiating the institutions of heterosexuality that have come to oversaturate the social imaginary. She shows that the kinds of arguments that crop up in the writings of people like Andrew Sullivan are not just right-wing fantasies. "In some queer work," she writes, "the very fact of attachment has been cast as only punitive and constraining because already socially constructed. . . . Radical anti-normativity throws out a lot of babies with a lot of bathwater. . . . An enormous fear of ordinariness or normalcy results in superficial accounts of the complex imbrication of sexuality with other aspects of social and psychic life, and in far too little attention to the dilemmas of the average people that we also are."[21]

We think our friend Biddy might be referring to us, although in this segment she cites no one in particular. We would like to clarify the argument. To be against heteronormativity is not to be against norms. To be against the processes of normalization is not to be afraid of ordinariness. Nor is it to advocate the "existence without limit" she sees as produced by bad Foucauldians ("EH," p. 123). Nor is it to decide that sentimental identifications with family and children are waste or garbage, or make people into waste or garbage. Nor is it to say that any sex called "lovemaking" isn't lovemaking; whatever the ideological or historical burdens of sexuality have been, they have not excluded, and indeed may have entailed, the ability of sex to count as intimacy and care. What we have been arguing here is that the space of sexual culture has become obnoxiously cramped from doing the work of maintaining a normal metaculture. When Biddy Martin calls us to recognize ourselves as "average people," to relax from an artificially stimulated "fear of normalcy," the image of average personhood appears to be simply descriptive ("EH," p. 123). But its averageness is also normative, in exactly the sense that Foucault meant by "normalization": not the imposition of an alien will, but a distribution around a statistically imagined norm. This deceptive appeal of the average remains heteronormative, measuring deviance from the mass. It can also be consoling, an expression of a utopian desire for unconflicted personhood. But this desire cannot be satisfied in the current conditions of privacy. People feel that the price they must pay for social membership and a relation to the future is identification with the heterosexual life narrative; that they are individually responsible for the rages, instabilities, ambivalences, and failures they experience in their intimate lives, while the fractures of the contemporary United States shame and sabotage them everywhere. Heterosexuality involves so many practices that are not sex that a world in which this hegemonic cluster would not be dominant is, at this point, unimaginable. We are trying to bring that world into being.

3   Queer Counterpublics

By queer culture we mean a world-making project, where "world," like "public," differs from community or group because it necessarily includes more people than can be identified, more spaces than can be mapped beyond a few reference points, modes of feeling that can be learned rather than experienced as a birthright. The queer world is a space of entrances, exits, unsystematized lines of acquaintance, projected horizons, typifying examples, alternate routes, blockages, incommensurate geographies.[22] World making, as much in the mode of dirty talk as of print-mediated representation, is dispersed through incommensurate registers, by definition *unrealizable* as community or identity. Every cultural form, be it a novel or an after-hours club or an academic lecture, indexes a virtual social world, in ways that range from a repertoire of styles and speech genres to referential metaculture. A novel like Andrew Holleran's *Dancer from the Dance* relies much more heavily on referential metaculture than does an after-hours club that survives on word of mouth and may be a major scene because it is only barely coherent *as* a scene. Yet for all their differences, both allow for the concretization of a queer counterpublic. We are trying to promote this world-making

project, and a first step in doing so is to recognize that queer culture constitutes itself in many ways other than through the official publics of opinion culture and the state, or through the privatized forms normally associated with sexuality. Queer and other insurgents have long striven, often dangerously or scandalously, to cultivate what good folks used to call criminal intimacies. We have developed relations and narratives that are only recognized as intimate in queer culture: girlfriends, gal pals, fuckbuddies, tricks. Queer culture has learned not only how to sexualize these and other relations, but also to use them as a context for witnessing intense and personal affect while elaborating a public world of belonging and transformation. Making a queer world has required the development of kinds of intimacy that bear no necessary relation to domestic space, to kinship, to the couple form, to property, or to the nation. These intimacies *do* bear a necessary relation to a counterpublic – an indefinitely accessible world conscious of its subordinate relation. They are typical both of the inventiveness of queer world making and of the queer world's fragility.

Nonstandard intimacies would seem less criminal and less fleeting if, as used to be the case, normal intimacies included everything from consorts to courtiers, friends, amours, associates, and coconspirators.[23] Along with the sex it legitimates, intimacy has been privatized; the discourse contexts that narrate true personhood have been segregated from those that represent citizens, workers, or professionals.

This transformation in the cultural forms of intimacy is related both to the history of the modern public sphere and to the modern discourse of sexuality as a fundamental human capacity. In *The Structural Transformation of the Public Sphere*, Habermas shows that the institutions and forms of domestic intimacy made private people private, members of the public sphere of private society rather than the market or the state. Intimacy grounded abstract, disembodied citizens in a sense of universal humanity. In *The History of Sexuality*, Foucault describes the personalization of sex from the other direction: the confessional and expert discourses of civil society continually posit an inner personal essence, equating this true personhood with sex and surrounding that sex with dramas of secrecy and disclosure. There is an instructive convergence here in two thinkers who otherwise seem to be describing different planets.[24] Habermas overlooks the administrative and normalizing dimensions of privatized sex in sciences of social knowledge because he is interested in the norm of a critical relation between state and civil society. Foucault overlooks the critical culture that might enable transformation of sex and other private relations; he wants to show that modern epistemologies of sexual personhood, far from bringing sexual publics into being, are techniques of isolation; they identify persons as normal or perverse, for the purpose of medicalizing or otherwise administering them as individuals. Yet both Habermas and Foucault point to the way a hegemonic public has founded itself by a privatization of sex and the sexualization of private personhood. Both identify the conditions in which sexuality seems like a property of subjectivity rather than a publicly or counterpublicly accessible culture.

Like most ideologies, that of normal intimacy may never have been an accurate description of how people actually live. It was from the beginning mediated not only by a structural separation of economic and domestic space but also by opinion culture, correspondence, novels, and romances; Rousseau's *Confessions* is typical both of the ideology and of its reliance on mediation by print and by new, hybrid forms of life narrative. Habermas notes that "subjectivity, as the innermost core of the private, was always oriented to an audience,"[25] adding that the structure of this intimacy includes a fundamentally contradictory relation to the economy:

> To the autonomy of property owners in the market corresponded a self-presentation of human beings in the family. The latter's intimacy, apparently set free from the constraint of society, was the seal on the truth of a private autonomy exercised in competition. Thus it was a private autonomy denying its economic origins . . . that provided the bourgeois family with its consciousness of itself.[26]

This structural relation is no less normative for being imperfect in practice. Its force is to prevent the recognition, memory, elaboration, or institutionalization of all the nonstandard intimacies that people have in everyday life. Affective life slops over onto work and political life; people have key self-constitutive relations with strangers and acquaintances; and they have eroticism, if not sex, outside of the couple form. These border intimacies give people tremendous pleasure. But when that pleasure is called sexuality, the spillage of eroticism into everyday social life seems transgressive in a way that provokes normal aversion, a hygienic recoil even as contemporary consumer and media cultures increasingly trope toiletward, splattering the matter of intimate life at the highest levels of national culture.

In gay male culture, the principal scenes of criminal intimacy have been tearooms, streets, sex clubs, and parks – a tropism toward the public toilet.[27] Promiscuity is so heavily stigmatized as nonintimate that it is often called anonymous, whether names are used or not. One of the most commonly forgotten lessons of AIDS is that this promiscuous intimacy turned out to be a lifesaving public resource. Unbidden by experts, gay people invented safer sex; and, as Douglas Crimp wrote in 1987:

> we were able to invent safe sex because we have always known that sex is not, in an epidemic or not, limited to penetrative sex. Our promiscuity taught us many things, not only about the pleasures of sex, but about the great multiplicity of those pleasures. It is that psychic preparation, that experimentation, that conscious work on our own sexualities that has allowed many of us to change our sexual behaviours – something that brutal "behavioral therapies" tried unsuccessfully for over a century to force us to do – very quickly and very dramatically. . . . All those who contend that gay male promiscuity is merely sexual *compulsion* resulting from fear of intimacy are now faced with very strong evidence against their prejudices. . . . Gay male promiscuity should be seen instead as a positive model of how sexual pleasures might be pursued by and granted to everyone if those pleasures were not confined within the narrow limits of institutionalized sexuality.[28]

AIDS is a special case, and this model of sexual culture has been typically male. But sexual practice is only one kind of counterintimacy. More important is the critical practical knowledge that allows such relations to count as intimate, to be not empty release or transgression but a common language of self-cultivation, shared knowledge, and the exchange of inwardness.

Queer culture has found it necessary to develop this knowledge in mobile sites of drag, youth culture, music, dance, parades, flaunting, and cruising – sites whose mobility makes them possible but also renders them hard to recognize as world making because they are so fragile and ephemeral. They are paradigmatically trivialized as "lifestyle." But to understand them only as self-expression or as a demand for recognition would be to misrecognize the fundamentally unequal material conditions whereby the institutions of social reproduction are coupled to the forms of hetero culture.[29] Contexts of queer world making depend on parasitic and fugitive elaboration through gossip, dance clubs, softball leagues, and the phone-sex ads that increasingly are the commercial support for print-mediated left culture in general.[30] Queer is difficult to entextualize *as* culture.

This is particularly true of intimate culture. Heteronormative forms of intimacy are supported, as we have argued, not only by overt referential discourse such as love plots and sentimentality but materially, in marriage and family law, in the architecture of the domestic, in the zoning of work and politics. Queer culture, by contrast, has almost no institutional matrix for its counterintimacies. In the absence of marriage and the rituals that organize life around matrimony, improvisation is always necessary for the speech act of pledging, or the narrative practice of dating, or for such apparently noneconomic economies as joint checking. The heteronormativity in such practices may seem weak and indirect. After all, same-sex couples have sometimes been able to invent versions of such practices. But they have done so only by betrothing themselves to the couple form and its language of personal significance, leaving untransformed the material and ideological conditions that divide intimacy from history, politics, and publics. The queer project we imagine is not just to destigmatize those average intimacies, not just to give access to the sentimentality of the couple for persons of the same sex, and definitely not to certify as properly private the personal lives of gays and lesbians.[31] Rather, it is

to support forms of affective, erotic, and personal living that are public in the sense of accessible, available to memory, and sustained through collective activity.

Because the heteronormative culture of intimacy leaves queer culture especially dependent on ephemeral elaborations in urban space and print culture, queer publics are also peculiarly vulnerable to initiatives such as Mayor Rudolph Giuliani's new zoning law. The law aims to restrict any counterpublic sexual culture by regulating its economic conditions; its effects will reach far beyond the adult businesses it explicitly controls. The gay bars on Christopher Street draw customers from people who come there because of its sex trade. The street is cruisier because of the sex shops. The boutiques that sell freedom rings and "Don't Panic" T-shirts do more business for the same reasons. Not all of the thousands who migrate or make pilgrimages to Christopher Street use the porn shops, but all benefit from the fact that some do. After a certain point, a quantitative change is a qualitative change. A critical mass develops. The street becomes queer. It develops a dense, publicly accessible sexual culture. It therefore becomes a base for nonporn businesses, like the Oscar Wilde Bookshop. And it becomes a political base from which to pressure politicians with a gay voting bloc.

No group is more dependent on this kind of pattern in urban space than queers. If we could not concentrate a publicly accessible culture somewhere, we would always be outnumbered and overwhelmed. And because what brings us together is sexual culture, there are very few places in the world that have assembled much of a queer population without a base in sex commerce, and even those that do exist, such as the lesbian culture in Northampton, Massachusetts, are stronger because of their ties to places like the West Village, Dupont Circle, West Hollywood, and the Castro. Respectable gays like to think that they owe nothing to the sexual subculture they think of as sleazy. But their success, their way of living, their political rights, and their very identities would never have been possible but for the existence of the public sexual culture they now despise. Extinguish it, and almost all *out* gay or queer culture will wither on the vine. No one knows this connection better than the right.

Conservatives would not so flagrantly contradict their stated belief in a market free from government interference if they did not see this kind of hyperregulation as an important victory.

The point here is not that queer politics needs more free-market ideology, but that heteronormative forms, so central to the accumulation and reproduction of capital, also depend on heavy interventions in the regulation of capital. One of the most disturbing fantasies in the zoning scheme, for example, is the idea that an urban locale is a community of shared interest based on residence and property. The ideology of the neighborhood is politically unchallengeable in the current debate, which is dominated by a fantasy that sexual subjects only reside, that the space relevant to sexual politics is the neighborhood. But a district like Christopher Street is not just a neighborhood affair. The local character of the neighborhood depends on the daily presence of thousands of nonresidents. Those who actually live in the West Village should not forget their debt to these mostly queer pilgrims. And we should not make the mistake of confusing the class of citizens with the class of property owners. Many of those who hang out on Christopher Street – typically young, queer, and African American – couldn't possibly afford to live there. Urban space is always a host space. The right to the city extends to those who use the city.[32] It is not limited to property owners. It is not because of a fluke in the politics of zoning that urban space is so deeply misrecognized; normal sexuality requires such misrecognitions, including their economic and legal enforcement, in order to sustain its illusion of humanity.

4 Tweaking and Thwacking

Queer social theory is committed to sexuality as an inescapable category of analysis, agitation, and refunctioning. Like class relations, which in this moment are mainly visible in the polarized embodiments of identity forms, heteronormativity is a fundamental motor of social organization in the United States, a founding condition of unequal and exploitative relations throughout even straight society. Any social theory that miscomprehends this participates in their reproduction.

The project of thinking about sex in public does not only engage sex when it is disavowed or suppressed. Even if sex practice is not the object domain of queer studies, sex is everywhere present. But where is the tweaking, thwacking, thumping, sliming, and rubbing you might have expected – or dreaded – in a paper on sex? We close with two scenes that might have happened on the same day in our wanderings around the city. One afternoon, we were riding with a young straight couple we know, in their station wagon. Gingerly, after much circumlocution, they brought the conversation around to vibrators. These are people whose reproductivity governs their lives, their aspirations, and their relations to money and entailment, mediating their relations to everyone and everything else. But the woman in this couple had recently read an article in a women's magazine about sex toys and other forms of nonreproductive eroticism. She and her husband did some mail-order shopping and have become increasingly involved in what from most points of view would count as queer sex practices; their bodies have become disorganized and exciting to them. They said to us: you're the only people we can talk to about this: to all of our straight friends this would make us perverts. In order not to feel like perverts, they had to make *us* into a kind of sex public.

Later, the question of aversion and perversion came up again. This time we were in a bar that on most nights is a garden-variety leather bar, but that, on Wednesday nights, hosts a sex performance event called "Pork." Shows typically include spanking, flagellation, shaving, branding, laceration, bondage, humiliation, wrestling – you know, the usual: amateur, everyday practitioners strutting for everyone else's gratification, not unlike an academic conference. This night, word was circulating that the performance was to be erotic vomiting. This sounded like an appetite spoiler, and the thought of leaving early occurred to us but was overcome by a simple curiosity: what would the foreplay be like? Let's stay until it gets messy. Then we can leave.

A boy, twentyish, very skateboard, comes on the low stage at one end of the bar, wearing lycra shorts and a dog collar. He sits loosely in a restraining chair. His partner comes out and tilts the bottom's head up to the ceiling, stretching out his throat. Behind them is an array of foods. The top begins pouring milk down the boy's throat, then food, then more milk. It spills over, down his chest and onto the floor. A dynamic is established between them in which they carefully keep at the threshold of gagging. The bottom struggles to keep taking in more than he really can. The top is careful to give him just enough to stretch his capacities. From time to time a baby bottle is offered as a respite, but soon the rhythm intensifies. The boy's stomach is beginning to rise and pulse, almost convulsively.

It is at this point that we realize we cannot leave, cannot even look away. No one can. The crowd is transfixed by the scene of intimacy and display, control and abandon, ferocity and abjection. People are moaning softly with admiration, then whistling, stomping, screaming encouragements. They have pressed forward in a compact and intimate group. Finally, as the top inserts two, then three fingers in the bottom's throat, insistently offering his own stomach for the repeated climaxes, we realize that we have never seen such a display of trust and violation. We are breathless. But, good academics that we are, we also have some questions to ask. Word has gone around that the boy is straight. We want to know: What does that mean in this context? How did you discover that this is what you want to do? How did you find a male top to do it with? How did you come to do it in a leather bar? Where else do you do this? How do you feel about your new partners, this audience?

We did not get to ask these questions, but we have others that we can pose now, about these scenes where sex appears more sublime than narration itself, neither redemptive nor transgressive, moral nor immoral, hetero nor homo, nor sutured to any axis of social legitimation. We have been arguing that sex opens a wedge to the transformation of those social norms that require only its static intelligibility or its deadness as a source of meaning.[33] In these cases, though, paths through publicity led to the production of nonheteronormative bodily contexts. They intended nonheteronormative worlds because they refused to pretend that privacy was their ground; because they were forms of sociability that unlinked money and family from the scene of the good life, because they made sex the consequence of public mediations and collective self-activity in a way that made for unpredicted pleasures; because, in turn, they attempted to make a context of support for their practices; because their pleasures were not purchased by a redemptive pastoralism of sex, nor by mandatory amnesia about failure, shame, and aversion.[34]

We are used to thinking about sexuality as a form of intimacy and subjectivity, and we have just demonstrated how limited that representation is. But the heteronormativity of US culture is not something that can be easily rezoned or disavowed by individual acts of will, by a subversiveness imagined only as personal rather than as the basis of public-formation, nor even by the lyric moments that interrupt the hostile cultural narrative that we have been staging here. Remembering the utopian wish behind normal intimate life, we also want to remember that we aren't married to it.

Notes

1 On public sex in the standard sense, see Pat Califia, *Public Sex: The Culture of Radical Sex* (Pittsburgh, 1994). On acts and identities, see Janet E. Halley, "The Status/Conduct Distinction in the 1993 Revisions to Military Antigay Policy: A Legal Archaeology," *GLQ* 3 (1996): 159–252. The classic political argument for sexual derepression as a condition of freedom is put forth in Herbert Marcuse, *Eros and Civilization: A Philosophical Inquiry into Freud* (Boston, 1966). In contemporary prosex thought inspired by volume 1 of Michel Foucault's *The History of Sexuality*, the denunciation of "erotic injustice and sexual oppression" is situated less in the freedom of individuals than in analyses of the normative and coercive relations between specific "populations" and the institutions created to manage them (Gayle Rubin, "Thinking Sex: Notes for a Radical Theory of the Politics of Sexuality," in *Pleasure and Danger: Exploring Female Sexuality*, ed. Carole S. Vance [Boston, 1984], p. 275). See also Michel Foucault, *The History of Sexuality: An Introduction*, vol. 1 of *The History of Sexuality*, trans. Robert Hurley (New York, 1978).

2 By heteronormativity we mean the institutions, structures of understanding, and practical orientations that make heterosexuality seem not only

coherent – that is, organized as a sexuality – but also privileged. Its coherence is always provisional, and its privilege can take several (sometimes contradictory) forms: unmarked, as the basic idiom of the personal and the social; or marked as a natural state; or projected as an ideal or moral accomplishment. It consists less of norms that could be summarized as a body of doctrine than of a sense of rightness produced in contradictory manifestations – often unconscious, immanent to practice or to institutions. Contexts that have little visible relation to sex practice, such as life narrative and generational identity, can be heteronormative in this sense, while in other contexts forms of sex between men and women might *not* be heteronormative. Heteronormativity is thus a concept distinct from heterosexuality. One of the most conspicuous differences is that it has no parallel, unlike heterosexuality, which organizes homosexuality as its opposite. Because homosexuality can never have the invisible, tacit, society-founding rightness that heterosexuality has, it would not be possible to speak of "homonormativity" in the same sense. See Michael Warner, "Fear of a Queer Planet," *Social Text*, no. 29 (1991): 3–17.

3 See *Time*, special issue, "The New Face of America." Fall 1993. This analysis reworks materials in Lauren Berlant, *The Queen of America Goes to Washington City: Essays on Sex and Citizenship* (Durham, N.C., 1997), pp. 200–8.

4 For a treatment of the centrality of "blood" to US nationalist discourse, see Bonnie Honig, *Democracy and the Foreigner* (Princeton, NJ, 2001).

5 See, for example, William J. Bennett, *The De-Valuing of America: The Fight for Our Culture and Our Children* (New York, 1992); Peter Brimelow, *Alien Nation: Common Sense about America's Immigration Disaster* (New York, 1995); and William A. Henry III, *In Defense of Elitism* (New York, 1994).

6 On the family form in national rhetoric, see Jay Fliegelman, *Prodigals and Pilgrims: The American Revolution against Patriarchal Authority, 1750–1800* (Cambridge, 1982), and Shirley Samuels, *Romances of the Republic: Women, the Family, and Violence in the Literature of the Early American Nation* (New York, 1996). On fantasies of genetic assimilation, see Robert S. Tilton, *Pocahontas: The Evolution of an American Narrative* (Cambridge, 1994), pp. 9–33, and Elise Lemire, "Making Miscegenation" (Ph.D. diss., Rutgers University, 1996).

7 The concept of welfare state governmentality has a growing literature. For a concise statement, see Jürgen Habermas, "The New Obscurity: The Crisis of the Welfare State and the Exhaustion of Utopian Energies," *The New Conservatism: Cultural Criticism and the Historians' Debate*, trans. Shierry Weber Nicholsen (Cambridge, Mass., 1989), pp. 48–70. Michael Warner has discussed the relation between this analysis and queer culture in his "Something Queer about the Nation-State," in *After Political Correctness: The Humanities and Society in the 1990s*, ed. Christopher Newfield and Ronald Strickland (Boulder, Colo., 1995), pp. 361–71.

8 *Congressional Record*, 101st Cong., 1st. sess., 1989, 135, pt. 134:12967.

9 Political geography in this way produces systematic effects of violence. Queers are forced to find each other in untrafficked areas because of the combined pressures of propriety, stigma, the closet, and state regulation such as laws against public lewdness. The same areas are known to gay-bashers and other criminals. And they are disregarded by police. The effect is to make both violence and police neglect seem like natural hazards, voluntarily courted by queers. As the 1997 documentary film *Licensed to Kill* illustrates, antigay violence has been difficult to combat by legal means: victims are reluctant to come forward in any public and prosecutorial framework, while bashers can appeal to the geographic circumstances to implicate the victims themselves. The legal system has helped to produce the violence it is called upon to remedy.

10 See Eve Kosofsky Sedgwick, *Epistemology of the Closet* (Berkeley, 1992).

11 Gay and lesbian theory, especially in the humanities, frequently emphasizes psychoanalytic or psychoanalytic-style models of subject-formation, the differences among which are significant and yet all of which tend to elide the difference between the categories male/female and the process and project of heteronormativity. Three propositional paradigms are relevant here: those that propose that human identity itself is fundamentally organized by gender identifications that are hardwired into infants; those that equate the clarities of gender identity with the domination of a relatively coherent and vertically stable "straight" ideology; and those that focus on a phallocentric Symbolic order that produces gendered subjects who live out the destiny of their positioning in it. The psychoanalytic and philosophical insights and limits of these models (which, we feel, underdescribe the practices, institutions, and incongruities of heteronormativity) require further engagement. For the time being, these works stand in as the most

challenging relevant archive: Judith Butler, *Bodies that Matter: On the Discursive Limits of "Sex"* (New York, 1993); Luce Irigaray, *Speculum of the Other Woman*, trans. Gillian C. Gill (Ithaca, N.Y., 1985) and *This Sex Which Is Not One*, trans. Catherine Porter and Carolyn Burke (Ithaca, N.Y., 1985); Teresa de Lauretis, *The Practice of Love: Lesbian Sexuality and Perverse Desire* (Bloomington, Ind., 1994); Kaja Silverman, *Male Subjectivity at the Margins* (New York, 1992); and Monique Wittig, *The Straight Mind and Other Essays* (Boston, 1992). Psychoanalytic work on sexuality does not always latch acts and inclinations to natural or constructed "identity": see, for example, Leo Bersani, *Homos* (Cambridge, Mass., 1995) and "Is the Rectum a Grave?" in *AIDS: Cultural Analysis/Cultural Activism*, ed. Douglas Crimp (Cambridge, Mass., 1988).

12 The notion of metaculture we borrow from Greg Urban. See Greg Urban, *A Discourse-Centered Approach to Culture: Native South American Myths and Rituals* (Austin, Tex., 1991) and *Noumenal Community: Myth and Reality in an Amerindian Brazilian Society* (Austin, Tex., 1996). On normalization, see Foucault, *Discipline and Punish: The Birth of the Prison*, trans. Alan Sheridan (New York, 1979), pp. 184–5 and *The History of Sexuality*, p. 144. Foucault derives his argument here from the revised version of Georges Canguilhem, *The Normal and the Pathological*, trans. Carolyn R. Fawcett and Robert S. Cohen (New York, 1991).

13 Here we are influenced by Eli Zaretsky, *Capitalism, the Family, and Personal Life* (New York, 1986), and Stephanie Coontz, *The Social Origins of Private Life: A History of American Families, 1600–1900* (London, 1988), though heteronormativity is a problem not often made visible in Coontz's work.

14 On privatization and intimacy politics, see Berlant, *The Queen of America Gose to Washington City*, pp. 1–24 and "Feminism and the Institutions of Intimacy," in *The Politics of Research*, ed. E. Ann Kaplan and George Levine (New Brunswick, N.J., 1997), pp. 143–61; Honig, *Democracy and the Foreigner*; and Rosalind Pollack Petchesky, "The Body as Property: A Feminist Re-vision," in *Conceiving the New World Order: The Global Politics of Reproduction*, ed. Faye D. Ginsburg and Rayna Rapp (Berkeley, 1995), pp. 387–406. On privatization and national-capitalism, see David Harvey, *The Condition of Postmodernity: An Enquiry into the Origins of Cultural Change* (Oxford, 1989), and Mike Davis, *City of Quartz: Excavating the Future in Los Augeles* (New York, 1992).

15 This language for community is a problem for gay historiography. In otherwise fine and important studies such as Esther Newton's *Cherry Grove, Fire Island: Sixty Years in America's First Gay and Lesbian Town* (Boston, 1993), or Elizabeth Lapovsky Kennedy and Madeline D. Davis's *Boots of Leather, Slippers of Gold: The History of a Lesbian Community* (New York, 1993), or even George Chauncey's *Gay New York: Gender, Urban Culture, and the Makings of the Gay Male World, 1890–1940* (New York, 1994), community is imagined as whole-person, face-to-face relations – total, experiential, proximate, and saturating. But queer worlds seldom manifest themselves in such forms. Cherry Grove – a seasonal resort depending heavily on weekend visits by New Yorkers – may be typical less of a "gay and lesbian town" than of the way queer sites are specialized spaces in which transits can project alternative worlds. John D'Emilio's *Sexual Politics, Sexual Communities: The Making of a Homosexual Minority in the United States, 1940–1970* is an especially interesting example of the imaginative power of the idealization of local community for queers: the book charts the separate tracks of political organizing and local scenes such as bar life, showing that when the "movement" and the "subculture" began to converge in San Francisco, the result was a new formation with a new utopian appeal: "A 'community,'" D'Emilio writes, "was in fact forming around a shared sexual orientation" (John D'Emilio, *Sexual Politics, Sexual Communities: The Making of a Homosexual Minority in the United States, 1940–1970* [Chicago, 1983], p. 195). D'Emilio (wisely) keeps scare quotes around "community" in the very sentence declaring it to exist in fact.

16 Artemidorus, *Oneirocritica* 1.2, quoted in David M. Halperin, "Sex before Sexuality: Pederasty, Politics, and Power in Classical Athens," in *Hidden from History: Reclaiming the Gay and Lesbian Past*, ed. Martin Bauml Duberman, Martha Vicinus, and Chauncey (New York, 1989), p. 49.

17 Halperin, "Sex before Sexuality," P. 49.

18 Studies of intimacy that do not assume this "web of mutuality," either as the self-evident nature of intimacy or as a human value, are rare. Roland Barthes's *A Lover's Discourse: Fragments*, trans. Richard Howard (New York, 1978), and Niklas Luhmann's *Love as Passion*, trans. Jeremy Gaines and Doris L. Jones (Cambridge, Mass., 1986) both try, in very different ways, to describe analytically the production of intimacy. More typical is Anthony Giddens's attempt to theorize inti-

macy as "pure relationship" in *The Transformation of Intimacy: Sexuality, Love, and Eroticism in Modern Societies* (Cambridge, 1992). There, ironically, it is "the gays who are the pioneers" in separating the "pure relationship" of love from extraneous institutions and contexts such as marriage and reproduction.

19 Berlant and Warner, "What Does Queer Theory Teach Us about *X*?" *PMLA* 110 (May 1995): 345.

20 Bennett, quoted in Maureen Dowd, "Talk Is Cheap," *New York Times*, 26 Oct. 1995, p. A25.

21 Biddy Martin, "Extraordinary Homosexuals and the Fear of Being Ordinary," *differences* 6 (Summer–Fall 1994): 123; hereafter abbreviated "EH."

22 In some traditions of social theory, the process of world making as we describe it here is seen as common to all social actors. See, for example, Alfred Schutz's emphasis on the practices of typification and projects of action involved in ordinary knowledge of the social in *The Phenomenology of the Social World*, trans. George Walsh and Frederick Lehnert (Evanston, Ill., 1967). Yet in most contexts the social world is understood, not as constructed by reference to types or projects, but as instantiated whole in a form capable of reproducing itself. The family, the state, a neighborhood, the human species, or institutions such as school and church – such images of social being share an appearance of plenitude seldom approached in contexts of queer world making. However much the latter might resemble the process of world construction in ordinary contexts, queer worlds do not have the power to represent a taken-for-granted social existence.

23 See, for example, Alan Bray, "Homosexuality and the Signs of Male Friendship in Elizabethan England," *History Workshop* 29 (Spring 1990): 1–19; Laurie J. Shannon, "Emilia's Argument: Friendship and 'Human Title' in *The Two Noble Kinsmen*," *ELH* 64 (Fall 1997); and *Passions of the Renaissance*, trans. Arthur Goldhammer, ed. Roger Chartier, vol. 3 of *A History of Private Life*, ed. Philippe Ariès and Georges Duby (Cambridge, Mass., 1989).

24 On the relation between Foucault and Habermas, we take inspiration from Tom McCarthy, *Ideals and Illusions* (Cambridge, Mass., 1991), pp. 43–75.

25 Habermas, *The Structural Transformation of the Public Sphere: An Inquiry into a Category of Bourgeois Society*, trans. Thomas Burger and Frederick Lawrence (Cambridge, Mass., 1991), p. 49.

26 Ibid., p. 46.

27 On the centrality of semipublic spaces like tearooms, bathrooms, and bathhouses to gay male life, see Chauncey, *Gay New York*, and Lee Edelman, "Tearooms and Sympathy, or, Epistemology of the Water Closet," in *Nationalisms and Sexualities*, ed. Andrew Parker et al. (New York, 1992), pp. 263–84. The spaces of both gay and lesbian semipublic sexual practices are investigated in *Mapping Desire: Geographies of Sexualities*, ed. David Bell and Gill Valentine (New York, 1995).

28 Douglas Crimp, "How to Have Promiscuity in an Epidemic," *October*, no. 43 (Winter 1987): 253.

29 The notion of a demand for recognition has been recently advanced by a number of thinkers as a way of understanding multicultural politics. See, for example, Axel Honneth. *The Struggle for Recognition: The Moral Grammar of Social Conflicts*, trans. Joel Anderson (Cambridge, 1995), or *Multiculturalism: Examining the Politics of Recognition*, ed. Amy Gutmann (Princeton, N.J., 1994). We are suggesting that although queer politics does contest the terrain of recognition, it cannot be conceived as a politics of recognition *as opposed to* an issue of distributive justice; this is the distinction proposed in Nancy Fraser's "From Redistribution to Recognition? Dilemmas of Justice in a 'Postsocialist' Age," *New Left Review*, no. 212 (July–Aug. 1995): 68–93; rept. in her *Justice Interruptus: Critical Reflections on the "Postsocialist" Condition* (New York, 1997).

30 See Sedgwick, *Epistemology of the Closet*, and Yvonne Zipter, *Diamonds Are a Dyke's Best Friend: Reflections, Reminiscences, and Reports from the Field on the Lesbian National Pastime* (Ithaca, N.Y., 1988).

31 Such a politics is increasingly recommended within the gay movement. See, for example, Andrew Sullivan, *Same-Sex Marriage, Pro and Con* (New York, 1997); Michelangelo Signorile, *Life Outside: The Signorile Report on Gay Men, Sex, Drugs, Muscles, and the Passages of Life* (New York, 1997); Gabriel Rotello, *Sexual Ecology: AIDS and the Destiny of Gay Men* (New York, 1997); William N. Eskridge, Jr., *The Case for Same-Sex Marriage: From Sexual Liberty to Civilized Commitment* (New York, 1996): *Same-Sex Marriage: The Moral and Legal Debate*, ed. Robert M. Baird and Stuart E. Rosenbaum (Amherst, N.Y., 1996); and Mark Strasser, *Legally Wed: Same-Sex Marriage and the Constitution* (Ithaca, N.Y., 1997).

32 The phrase "the right to the city" is Henri Lefebvre's, from his *Le Droit à la ville* (Paris, 1968); trans. Eleonore Kofman and Elizabeth

Lebas, under the title "The Right to the City," *Writings on Cities* (Oxford, 1996), pp. 147–59. See also Manuel Castells, *The City and the Grassroots* (Berkeley, 1983).

33 On deadness as an affect and aspiration of normative social membership, see Berlant, "Live Sex Acts (Parental Advisory: Explicit Material)," *The Queen of America Goes to Washington City*, pp. 59–60, 79–81.

34 The classic argument against the redemptive sex pastoralism of normative sexual ideology is made in Bersani, "Is the Rectum a Grave?"; on redemptive visions more generally, see his *The Culture of Redemption* (Cambridge, Mass., 1990).

Part IV

Transnationalizing Sexualities

12

Dying to Tell
Sexuality and Suicide in Imperial Japan

Jennifer Robertson

[The Japanese] play up suicide as Americans play up crime and they have the same vicarious enjoyment of it. They choose to dwell on events of self-destruction instead of on destruction of others. . . . [Suicide] meets some need that cannot be filled by dwelling on other acts.

Benedict (1946) 1974, 167

To mention suicide and Japan in the same sentence is to bring to bear a set of stereotypes that continue to shape Western perceptions of non-Western cultures.

Wolfe 1990, xiii

Introduction: "Homosexual Elegy"

On February 17, 1935, the humor column of the *Asahi Shinbun*, a nationally distributed daily newspaper, was devoted to spoofing an attempted lesbian double suicide that had taken place about three weeks earlier. The "feminine" partner was Saijô Eriko, a 23-year-old "woman's role player" (*musumeyaku*) in a popular all-female revue, and the "masculine" partner, 27-year-old Masuda Yasumare, an affluent and zealous fan of the actress.[1] (Yasumare was a masculine name that she chose for herself; her parents had named her Fumiko.) One amateur songwriter contributed a ballad titled "Homosexual Elegy" (Dôseiai Hika), translated below.

Her love for a woman
Was greater than her parents' love for her,
And her older sister was cold-hearted.

She blushed and her heart danced when first
   they met.
But because they are two women together,
The fan's life is short.

Dashing from east to west,
Theirs was a passionate love
In a baneful world
Only to succumb to nihilism.
When will it fade, the anger in her heart?
For lesbians, the answer is suicide.
Because they are not man and woman,
The fan's grief is deep.

As the masculine partner, Masuda was singled out as aggressive and deviant and cast as the more pathetic of the two, owing to her "unladylike" appearance and behavior. She belonged to the urban upper class whose female constituents were expected to epitomize the Good Wife, Wise Mother gender role santioned by the Meiji Civil Code, based on the German model and operative

187

from 1898 to 1947. Moreover, as a "masculinized" (*danseika*) female, Masuda was one of the "problem women" associated with the so-called Woman Problem (*fujin mondai*), a term coined around 1900 as a euphemism for issues related to females' civil rights and the struggle of the New Woman (*atarashii onna*) for full citizenship and equality; including voting rights and autonomy (or agency) (see Koyama 1982, 1986; Sievers 1983; and Nolte and Hastings 1991). Obviously, not all New Women were lesbians, but all were castigated by conservative pundits as problematic and "masculine" females in contrast to the codified model of femaleness.

In addition to these verses, readers submitted different genres of satirical commentary on the incident, including ballad dramas and comic dialogues (Modan otona tôsei manga yose 1935). A pun-filled ballad titled "Suicide Journey of a Flapper and a Mannish Woman" (Datemusume dansô michiyuki) referred to the feminine partner as a "flapper" and a "revue girl" whose last dance (*dansu*) was with a female cross-dresser (*dansô*). The couple's suicide attempt was sensationalized widely in the mass media, including in *Fujin Kôron* (Women's Review) and *Chûô Kôron* (Central Review), two of the most prominent mainstream magazines in which articles addressing the intersection of sexuality, sexology, and modernity appeared on a regular basis.[2]

Three years before Masuda and Saijô tempted fate, the successful double suicide of a heterosexual couple, a Keio University student and the daughter of a wealthy (Christian) household, was similarly sensationalized, and elegies were published in the mass media memorializing the exquisite purity of their love – needless to say, the poems were not submitted to humor columns. The two had decided to commit suicide together by drowning (in a mountain lake southwest of Tokyo) after the woman's parents took steps to force her into an arranged marriage. Arranged marriage preparations motivated many women (and men) to commit, or attempt to commit, suicide regardless of their sexual orientation. A comparison of "Homosexual Elegy" with a poem on the heterosexual couple's suicide, titled "A Love Consummated in Heaven" (Tengoku ni musubareru koi),[3] suggests the different narrative treatment of the psychological circum-

stances and at least initial public reception of homosexual (*dôseiai*) and heterosexual (*iseiai*) double suicides. (The differential treatment was also apparent in the Japanese social-scientific literature on double suicide, as I discuss below.) The poem introduces the atmosphere defining the incident, followed by first the man's lament, then the woman's, and ends in a joint declaration by the couple.

> This evening's farewell, the moon also
> Dims with grief; in Sagami Bay
> The fire lures of fishermen are damp with
> tears.
> So fleeting is love in this life.
>
> With you the bride of another,
> How will I live? How can I live?
> I too will go. There where Mother is,
> There beside her,
> I will take your hand.
>
> God alone knows
> That our love has been pure.
> We die, and in [Heaven],
> I will be your bride.
>
> Soon, we will fade away happily:
> Spring flowers on Mount Sakata.[4]

It is quite clear that this poem was not intended as a spoof or critique of the practice of double suicide, and the incident inspired a popular movie of the same title (Seidensticker 1990, 35). The pristine love of the couple is celebrated, and all of nature, from the moon to the fishermen, weeps with grief tinged with bittersweet joy for their union in Heaven. The lesbian couple, on the other hand, and specifically the "masculine" partner, is portrayed as a casualty of, to use today's jargon, a dysfunctional family, represented by insufficient parental love and a cold-hearted older sister. Their attempted suicide is characterized as an act provoked by nihilistic anger, as opposed to visions of conjugal bliss in another life.

Masculinized Females as Social Disorder

Juxtaposed, these two cases underscore the common sense or dominant notion in Japan past and present about the dichotomous constructions of sex, gender, and sexuality. In modern

Dying to Tell

Japan, as in the United States, a person's gender is assigned, and heterosexuality assumed, at birth on the initial basis of genital type, but this is neither an immutable assignment nor an unproblematic assumption.[5] Although, in the case of Japan, the existence of two sexes and two genders is taken for granted, female gender (femininity) and male gender (masculinity) are not ultimately regarded as the exclusive province of female- and male-sexed bodies, respectively. Sex, gender, and sexuality may be popularly perceived as irreducibly joined, but this remains a situational, and not a permanently fixed, condition.

The introduction and coinage in the late nineteenth century of the new social scientific terms "homosexual" (*homosekushuaru*, also *dôseiai*) and "heterosexual" (*heterosekushuaru*, also *iseiai*) obfuscated actual sexual practices that were far more complex and boundary-blurring than the models of and for them. "Homosexual" and "heterosexual" were conveniently superimposed on the existing dominant dichotomous construction of sex, gender, and sexuality and stimulated a new, psychoanalytic exploration of their relationship. However, these terms, especially in their official Japanese translations of *dôseiai* and *iseiai*, were not used consistently and were qualified on the basis of extenuating circumstances and definition-stretching practices. For example, depending on the context, *dôseiai* was used to describe either a relationship that involved a same-gender, same-sex couple (e.g., two feminine females or two masculine males) or a same-sex, different-gender couple (e.g., a "butch–fem"-type female couple or a "butch–nellie"-type male couple). Masuda and Saijô clearly were constructed in the mass media as an *ome* or "butch–fem"-type couple – that is, a couple consisting of what was perceived as a masculine woman and a feminine woman.[6] Initially, they were ridiculed openly – as in the instance of the humor column – not for the simple fact of their unconventional relationship but for other reasons, including their public and publicized conduct, their celebrity and affluence, and, most important, their apparent eschewal of heterosexual marriage and motherhood.

Japanese pundits have been adept at selectively adapting for domestic and often dominant purposes institutions and terminologies that were first established and coined outside of Japan. One of the earliest such sources was China, and since the sixteenth century, Europe has served as an important antecedent. It was in the late nineteenth century that Euro-American loanwords and Japanese neologisms in the new field of sexology rapidly made their way into professional and lay parlance alike, evidenced not only in a wide range of printed media, including translations of foreign texts, but also by the many dictionaries devoted to introducing and defining such words. Among the loanwords and Japanese social scientific neologisms that were household words by the early 1900s were, in addition to homosexual and heterosexual, "fan" (*fuan*), "love letter" (*rabu retâ*), "lesbian" (*rezubian*), and *garuson* (garçon), in reference to a mannish woman. Other, somewhat less conspicuous loanwords referring to same-sex sexual practices were "sapphism" (*saffuo*), "tribadism" (*tsuribadeizumu*), and "uranism" (*uranizumu*), among others (Hayashi 1926; Ôsumi 1931).

Obviously, social and sexual practices labeled and categorized in the "feudal" Edo period (1603–1867) were undertaken and perceived differently in the succeeding Meiji period (1868–1911) and onward, when the country embarked on a course of modernization, industrialization, and selective Westernization. In fact, a growing if grudging acknowledgment, and new interpretation, of sexual relations between females prompted the introduction of the term *dôseiai* to distinguish their activities from those of males, although before long the neologism became a standard word for homosexuality in general, regardless of the sex of the individuals involved (Furukawa 1994, 115). Among the "indigenous" terms for lesbians and lesbianism are *aniki* (older brother), *dansô no reijin* (beautiful person [female] in men's clothes), *gôin* (joint licentiousness), *imoto* (younger sister), *join* (female licentiousness), *joshoku* (female eroticism), *kaiawase* (matching shells), *mesu* (female [animal]), *musumeyaku* (woman's role-player), *neko* (pussy[cat], similar in meaning to "fem"), *onêsama* (older sister), *osu* (male [animal]), *otokoyaku* (man's role-player), *shirojiro* (pure white, with etymological implications of falseness and feigned ignorance), *tachi* (an abbreviation of *tachiyaku*, or "lead-

189

ing man," similar in meaning to "butch"), and *tomogui* ("eat each other") (Sugahara 1971, 4–5; Robertson 1998b, 19–20). Japanese lesbian feminists today translate butch and fem as *tachi* and *neko*, and often use the loanwords *butchi* and *fuemu* (Minakawa 1987, 23). Another Japanese term for butch often encountered today is *onabe*, or shallow pot, a play on *okama*, or deep pot, a slang word for a feminine homosexual male (i.e., a "bottom"). In short, indigenous and foreign-derived words alike were and are historically and culturally specific to the Japanese discourse of sexuality.

The works of Sigmund Freud, Richard von Krafft-Ebing, Edward Carpenter, Havelock Ellis, Magnus Hirschfeld, Otto Weininger, and others were imported directly to Japan where they were translated, often by Japanese scholars who had studied abroad, and employed immediately in the identification of social problems and their analysis and resolution, exercises in which the state became increasingly invested (see Furukawa 1994; Frühstück 1996, 1998). For Japanese social scientists and critics, the loanwords "homosexual" and "heterosexual" helped to explain historical phenomena in a new way and to devise new categories of pathological phenomena, such as "female" psychology, neurasthenia, and fandom. Like all other methods of classification and analysis, these terms and their definitions both opened up new insights and closed off others.

For many critics, moral depravity accompanying the growth of the modernizing (or Westernizing) city seemed to be the only viable explanation for *ome* or butch–fem relationships among bourgeois urban women, at least until the advent of all-female revues, whose men's role players (*otokoyaku*) inspired new ideas to account for the increasingly visible masculinized female (Robertson 1992). Whereas the Japanese Good Wife, Wise Mother was praised by conservatives as the embodiment of social stability and cultural integrity, her alter ego, the Western Masculinized Female – and New Woman in general – was perceived as the embodiment of social instability. As Sharon Sievers has shown, national cultural identity in Imperial Japan was premised on a sexual division of symbolic labor, where crew-cut males in dark suits evinced the nation's modernization program, and kimono-clad females with chignons represented the longevity and continuity of Japanese tradition, itself a modern product. (In fact, short hair for women was made illegal in 1872, although this law was routinely flouted and rarely enforced [Sievers 1983, 14–15].)

The place of class in the overlapping discourses of sex, gender, and nationality cannot be underestimated. Some females, in the first half of the twentieth century at least, passed as men in order to secure employment as rickshaw drivers, construction supervisors and laborers, fishers, department store managers, grocers, and so on (Tomioka 1938, 103). "Passing" was associated unequivocally with sexual deviancy in the case of urban middle- and upper-class girls and women who, it was argued, wore masculine attire not to secure a livelihood but as an outward expression of their moral depravity. As privileged and educated – in short, bourgeois – girls and women, they were supposed to fulfill the state-sanctioned Good Wife, Wise Mother gender role. Consequently, those who resisted were vilified in journal and newspaper articles on mannish women and roundly critiqued in texts and treatises on "female" psychology (Sugita 1929, 1935; Sakabe 1934; Yasuda 1935; Ushijima 1943).

The modern(izing) state discouraged gender ambivalence and sexual confusion, which were associated with social disorder (Watanabe and Iwata 1989, 127), and the steady militarization of the society heightened the delineation of sex and gender. On the surface at least, it seems that the state got its way: a one-day survey of 1,180 people in Ginza, Tokyo's premier boulevard, conducted by culture critic Kon Wajirô in 1925, revealed that 67 percent of males wore Western-style outfits, while all but 1 percent of females appeared in Japanese dress (cited in Silverberg 1992, 38). Nevertheless, the 1 percent (and probably more) of females who did wear "modern" clothes rankled critics who believed that one dreadful effect of the select Westernization of social, political, and economic institutions was the apparent masculinization of *the* Japanese Woman and the neglect of Japanese customs (Tachibana 1890; Nogami 1920; see also Roden 1990; Silverberg 1991). Moreover, as Donald Roden reports, "the expression and representation of gender ambivalence captured the imagination of the literate urban populace" in the 1910s and 1920s, sparking a heated debate in the media between conservatives and liberals (Roden 1990, 43).

Whereas Roden claims that debates about gender and sexual ambivalence were directed at males and females equally, my extensive perusal of hundreds of contemporary newspaper, magazine, and journal articles leads me to different conclusions: females almost exclusively were singled out as the source of sexual deviance and social disorder and as the targets of acrimonious debates about the relationship among sex, gender, and sexuality.[7] If the sexes were converging, as some pundits argued (e.g., Nogami 1920), it was because the masculinization of females was compromising the masculinity of males, who appeared more feminine in contrast; that is, the markers distinguishing male from female, masculine from feminine were losing their polarity. The dialectical dynamics of sex and gender were experienced as a zero-sum game. Because the nation itself was personified in contrastive gendered terms, it would not do to have androgynous females (and males) wreaking symbolic havoc. Gendering New Japan, as the imperial nation was called, was an ongoing project that was constantly adapted to extenuating circumstances. As I have illustrated in an article on the culture of Japanese imperialism, when the martial spirit of the Japanese was at issue, the West and Euro-American cultural productions were cast as feminine and feminizing, in the "bad" sense of unmanly and emasculating. Contrarily, the nation was personified as feminine, in the "good" sense of traditional, when the superior cultural sensibility and artistic achievements of the Japanese were publicized (Robertson 1995). Mannish girls and women were therefore deemed un–Japanese.[8]

The press propagated a negative definition of the New Woman, describing her as "an indulgent and irresponsible young Japanese woman who used her overdeveloped sexuality to undermine the family and to manipulate others for her own selfish ends" (Sievers 1983, 175). Whether or not actual females claimed the label, the New Woman was a cultural construct – a trope of and for social disorder in the eyes of the state (Silverberg 1991; cf. Smith-Rosenberg 1985, 245–96). The "feminization of males" (*danshi no*

joseika) was a consequence of the "masculinization of females" (*joshi no danseika*), and while the former was worrisome, it was the latter condition at which critics directed their fearful anger (see Roden 1990). For conservatives, whose collective voice was amplified in the press, the masculinized female (and mannish lesbian) embodied social disorder – she eschewed conventional femininity, flouted the Good Wife, Wise Mother model of gender sanctioned by the civil code, and disrupted Japanese tradition.

Siting Double Suicide

Suicide is a key component of a Japanese national allegory, as Alan Wolfe argues in his exploration of the relation between the concept of national suicide and autobiographical writing (1990, 14–15, 215–17). "Problem women" who, in the 1930s, chose suicide were squarely situated within this allegory. For female couples to commit or attempt double suicide was tantamount to their making a public(ized) claim for sexual citizenship and subjectivity through an act of ultimate resolve valorized for centuries in literature and reified as a quintessentially Japanese expression of sincerity and purity of intention. The suicide and parasuicide attempts, notes, and letters of lesbians constituted an important voice in contested debates about the relationship between sexuality and nationality in a modern(izing) Japan. Responding to the preponderance of such attempts reported in the press, one prominent sexologist, Yasuda Tokutarô, wondered, "Why are there so many lesbian double suicides reported in the society column of the daily newspapers? One can only infer that females these days are monopolizing homosexuality" (Yasuda 1935, 150).[9] Moreover, lesbian suicide attempts effectively highlighted the connection between self/social destruction and self/social reconstruction.

Before examining lesbian (double) suicide attempts in greater detail, the category and subcategories of double suicide must be placed, briefly, in historical and anthropological context. The several Anglophone works that deal analytically with Japanese suicide avoid mention of homosexual double suicide even though this particular category figures, quite prominently in some cases, in the Japanese social scientific literature on suicide.[10] Likewise, whereas the long history in Japan of same-sex sexual relations between males (specifically Buddhist priests, samurai, and Kabuki actors) is well accounted for, if largely descriptively (e.g., Leupp 1995), until very recently, sexual relations between females in general have remained largely unrecognized, unacknowledged, invisible, and inaccessible in the postwar scholarly literature in and on Japan.[11]

However, unlike in the bridled Japanese and Anglophone scholarship of today, various types of lesbian practice, including double suicide, were widely and openly highlighted, discussed, sensationalized, and analyzed in the scholarly and popular media of early twentieth-century Japan. The involuted complexities of sexual practices and the instability of categories thereof, together with a perceived and internalized stigma on lesbian subjects, jointly have induced Japan scholars to disregard even what captivated the Japanese public and scholarly community at a given historical moment. Ironically, the space of sociosexual (in)difference is evident *not* in the popular cultural discourse shaping a specific period but in the academic scholarship on Japan. The persistence of the dominant sex-gender ideology that females are objects of male desire and not the subjects of their own desire, effectively inhibits both naming that desire and identifying multiple modes of female *and* male sexualities in Japan. Attending to the early debates on sexuality and conveying a sense of the contested rhetorical climate in which they took place are a necessary beginning for a more complete (and more responsible) anthropology of sexuality, gender ideology, and associated practices today.

Double suicide is often translated as "love suicide" in keeping with the nuances of the Japanese terms *shinjû* (hearts contained) and *jôshi* (love death). As Takie Lebra notes, the "theme of inseparability stands out not only in the motivation or goal, but also in the method [of suicide]" (Lebra 1976, 195–6). Whereas prior to the seventeenth century, *shinjû* denoted "milder pledges of love such as exchanging oaths or tearing out a fingernail," it has since meant both a double suicide by lovers and any suicide involving the death of more than one person, such as *oyako shinjû* (parent[mother]–child suicide), *fufu shinjû* (married-couple suicide), *shimai jôshi* (sisters suicide), and *muri shinjû* (forced or coerced suicide) (Keene 1976, 253; Lebra 1976, 195). Since the early twentieth century, *dôseiai shinjû* and *dôseiai jôshi* have been the most common terms used for homosexual double suicide.[12]

Double suicide qua love suicide is distinguished from *junshi*, or the death of one or more persons as martyrs for a cause or to prove their loyalty to a deceased superior. *Seppuku* refers to ritual disembowelment and was used historically (albeit limitedly) not only for voluntary death but also as a penalty reserved for members of the elite samurai class. This largely proscribed yet much glamorized practice, along with the military's legitimation of institutionalized suicide during World War II, have informed the creation of a naturalizing link between suicide and Japaneseness in the minds of Japanese and non-Japanese alike.[13] Most of the literature on suicide on which such "copulative conjunctions" (Wolfe 1990, xiii) are made, however, is based on literary portrayals of suicide taken at face value and on the generalization of the "logic" of war, military strategy, and wartime xenophobia. Finally, all of the types of suicide noted above are, in turn, distinguished from the "ordinary" solitary suicide referred to generically as *jisatsu* (killing of the self).

Lesbian Double Suicide: the Practice

In his book on Tokyo since the great earthquake of 1923, Edward Seidensticker makes note of the high incidence of suicides and double suicides in the 1930s and connects these acts to the "nervous and jumpy" national and international climate. The Japanese government withdrew from the League of Nations in 1933 after rejecting a demand for the Kwantung Army to withdraw from Manchuria, where they had established the puppet ("The Last Emperor") state of Manchukuo in 1932. Parts of Manchuria had been under Japanese control since 1906; the Kwantung Army plotted to occupy that country in 1931, which led to the outbreak of a full-scale war with China in 1937, a development marked as the "beginning" of

World War II for Japan. Seidensticker suggests that the Japanese government's withdrawal from the League provoked feelings of isolation and apprehension among ordinary citizens which, with the economic depression, exacerbated the despondency, illness, and family difficulties that motivate suicidal acts (Seidensticker 1990, 35, 37). The decision to withdraw from the League also appeared to have quickened the resolve of the Japanese state to pursue a zealous and aggressive course as an anticolonial colonizer. Okinawa, Taiwan, Korea, and Micronesia had already been under Japanese rule for decades by this time, and in 1940 the military state proclaimed the formation of a Greater East Asia Co-Prosperity Sphere, with Japan as the nucleus, as the key to the liberation of the rest of Asia and the Pacific from European and American imperialism.

One might productively interpret lesbian double suicides as both signifying and symptomatic of another dimension of national isolation and apprehension, not only on the part of the females involved but also on the part of culture critics obsessed with the figure of the masculinized female, and especially the mannish lesbian (cf. Smith-Rosenberg 1985, 245–96). Yasuda Tokutarô's rhetorical question noted above about females' monopoly on suicide and homosexuality points to this other dimension. Unlike the majority of his contemporaries, Yasuda was unusual in looking favorably upon Japanese lesbian practices as representing female and ultimately cultural emancipation, in that mutual cooperation between females and males would insure that neither would be reduced to servile status (Yasuda 1935, 152; see Roden 1990, 54). His interest, in his words, in the "widespread phenomenon of same-sex love among females" was provoked by press coverage of Masuda Yasumare and Saijô Eriko's attempted double suicide, to which I now return (Yasuda 1935, 146).

What were the circumstances of the female couple's attempted "love suicide"? The media focused mostly on Masuda, whose masculine appearance was perceived not only as a marker of aggression but also as subversive and dangerous. Saijô, in contrast, was treated more leniently for the likely reason that her comparatively feminine, if problematically "modern,"

appearance was perceived as less threatening than Masuda's blatantly maverick aspect. It is also likely that as a revue girl (rebyû gâru), a vocation associated with wanton women, Saijô's conduct was already marked as beyond the pale (cf. Asagawa 1921; Ozaki 1986). Masuda, though, was singled out as proof of the "recent, disturbing increase in the 1920s and 1930s in lesbian affairs between upper class girls and women," affairs that presumably "in the past, were associated with lower class status" (Kore mo jidaisô ka 1935).

Saijô, the feminine partner, published an autobiographical account of the suicide attempt two months after the event in *Fujin Kôron*.[14] I recount most of Saijô's story to provide readers with a sense of its tone and colorful characterizations. Saijô begins by recalling how she first met Masuda backstage after a show in May 1934 at an Osaka theater: the actress was stepping out of her bath wrapped in a towel when Masuda approached and struck up a short conversation. The cross-dressed fan's physical beauty, especially her straight, white teeth, round "Lloyd" spectacles, and "Eton crop" (a short hairstyle) impressed Saijô, and the visits became a daily affair. Come autumn, after half a year of constant contact at different venues in eastern and western Japan, Saijô reports that Masuda's letters to her grew intensely passionate; the handsome fan would write such things as, "I can't bear to be apart from you for even a moment." "Although these letters could be interpreted as expressions of lesbian love," the actress explains, "I viewed them as the confessions of a sincere fan" (Saijô 1935, 170).

Saijô's admission of the fuzzy boundary between fandom and lesbian desire played into the dominant perception of female fans of the all-female revue as pathological and socially problematic. "Fan" was often used as a euphemism for lesbian (or for a girl or woman with lesbian proclivities), and fandom was identified as a serious illness marked by an inability to distinguish between sexual fantasies (themselves problematic phenomena in women) and actual lesbian practices (Hogosha wa kokoro seyo 1935; Kore mo jidaisô ka 1935; Robertson 1998b, chaps. 4, 5).

In her account, Saijô refers to herself by her first name, Eriko, and characterizes herself as a gullible actress – as highly impressionable and thus "naturally inclined" to become absorbed into Masuda's charismatic aura. She waxes nostalgic about their walks, hand in hand, along the bay: "For those who didn't know us, we probably looked just like [heterosexual] lovers" (Saijô 1935, 171). The couple traveled widely in the Kansai area, and New Year's Day 1935 found them together in bed in a Kyoto hotel. Saijô claims that by that point she had wearied of the intensity of their relationship and wanted to return to Tokyo, where she had a photo shoot scheduled for the first week of January. But whenever she mentioned the word "return home" (*kaeru*), Masuda became deathly pale and stern, and Saijô would lose her courage to insist.

They spent the next several days on a ferryboat to Beppu on the island of Kyushu – a "gateway to death," as Saijô describes the experience (Saijô 1935, 172). Travel provided this and other same-sex couples an opportunity for extraordinary activities and practices that could not be practically sustained in the more mundane realm of everyday life (cf. Ôhara 1973, 244–5). A couple would often travel for several days to a particular suicide site, enjoying each other's intimate company to an unprecedented degree. It was on the trip to Beppu that Masuda first recited to Saijô the sad story about her sterile, dysfunctional, and fatherless family. Masuda's father had separated from his wife shortly after his brokerage firm went bankrupt and set up housekeeping with a mistress with whom he eventually produced six children (Dansô no reijô no kashutsu jiken 1935).

Much to her apparent chagrin, Saijô's chronic appendicitis flared up shortly after they arrived in Beppu, and the actress was hospitalized for three days. The doctor encouraged her to return to Kyoto by train, which was faster and more comfortable than a ferryboat. Back in Kyoto, the tension between the two women escalated, although they "fought silently." When Saijô insisted on returning to Tokyo, Masuda threatened to commit suicide.

Meanwhile, Masuda's mother had hired a private investigator to locate the itinerant couple, at which point the press, alerted and ready to exploit the splashy story, filed daily reports on the couple's saga, noting that their real "suicide journey" (*michiyuki*) began on the night of January 23 (Dansô no reijin 1935) when, after a "storybook-like" chase involving trains and cars, the couple was apprehended in Nagoya by the private investigator. Masuda's mother and sister blamed the revue actress for the love-struck fan's transgressions, including the theft of money and stock certificates out of which their travels were paid and fancy gifts bought. Masuda was sent back to her mother's house in Osaka, and Saijô retired to her parents' home in Tokyo.

That was not the end of their relationship, however. Late at night on January 27, Saijô received a telephone call from Masuda, who had fled to Tokyo the previous night and was staying at a city hotel. (The press described her escape as a matter of "re-entering the fickle world of sexual desire" [Dansô no reijin 1935].) Saijô went immediately to the hotel, her father in tow. Feeling sorry for her "special friend," Saijô, "at [her] father's urging," prepared to spend the night with Masuda, who recounted her escape.[15] Apparently Masuda had fooled her mother into thinking that she was asleep in bed by stuffing cushions under her blankets. Breaking open the terrace door, she climbed over a tall wall to freedom, cutting her hands badly in the process. Borrowing money from a neighbor, she made her way to Tokyo, vowing never to return to her family from hell. Before leaving, she left a note on her bed instructing her mother and sister not to pursue her – advice they ignored.

Masuda and Saijô conspired to move secretly to another city hotel in order to avoid the droves of pesky newspaper reporters who had tracked the handsome fan to Tokyo. At around midnight, they pushed their beds together and "went to sleep." No mention is made in Saijô's account of a double suicide pact or the ingestion of tranquilizers and sleeping pills. The narrative as a whole is crafted defensively, with the actress represented as a victim of her fan's willful passion. Acknowledging the widespread press coverage of the attempted double suicide, Saijô allows the reader to supply the missing details and notes simply that she was shocked to find herself awake in the morning.[16] Looking at Masuda's "peacefully sleeping form," Saijô read the masculine female's suicide note, which was reprinted in her *Fujin Kôron* article as follows:

Eriko [Saijô's first name].

Even though it seems as though we've known each other forever, ours was a very short-lived relationship. But you more than anyone have left a deep and everlasting impression on my heart. What this means not even I know for sure. What I do know is that I loved you (*suki deshita*) unconditionally. Now as I approach the end of my life, I can say that I never thought that I would become so profoundly indebted to you. In any case, thank you; thank you very very much. I don't know how I can thank you enough. No, it's not merely thanks; I will die indebted (*osewa*) to you and that is a happy thought. My incorrigibly selfish ways have caused you much grief. Please forgive me. Once I had made the decision to die, I cried and cried thinking of all that we've shared and how much I would miss you. And I realized how sad it is to die alone. To be perfectly honest, I wanted you to die with me. But I am aware of your circumstances, and you always assumed a rational stance in contrast to my emotional one. So, I'll go alone after all. Goodbye.

Yasumare [Masuda's self-selected first name]
January 28, evening (Saijô 1935, 178)

Masuda's letter was likely edited by Saijô or someone else in a way that exonerated the revue actress from any complicity in a double suicide attempt. Saijô also appears as rational to Masuda's emotional. Perhaps this was a strategy designed to minimize the incident's damage to her acting and modeling career? In any case, shortly after her double suicide attempt, Saijô left the Shôchiku Revue to pursue a career in film. She all but disappeared from that revue's fan magazines, where she had been featured regularly before the incident.

In concluding her tale of love and suicide, Saijô reveals that she was able to deal influentially with the Masuda family lawyer, requesting that her masculine partner be allowed the unprecedented step of forming a branch household (*bunke*) and living independently, as if Masuda were, in fact, male. And when Masuda's estranged father visited his daughter in the hospital, Saijô criticized him for being an absentee father. Saijô herself vowed henceforth to keep a close watch on Masuda's behavior. Self-interest aside, Saijô's and others' accounts (see Tani 1935) of the couple's ordeal in prominent mainstream magazines effectively parried the earlier disparaging treatment of their double suicide attempt in the humor column of the *Asahi Shinbun*.

Lesbian Suicide: The Theories

Some Japanese scholars and clinicians have regarded the double or love suicide in general as a peculiarly Japanese practice informed by the Buddhist belief in reincarnation and the spirit of martyrdom in the Way of the Samurai (*bushidô*). Others have disagreed, providing historical evidence of the practice elsewhere in Asia and in Europe (Ôhara 1965, 186–8). Still others have linked lesbian practices, including double suicide, to the more recent, insidious effects and social ramifications of Westernization.

Quite a few Japanese psychiatrists and social critics of the time assumed that females' "natural" passivity and hormone-provoked melancholia made them susceptible to neurasthenia (*shinkeishitsu*), which in turn occasioned a pessimism expressed in the form of homosexuality. Their melancholia was exacerbated, in turn, by homosexual practices that made them further susceptible to suicidal impulses (Tamura 1913; Shôjo no hi no sei mondai 1934; Fukushima [1935] 1984, 562). Pundits and critics also asserted that all-female revues on the subject of romantic love and its ephemerality, together with certain European films, such as the antipatriarchal *Mädchen in Uniform*, first shown in Japan in 1933 to sold-out audiences, valorized both lesbianism and suicide (Shôjo no hi no sei mondai 1934, 9).[17]

"Homosexual Elegy," translated at the beginning of this article, parrots the various explanations for lesbian sexuality and double suicide popularized in the press. For example, a 1935 newspaper article on the recent fad among girls and women of dressing as men included an interview with a physician, Saitô Shigeyoshi, who cited the theories of bisexuality proposed by Weininger in explaining female transvestism in Japan (Kore mo jidaisô ka 1935). Weininger's formulations contributed to the "psychiatric style of reasoning" that emerged in the late nineteenth century in America, Europe, and Japan (see also Davidson 1987). Today, his *Sex and Character* (Weininger 1906) is recognized as racism (anti-Semitism) and misogyny in the guise of scientific analysis.

On the one hand, Weininger, like many of his Japanese counterparts, linked female anatomy to such negative characteristics as chronic immaturity, emotionalism, and a preoccupation with sexuality. On the other hand, he alluded to the transformative effects of gender, suggesting that "homosexuality in a woman is an outcome of her masculinity and presupposes a higher degree of development." He also claimed that "the degree of emancipation and the proportion of maleness in the composition of a woman are practically identical," an observation that was shared by his Japanese readers and counterparts (quoted in Garber 1992, 225; cf. Sugita 1929).

In the newspaper article introducing Weininger, Saitô, the Japanese physician, acknowledges a long history of lesbian sexuality and mannish women in Japan but claims that the permanent condition was "more prevalent in the West," implying, as did others, that an incorrigibly masculinized female (in this case, a mannish lesbian) was thoroughly Westernized and therefore un-Japanese (Kore mo jidaisô ka 1935). Doubtless Saitô was also familiar with the work of Weininger's contemporary, Krafft-Ebing, whose *Psychopathia Sexualis* (1886) was standard reading for Japanese psychologists and sexologists. It was even appropriated as a template for *Hentai seiyokuron* (The theory of deviant sexual desire), coauthored by Habuto Eiji and Sawada Junjirô in 1915 (and reprinted eighteen times over the next decade) (Roden 1990, 45). Krafft-Ebing created a new "medico-sexual category, the Mannish Lesbian," in which he linked "women's rejection of traditional gender roles and their demands for social and economic equality to cross-dressing" (Smith-Rosenberg 1985, 272). What was a universal, if new, "medico-sexual" category for Krafft-Ebing was for Saitô a consequence of Westernization.

Masuda and Saijô were referred to disparagingly in the newspaper article as practicing a "deviant homosexual love" (*hentai dôseiai*). "Deviant," because same-sex, different-gender (e.g., butch–fem) relationships were regarded as abnormal, while same-sex, same-gender relationships, or passionate friendships among outwardly feminine couples, were and are regarded as part of a normal and self-limited stage in the female life cycle (Tamura 1913; Mochizuki 1959; Robertson 1989, 1992). Lesbianism, broadly defined as eroticized intimate relations between two females, was not itself an issue so long as it was self-limited and unmarked by the presence of a masculine partner. Provided sexual practices neither interfered with nor challenged the legitimacy of the twinned institutions of marriage and household, nor competed with heterosexist conventions in the public sphere, Japanese society accommodated (and still does) a diversity of sexual behaviors. To wit, social reproduction need not be synonymous with human reproduction (as in the case of adopted sons-cum-sons-in-law, a common strategy of household succession in Japan in the absence of a male heir), but the former must not be compromised by a politicized sexual identity that interferes with the latter.

Following their European and American counterparts, such as Ellis, some Japanese psychologists active in the early twentieth century drew a distinction between "real" or "permanent" (*shin*), and "provisional" or "transient" (*kari*) homosexuality in females. Unlike their European and American counterparts, they sometimes referred to the former condition as Western and the latter as Japanese. Whereas the former condition, embodied by the masculine woman, was deemed incurable, the latter condition, embodied by the feminine woman, supposedly resolved itself quickly once she married. Parents were reassured that "provisional lesbianism" was not the result of mental insufficiency or illness but rather should be perceived as a short-lived "spiritual hedonism" (*seishinteki kyôraku*) (Kore mo jidaisô ka 1935).

The works of the European and American sexologists named earlier "quickly captured the imagination of Japan's earliest students of psychology," amateurs and professionals alike (Roden 1990, 45; see also Hirschfeld 1935, 7–39). The application of these theories by Japanese scholars and clinicians was informed by an apparent contradiction: a subscription (sometimes on the level of academic lip service) to the universality of Euro-American psychological theories and a belief in Japanese uniqueness, which in turn was typified by a lack of both awareness and theoretical engagement with everyday sexual and gendered practices in Japan (Yoshimoto 1989, 25; see also Yasuda 1935). In this connection, the German sexologist and advocate of homosexual rights, Hirschfeld, reported that during his lecture tour of Japan in 1931 he encountered among his Japanese colleagues, many of whom had studied in Europe, an apparently "widespread ignorance of intersexual male and female types off the stage, and especially of the extent of homosexuality in general" (Hirschfeld 1935, 30).[18] He recorded the following illuminating account of his conversation with Miyake Kôichi, a professor of psychiatry:

> Professor Myaki [sic] . . . said when we first met: "Tell me, my dear Hirschfeld, how is it that one hears so much about homosexuality in Germany, England and Italy and nothing of it among us?"
>
> I answered: "That, my dear colleague, is because it is permitted by you and forbidden by us."
>
> "But it seems to be more prevalent in Europe," he continued. "In all my long practice I have never yet seen one single case."
>
> "I can scarcely believe that the phenomenon is rarer among you than among us," I replied, "but I shall be able to tell you better in a few weeks when I have done some investigating among specialists in the subject."
>
> I gave him my opinion shortly before I left, after I had had a chance to find out, from letters written me by Japanese and particularly from people who came to see me after my presence was known, that every form of homosexuality, in tendency as well as in expression, is precisely the same in Japan as in Europe. My old observation was again completely confirmed: the *individual sex type* is a far more important factor than the *racial type*. (Hirschfeld 1935, 30–1)

Despite a cultural history of same-sex sexual practices among males, not to mention the sensationalized coverage of homosexual love and its social implications, some of Hirschfeld's Japanese colleagues claimed to be unaware of the history and present situation of same-sex or homosexual practices in Japan – or they at least

maintained a public posture of ignorance – as is obvious from their published works. In an article on deviant sexual desire, for example, Ôsumi Tamezô focuses on homosexual practices *outside* of Japan, providing Japanese translations for English, French, and Latin terms (Ôsumi 1931). Roden suggests that Japanese sexologists writing for an educated but popular audience were obliged to grace their articles and books "with just enough pseudo-scientific information and prescriptive advice to limit government censorship without dampening the curiosity of their middle-class audience" (Roden 1990, 46). The use of Euro-American examples to illustrate allegedly universal (homo)sexual practices may have been, in part, a strategy to avoid official censure, which was considerable by the late 1930s. But what could account for earlier self-censoring practices?

Sabine Frühstück (1998) suggests that some German- and Austrian-trained sexologists, like Miyake, willfully dismissed those sexual practices which they felt would compromise Japan's international image as a "civilized" country, while others used new sexological categories to isolate and rebuke all types of New Women, and particularly the Mannish Lesbian. It might also be the case that Miyake and others like him simply did not recognize certain historical same-sex sexual practices in Japan as categorizable under the new sexological terminology adopted from continental *Sexualwissenschaft*.

Finally, not a few Japanese scholars claimed that their knowledge of Japanese sexual practices was gained indirectly, if not fortuitously, through the study of, for instance, German. Thus, even the progressive psychologist Yasuda Tokutarô, in a 1935 article on historical perspectives on homosexuality, credits his knowledge about Japanese (male) homosexual practices to German texts lent to him by the late Iwaya Sazanami, who, Yasuda claims, first "informed the world about the history of homosexual love in Japan" despite being publicly acknowledged only as a specialist in children's folklore (Yasuda 1935, 147).

Although Hirschfeld focused only on male homosexuals in his investigation (for the obvious reason of accessibility), he did discuss the topic of homosexuality with the leaders of the Japanese women's movement, including Ishimoto

Shizue and Ishikawa Fusae (Hirschfeld 1935, 12). If patriarchal critics regarded the New Woman and the Mannish Lesbian as examples of the worst ramifications of Westernization, Japanese feminists (and some male reformers) used "the West" in part as a rhetorical device to create a new discursive space in which to critique the patriarchal family-state system, sexual double standards, and political repression (see Sievers 1983). The West, in short, was deployed as a foil in contradictory ways with respect to the sex-gender system: by traditionalists and state ideologues as subversive and detrimental to the androcentric status quo, and by their adversaries as a type of counterdiscourse (whether registered in writing or in sartorial expression) through which to express what was otherwise politically difficult or even impossible and ideologically inconceivable. The evocation of the West was not about the specific countries and cultural areas grouped under that rubric but about contemporary social transformations in Japan; it was invoked as a discursive space for a range of adversarial cultural and political critiques (cf. Chen 1992, 688).

Dying to Tell

Suicides and attempted suicides generated a variety of narratives representing a spectrum of genres, including social scientific analyses, suicide notes, letters, wills, autobiographical accounts, magazine and newspaper articles, poems, dramatic chants, and so forth.[19] Masuda's suicide note to Saijô apparently was one of five she had prepared for members of her family, a close friend, and for the public (Nakano 1935, 164). Only the note to Saijô was made public, although it may have been doctored, as I have suggested. Significantly, the suicide and parasuicide narratives written by Japanese lesbians and published in the print media contradict the various dominant theories about both suicide and lesbianism such as those ventured by Komine Shigeyuki, a prominent sexologist. Two years after the Masuda-Saijô case, another lesbian suicide incident was featured in *Fujin Kôron*.

Briefly, the case involved a love triangle among three women (in their mid-twenties), one of whom was "malelike" and attractive. The

mannish lesbian and the younger of the feminine partners regarded themselves as "spiritually, a perfect married couple." The latter's parents took it upon themselves to arrange a marriage for their maverick daughter, a unilateral act that occasioned the couple's decision to commit double suicide. However, the masculine partner failed to show up at the appointed time and place, and in frustration and disappointment the younger, feminine woman drank poison alone. Her solo attempt at self-destruction failed, for she vomited the poison and survived. She then received a suicide letter from her partner that read, "Goodbye forever. I pray for your happiness. Please forgive my selfishness. My last wish is for you to return to the countryside and get married. 'D', forever beneath the ocean" (quoted in Ôhara 1973, 244–5).

"D," it turned out, had committed suicide with the older feminine partner. Enraged, the younger woman slashed her wrists but again did not succumb to her injuries. Her own suicide note (to her deceased lover) read: "I believed in you completely. . . . I can't let you sink alone into the frigid waters of the ocean." This incident was referred to in the newspapers as *shinjû sannin kurabu*, or "the suicide triangle club" (quoted in Ôhara 1973, 245).

Komine draws distinctions between heterosexual and homosexual double suicides. He claims that whereas a heterosexual couple's double suicide was premeditated and often provoked by their inability to marry, a homosexual couple's decision to commit double suicide was spontaneous and carried out for apparently "trivial" reasons. While Komine does not discount entirely the possibility of sexual desire between females, he does insist that "empathy and commiseration" (*dôjô*), and not frustrated sexual desire (sometimes in the guise of resistance or opposition to an arranged marriage), was the catalyst for lesbian double suicides (Komine 1985, 197–8).

The various narratives generated by the Masuda-Saijô attempted double suicide and others demonstrate that the women's decision to die was neither spontaneous nor motivated by petty concerns. Moreover, although a couple's frustration at the futility of maintaining their romantic relationship was underplayed, there seemed to be a public consensus about both the "causes" of lesbianism and the suicidal effects of melancholia, loneliness, a dysfunctional family, and/or parental efforts to force a woman into an arranged marriage – causes that were hardly trivial. This was a consensus that coexisted with attempts in the press to trivialize female couples and their tribulations.

Komine tabulates the numbers of female same-sex double suicides (or love suicides [*joshi dôseijôshi*]) reported in the daily press between 1925 and 1935, acknowledging that the actual figures were probably much higher (Komine 1985, 232).[20] The haphazard quality of suicide statistics in the early twentieth century, in terms of collection, categorization, and interpretation, make it difficult to determine accurately both the number of suicides and which of the double suicides actually involved lesbian couples. Clearly, a proportion significant enough to attract critical attention were committed by lesbians. Komine himself suggests this in his study of homosexual double suicide, although he warns that not only are double suicides committed by female couples hidden in statistics for heterosexual suicides, such as in cases involving a man and two women, but that not all female double suicides involved lesbians, as in cases involving siblings (1985, 176). According to Komine's data, there were 342 incidents of "female same-sex double (or 'love') suicide" (totaling *at least* twice as many females) reported in the press between 1925 and 1935. His category *joshi dôseijôshi* is ambiguous; given the subject of his book, Komine most probably means "lesbian double suicides," although it is not entirely clear whether he adjusted his statistics for the possibility that some of these suicides (or attempts) involved female siblings or love triangles (e.g., two women in love with the same man).

More than half of these acts occurred during the "nervous and jumpy" years of 1932 and 1935. Komine claims that confirmed lesbian double suicides amounted to about 31 percent of all suicides (1985, 174–5). The average age of the women at the time of their resolve to die was between twenty and twenty-five years. The vast majority of lesbian double suicides involved factory workers, waitresses, and nurses, in that order; prostitutes constituted the majority of female actors in the case of heterosexual double

suicides (178, 174). Komine reports that whereas the actors in heterosexual double suicides tended to be of different social statuses and classes – for example, a male novelist and a female prostitute, a wealthy housewife and a chauffeur – the vast majority (more than 80 percent) of partners in homosexual double suicides were of the same social status, class, or occupation (175).

As I have noted, one reason the Masuda-Saijô attempted suicide generated so much interest and attention was their social prominence: Masuda's upper-class status and Saijô's celebrity status. However, their statuses alone did not clinch their notoriety, for the newspapers and magazines of those and earlier years were filled with accounts and analyses of female homosexual practices and their consequences. Widespread press and magazine coverage facilitated the public intertextuality of lesbian practices and acts (both successful and unsuccessful) of double suicide, although the majority of actors in these incidents were but names and statistics without faces. Doubtless a widely publicized lesbian double suicide attempt on June 12, 1934, was familiar to Masuda and Saijô, just as the partners in that attempt were inspired to die after reading an article about a female student from Tokyo who jumped into the crater of Mount Mihara on the offshore island of Ôshima. The student "took along a friend to attest to the act and inform the world of it" (Seidensticker 1990, 36).[21]

The June 1934 case concerned a love triangle involving a so-called masculinized female (age 23) to whom two feminine females (ages 18 and 23) were attracted. All three worked at a Tokyo coffee shop where the cross-dressed, mannish partner was a manager and the other two waitresses.[22] The many newspaper articles on the case quoted the women as recognizing that in society at present a bona fide love relationship was only possible as a couple and not as a threesome. Acting on that realization, the "kind-hearted" older feminine partner decided to withdraw from the group to simplify matters. One morning in early June she left suicide notes at her sister's and brother's homes and proceeded to a park were she swallowed an overdose of tranquilizers. She later recovered (Dôseiai no onna san'nin shinjû 1934; Dôseiai no seisan 1934).

Meanwhile, the couple had resolved, independent of the third woman, to die together, and set out on a two-day suicide journey to the offshore island of Ôshima where they planned to throw themselves into the volcanic crater. The masculine partner had chosen this particular mode of death inspired by the aforementioned student's suicide there the previous year (apparently most suicidal females elected either to drown themselves or to swallow tranquilizers or sleeping pills [Komine 1985, 183]). In an autobiographical account summarized below, she recounts how the pair spent the night at an inn, "thinking only of death," and how she held her partner close to her as they stood in the thick fog that hugged the coast (Sakuma 1934, 82).

Alerted by the siblings of the estranged partner, the press trailed the couple to Ôshima, updating readers on their whereabouts and activities. The masculine partner was described as sporting short hair and dressed like a man's role player in the all-female revue theater. She cut a dapper figure in her white knickerbockers, red jacket, two-tone shoes, and panama hat. The feminine partner wore a Western-style dress, short socks, and straw thongs. Guided by the island's residents, who had easily spotted the two climbers, the paparazzi caught up with the couple shortly after the proprietor of a summit teahouse, sensing their melancholia, had grabbed them as they headed toward the crater. One of the several photographs of the couple published in the press shows them standing together, heads bowed in dejection at having failed in their mission. Only after their capture did they learn from reporters of their estranged partner's attempted suicide two days earlier (Watashi wa koi no shorisha 1934).

Two months later, Sakuma Hideka, the masculine partner, published an autobiographical account of the incident in *Fujin Gahô* (Women's Illustrated News), a mainstream women's magazine. A staff reporter prefaced the account by claiming that "everyone has experienced homosexual love at least once, but no one has written about its mysteries until now" (Sakuma 1934, 82). After asking for everyone's forgiveness, Sakuma dismisses categorically the rumors that were spread like wildfire through the press of her "father's alcoholism," her grandmother's "geisha past," her impoverished, dysfunctional family, and her alleged "biological maleness" and "ability to impregnate women." She also criticizes sharply the newspapers' role in trivializing her ordeal by inviting readers to submit satirical songs about the incident (as the press did a year later in the Masuda-Saijô case) (82).

It is clear that Sakuma understood the link between economic autonomy and self-representation and subjectivity, for she makes the radical argument that, provided they could support themselves, why shouldn't two women (much less three) in love with each other be able to live together in the same way that heterosexual couples can and do? "I don't hate men, I've just felt closer to women since graduating from girl's high school," she declares.[23] As for her so-called masculine appearance, Sakuma explains that "although I may have assumed a man's role, I am neither physically nor mentally malelike." And she stresses that by wearing trousers, she is not impersonating males but rather wearing what is most convenient and comfortable given the demands of her managerial job. Sakuma closes her narrative by lamenting her loneliness (83). Meanwhile, notoriety was good for business, and large, expensive ads for the coffee shop where Sakuma worked began appearing in the press (e.g., "Yaesuen" 1934, 3).

More vividly than the actress Saijô's autobiographical account, the manager Sakuma's account suggests an apparently ironic connection between the resolve to commit suicide and the resolve to challenge on some level a family-state system that rendered women docile and subservient. Historically in Japan, suicide or attempted suicide was recognized, and to some extent valorized, as an empowering act that illuminated the purity and sincerity of one's position and intentions. A suicide letter corroborated these virtues by documenting one's motives. In other words, suicide was a culturally intelligible act that turned a private condition into a public matter.

Obviously, attempted (or unsuccessful) suicides have more direct political capital, for, as in this case, the women live to tell in greater complexity about the circumstances informing their resolve to die, and they live to act on their resolve and to encourage action on the sometimes radical vision articulated in their suicide notes. Saijô, for example, claims in her account that she was able to deal influentially with the Masuda family lawyer regarding the unprecedented establishment of a branch household for her masculine partner. And Sakuma's article about her attempted double suicide introduces to mainstream audiences ideas and arguments about self-representation and the connection between economics and gender ideology that were (and still are) quite radical.

Lesbian suicide and parasuicide letters and accounts collectively constituted another voice, whether explicitly controversial or defensive, or both, in heated public debates about the articulation of sexuality, gender ideology, cultural identity, and (inter)national image. Moreover, like acts and attempts of suicide themselves, these texts, including those that doubled as love letters, were both private explorations and public proclamations – "public" because the art of writing letters consists in making one's views known to a correspondent, whether that person be a lover, parent, sibling, or anonymous reader. Suicide notes in this sense were an extension of, and not a substitute for, lesbian practices. Largely as a result of the cultural intelligibility of suicide in Japan, stories of suicide and attempted suicide seem to have served as an effective way to get controversial ideas into print and integrated with the popular discourse of sexuality. I have reviewed the circumstances of only several of the hundreds of cases of lesbian suicide and parasuicide reported, yet these several cases generated a significant number of newspaper and magazine articles and analyses, whether sympathetic or hostile.

Clearly there is more to suicide than simply the "cultural appeal [in Japan] of masochistic behavior" (Lebra 1976, 200). Lesbian double suicides and attempted suicides were predicated on – and both used and criticized as a trope for – a revolt against the normalizing functions of tradition (qua the Good Wife, Wise Mother) as sanctioned by the civil code. Double suicide itself was a mode of death eulogized and allegorized in literature, particularly since the late seventeenth century, but when linked with women's unconventional sexual affinities and practices, lesbian suicide and parasuicide accounts drew attention to the symbolic death of the traditional Japanese Woman and the emergence on the public stage of new and more complex female actors.

Notes

All translations from Japanese to English are mine except when noted otherwise. Japanese names and authors published in Japanese are presented with the family name followed by the given name.

1   Saijô was a member of the all-female Shôchiku Revue founded in Tokyo in 1928, fifteen years after its arch rival, the Takarazuka Revue, was established in the city of Takarazuka near Osaka. The Shôchiku Revue later established an Osaka branch, and the Takarazuka Revue opened a Tokyo theater in 1934. For more information about all-female revues, see Robertson 1998b.

2   By the 1930s, the population of 65 million purchased 10 million copies of daily newspapers, and the number of registered magazines and journals was 11,118. Print culture was available to all classes of consumers (Silverberg 1993, 123–4), and the Masuda-Saijô "love story" was circulated countrywide. Fiction writers also capitalized on the erotics of lesbian double suicide. Tanizaki Junichirô's serial novel *Manji* (originally published in 1928–30) focused on an obsessive triangulated relationship involving a married woman, a bisexual femme fatale, and the former's husband, and their attempted double (actually triple) suicide (Tanizaki 1995). My article reports on actual cases of lesbian suicide and not on its representation in fiction.

3   The poem was subtitled "The Philosophy of Suicide" (Shinjû no fuirosofui).

4   The Japanese text is in Ôhara 1965, 210. Verses two and three appear in English in Seidensticker 1990, 35, and I have deferred to his translation, with one exception: I changed the original *tengoku* in the third verse from "paradise" to "Heaven," to underscore the woman's Christian faith. The remaining verses are my translations.

5   While this method of gender assignment is most typical of but not limited to Anglo-Americans, the lack of specific information on the assignment and assumption of "female" or "male" gender among non-Anglos makes me reluctant to generalize for all Americans. To generalize a "Japanese" notion of gender admittedly is problematic, given the various ethnic groups comprised in that superficially "homogenous" society, although "Japanese" arguably is a more inclusive signifier than is "American." In this connection, I should also note that although I am familiar with much of the scholarly literature on the relationship among cross-dressing, sexuality,

Jennifer Robertson

and gender ideology and cite some relevant sources, I have kept comparisons to a minimum, partly for reasons of space, but also because I am in a better position to provide otherwise inaccessible and stereotype-bending information about Japan to scholars that augments the larger – mostly Eurocentric – literature.

6 *Ome* or *ome no kankei* ("male–female relations") were the expressions often used to identify lesbian couples. *Ome* is an abbreviation of *osu* and *mesu*, terms reserved to distinguish between male and female animals. They become pejorative when used to label humans, as in this case.

7 Roden does acknowledge in passing that it was the New Woman and not her male counterpart who "triggered" the debates about the relationship among sex, gender, and sexuality, although his essay as a whole suggests that unconventional males and females were criticized to equal degrees in the media (Roden 1990, 43). The one exception to the overwhelming focus on the "woman problem" and its "problem women" was a Manichaean debate in the mass media about the place of Kabuki *onnagata*, or woman's role player, in modern Japan: was he a naturalized and necessary tradition or unnatural, perverse, and anachronistic? As I discuss elsewhere (Robertson 1998b, 56–9), "tradition" won over charges of perversity. Briefly, the valorization of tradition as part of the spiritual mobilization of the people during the wartime period (roughly 1931–45) included the promotion of Kabuki as a classical Japanese theater arts form, a status that insured its central place in the cultural archive of the Japanese Empire as a living symbol of Japanese cultural superiority.

8 I discuss at length the feminine and maternal personification of Japanese tradition in Robertson (1998a).

9 Parasuicide refers both to the attempted suicide and the "suicide gesture," usually in reference to individuals who are not actually trying to kill themselves (Buhrich and Loke 1988).

10 Among the major Anglophone works dealing with Japanese suicide are Benedict (1946) 1974; Seward 1968; De Vos 1973; Lebra 1976; and Pinguet (1984) 1993. Japanese works in which homosexual double-suicide figures quite prominently include Yamana 1931; Ôhara 1965, 1973; Tatai and Katô 1974; and Komine 1985.

11 Recent works addressing lesbian practices include the "lesbian special issues" of the "alternative" journals *Bessatsu Takarajima* (1987) and *Imago* (1991); Yoshitake 1986; Roden 1990; and

Furukawa 1994. Privately circulated newsletters (printed by women's/feminist/lesbian groups, for example) are another source of information about Japanese female sexualities.

12 For additional terminology, see Ôhara 1965, 186–7. I am not interested here in reviewing the sociopsychological literature on suicide or in exploring the sociology of suicide per se. If the suicide actors were female, the prefix *joshi* or *josei* (female) preceded the generic (androcentric) expression. Another term used, albeit inconsistently, for ostensibly nonlesbian female same-sex suicide is *onna dôshi shinjû* (double suicide of like-minded girls/women).

13 This "naturalized link" was symbolized vividly by the brief deployment at the end of the war of kamikaze and suicide submarines (*raiden*) and by the mass suicides of Japanese civilians in Saipan (1944) and Okinawa (1945).

14 The details of this incident are drawn from Saijô's account unless otherwise indicated (Saijô 1935).

15 Saijô claims that her father urged her to stay close to Masuda, whom they felt was suicidal, until someone from the Masuda family could come and fetch her. Although Saijô's parents are rarely mentioned in the various accounts of the double suicide attempt, when they are, it is always in a kindly light.

16 If the story filed by a veteran reporter for the *Fujin Kôron* and friend of Saijô's father is accurate, then the actress's account is disingenuous. Apparently, the reporter interviewed a woozy Saijô after she had swallowed an overdose of sleeping pills. Following her back to her room, he found Masuda in a near coma and called for medical help (Nakano 1935).

17 *Mädchen in Uniform* was released in Germany in 1931. It was based on the play *Gestern und Heute* (Yesterday and today) by Christa Winsloe, who also republished it as a novel, *Das Mädchen Manuela* (The child Manuela). B. Ruby Rich interprets *Mädchen*, which takes place in a girls' boarding school, as a "film about sexual repression in the name of social harmony, about the absent patriarchy and its forms of presence, about bonds between women which represent attraction instead of repulsion, and about the release of powers that can accompany the identification of a lesbian sexuality. . . . [The film] offers a particularly clear example of the interplay between personal and collective politics – and the revolutionary potential inherent in the conjunction of the two" (Rich 1983, 44). A Japanese critic writing in 1935 declared that "the film [*Mädchen*] offers clues as to why

female sexual perversion (*josei no seiteki tôsaku*) is increasing" (Shôjo no hi no sei mondai 1934).

18 The lectures in Japan during the months of March and April were part of Hirschfeld's world tour that year. While in Japan, Hirschfeld lectured at scholarly conferences on the "status of sex pathology," one of which was the first sexological lecture at the University of Tokyo, and gave public lectures in Tokyo and Osaka sponsored by the *Asahi Shinbun*, a leading newspaper. Not only were all his lectures translated directly into Japanese, but Japanese abstracts of his talks were distributed to the audiences, and "long illustrated reports" of the University of Tokyo lecture were published in several medical journals (Hirschfeld 1935, 10–11). Hirschfeld's explorations and theories about homosexuality continue to be employed by Japanese social scientists, sexologists, and critics writing today (e.g., Watanabe 1990). The "stage" in question is both the all-male Kabuki theater, and specifically the *onnagata*, or "woman's role Player," and the all-female revue theater's *otokoyaku*, or "man's role player."

19 There are several Japanese books specifically on the subject of wills and suicide notes, including Yamana 1931 and Ôhara 1963.

20 Komine also tabulates the number of male homosexual double suicides (Komine 1985, 202–32). I have focused exclusively on lesbian double suicides.

21 Seidensticker writes that this particular suicide triggered a vogue for jumping into the same crater, "and by the end of 1933, about a thousand people had plunged into it, the majority of whom were male" (Seidensticker 1990, 36). Suicide and attempted suicide venues seem to follow trends, and in the 1930s a disproportionate number of people attempted to end their lives by hurling themselves into Mount Mihara.

22 The press noted that the fact that all three lived with seventeen other women in an attached dorm increased the likelihood of their lesbianism – an argument premised on a type of demographic determinism (Dôseiai no onna san'nin shihjû 1934).

23 Girls' schools and the all-female revues, along with their (unmarried) teachers and members, were singled out by sexologists and social critics as the sites and agents of homosexuality among females (Tamura 1913; Sugita 1935; Ushijima 1943; cf. Smith-Rosenberg 1985, 266, and Vicinus 1989). Thus, the critics' perception of the deleterious effects of the German film *Mädchen in Uniform* on girls and women.

References

Asagawa Kiyo. 1921. "Joyû to onnayakusha" (Actresses and women's role players). *Josei Nihonjin* 4:112–13.

Benedict, Ruth. (1946) 1974. *The Chrysanthemum and the Sword*. New York: Meridian.

Bessatsu Takarajima. 1987. Onna o aisuru onnatachi no monogatari (A tale of women who love women). Special issue, no. 64.

Buhrich, Neil, and Carlson Loke. 1988. "Homosexuality, Suicide, and Parasuicide in Australia." *Journal of Homosexuality* 15(1–2):113–29.

Chen, Xiaomei. 1992. "Occidentalism as Counter discourse: 'He Shang' in Post-Mao China." *Critical Inquiry* 18(4):686–712.

"Dansô no reijin" (Cross-dressed beauty). 1935. *Asahi Shinbun*, January 28, Osaka morning edition, p. 11.

"Dansô no reijô no kashutsu jiken" (The cross-dressed beauty's escape from her home). 1935. *Fujô Shinbun*, February 3, p. 3.

Davidson, Arnold. 1987. "Sex and the Emergence of Sexuality." *Critical Inquiry* 14(1):16–48.

De Vos, George. 1973. *Socialization for Achievement: Essays on the Cultural Psychology of the Japanese*. Berkeley: University of California Press.

"Dôseiai no onna san'nin shinjû" (The suicide of three lesbians). 1934. *Asahi Shinbun*, June 13, Tokyo evening edition, p. 2.

"Dôseiai no seisan" (Settlement of differences among lesbians). 1934. *Asahi Shinbun*, June 13, Tokyo morning edition, p. 11.

Frühstück, Sabine. 1996. "Die Politik der Sexualwissenschaft: Zur Produktion und Popularisierung sexologischen Wissens in Japan, 1900–1941" (The politics of sexology: The creation and popularization of the science of sexuality in Japan, 1900–1941). Ph.D. dissertation, University of Vienna, Institute for Japanese Studies.

———. 1998. "Then Science Took Over: Sex, Leisure and Medicine at the Beginning of the Twentieth Century." In *The Culture of Japan as Seen through Its Leisure*, ed. Sepp Linhart and Sabine Frühstück, 59–79. Albany, N.Y.: SUNY Press.

Fukushima Shirô. (1935) 1984. *Fujinkai sanjûgonen* (Thirty-five years of Women's World). Tokyo: Fuji Shuppansha.

Furukawa, Makoto. 1994. "The Changing Nature of Sexuality: The Three Codes Framing Homosexuality in Modern Japan," trans. Alice Lockyer. *U.S.–Japan Women's Journal* (English supp.) 7:98–127.

Garber, Marjorie. 1992. *Vested Interests: Cross-Dressing and Cultural Anxiety*. New York: Harper Perennial.

Habuto Eiji and Sawada Junjirô. 1925. Hentai seiyokuron (Treatise on deviant sexual desire). 18th ed. Tokyo: Sun'yôdô.

Hagiwara Hiroyoshi. 1954. *Takarazuka kageki 40nenshi* (Forty-year history of the Takarazuka Revue). Takarazuka: Takarazuka Kagekidan Shuppanbu.

Hayashi Misao. 1926. "Danjo to shiyû" (Man and woman, male and female). *Nihon Hyôron* 3:319–25.

Hirschfeld, Magnus. 1935. *Women East and West: Impressions of a Sex Expert.* London: William Heinemann (Medical Books) Ltd.

"Hogosha wa kokoro seyo – byôteki na fuan buri" (Guardians, beware of pathological fandom). 1935. *Asahi Shinbun*, January 31, Tokyo morning edition, p. 8.

Imago. 1991. *Tokushû: Rezubian* (Special issue: Lesbian), vol. 2, no. 8.

Keene, Donald. 1976. *World within Walls: Japanese Literature of the Pre-Modern Era, 1600–1867.* New York: Grove Press.

Komine Shigeyuki. 1985. *Dôseiai to dôseiai shinjû no kenkyû* (A study of homosexuality and homosexual double suicide). Tokyo: Komine Kenkyûjo.

"Kore mo jidaisô ka" (Is this too the shape of the times?). 1935. *Asahi Shinbun*, January 30, Tokyo morning edition, p. 7.

Koyama Shizuko. 1982. Kindaiteki joseikan to shite no rôsaikenbo shisô (The Good Wife, Wise Mother as a modern idea about women). *Joseigaku Nenpô* 3:1–8.

——. 1986. Rôsaikenboshugi no reimei (The dawn of Good Wife, Wise Motherism). *Joseigaku Nenpô* 7:11–20.

Krafft-Ebing, Richard von. 1886. *Psychopathia Sexualis.* Stuttgart: F. Enke.

Lebra, Takie. 1976. *Japanese Patterns of Behavior.* Honolulu: University of Hawaii Press.

Leupp, Gary. 1995. *Male Colors: The Construction of Homosexuality in Tokugawa Japan (1603–1868).* Berkeley: University of California Press.

Minakawa Yôko. 1987. "Tachi: Kono kodokuna ikimono" (Butch: This lonely creature). *Bessatsu Takarajima* 64:18–23.

Mochizuki, Mamor[u]. 1959. "Cultural Aspects of Japanese Girl's Opera." In *Japanese Popular Culture*, ed. Hidetoshi Kato, 165–74. Tokyo: Charles E. Tuttle.

"Modan otona tôsei manga yose" (The latest variety comics for modern adults). 1935. *Asahi Shinbun*, February 17, Osaka evening edition, p. 4.

Nakano Eitarô. 1935. "Dansô no reijin to Saijô Eriko: Dôseiaishi misui no ikisatsu" (The cross-dressed beauty and Saijô Eriko: The circumstances of their double suicide attempt). *Fujin Kôron* 3:161–7.

Nogami Toshio. 1920. "Gendai seikatsu to danjo ryôsei no sekkin" (The association of modern life and androgyny). *Kaizô* 2(4):185–204.

Nolte, Sharon, and Sally Hastings. 1991. "The Meiji State's Policy towards Women, 1890–1910." In *Recreating Japanese Women, 1600–1945*, ed. Gail Bernstein, 151–74. Berkeley: University of California Press.

Ôhara, Kenshirô. 1963. *Isho no kenkyû* (A study of wills and suicide notes). Tokyo: Nihon Bungeisha.

——. 1965. *Nihon no jisatsu: Kodoku to fuan no kaimei* (Suicide in Japan: An interpretation of loneliness and anxiety). Tokyo: Seishin Shobô.

——. 1973. *Shinjûkô: Ai to shi no byôri* (A treatise on double suicide: The pathology of love and death). Tokyo: Rogosu Sensho.

Ozaki Hirotsugu. 1986. "Sannin no joyû o chûshin ni" (Focusing on three actresses). In *Meiji no joyûten* (Exhibition of Meiji-period actresses), ed. Hakubutsukan, Meiji-mura, 10–16. Nagoya: Nagoya Tetsudô.

Ôsumi Tamezô. 1931. "Hentai seiyoku" (Deviant sexual desire). *Hanzai Kagaku* 4:75–83.

Pinguet, Maruice. (1984) 1993. *Voluntary Death in Japan*, trans. Rosemary Morris. Cambridge: Polity Press.

Rich, B. Ruby. 1983. "Maedchen in Uniform: From Repressive Tolerance to Erotic Liberation." *Jump Cut* 24/25:44–50.

Robertson, Jennifer. 1989. "Gender-Bending in Paradise: Doing 'Female' and 'Male' in Japan." *Genders* 5:48–69.

——. 1992. "The Politics of Androgyny in Japan: Sexuality and Subversion in the Theater and Beyond." *American Ethnologist* 19(3):419–42.

——. 1995. "Mon Japan: Theater as a Technology of Japanese Imperialism." *American Ethnologist* 22(4):970–96.

——. 1998a. "It Takes a Village: Internationalization and Nostalgia in Postwar Japan." In *Mirror of Modernity: Invented Traditions in Modern Japan*, ed. Stephen Vlastos, 209–39. Berkeley: University of California Press.

——. 1998b. *Takarazuka: Sexual Politics and Popular Culture in Modern Japan.* Berkeley: University of California Press.

Roden, Donald. 1990. "Taishô Culture and the Problem of Gender Ambivalence." In *Culture and Identity: Japanese Intellectuals during the Interwar Years*, ed. J. Thomas Rimer, 37–55. Princeton, N.J.: Princeton University Press.

Saijô Eriko. 1935. "Dansô no reijin Masuda Fumiko no shi o erabu made" (Up until Masuda Fumiko, the cross-dressed beauty, chose death). *Fujin Kôron* 3: 168–78.

Sakabe Kengi. 1934. *Fujin no shinri to futoku no kisô*

(The foundation of women's psychology and morality). Tokyo: Hokubunkan.

Sakuma Hideka. 1934. "Jôshi o ketsui suru made" (Until [we] resolved to commit love suicide). *Fujin Gahô* 8:82–83.

Seidensticker, Edward. 1990. *Tokyo Rising: The City since the Great Earthquake.* New York: Knopf.

Seward, Jack. 1968. *Hara-Kiri: Japanese Ritual Suicide.* Rutland, Vt.: Charles E. Tuttle.

"Shôjo no hi no sei mondai: Haru no mezame" (Girls' day and the problem of sex: Spring awakening). 1934. *Asahi Shinbun*, June 18, Tokyo morning edition, p. 9.

Sievers, Sharon. 1983. *Flowers in Salt: The Beginnings of Feminist Consciousness in Modern Japan.* Stanford, Calif: Stanford University Press.

Silverberg, Miriam. 1991. "The Modern Girl as Militant." In *Recreating Japanese Women, 1600–1945*, ed. Gail Bernstein, 239–66. Berkeley: University of California Press.

——. 1992. "Constructing the Japanese Ethnography of Modernity." *Journal of Asian Studies* 51(1):30–54.

——. 1993. "Constructing a New Cultural History of Prewar Japan." In *Japan in the World*, ed. Masao Miyoshi and H. D. Harootunian, 115–43. Durham, N.C.: Duke University Press.

Smith-Rosenberg, Carroll. 1985. *Disorderly Conduct: Visions of Gender in Victorian America.* New York and Oxford: Oxford University Press.

Sugahara Tsûsai. 1971. *Dôseiai* (Homosexuality). Tokyo: San'aku Tsuihô Kyôkai.

Sugita Naoki. 1929. "Seihonnô ni hisomu sangyaku-sei" (Sado-masochistic qualities latent within sexual instinct). *Kaizô* 4:70–80.

——. 1935. "Shôjo kageki netsu no shinden" (All-female revue; a sanctuary for feverish infatuation). *Fujin Kôron* 4:274–8.

Tachibana Kaoru. 1890. "Fûzoku hôtan" (Forsaking custom). *Fûzoku Gahô* 14:15–16.

Tatai Kichinosuke and Katô Masa'aki. 1974. *Nihon no jisatsu o kangaeru* (A consideration of suicide in Japan). Tokyo: Igaku Shoin.

Tamura Toshiko. 1913. "Dôseiai no koi" (Same-sex love). *Chûô Kôron* 1:165–8.

Tani Kazue. 1935. "'Dansô no reijin' no jogakusei jidai o kataru" (On the girls' school years of the "cross-dressed beauty"). *Hanashi* 4:250–6.

Tanizaki Junichirô. 1995. *Quicksand*, trans. Howard Hibbett. New York: Vintage Books.

Tomioka Naomichi. 1938. "Dansei josô to josei dansô" (Males in women's clothing, females in men's clothing). *Kaizô* 10:98–105.

Ushijima Yoshitomo. 1943. *Joshi no shinri* (Female psychology). Tokyo: Ganshodô.

Vicinus, Martha. 1989. "Distance and Desire: English Boarding School Friendships, 1870–1920." In *Hidden from History: Reclaiming the Gay and Lesbian Past*, ed. Martin Duberman, Martha Vicinus, and George Chauncey, 212–29. New York: New American Library.

Watanabe Tsuneo. 1990. "Serufu rabu: Otoko to iu yokuatsu kara nogareru tame ni" (Self love: In order to escape the oppression of maleness). *Bessatsu Takarajima* 107:80–90.

Watanabe Tsuneo and Jun'ichi Iwata. 1989. *The Love of the Samurai: A Thousand Years of Japanese Homosexuality*, trans. D. R. Roberts. London: GMP.

"Watashi wa koi no shorisha" (I am a survivor of love). 1934. *Asahi Shinbun*, June 14, Tokyo morning edition, p. 11.

Weininger, Otto. 1906. *Sex and Character* New York: G. P. Putnam's Sons.

Winsloe, Christa. 1975. *The Child Manuela.* New York: Arno Press.

Wolfe, Alan. 1990. *Suicidal Narrative in Modern Japan.* Princeton, N.J.: Princeton University Press.

"Yaesuen" (Advertisement for the Yaesuen coffee shop). 1934. *Asahi Shinbun*, June 24, Tokyo morning edition, p. 3.

Yamana Shôtarô. 1931. *Nihon jisatsu jôshiki* (A history of suicide and love suicide in Japan). Tokyo: Ôdôkan Shoten.

Yasuda Tokutarô. 1935. "Dôseiai no rekishikan" (Historical perspectives on homosexuality). *Chûô Kôron* 3:146–52.

Yoshimoto, Mitsuhiro. 1989. "The Postmodern and Mass Images in Japan." *Public Culture* 1(2):8–25.

Yoshitake Teruko. 1986. *Nyonin Yoshiya Nobuko* (The woman Yoshiya Nobuko). Tokyo: Bunshun Bunko.

13

Nostalgia, Desire, Diaspora
South Asian Sexualities in Motion

Gayatri Gopinath

In *Funny Boy*, Sri Lankan–Canadian writer Shyam Selvadurai's 1994 novel in six stories, the upper-middle-class Sri Lankan Tamil narrator traces a seven-year period of his childhood and adolescence that preceded the Tamil–Sinhalese riots of 1983 and his family's subsequent migration to Canada.[1] This experience of migration is the grounds upon which the narrative unfolds; the novel is structured in terms of remembrance, with the narrator, Arjie, recalling a "remembered innocence of childhood . . . now colored in the hues of a twilight sky" (5). Such a phrase, coming early on in the novel, seems to signal that the text can be comfortably contained within a conventional genre of exile literature, one that evokes from the vantage point of exile an idyllic, coherent, preexilic past shattered by war and dislocation. Similarly, the novel's parallel narrative of Arjie's sexual awakening initially locates the text within an established genre of "coming out" stories, where the protagonist grows into an awareness of his "true," homosexual identity. Yet while *Funny Boy* references the familiar narratives of exile and "coming out," it reworks the conventions of these genres as well as the very notions of exile and sexual subjectivity. In this article, I will read Selvadurai's novel alongside two other South Asian diasporic narratives of sexuality[2] – Indian–Canadian filmmaker Deepa Mehta's 1996 film *Fire* and a scene from the popular 1993 Hindi film *Hum aapke hain koun* – to interrogate

our understandings of nostalgia, "home," and desire in a transnational frame.

Nonheteronormative Sexuality and the Nation

An important body of feminist criticism has emerged in the past decade that examines the complicity of nationalist discourses with gender hierarchies and demonstrates how the figure of the woman in nationalist discourse acts as a primary marker of an essential, inviolable communal identity or tradition.[3] Anne McClintock and others have argued that a gender critique of nationalism reveals the ways in which the nation is construed in terms of familial and domestic metaphors, where "the woman" is enshrined as both the symbolic center and boundary marker of the nation as "home" and "family."[4] Deniz Kandiyoti, following Benedict Anderson, further explicates this conflation of "woman," "home," "family," and "nation" by pointing out that "nationalism describes its object using either the vocabulary of kinship (motherland, *patria*) or home (*heimat*) in order to denote something to which one is 'naturally' tied . . . The association of women with the private domain reinforces the merging of the nation/community with the selfless mother/devout wife."[5] The nation (as many critics have asserted) is a nostalgic construction, one that evokes an archaic past and authentic communal identity to assert and legitimize its project of modernization.[6] Women's bodies, then, become crucial to nationalist discourse in that they serve not only as the site of biological reproduction of national collectivities,[7] but as the very embodiment of this nostalgically evoked communal past and tradition.

If recent work on gender and nationalism has enabled us to see the ways in which women become emblematic of the concept of "home" as nation, as feminized domestic space, and as a site of pure and sacred spirituality,[8] much less attention has been paid to the production and deployment of nonheteronormative, or "queer," sexuality within colonial, anticolonial nationalist, and contemporary nationalist discourses.[9] Given the increasing recognition that sexuality historically secures the grounds for the production of gendered colonial and bourgeois nationalist subjects,[10] it is somewhat surprising that some recent attempts to consider the imbrication of discourses of nationalism and women's sexuality still presume the heterosexuality of the female subject.[11] By failing to examine the existence and working of alterior sexualities within dominant nationalisms, such analyses leave intact hegemonic constructions of the nation as essentially heterosexual. Whereas "the woman" carries a powerful symbolic freight in the constitution of the nation, a nonheteronormative subject necessarily has a very different relation to the constructions of "home" and "family" upon which nationalism depends.

Within the familial and domestic space of the nation as imagined community, nonheteronormative sexuality is either criminalized,[12] or disavowed and elided; it is seen both as a threat to national integrity and as perpetually outside the boundaries of nation, home, and family. As M. Jacqui Alexander states in an important essay discussing the 1991 Sexual Offenses and Domestic Violence Act in the Bahamas:

> The nation has always been conceived in heterosexuality, since biology and reproduction are at the heart of its impulse. The citizenship machinery is also located here, in the sense that the prerequisites of good citizenship and loyalty to the nation are simultaneously sexualized and hierarchized into a class of good, loyal, reproducing heterosexual citizens, and a subordinated, marginalized class of non-citizens.[13]

Alexander's comment is instructive because it makes explicit the fact that the nation demands heterosexuality as a prerequisite of "good citizenship," since it depends on the family as a reproductive unit through which the stability of gender roles and hierarchies is preserved. Heterosexuality, in other words, is fundamental to the way in which the nation imagines itself. Alexander goes on to elaborate upon the interplay of nation and nostalgia as understood by other critics by noting that the archaic past produced within nationalism is one of "sexual 'purity' . . . imagined within a geography (and a home) that only heterosexuals inhabit" (85). If women under nationalism, as I noted earlier, are figured as "inherently atavistic – the conservative repository of the national archaic"[14] – nonheteronormative subjects, conversely, are written out of national memory entirely. Thus, within a nationalist logic where women embody the past and that past is figured as heterosexual, the nonheterosexual female in particular is multiply excluded from the terms of national belonging and "good citizenship."

It is true that, as Alexander points out, the charge of sexual "impurity" or "perversion" is not leveled solely against lesbians and gay men but extends to all those who cannot be located within the strict confines of middle-class heteronormativity: prostitutes, those who are HIV infected, and working-class and single women, for instance.[15] "Perversion" then, may most clearly mark the figure of the homosexual, but it is certainly not contained by or exclusive to it. Nevertheless, it is worth specifying the different forms of violence and disciplinary mechanisms that mark the various bodies within this "marginalized class of noncitizens," as each subject position engenders its own highly particular forms of resistance to, and at times accommodation with, nationalist logic. This essay, then, is a small part of a much larger project that begins the work of identifying the ways in which those who occupy one "perverse" subject position – a "queer South Asian diasporic subjectivity" – reimagine and reconstitute their particular, fraught relation to multiple national sites, and as such, demand a rethinking of the very notions of "home" and nostalgia.[16] My contention here is that a consideration of a queer diasporic subject prompts a different understanding of the mechanisms by which national belonging is internalized in the constitution of "modern" national subjects. More specifically, I want to point to some of the ways in which queer diasporic subjects – especially those who are women – negotiate their elision from national memory, as well as their function both as threat to home/family/nation and as perenially outside the confines of these entities. I stress queer female subjectivity in the diaspora because dominant diasporic articulations of community and identity intersect with patriarchal nationalist logic in its figuring of "woman" as bearer and guardian of communal tradition.[17]

Queer Sexuality and the Diaspora

As Anannya Bhattacharjee has shown in her work on domestic violence within Indian immigrant communities in the United States, immigrant women are positioned by an immigrant male bourgeoisie as repositories of an essential "Indianness." Thus, any form of transgression on the part of women may result in their literal and symbolic exclusion from the multiple "homes" that they as immigrant women inhabit: the patriarchal, heterosexual household, the extended "family" made up of an immigrant community, and the national spaces of both India and the United States.[18] Within the patriarchal logic of an Indian immigrant bourgeoisie, then, a "nonheterosexual Indian woman" occupies a space of impossibility, in that not only is she excluded from these various "home" spaces but, quite literally, she simply cannot be imagined.

The impossibility of imagining such a subject within dominant diasporic and nationalist logics has been made all too apparent by the ongoing battle in New York City between the South Asian Lesbian and Gay Association (SALGA) and a group of Indian immigrant businessmen known as the Federation of Indian Associations (FIA) over SALGA's inclusion in the FIA-sponsored annual India Day Parade. The parade, which ostensibly celebrates India's independence day, makes explicit the ways in which an Indian immigrant male bourgeoisie (embodied by the FIA) reconstitutes anticolonial and contemporary nationalist discourses of

communal belonging by positioning "India" as Hindu, patriarchal, middle-class, and free of homosexuals. In 1995, the FIA denied both SALGA and Sakhi for South Asian Women (an anti-domestic violence women's group) the right to march in the parade on the grounds that both groups were, in essence, "antinational." In 1996, however, the FIA allowed Sakhi to participate while continuing to deny SALGA the right to march. The FIA, as self-styled arbiter of communal and national belonging, thus deemed it appropriate for women to march as "Indian women" – even, perhaps, as "feminist Indian women" – but it could not envision women marching as "Indian queers" or "Indian lesbians"; clearly the probability that lesbians may indeed exist within Sakhi was not allowed for by the FIA.

I mention the controversy surrounding the India Day Parade here because it highlights how hegemonic nationalist discourses, reproduced in the diaspora, position "woman" and "lesbian" as mutually exclusive categories to be disciplined in different ways. Within patriarchal diasporic logic, the "lesbian" can only exist outside the "home" (as household, community, and nation of origin), whereas the "woman" can only exist within it. Indeed the "lesbian" is seen as "foreign," as a product of "being too long in the West," and she is therefore annexed to the "host" nation where she may be further elided – particularly if undocumented – as a nonwhite immigrant within both a mainstream (white) lesbian and gay movement and the larger body of the nation-state.

Given the illegibility and unrepresentability of a nonheteronormative (female) subject within patriarchal and heterosexual configurations of both nation and diaspora, the project of locating a queer South Asian diasporic subject – and a queer female subject in particular – may begin to challenge the dominance of such configurations. To this end, I want to suggest here some reading strategies by which to render queer subjects intelligible and to mark the presence of what Alexander terms an "insurgent sexuality" that works within and against hegemonic nationalist and diasporic logic. Indeed, the representations of nonheteronormative desire within the three texts that I consider here call for an alternative set of reading practices, a "queer diasporic" reading that juxtaposes wildly disparate texts and traces the cross-pollination between the various sites of nonnormative desires that emerge within them. On the one hand, such a reading renders intelligible the particularities of same-sex desiring relations within spaces of homosociality and presumed heterosexuality, and, on the other hand, it deliberately wrenches particular scenes and moments out of context and extends them further than they would want to go. It would exploit the tension in the texts between the staging of female homoerotic desire as simply a supplement to a totalizing heterosexuality and the potentiality that they raise for a different logic and organization of female homoerotic desire. A queer diasporic reading and viewing practice conceptualizes a viewing public as located within multiple diasporic sites and the text itself as accruing multiple, sometimes contradictory meanings within these various locations. In other words, I place these texts within a framework of a queer South Asian diaspora, one that allows us to conceive of both the text and the viewer in motion; scenes and moments in popular culture that in their "originary" locations simply reiterate conventional nationalist and gender ideologies may, in a South Asian diasporic context, become the very foundation of queer culture. Furthermore, as I hope to demonstrate, queer diasporic readings within such a framework allow us to read nonheteronormative arrangements within rigidly heterosexual structures and to recognize the ways in which queer articulations of desire and pleasure both draw from and infiltrate popular culture. While queer reading practices alone cannot prevent the violences of heteronormativity, they do intervene in formulations of "home" and diaspora that – in their elision and disavowal of the particularities of queer subjectivities – inevitably reproduce the heteronormative family as central to national identity.

This framework of a queer South Asian diaspora produces linkages between the various representations of queer desire and cultural practices among South Asians in migrancy. It enables us to consider formations of queer desire and pleasure in radically particular sites, as well as in the context of movement and migration. Reading these texts as both constituting and constituted by a queer South Asian diaspora also resituates the conventions by which homosexuality has traditionally been encoded in an Anglo-American context. Queer sexualities as articulated by the texts I consider here reference familiar tropes and signifiers of Anglo-American homosexuality – such as the coming-out narrative and its attendant markers, secrecy and disclosure, as well as gender inversion and cross-dressing – while investing them with radically different and distinct significations. It is through a particular deployment of South Asian popular culture that this defamiliarization of conventional markers of homosexuality takes place, and that alternative strategies for signifying nonheteronormative desire are subsequently produced. These alternative strategies suggest a mode of reading and "seeing" same-sex eroticism that challenges modern epistemologies of visibility, revelation, and sexual subjectivity. Indeed, the notion of a queer South Asian diaspora can be seen as a conceptual apparatus that poses a critique of modernity and its various narratives of progress and development.[19] A queer South Asian diasporic geography of desire and pleasure stages this critique on multiple levels: it rewrites colonial constructions of Asian sexualities as anterior, premodern, and in need of Western political development – constructions that are recirculated by contemporary gay and lesbian transnational politics[20] – while simultaneously interrogating different South Asian nationalist narratives that imagine and consolidate the nation in terms of organic heterosexuality.

Pigs Can't Fly

"Pigs Can't Fly," the first story in Selvadurai's novel *Funny Boy*, lays out the complex system of prohibition, punishment, and compulsion that governs and structures gender differentiation. The story tells of the childhood game Bride–Bride that Arjie and his girl cousins play in the house of their grandparents, and which entails an elaborate performance of a marriage ceremony. For Arjie, dressing up as the bride – complete with shimmering white sari, flowers, and jewelry – is a way of accessing a particular mode of hyperbolic femininity embodied both by his mother and by the popular Sri Lankan female film stars of the day. The pleasure Arjie takes in this activity causes intense embarrassment and consternation on the part of the adults, who decree that henceforth Arjie is to play with the boys. Arjie's eventual traumatic banishment from the world of the girls and his forced entry into proper gender identification are figured in terms of geography and spacialization, of leaving one carefully inscribed space of gender play and entering another of gender conformity: Arjie is compelled to leave the inner section of the compound inhabited by the girls and enter the outer area where the boys congregate. Similarly, he is barred from watching his mother dress in her room, which throughout his childhood has been the site of his most intense spectatorial pleasure.[21]

The game itself, brilliantly titled Bride–Bride (not Bride–Groom), offers a reconfiguration of the contractual obligations of heterosexuality and gender conformity. Arjie installs himself in the most coveted role – that of bride – and makes it abundantly clear that the part of groom occupies the lowest rung of the game's hierarchy. Indeed, the game is predicated on the apparent nonperformativity of masculinity,[22] as opposed to the hyperbolic feminine performance of Arjie as bride. The game's title then references both the unimportance of the groom and the pleasure derived from Arjie's performance of hyperfemininity, as well as the potentiality of a female same-sex eroticism that dispenses with the groom altogether. Arjie thus sutures himself into the scene of marriage, radically displacing it from the scene of heterosexuality and calling into question the very logic and authority of heteronormativity. "Pigs Can't Fly," then, encodes gender differentiation within multiple narratives, not all of which are necessarily pathologizing. While Arjie's father reads Arjie's cross-gender identification as unnatural and perverse, his mother is unable to come up with a viable explanation for the logic of gender conformity. When pushed by Arjie to explain why he can no longer watch her dress or play with the girls, she resorts to a childhood nursery rhyme, stating, "Because the sky is so high and pigs can't fly, that's why" (19). Her answer attempts to grant to the fixity of gender roles the status of universally recognized natural law and to root it in "common sense"; however,

such an explanation fails to satisfy Arjie, and his mother seems equally unconvinced but unable to imagine an alternative "order of things." Thus, gender conformity and nonconformity are narrativized through competing discourses in the story, where the rhetoric of nonconformity as perversion is undercut by Arjie's mother making apparent the nonsensical nature of gender codification, as well as by the antinormative performance of gender in Bride–Bride.

Arjie's sexual encounters with a Sinhalese classmate, Shehan, and his realization that such homoerotic sex has pushed him outside the purview of "family," as he has known it, can initially be read within the narrative tradition of the coming-out story. Such narratives can be characterized as journeys toward an essential wholeness, toward the discovery of a true, gay identity through a teleological process of individuation that is granted representative status. Indeed, the novel's title, *Funny Boy*, can be read as a reference to Edmund White's 1982 narrative of gay coming-of-age in the fifties, *A Boy's Own Story*.[23] However, unlike White's text, where sexuality is privileged as the singular site of radical difference and the narrator's sole claim to alterity, sexuality in *Funny Boy* is but one of many discourses, such as ethnic identity and forced migration, that speak to multiple displacements and exiles. Thus, gender inversion in "Pigs Can't Fly" is not really a primary marker of Arjie's latent homosexuality, a childhood signifier of adult homosexuality as charted along a linear narrative of sexual development that ends with a fully realized "gay" subject. Rather, cross-gender identification in the story takes on numerous complex valences, given the novel's engagement with questions of loss and memory in the context of diasporic displacement. It is from the vantage point of "a new home . . . in Canada" that the narrator remembers the intense pleasure derived from the ritual of becoming "like the goddesses of the Sinhalese and Tamil cinema, larger than life" (5) and of watching his mother dress. Thus the narrator's evocation of these remembered instances of cross-gender identificatory practices and pleasures becomes a means of negotiating the loss of "home" as a fantasied site of geographic rootedness, belonging, and gender and erotic play. Indeed, if "home," as Dorinne Kondo states, is, for "peoples in diaspora," that which "we cannot not want,"[24] home for a queer diasporic subject becomes not only that which "we cannot not want" but also that which we cannot and could never have. Home in the queer fantasy of the past is the space of violent (familial and national) disowning.

Cross-Gender Identification and Queer Diasporic Memory

Cross-gender identification – through the game of Bride–Bride and in his mother's dressing room – allows Arjie to momentarily lay claim to domestic space and its gendered arrangements. The remembrance of such moments, then, mediates the multiple alienations of the queer diasporic subject from "home" as familial, domestic, and national space. Sri Lankan popular culture – the images of "the Malini Fonsekas and the Geeta Kumarasinghes" – acts as the vehicle through which "home" is conjured into being, mourned, and reimagined. The various meanings that the novel ascribes to Arjie's cross-dressing echoes anthropologist Martin Manalansan's depiction of the uses of drag within contemporary gay Filipino communities in New York City. Manalansan finds that for diasporic Filipino gay men, drag is inextricably intertwined with nostalgia, in that it evokes "the image and memory of the Filipino homeland while at the same time acknowledging being settled in a 'new home' here in the U.S."[25] Similarly, the narrator's memory of cross-dressing in *Funny Boy* negotiates multiple cultural and geographic sites while suggesting the uses of nostalgia for queer diasporic subjects.

Indeed, Arjie's performance of what we can term "queer femininity" radically reconfigures hegemonic nationalist and diasporic logic, which depends on the figure of the "woman" as a stable signifier of "tradition." Within a queer diasporic imaginary, the "lost homeland" is represented not by the pure and self-sacrificing wife and mother, but rather by a queer boy in a sari. . . .

The novel's final section makes all the more evident the ways in which "home" is reconfigured in queer diasporic memory. Here, Arjie has sex with Shehan for the last time before leaving with his family for Canada after the 1983 riots.

The smell of Shehan's body lingering on his clothes becomes "a final memento," not only of a remembered scene of homoerotic desire but of Sri Lanka, of "home," itself. The text thus "queers" the space of Sri Lanka as "home" by disrupting the logic of nationalism, which consolidates "the nation" through normative hierarchical sexual and gender arrangements that coalesce around the privatized, bourgeois domestic space of "home" as a site of sanitized heterosexuality. The mapping of homoeroticism onto the national space of "Sri Lanka" also reverses the standard notion of a "gay" subject having to leave a "third world" site of gender and sexual oppression in order to "come out" into the more liberated West. As such, it disorganizes the conventional coming-out narrative that "begins with an unliberated, 'prepolitical' homosexual practice and that culminates in a liberated, 'out,' politicized, 'modern' 'gay' subjectivity."[26] This moment in the narrative encapsulates the text's deployment of what I would call a generative or enabling nostalgia and homesickness, where the "home" that is evoked signifies multiply: as both national space and domestic space, it is the site of homoerotic desire and cross-gender identification and pleasure, of intense gender conformity and horrific violence, of multiple leave-takings and exiles. Thus, the text also complicates the axes of a conventional exilic novel with fixed points of origin and departure. Instead, the stories detail the layered crises and multiple losses, the leave-takings and exiles that occur within the site of "home" itself.

Female Homosociality, Queer Femininity

Arjie's game of Bride–Bride not only references a particular mode of hyperbolic femininity and cross-gender identificatory pleasure, it also suggests the possibility of a female homoeroticism located within the home and working through the absence and irrelevance of the groom. Since the moments of cross-dressing that I have thus far discussed tend to privilege a gay male diasporic subject, I want to detach Arjie's performance of queer femininity from a narrative of queer boyhood and instead use it to locate a queer female subject within multiple "home" spaces. For a staging of the game of Bride–Bride within a female homosocial context, then, we can turn to the recent independent film *Fire*, which depicts the relationship between two brides, that is, two sisters-in-law in the North Indian urban home of a middle-class extended family. Filmmaker Deepa Mehta quickly establishes the familiar familial violences and compulsions that underlie this space of home: both women (ironically named Radha and Sita)[27] do most of the labor for the family business while their husbands alternately abuse or ignore them; this eventually precipitates their turning to each other for sex and emotional sustenance.

The film renders explicit the female homoerotic desire hinted at in Arjie's game of Bride–Bride by producing a complicated relay between female homosociality and female homoerotic practices. In one scene, for instance, Sita massages Radha's feet at a family picnic, transforming a daily female homosocial activity into an intensely homoerotic one while the other members of the family unwittingly look on. The slide from female homosociality into female homoeroticism in this scene, as well as in another where Radha rubs oil into Sita's hair, serves to locate female same-sex desire and pleasure firmly within the confines of the home and "the domestic," rather than occurring safely "elsewhere."[28] This emergence of female homoeroticism at the interstices of heterosexuality interrupts, as Geeta Patel phrases it, the "apparently necessary slide from marriage into heterosexuality," and denaturalizes the linkages between heterosexuality and the domestic.[29] This articulation of female same-sex desire within the space of the domestic directly confronts and disrupts contemporary nationalist constructions of the bourgeois Hindu home as the reservoir of essential national cultural values, embodied in the figure of the Hindu woman as chaste, demure, and self-sacrificing.[30]

Furthermore, the erotic interplay between Radha and Sita speaks to a specific modality of South Asian femininity through which – in a middle-class context – lesbian desire is articulated within sites of extreme heteronormativity. The trope of dressing and undressing that threads through *Funny Boy* marks *Fire* as well: in the absence of their husbands, the two women indulge not only in dressing each other but in dressing for each other, donning heavy silk saris, makeup, and gold jewelry in a performance of the hyperbolic femininity that Selvadurai's narrator also references. Their eroticization of a particular aesthetic of Indian femininity brings to mind the problematic sketched out by Kaushalya Bannerji in the South Asian lesbian and gay anthology *A Lotus of Another Color*.[31] Bannerji remarks upon her alienation from a white lesbian aesthetic of androgyny, given her "fondness for bright colors, long hair, jewelry" – bodily signs that have multiple meanings for her as an Indian Canadian woman but read within a white lesbian context simply as markers of a transparent "femme" identity. Bannerji's presentation of a South Asian femininity elicits fetishistic responses from white lesbians, whereas for her, this particular aesthetic is a means of negotiating and reconciling categories of both ethnic and sexual identity. Similarly, the two protagonists in *Fire* derive pleasure from a particular, middle-class version of South Asian (and specifically North Indian) femininity that sometimes slips into an equally class-marked articulation of female homoerotic desire.[32]

Clearly, then, the "mythic mannish lesbian" (to use Esther Newton's term)[33] that haunts Euramerican discourses of twentieth-century lesbian sexuality is not the dominant modality through which female same-sex desire can be read here; rather, within the context of the middle-class home in the film, it is Radha and Sita's performance of queer femininity that emerges as the dominant mode or aesthetic through which female same-sex desire is rendered intelligible. As such, the film suggests an alternative trajectory of representing female homoeroticism in a South Asian context – one that is at odds with conventional Euramerican "lesbian" histories that chart a developmental narrative from a nineteenth-century model of asexual "romantic friendship" between bourgeois women in privatized, domestic, gender-segregated spaces to a contemporary modern, autonomous, "lesbian" identity, sexuality, and community.[34] The film's depiction of the ways in which this privatized, seemingly sanitized "domestic" space can simultaneously function as a site of intense female homoerotic pleasure and practices calls into question a narrative of "lesbian" sexuality as needing to emerge from a private, domestic sphere into a public, visible, "lesbian" subjectivity.[35] *Fire* then, like *Funny Boy*, refuses to subscribe to the notion that the proper manifestation of same-sex eroticism is within a "politics of visibility" in the public sphere. Rather, it suggests that in a South Asian context, what constitutes "lesbian" desire may both look and function differently than it does within Euramerican social and historical formations, and draw from alternative modes of masculinity and femininity. In other words, the film makes explicit the ways in which not all female same-sex desire culminates in an autonomous "lesbianism," and not all "lesbianism" is at odds with domestic marital arrangements.

The film in a sense references this problematic of visuality and identity in its opening scene, which recurs throughout the film. The scene is that of Radha's dreamscape: a wide, open field of yellow flowers, where Radha's mother exhorts a young Radha to "see the ocean" lying at the limits of the landlocked field. This exhortation to "see" differently, to "see" without literally seeing, speaks to the need for a particular strategy of reading sexuality outside dominant configurations of visibility, desire, and identity. I am not asserting here that the film depicts an authentic, autonomous, or indigenous form of lesbian desire; rather, it suggests an alternative mode of reading and "seeing" nonnormative erotic and gender configurations as they erupt within sites of extreme heteronormativity. The film thus enacts the critique articulated by Manalansan of transnational gay and lesbian globalizing discourse, which in its privileging of Western definitions of same-sex sexual practices "risks duplicating an imperial gaze in relation to nonwestern non-metropolitan sexual practices and collectivities."[36]

Insofar as the two women come together because of the failures of their respective marriages, however, *Fire* recenters heterosexuality by relying on a conventional framing of "lesbian" desire as the result of failed heteronormative arrangements. Yet one particular scene in the film hints at an alternative organization of female same-sex desire, and perhaps exceeds the film's narrative framing of "lesbian" desire as simply an auxiliary to heterosexuality. In it, Sita (dressed in a suit with her hair slicked back) and Radha (as a Hindi film heroine) engage in a playful lip-synching duet that both inhabits and ironizes the genre of popular Hindi film songs. Whereas Radha's fantasy space is that of the field that gives way to the ocean, this evocation of popular Hindi film becomes Sita's fantasied site of erotic and gender play. This scene of cross-gender identification stands apart from an earlier scene of playful cross-dressing where Sita discards her sari and dons her husband's jeans and smokes his cigarettes as a way of temporarily laying claim to male authority, freedom, and privilege. In the later scene, cross-dressing is not a means for claiming male privilege but rather functions as an articulation of same-sex desire; echoing *Funny Boy*, the film suggests that if one mode for making lust between women intelligible is through the representation of hyperbolic femininity, another is through the appropriation of popular culture and its particular gender dynamics.

Female Same-Sex Desire and South Asian Popular Culture

We can read this scene in *Fire* as referencing a strikingly similar female cross-dressing scene in the immensely popular 1993 mainstream Hindi film *Hum aapke hain koun*. This sequence takes place during a woman-only celebration of an upcoming marriage, around which the film's entire plot revolves. Into this space of female homosociality enters a woman cross-dressed as the film's male hero, in an identical white suit, who proceeds to dance suggestively with the heroine (played by Madhuri Dixit) and with various other women in the room. What follows is an elaborate dance sequence where the cross-dressed woman and Dixit engage in a teasing, sexualized exchange that parodies the trappings of conventional middle-class Hindu family arrangements (that is marriage, heterosexuality, domesticity, and motherhood). Halfway through the song, however, order is apparently restored as the cross-dressed interloper is chased out of the room by the "real" hero (Salman Khan). The cross-dressed woman disappears from both the scene and indeed the entire film, and Salman Khan proceeds to claim his rightful place opposite Dixit. What meanings, then, can we ascribe to these instances in both *Fire* and *Hum aapke* of an explicitly gendered erotics between women? Clearly, neither scene is purely transgressive of conventional gender and sexual hierarchies: in *Fire*, the gendered erotic interplay of the two women can be seen as simply an articulation of their desire for each other in the absence of "real" men, while in *Hum aapke* the cross-dressed woman seems merely to hold the place of the "real" hero until he can make his entrance, that is, to hold in place the hierarchical gendered relations in the scene.[37] Indeed, the film can afford such a transparent rendering of female-female desire precisely because it remains so thoroughly convinced of the hegemonic power of its own heterosexuality. However, the fact that gender reversal in *Hum aapke* occurs within a space of female homosociality renders the implied homoeroticism of the scene explicit to both the characters and to the film's audience, and by doing so, makes it eminently available for a queer diasporic viewership. For a queer South Asian viewing subject, then, the scene foregrounds the ways in which South Asian popular culture acts as a repository of queer desiring relations; it also marks the simultaneous illegibility of those relations to a heterosexual viewing public and their legibility in a queer South Asian diasporic context.[38]

It is critical to note that upon *Hum aapke*'s release, the popular press attributed its tremendous and sustained popularity to its return to "family values," a phrase that apparently referred to the film's rejection of the sex and violence formulas of other popular Hindi movies. However, this phrase speaks more to the ways in which the film works within Hindu nationalist discourses of the nation by articulating a desire for a nostalgic "return" to an impossible ideal, that of supposedly "traditional" Hindu family and kinship arrangements that are staunchly middle class and heterosexual. The incursion of female homoerotic desire into this ultraconventional Hindu marriage plot – both suggested and contained by the scene between Dixit and her cross-dressed partner – threatens the presumed seamlessness of both familial and nationalist narratives by calling into question the

functionality and imperviousness of heterosexual bonds.

Pigs with Wings

The nostalgia evoked by the film is quite unlike the longing in *Funny Boy* for a space of "home" that is permanently and already ruptured, rent by colliding and colluding discourses around class, sexuality, and ethnic identity. *Funny Boy* lays claim to both the space of "home" and the nation by making both the site of nonheteronormative desire and pleasure in a nostalgic diasporic imaginary. Such a move disrupts nationalist logic by forestalling any notion of queer or nonheteronormative desire as insufficiently authentic. *Funny Boy* thus refuses to subsume sexuality within a larger narrative of ethnic, class, or national identity, or to subsume these other conflicting trajectories within an overarching narrative of "gay" sexuality. Within *Funny Boy* as well as in *Fire* and *Hum aapke*, sexuality functions not as an autonomous narrative but instead as enmeshed and immersed within multiple discourses. Clearly, none of these texts allow for a purely redemptive recuperation of same-sex desire, conscribed and implicated as it is within class, religious, and gender hierarchies. Indeed, it is precisely in the friction between these various competing discourses that queer pleasure and desire emerge. In both *Fire* and *Hum aapke*, for instance, female homoerotic pleasure is generated and produced by the very prohibitions around class, religion, and gender that govern and discipline the behavior of middle-class women.

Throughout this essay, I have attempted to gesture toward the ways in which nation and diaspora are refigured within a queer diasporic imaginary. Nostalgia as deployed by queer diasporic subjects is a means for imagining oneself within those spaces from which one is perpetually excluded or denied existence. If the nation is "the modern Janus," a figure that gazes at a primordial, ideal past while at the same time facing a modern future,[39] a queer diaspora instead recognizes the past as a site of intense violence as well as pleasure; it acknowledges the spaces of impossibility within the nation and their translation within the diaspora into new logics of affiliation. The logic of "pigs can't fly" becomes transformed, in the diaspora, into the alternative queer diasporic logic that allows for two brides in bed together, a marriage without a groom, pigs with wings. In other words, a queer diasporic logic displaces heteronormativity from the realm of natural law and instead launches its critique of hegemonic constructions of both nation and diaspora from the vantage point of an "impossible" subject.

Notes

1 Shyam Selvadurai, *Funny Boy* (Toronto: McClelland and Stewart, 1995). Subsequent references to this work will be given in parentheses in the text.

2 I use the term "South Asian" throughout this article to reference a particular diasporic political formation that locates itself outside the national boundaries of any one national site (such as Bangladesh, Bhutan, India, Nepal, Pakistan, or Sri Lanka). However, I am also aware of the regional hierarchies that may be resurrected within the term. For a cogent explication of the oppositional uses and limits of the term "South Asian" among activists in the United States see Anannya Bhattacharjee, "The Public/Private Mirage: Mapping Homes and Undomesticating Violence Work in the South Asian Immigrant Community," in *Feminist Genealogies, Colonial Legacies, Democratic Futures*, ed. M. Jacqui Alexander and Chandra T. Mohanty (New York and London: Routledge, 1997), 309.

3 A few examples of such work include Partha Chatterjee, *The Nation and Its Fragments* (Princeton, N.J.: Princeton University Press, 1993); Anne McClintock, *Imperial Leather: Race, Gender, and Sexuality in the Colonial Contest* (New York and London: Routledge, 1993); Floya Anthias and Nira Yuval Davis, eds., *Women–Nation–State* (London: Macmillan, 1989); and Deniz Kandiyoti, "Identity and Its Discontents: Women and the Nation," in *Colonial Discourse and Post-colonial Theory*, ed. Patrick Williams and Laura Chrisman (New York: Columbia University Press, 1994), 376–91.

4 McClintock, *Imperial Leather*, 354.

5 Kandiyoti, "Identity and Its Discontents," 382.

6 See, for instance, Tom Nairn, *The Break-up of Britain: Crisis and Neo-nationalism* (London: Verso, 1981); Homi K. Bhabha, ed., *Nation and Narration* (New York and London: Routledge, 1991); Benedict Anderson, *Imagined Communities* (London: Verso, 1991); and Kandiyoti, "Identity and Its Discontents."

7 Anthias and Yuval Davis, *Women–Nation–State*, 7.

8 Inderpal Grewal, *Home and Harem: Nation, Gender, Empire, and the Cultures of Travel* (Durham, N.C.: Duke University Press, 1996), 7.

9 I use the term "queer" throughout this article to suggest a range of nonheteronormative sexual practices and desires that may not necessarily coalesce around categories of identity.

10 For an exemplary study of sexuality and colonialism see Mrinalini Sinha, *Colonial Masculinity: The "Manly Englishman" and the "Effeminate Bengali" in the Late Nineteenth Century* (Manchester, England: Manchester University Press, 1995).

11 For one recent instance of this particular blindspot in feminist critiques of nationalism see Kumari Jayawardena and Malathi de Alwis, eds., *Embodied Violence: Communalising Women's Sexuality in South Asia* (New Delhi: Kali for Women, 1996).

12 In India, for instance, Section 377 of the Indian Penal Code bans same-sex sexual relations as "unnatural offences." The law was initially instituted under British colonial rule in the 1830s, which makes explicit the complicity of colonial and anticolonial nationalist framings of sexuality.

13 M. Jacqui Alexander "Erotic Autonomy As a Politics of Decolonization: An Anatomy of State Practice in the Bahamas Tourist Economy," in Alexander and Mohanty, *Feminist Genealogies*, 84.

14 McClintock, *Imperial Leather*, 359.

15 Alexander, "Erotic Autonomy," 97.

16 For work that begins to trace the contours of queer South Asian subjectivity see, for instance, Geeta Patel, "Homely Housewives Run Amok: Lesbians in Marital Fixes," *Public Culture* (forthcoming); Gayatri Gopinath, "Homo-Economics: Queer Sexualities in a Transnational Frame," in *Burning Down the House: Recycling Domesticity*, ed. Rosemary M. George (New York: Westview/Harper Collins, 1998); and Rakesh Ratti, ed., *A Lotus of Another Color: An Unfolding of the South Asian Gay and Lesbian Experience* (Boston: Alyson, 1993).

17 For further discussion of how diasporic articulations of community and identity both replicate and challenge the masculinist logic of conventional nationalisms see Gayatri Gopinath, "'Bombay, U.K., Yuba City': Bhangra Music and the Engendering of Diaspora," *Diaspora* 4, no. 3 (winter 1995): 303–22.

18 Bhattacharjee, "The Public/Private Mirage," 308–29. See also Anannya Bhattacharjee, "The

Habit of Ex-nomination: Nation, Woman, and the Indian Immigrant Bourgeoisie," *Public Culture* 5, no. 1 (fall 1992): 19–46.

19 The imbrication of narratives of "progress," "modernity," and "visibility" is made obvious in what Alexander terms "prevalent metropolitan impulses that explain the absence of visible lesbian and gay movements [in non-Western locations] as a defect in political conciousness and maturity, using evidence of publicly organized lesbian and gay movements in the U.S. . . . as evidence of their originary status (in the West) and superior political maturity" (Alexander, "Erotic Autonomy," 69).

20 See Martin Manalansan, "In the Shadows of Stonewall: Gay Transnational Politics and the Diasporic Dilemma," in *The Politics of Culture in the Shadow of Capital*, ed. Lisa Lowe and David Lloyd (Durham, N.C.: Duke University Press, 1997), for an important interrogation of contemporary gay transnational politics.

21 In its depiction of the "inner" as a female site but also a site of gender play and reversal, the story refigures in interesting ways anticolonial nationalist framings of space that posit the "inner" as a space of essential spirituality and tradition, embodied by "woman," as opposed to the "outer," male sphere of progress, materiality, and modernity. For an analysis of the creation of "inner" and "outer" spheres in anticolonial nationalist discourse see Partha Chatterjee, "The Nationalist Resolution to the Woman's Question," in *Recasting Women: Essays in Colonial History*, ed. Kumkum Sangari and Sudesh Vaid (New Delhi: Kali for Women, 1989), 233–54.

22 See Judith Halberstam, *Female Masculinity* (Durham, N.C.: Duke University Press, 1998), for a discussion of masculine nonperformativity in the context of female "drag king" performances.

23 See Robert McRuer, "Boys' Own Stories and New Spellings of My Name: Coming Out and Other Myths of Queer Positionality," *Genders* 2, no. 1 (1994): 260–83, for a critique of the coming-out narrative as "necessary for understanding one's (essential) gay identity" (267) and of Edmund White's novel in particular.

24 Dorinne Kondo suggests this formulation of "home" in her essay on Asian American negotiations of community and identity, "The Narrative Production of 'Home,' Community and Political Identity in Asian American Theater," in *Displacement, Diaspora, and Geographies of Identity*, ed. Smadar Lavie and Ted Swedenburg (Durham, N.C.: Duke University Press, 1996), 97.

25 Martin Manalansan, "Diasporic Deviants/Divas: How Filipino Gay Transmigrants 'Play with the World'" in *Homosexuality in Motion: Gay Diasporas and Queer Peregrinations*, ed. Cindy Patton and Benigno Sanchez-Eppler (Durham, N.C.: Duke University Press, 2000).

26 Manalansan, "Diasporic Deviants/Divas," 3.

27 In Hindu mythology, Sita proves her chastity to her husband, Ram, by immersing herself in fire; she thereby embodies the ideals of womanly virtue and self-sacrifice. Radha, similarly, is the devoted consort of the god Krishna, who is famous for his womanizing. The irony in the film's naming of the two female protagonists lies in their refusal to inhabit these overdetermined roles of woman as devoted, chaste, and self-denying.

28 I have further explored this particular relation between female homoeroticism and female homosociality in a South Asian context in a discussion of Ismat Chughtai's short story "The Quilt." See Gopinath, "Homo-Economics."

29 See Patel, "Homely Housewives," 7.

30 See Chatterjee, "Nationalist Resolution," for an analysis of the ways in which anticolonial nationalism used the figure of the woman as a bearer of inviolate tradition in order to imagine the independent nation.

31 Kaushalya Bannerji, "No Apologies," in Ratti, *Lotus of Another Color*, 59–64.

32 Outside the confines of the middle-class North Indian home depicted in *Fire*, female homoerotic desire may manifest itself in forms other than that of hyperbolic or queer femininity. As Geeta Patel has noted in her discussion of the controversy around the 1987 "marriage" of two policewomen in central India, the police barracks in which the two women lived constituted a site of complicated and explicitly gendered erotic relations between women. See Patel, "Homely Housewives," 14–22.

33 Esther Newton, "The Mythic Mannish Lesbian: Radclyffe Hall and the New Woman," in *Hidden from History: Reclaiming the Gay and Lesbian Past*, ed. Martin Duberman et al. (New York: Meridian, 1989), 281–93.

34 See ibid. for a critique of nineteenth-century "romantic friendships" as protolesbian/feminist relationships.

35 Clearly, a Euramerican bourgeois space of "home" is not akin to the domestic space represented in *Fire*, given that the latter is marked by a history of British colonialism, anticolonial nationalism, and contemporary Indian (and Hindu) nationalist politics.

36 Manalansan, "Under the Shadows," 6.

37 *Hum aapke*'s brief interlude of gender reversal and implied female homoeroticism seems to locate the film within Chris Straayar's definition of the "temporary transvestite film," those that "offer spectators a momentary, vicarious trespassing of society's accepted boundaries for gender and sexual behavior. Yet one can relax confidently in the orderly [heterosexual] demarcations reconstituted by the films' endings" (Chris Straayar, *Deviant Eyes, Deviant Bodies: Sexual Reorientations in Film and Video* [New York: Columbia University Press, 1996], 44).

38 These scenes of cross-dressing and gender reversal can also be read as gesturing toward the gendered arrangements of female same-sex desire that Patel details, and that shadow the middle-class domestic locations of both *Fire* and *Hum aapke*.

39 McClintock, *Imperial Leather*, 358.

14

The Perfect Path
Gay Men, Marriage, Indonesia

Tom Boellstorff

In a 1997 ad for Ciputra Hotels that appeared in the Indonesian national airline's in-flight magazine, a smiling Balinese dancer in bejeweled "traditional" garb stands juxtaposed to glittering hotel facades. The ad proclaims that "Indonesia is *also* home to Asia's newest hotel concept. . . . While tradition thrives in Indonesia, the world's most modern concepts are equally at home." Presumably, one of these "modern concepts" is the "Western" male business traveler, who will feel "at home" under the domestic attentions of the female staff.[1]

It hardly takes a subversive reading to see that the ad constructs Indonesia as a hybrid of tradition, gendered female, and modernity, gendered male. This binarism has a long history, extending from colonialism to modernization theory. Many non-"Western" intellectuals have addressed its symbolic violence, including the man many consider Indonesia's greatest living author, Pramoedya Ananta Toer. His novel *Footsteps*, which opens in 1901, is set in the late colonial period but speaks by analogy to the Indonesia of the 1970s and 1980s, when it was written. The protagonist, Minke, has just come from Surabaya to the capital, known informally as Betawi. Alone and poor but on his way to medical school and a "modern" career, Minke frames his arrival as a change of time as well as place:

> Into the universe of Betawi I go – into the universe of the twentieth century. And, yes, to you too, nineteenth century – farewell! . . . People

say only the modern man gets ahead in these times. In his hands lies the fate of humankind. You reject modernity? You will be the plaything of all those forces of the world operating outside and around you. I am a modern person. . . . And modernity brings the loneliness of orphaned humanity, cursed to free itself from unnecessary ties of custom, blood – even from the land, and if need be, from others of its kind.[2]

Through Minke's voice, Toer questions the perfect path of modernist teleology, with its assumption that "footsteps" to the future necessarily lead to a homogenized subjectivity that denies the local, the "others of its kind." One can well imagine Minke as the modern business traveler, building his career, reading an in-flight magazine, experiencing the "loneliness of orphaned humanity," and hoping to find a home. But where would Minke's footsteps have taken him if he had flown into Jakarta International Airport in 1999, rather than disembarked on its shores in 1901? How would he think of the relationship between past and future, tradition and modernity, self and other? There is no doubt that the forces of globalization have grown and shifted tremendously in recent decades. But many scholars of transnationalism question whether this growth implies homogenization or instead may result in new forms of difference. As Arjun Appadurai notes, the contemporary moment is marked by disjunctions in the global movement of images, commodities, and persons and by "a new role for the imagination in social life."[3]

On the most fundamental symbolic level, for instance, the Ciputra Hotels ad requires that the woman staring out at the prospective customer not be lesbian. Her heterosexuality structures the very opposition between tradition and modernity on which the ad's semiotic logic rests. This logic is part and parcel of a system of governmentality in which the Indonesian state strives to efface the distinction between itself and society through metaphors of the heterosexual, middle-class family. Such heteronormativity raises the question of why there are *lesbi* and *gay* subjectivities in Indonesia, the fourth most populous nation, at all. By exploring the "homoscapes" in which some non-"Western" subjects identify as lesbian or gay – in particular, by exploring the "mystery" of gay-identified men's marriages to women in Indonesia – I hope to clarify the processes of "reterritorialization" and "localization" identified by scholars of globalization.[4] What is the history and social context of these subjectivities? These are the kinds of questions that came to my mind when I first saw this ad on my way to Indonesia to begin fieldwork.

My consideration of these questions took place in a postcolonial frame. By *postcolonial*, whose scope and validity remain ambiguous, I refer to a theoretical stance according to which the emergence of nations in the formerly colonized world poses a new set of questions about belonging, citizenship, and the self. I turn to creative uses of this framework by such scholars as Homi K. Bhabha, Partha Chatterjee, Stuart Hall, Akhil Gupta, and Gayatri Chakravorty Spivak rather than to analyses that reject "postcoloniality" by claiming that it implies that colonialism is "past," that economic forces are irrelevant, or that all nations follow the same path.[5] One theme of this essay is that in LGQ studies a more serious engagement with postcoloniality as a category of analysis might improve our understanding of sexualities outside the "West."[6]

In this essay I focus on people outside the "West" who use the terms *gay, lesbian*, and *bisexual*, or close variants of them, rather than on the "indigenous" homosexualities and transgenderisms that have hitherto been the almost exclusive concern of the "ethnocartography" of homosexuality.[7] (In the case of Indonesia, the subjectivities I refer to are *gay* and *lesbi*.) While attention to lesbian, gay, and bisexual subjectivities outside the "West" is certainly increasing, Kath Weston's 1993 observation that "in the international arena, the 'salvage anthropology' of indigenous homosexualities remains largely insulated from important new theoretical work on postcolonial relations" continues to be distressingly valid in 1999.[8] This provincialism originates in the perceived incompatibility between postcoloniality, on the one hand, and persistent narratives of a "global movement" within LGQ studies, on the other. While such narratives are politically salutary – indeed, a strategic essentialism may be warranted in some contexts, given the dominance of "development" as a rubric for conceptualizing global change[9] – they have limited LGQ studies' awareness of the ethnocentrism of many of its assumptions about what constitutes activism, visibility, politics, social movements, and even identity. In response, I view this essay as representing a category of scholarship that might be termed "postcolonial LGQ studies."

I am struck by the predictable manner in which interpretations of non-"Western" gay and lesbian subjectivities fall into two reductionisms in LGQ studies. In the first, these subjectivities are said to be "just like" lesbian and gay subjectivities in a homogenized "West." They represent the transcendental gay or lesbian subject, characterized by a supposed essential *sameness* that has been there all along, hidden under a veneer of exotic cultural difference. (Such an understanding recalls Bhabha's analysis of colonial mimicry, "the desire for a reformed, recognizable Other, *as a subject of difference that is almost the same, but not quite*," and is represented in texts like *The Global Emergence of Gay and Lesbian Politics: National Imprints of a Worldwide Movement*.)[10] I want to point out how teleologies like this converge with Minke's "footsteps" to modernity, critiqued in Toer's novel.

The second reductionism, the opposite of the first, assumes that these gay men and lesbians suffer from false consciousness and are traitors to their "traditional" subjectivities, victims of (and, ultimately, collaborators with) a global gay imperialism. They represent the McDonalds–ized, inauthentic gay or lesbian subject, alienated from its indigenous *Geist*. From this perspective, these subjectivities have an essential *difference*, hidden under the veneer of the terms *lesbian* and *gay*. So the "footsteps" of traveling LGQ theorists go in circles around the "sameness" or "difference" of non-"Western" gay and lesbian people with respect to gay and lesbian people elsewhere. The issue of sameness and difference extends to concerns about postcolonial subjectivity beyond LGQ studies; it is in fact one of the animating concerns of anthropology in the twentieth century. My work has been motivated in part by a search for a way of talking about sameness and difference that avoids these reductionisms. Such a way might point toward less teleological paths of theory and identity in LGQ studies.

Considering the importance of postcoloniality in this way has led me to recall that in the last twenty years there has appeared, outside LGQ studies, a sophisticated body of literature exploring Indonesia from a postcolonial perspective.[11] Yet the scholars who have contributed to it have paid scant attention to *lesbi* and *gay* subjectivities, even though most US-based Indonesianists of the past fifteen years were taught Indonesian by Dédé Oetomo, a Cornell-trained anthropologist who has written on *gay* identities in Indonesia.[12] In this essay I use ethnographic material from Indonesia to interrogate the complementary lacunae in Indonesian studies and LGQ studies in search of a third framing of *gay* and *lesbi* subjectivities. Historical context plays a role as well. Both *Footsteps* and *Imprints* employ a path metaphor either to critique or to celebrate globalization as developmental and homogenizing. In 1990, however, an Indonesian sociologist discovered in a Jakarta archive a remarkable manuscript written by a man named Sucipto, who had had sex only with men and had participated in a community of like-minded men in 1920s colonial Java. Sucipto titled his writings *The Perfect Path*. The relationship between his "perfect path" and contemporary *lesbi* and *gay* subjectivities cannot be reduced to a Procrustean modernist path. The contingent appropriation of concepts of homosexuality makes for subjectivities that are irre-

ducible to those in the "West," even if the terms are similar. *Gay* and *lesbi* are not just "gay" and "lesbian" with a foreign accent.

An important caveat is that in this essay I focus on *gay* men.[13] In some sense "gay" and "lesbian" moved to Indonesia as one concept, "gayandlesbian"; thus homosexuality has implied heterosociality in some circumstances.[14] But despite an impressive record of cogendered community, the "*gay* archipelago" I describe is decidedly gendered male.[15] The case study I employ is the "mystery" of *gay* men's marriages to women. In the larger project from which this essay is derived I explore the specificities of *lesbi* subjectivity in Indonesia from historical and contemporary perspectives, building on existing analyses of Indonesian women's same-sex and transgendered subjectivities.[16]

Sameness versus Difference, Local versus Global: Reconceiving Two Binarisms

I develop my argument for a postcolonial perspective via two binarisms that permeate most discussions of LGQ identities outside the "West": sameness versus difference and local versus global. In regard to the vexed binarism of sameness and difference, the issue is not the world's becoming more the same *or* more different under globalization (neither homogenization nor heterogenization per se) but the transformation of the very yardsticks by which one decides whether something is the same or different in the first place, that is, the reconfiguration of the grid of similitude and difference. In *The Order of Things* Michel Foucault characterizes shifts in Western European thought in terms of conceptualizations of sameness and difference.[17] What analytic purchase might be gained by positing, under some circumstances at least, a postcolonial "order of things" in which relationships between same and other were characterized not as boundaries transgressed but as boundaries blurred, not as borders crossed but as borderlands inhabited, not as spheres adjoined but as archipelagoes intertwined?[18] This approach might help theorize the inequalities of globalization (oppression does not require distinct boundaries), and the fact that globalization is not rendering the state irrelevant, in a way that still accounts for the fact that *gay* and *lesbi* Indonesians find their subjectivities authentic.

The second issue is the revamping of the local–global binarism. Building from emic cultural logics of a *gay* archipelago, I argue that *gay* and *lesbi* are translocal subjectivities for which the local–global binarism is conceptually and methodologically insufficient. The isomorphism between difference and distance is broken; sameness is measured not in terms of concentric spheres of decreasing familiarity but archipelagically, so that someone thousands of miles away might be "closer" than someone next door. This phenomenon is not a cosmopolitanism by which national subjects (usually urban elites) imagine themselves as part of a community that transcends the nation, sharing structures of feeling and patterns of migration above local (usually poorer) communities.[19] Nor is it a diaspora in which gay or lesbian selves disperse from an originary homeland, or a hybridity in which two prior unities turn difference into sameness via an "implicit politics of heterosexuality."[20] *Gay* and *lesbi* Indonesians construct themselves as part of a community that, while it includes non-Indonesians in complex ways, transforms rhetorics of nationalism and locality as well. The dialectic between immanence and transcendence sets these subjectivities apart from cosmopolitan, diasporic, or hybrid ones.

The production of translocality in *gay* and *lesbi* subjectivities presents a problem for some theories of globalization, for it is not predicated on the movement of people; most *lesbi* and *gay* Indonesians are working-class, do not speak English, have never traveled abroad, and have no contact with non-Indonesian lesbians and gay men.[21] A majority live in the towns and even the households where they grew up. Nevertheless, most see not only their selves but their social places as figurations of a simultaneously national and global community. To explore how translocal subjectivities could arise without the movement of people, my research needed to be translocal as well. I conduct ethnography in three primary urban sites – Surabaya (East Java), Denpasar/Kuta (Bali), and Ujung Pandang (South Sulawesi) – but in a profound sense I do not regard my work as comparative. I am certainly interested in differences and similarities between my sites, but I also view my work as taking place in one site, Indonesia.[22] While extralocal affiliations are common throughout Indonesia, impacted not only by nationalism and capitalism but by world religions like Islam and Christianity, *gay* and *lesbi* subjectivities exhibit translocality to a heightened degree. Significantly, there are local places and organizations for *lesbi* women and *gay* men and a national network but no intermediate Java-wide or Bali-wide organizations. Throughout the remainder of this essay I show why, while *gay* and *lesbi* Indonesians are aware of their ethnicities, the idea of a specifically Javanese or Balinese *gay* or *lesbi* self is currently unthinkable: there is a meaningful incompatibility between ethnicity and *gay* or *lesbi* subjectivity. Anthropologists looking in Surabaya for gay Javanese people, *orang gay Jawa*, would fail. Instead, they would find people who, in the context of their sexual subjectivities, thought of themselves as *orang gay Indonesia*.

Gay Worlds and Archipelagoes

In the early 1980s some Indonesians began to take the "Western" terms *lesbian* and *gay* and transform them until they saw them as authentically Indonesian. Through everyday practices of spatial formation, pleasure, romance, bodily comportment, social imagination, and language (including the use of a slang involving not only lexical substitutions but unique inflections), they have articulated a community that they call the *dunia gay*, or "gay world."[23] For men, this world encompasses a range of places and activities, from strolling in air-conditioned shopping malls to hanging out in parks or by the side of a road at night, forging quasi-private sites in public space called *tempat ngeber*, or "flaunting places." That the *gay* (and occasionally *lesbi*) Indonesians who frequent such sites see them as transformed is illustrated by a contrast drawn by an informant in Bali. We were talking about the importance of friendship when he said, "[*Gay* men] might become friends in places like the *tempat ngeber* in the town square, but if we meet in a *tempat umum* [public place] like a movie theater or supermarket, we pretend we don't know each other." In terms of semiotics, bodily comportment, and community, he no longer experiences the town square as a public place.[24]

This man's emphasis on *tempat ngeber* as a place to make friends is significant. Under general conditions, when one is rarely far from the watchful eye of family, workplace, or school, *tempat ngeber* are sites where subjectivities are forged. The people who hang out there are only secondarily looking for sex; indeed, many come night after night with long-term lovers or a group of friends. Groups of two or three quietly conversing alternate with crowds of five to thirty engaged in "campy" [*ngondhek*] joking, gossip, and rapid-fire retorts, using slang extensively. *Gay* men and *lesbi* women define themselves in terms of "desiring the same," unlike transgenders, who see themselves as having the soul of one gender in the body of another. *Tempat ngeber*, then, are literal subject positions, forming both local communities and the persons who inhabit them. Some *tempat ngeber* comprise areas where "open" *gay* men are known to congregate (often under a streetlight), other areas where those who are more "closed" gather, and still others where sexual partners may be found regardless of self-identification. People's movements between these areas – on a given night but also in a general pattern over a period of weeks or months – not only reflect their subjectivities but reconstitute the relationships that form these subjectivities. Since *tempat ngeber* usually exist in public spaces and at night, access to them is limited for women, including *lesbi* women. But they and *gay* men also form subject positions in homes, salons, food stalls, and church groups; on volleyball teams; and in shopping malls or discos. Some *gay* men and *lesbi* women form organizations with varying degrees of formality and even publish magazines.[25]

It is widely felt that these groups, as well as the less formal subject positions of parks and homes, are linked in a national network. *Gay* men and *lesbi* women assume that *gay* and *lesbi* communities elsewhere in Indonesia share their subjectivities, differing only in the degree to which their members can be "open" and can interact with transgenders. Some *lesbi* and *gay* Indonesians experience communities outside their own directly through migration as they search for work (or attempt to escape from prying family members). In addition, many cities (particularly Solo, Yogyakarta, Denpasar, Malang, and Surabaya) put on performance events that attract *gay* men and *lesbi* from distant cities for two or three nights of revelry. Rural *gay* men say that these events give them a rare chance to move outside the limited world of pen pals and build a friendship network.

While many rural and some urban *gay* men and *lesbi* women are isolated from other *gay* men and *lesbi* women (due to the fear of discovery or to their not knowing where others can be found), most have a network of five to twenty friends who play a constant role in their lives. An all-*gay* volleyball team practices every afternoon on a crowded athletics field; a line of men waits to play, but many sit on the sidelines and exchange news. Agung, a *gay* man, lives with his parents in their boardinghouse. It has twelve rooms on the upper floor; over a period of two years five are rented to *gay* men, two to *gay* couples, and one to a *lesbi* woman. In the hallway between the rooms, conversations on long hot nights give way to meetings and the idea of an organization, until one day the mother decides that she dislikes Agung's crowd, and one by one they move elsewhere. A *lesbi* woman whose parents own a small restaurant finds temporary work for another *lesbi* woman in a nearby shop and advises her on a recent breakup. While the quotidian details of life come and go, *lesbi* or *gay* Indonesians who move from one city to another expect to find people who share their subjectivities and suspect where they may be found. For the larger number who do not move from one city to another, there remains a sense that these everyday experiences are part of an imagined community of *gay* and *lesbi* subjectivity extending across Indonesia.

Moreover, *gay* and *lesbi* Indonesians think that non-Indonesian lesbians and gay men share a set of beliefs, desires, and practices (even though only a few have known such people personally). At the end of interviews I always asked my informants if they had any questions. Some wanted to know if gay bars really existed or if I had met Leonardo DiCaprio, but just as often they responded politely that "I feel I already know everything about your life."[26] *Gay* men and *lesbi* women usually assume that these familiar others are "the same" in terms of same-sex desire and "different" in terms of social acceptance and political rights. (But the meanings of "desire" and "acceptance" may themselves be conflicted, as *gay* men's marriages to women indicate.) Here the role of social imagination, already important in the nation, takes on new significance. For example, in Surabaya most *tempat ngeber* are named after locations outside Indonesia: *Texas, Kalifor, Pattaya* (a tourist beach in Thailand), *Paris, Brasil*. Such names, by permitting embodied visits to locales simultaneously outside and inside Indonesia, sidestep the binarisms of same–different and local–global. Such *lesbi* and *gay* imaginings are not unique to *tempat ngeber*, but they provide a particularly clear example of them.

The *gay* world is a domain of everyday subjectivity and practice that parallels the regular world, but when the places of the *gay* world are linked in an imagined national or transnational community, distant but present, the metaphor shifts from world to archipelago. One group in Surabaya names itself (and its magazine, usually recognized as the national magazine) GAYa Nusantara, an intentional polysemy in which each term has a dual valence. *Gaya* is the Indonesian for "style," but the unusual capitalization highlights the term's similarity to *gay*. *Nusantara* means "archipelago" and is also a nationalist term for "Indonesia." Because adjectives follow the nouns they modify in Indonesian, while they usually precede them in English, the term *GAYa Nusantara* parses in a fourfold manner as "archipelago style," "Indonesia style," "gay Indonesia," and "gay archipelago." While this term is by no means used by or even known to all Indonesians who identify as *lesbi* or *gay*, it manifests a common way of translocalizing these subjectivities "archipelago-style," at the intersection of local, national, and transnational rhetorics of selfhood, sexuality, and community. In other words, the local does not form the ontological ground for these subjectivities, and *lesbi* and *gay* Indonesians do not see themselves in a position of simple exteriority or interiority *vis-à-vis* non-Indonesian gay and lesbian communities. State ideology frames Indonesia as an archipelago of ethnicities; *lesbi* and *gay* Indonesians co-opt this image by conceptualizing the sites of *lesbi* and *gay* identities as "islands," which at a higher resolution are reframed as a single island in a transnational archipelago of gay and lesbian community. While the Javacentric Indonesian state provides a familiar example of archipelagic inequality, archipelagoes are nevertheless composed of discontinuous sites, none of them subsumed by the others: they are not bounded domains with a necessary center and periphery. How are we to understand subjectivities that connect and confound traditional levels of analysis – and, arguably, lived experience in the "West" – namely, the local, regional, national, and international? . . .

Dubbing Culture: State Hegemony, Mass Media, and the Good Family

The archipelago concept, in the "unity in diversity" form in which it is articulated through the practices and statements of *lesbi* and *gay* Indonesians, is not a timeless cultural archetype but is quintessentially modern, a key structuring principle of the nation-building project. Its reformulation has been a crucial means by which the state has struggled to reinterpret the denizens of Alfred Russel Wallace's colonial-era "Malay Archipelago" as citizens of a postcolonial archipelago.[27] The *wawasan nusantara* or "archipelago concept" dates from the early period of nationalism, at the beginning of the twentieth century, but it gained new force in 1957 in the context of an international dispute over maritime boundaries.[28] In 1973 the Indonesian government decreed that the archipelago concept "gives life to national development in all its aspects – political, social, and cultural."[29] Public culture in Indonesia is replete with the image and ethos of the archipelago. Diversity subsumed in unity is a hallmark of the state's rhetoric of cultural citizenship; it is predicated on a distinction between "culture" and "politics" that frames ethnicity [*suku*] as a matter of religion and the arts, while the people [*bangsa*] are linked to politics, commerce, and, above all, modernity.[30]

Fifty-four years after national independence, this Indonesian subjectivity is as fully imagined as any ethnicity, with its own language, ritual practices, ideologies, and symbolic sites. That it is complexly imbricated with the state does not invalidate its everyday authenticity for many Indonesians. It has not supplanted ethnicity but interacts with it in an additive manner, since the valorization of pluralism is central to the state's self-presentation as an archipelagic container of diversity. *Gay* or *lesbi* Indonesians are not necessarily more nationalist than other citizens. At the same time, state rhetorics of the archipelago are not deployed in a utilitarian manner by pre-social *gay* and *lesbi* subjects; a man hanging out in *Texas* does not deploy the archipelago concept instrumentally, although it does facilitate his imagining that place and his self as linked to an imagined gay Texas elsewhere. The state stands as an inadvertent idiom for *gay* subjectivity, influencing the daily practices by which the *gay* archipelago is enacted, constituted, and maintained in all its marginality.

The state itself, however, pays little attention to these subjectivities. There is no political persecution of *gay* men and *lesbi* women or banning of their magazines; indeed, government officials have labeled homosexuality incompatible with Indonesian society only once, at the United Nations International Conference on Population and Development in Cairo in 1994.[31] But the state has played an accidental role in fostering these subjectivities, by encouraging the mass media as a means to build nationalism.[32] One afternoon, for example, Darta, an informant, told me this story:

> When I first heard the word *gay*, it was in the fifth or sixth grade [c. 1985], on the island of Ambon, where I grew up, near New Guinea. It was there that I first heard about *lesbi*. Earlier, you know – *gay* wasn't around yet. But *lesbi* was already in women's magazines. I read lots of those magazines because Mom was a regular subscriber. Mom and I loved reading the articles on sexual deviants. I was always effeminate, and one day she said *I* was *lesbi*, because she didn't know *gay*; the term wasn't public back then.[33] But eventually I learned the term *gay* as well. That was also from a magazine. There was some story about historic English royalty . . . Richard someone. When I saw that, I thought, "There are others like me."[34]

While Darta's prior identification as *lesbi* raises interesting questions about the disjunctural character of postcolonial sexualities, the element

of his story that I want to highlight is the role played by mass media. Most Indonesians do not learn of the terms *lesbi* and *gay* through non-Indonesian lesbians and gay men or through *lesbi* and *gay* magazines, which they usually access only after identifying as *lesbi* or *gay*. Most learn of these terms through imported programs – movies like *Cruising*, *The Wedding Banquet*, and *My Best Friend's Wedding*; television shows like *Melrose Place* – as well as through pop psychology advice columns and gossip columns on the sexual lives of celebrities.[35] Many informants recall a moment of recognition when "I knew that was me" or "I knew I was not the only one." Some "Western" lesbians and gay men may find such a moment of recognition familiar. However, the subjectivities that these Indonesians recognize (or misrecognize)[36] in mass media cannot be reduced to dominant "Western" models of sexual identity. Nor does a preexisting internal state of desire find its social label at this moment. Instead, the subject and the archipelagic frame encompassing its desires are mutually constructed.

To situate the moment of recognition or construction, it is once again necessary to bring in the postcolonial nation-state. The Indonesian state has become aware that its mass media policies have crossed a threshold beyond which they encourage not only nationalism but translocal subjectivities that threaten to spin beyond state control. Television stations in Indonesia, for example, rely heavily on imported programming (each imports about seven thousand shows a year), and they frequently dub these shows into Indonesian. In 1996, sensing an opportunity to further its language policy, the parliament, with Suharto's tacit approval, passed a draft law requiring that *all* foreign shows be dubbed.[37] An unusual debate between Suharto, the parliament, the army, and other pressure groups ensued, and in July 1997, after months of controversy, Suharto refused to sign the law – the first time in Indonesian history that such a constitutionally questionable act had taken place.[38] When the dust cleared in December 1997, the law had been changed to its exact opposite: all dubbing of foreign television shows was forbidden; only subtitles were permitted.[39]

The government has justified this about-face in terms of cultural contamination and the family. As one apologist explained: "Dubbing can . . . ruin the self-image of family members as a result of adopting foreign values that are 'Indonesianized.' . . . whenever Indonesians view television, films, or other broadcasts where the original language has been changed into our national language, those Indonesians will think that the performances in those media constitute a part of themselves. As if the culture behind those performances were also the culture of our people."[40] At the intersection of postcoloniality and globalization, the ability of Sharon Stone or Jim Carrey to speak Indonesian is no longer a welcome opportunity to build language skills and foster the prestige of Indonesian but instead threatens Indonesians' ability to differentiate themselves from the outside.[41] The fear is that the citizen will be alienated, as in Toer's novel, from "others of its kind." How might the emergence of *lesbi* and *gay* subjectivities, on ostensibly personal and social levels, parallel this controversy? How might we think of them in terms of "dubbing culture," an embodiment of subjectivities that, from a modernist perspective, appear disjunctural and inauthentic? How might dubbing culture be less like a path and more like an archipelago?

The Mystery of Gay Marriage

Despite the power of mass media, their influence is neither direct nor determining. Their transformative effects, and those of the archipelago concept, are nowhere more apparent than in the "mystery" of *gay* men's marriages to women. Walking along the dark riverbank in *Texas* one night toward a group of shadows leaning against a railing, I met Andy and four of his friends. Andy identified as *gay*, explaining that his boyfriend of ten years was married with two children. When I asked if the boyfriend should get divorced, he stared in shock: "Of course not. He needs descendants and a wife. I want to get married in five years – I already have a girlfriend. You mean you won't marry as long as you live?" When I nodded, the other men confronted me in astonishment: "How could you not want to get married? You'll be lonely when you get old! Everyone must have descendants."

In this story, *gay* men not only implicate me in their *gay* archipelago but also discuss a central concern of their lives, marriage. Most *gay* Indonesians marry and have children and see these actions as consistent with their subjectivities. Most also assume that gay men in the "West" marry women.[42] While in Indonesia, I always placed on my desk a picture of my partner that shows him standing with a female colleague. Most *gay*-identified men would point out this picture and say, "His wife is taller than he is!" My explanation that she was a friend and that neither my partner nor I wanted to marry a woman would be met with disbelief and pity. Many "Westerners" have reciprocated with their own misrecognition when assuming, as I once did, that *gay* identities are incompatible with marriage. They have failed to understand that not only the *gay* world but the *gay* self is archipelagic. What is distinctive about these identities *vis-à-vis* "normal" Indonesian sexuality is not same-sex sex (it is usually taken for granted that both men and women will engage in it, given the chance) but love, abiding romantic interest in the same gender.

The *gay* self is not internally homogeneous and integrated; instead, it is composed of multiple subjectivities constituted in, rather than ontologically anterior to, social relations. It is an additive and "dividual" self, consistent with selves identified by many scholars of Southeast Asia and Melanesia but, just as important, embodying state rhetorics of ethnonational identity.[43] *Gay* and *lesbi* Indonesians construct and are constructed by an overdetermined archipelagic idiom. Thus dominant "Western" notions of egosyntonic, unitary identity have been reconfigured in the Indonesian context: this homosexual self desires to marry. *Gay* persons are self-reflexive but not self-congruent. Could they become poster children for the ultimate postmodern subject? The mystery is more complex.

Ikbal was a friend of Andy; Ikbal's wife of five years lived in a nearby village with their child, while he cohabited in Surabaya with a male lover, Dodi. Hand in hand with Dodi at *Texas* almost every night, Ikbal frequently lectured other *gay* men on the obligation to marry and the joys it brought. It was a point of pride to him that his wife and parents "knew about him" and that he and Dodi had married cousins so they would never be separated. One day Ikbal insisted that I come to the village to meet his wife. Once there, however, we would stay in a nearby town with his parents until Sunday; he would end up spending only two hours with his wife before we had to return to Surabaya. En route to the meeting Ikbal told me about the months of sexual frustration he and his wife had experienced: they had been able to consummate their marriage only by admitting Dodi to their bed, where he lay alongside Ikbal and, as Ikbal's wife sobbed, stimulated him so that penetration could take place. On this Sunday, when he could delay his visit with his wife no longer, Ikbal warned me to be extra macho: "Now is the time to begin playacting." Apparently his family's knowledge of him was more fractured than I had suspected. As our little minibus, adrift in a green flowing sea of rice paddies, approached the village and a tense afternoon of silent squabbles and awkward smiles, Ikbal looked out the dusty window and almost whispered: "These parts of my life cannot be unified."[44]

Theoretical physicists may believe in God's creation; social constructionists may believe that they were born gay or lesbian. The mystery of *gay* men's marriages to women is that most *gay* men evince – simultaneously, within a single subjectivity – an archipelagic self to which marriage is not only compatible but pleasurable and a self for which it stymies a desire to integrate one's spheres of life into a single narrative trajectory.[45] Most *gay* men want to marry, but they also scheme how to delay or avoid it and how to maintain *gay* friendships and sex partners once married. This is a mystery not only to the "external," non-Indonesian observer but also to the men themselves; many of them, like Ikbal, experience it as a contradiction. One clue to it lies in the origins of the imperative to marry itself. While marriage is a powerful norm throughout Indonesia, the particular form of this imperative that *gay* men experience certainly does not stem from a primordial localism: I have found strikingly little regional, religious, or ethnic variation concerning *gay* men's ideologies of marriage. In some regions, like Java and South Sulawesi, it is not historically expected that all persons will wed and procreate.[46] Additionally, what limited sources we have suggest

that from the 1920s to the 1960s Indonesian men with same-sex subjectivities assumed that their subjectivities, like those of gay men and lesbians in the contemporary "West," precluded marriage to an opposite-sex spouse. What, then, is the origin of the imperative to marry?

A key element of Indonesian state ideology, apart from the archipelago concept, is the *azas kekeluargaan*, or "family principle," which holds that the family is the fundamental unit of the nation.[47] Crucially, this is not the extended family but the nuclear family, whose ubiquitous smiles illuminate television ads and government posters: husband, wife, and two children, with a car, a home with smooth white tile floors, a television set, and other paraphernalia of the new middle class. It is this "public domesticity" that the state equates with citizen subjectivity and summons into being through a range of development practices.[48] Children are necessary for continuing the nation and for supporting their elders in their old age. The state's ideal family converges with the rhetoric of globalization.

While a considerable body of work has pointed out the gender inequalities of the new international division of labor, less attention has been paid to its foundation in the naturalization of the heterosexual couple as the basic unit of the postcolonial nation. More effectively than Henry Ford's fabled management of his workers' lives ever could, the heterosexualization of the labor force constitutes the domains of public and private, locates the family as the unit of consumption, and naturalizes gender inequalities. Thus heterosexuality provides a critical suture between capitalist ideologies of production and nationalist ideologies of the nuclear, middle-class family as metonym for the nation. It is a moral economy linking economic production and citizenship. As constituted by these discourses, the unmarried self is an incomplete economic and national subject.[49] . . .

This notion of the family is strongly influenced by shifting economic rationalities. In 1982, following the oil boom, Suharto's technocratic ministers gained ground and enacted economic and fiscal reforms that resulted in massive inflows of capital, which accelerated a shift away from agriculture and toward the service and industrial sectors.[50] This shift led to the rise of a substantial middle class for the first time in Indonesian history; Daniel S. Lev dates its consumerist and self-reflexive consciousness to a special edition of the magazine *Prisma* on the "new middle class" in 1984, during the same period in which *lesbi* and *gay* subjectivities appeared in the form of a national network for the first time.[51] These economic changes did not affect *gay* and *lesbi* subjectivities in a determinist manner, nor were Indonesians suddenly able to travel to or to obtain lesbian and gay publications from the "West." Most *lesbi* and *gay* Indonesians make less than fifty dollars a month – working-class wages even by Indonesian standards. But many observers identify the Indonesian middle class in terms of aspiration and "mode of consumption." In Howard Dick's words: "Among the *rakyat* [lower classes], consumer durables are shared: it is anti-social to restrict the access of one's neighbors. Middle class households, by contrast, confine the enjoyment of such goods to members of the household. . . . In other words, there is 'privatization of the means of consumption.'"[52]

With this consumerist ethic comes a modernist, narrative self, defined in terms of autobiography. While far from universal, the notion of the self as something constructed is hardly new.[53] What is at issue in the Indonesian context is the conjunction of a fashioned self with a specific middle-class consumerism. It is not a fantasy of the sultan or the super-rich cosmopolitan who selects at will from the world's bounty. It is a circumscribed personhood-as-career in which, given limited resources, one negotiates and budgets one's life trajectory within a marketplace logic that guides the crafting of choices. The self becomes the self's profession: this middle-class subjectivity is a story that the self tells to itself about itself, rather than a story passed down primarily through kinship, ethnic, or religious background, as the stories of the lower and upper Indonesian classes historically were.[54] Like middle-class subjectivities, *gay* and *lesbi* subjectivities are not passed down through tradition; they become their own stories, and the telling of those stories becomes a problem. A palette of possible lives spreads out before the subject, whose only prohibition is not to choose. One self-consumes, struggling to forge one's self-story. Like M. C. Escher's image of two disembodied hands gripping pens, con-juring each other into existence on a drawing pad, the self and the self's story form a loop of personhood in which social others are secondary. As Escher's loop breaks down without the pens with which to draw, so the commodity forms the conduit by which the middle-class self writes its story. In this sense, the *gay* person is self-congruent. Is this the same old liberal, bourgeois subject that has received such scholarly attention?[55] The mystery is more complex.

My goal is not to adjudicate between apparently contradictory notions of *gay* personhood, the archipelagic and multiple (where marriage to women is not a problem) or the consumerist and congruent (where marriage to women is a problem).[56] Noting that both the archipelago concept and the family principle emerge in the shadow of the state, I wish to hold them in tension, as a mystery, because it is precisely in such a multiply mediated contact zone that *gay* subjectivities exist.[57] Neither concept of personhood is exclusive to Indonesia; at issue are the circumstances of their imbrication. In the context of a narrativized self that is also multiple, a *gay* self can be a married, procreating self. When a *gay* man turns to his lover in bed and tells him to marry, he is not confused about who he "really" is, nor is he internalizing homophobia or denying reality. He is expressing and perpetuating an identity best thought of as archipelagic (rather than cosmopolitan, diasporic, or hybrid). While I find the gender politics of this scenario disturbing, particularly for women like Ikbal's wife who have little power in their marriages, it is important to recognize the situated rationality at play in the production of these new inequalities.

The crucial point is that homosexuality (and sexuality more generally) is globalized not as a monolithic domain but as a multiplicity of beliefs and practices, elements of which can move independently of each other or not move at all.[58] In the case of *gay* and *lesbi*, the notion of homosexual identity has moved, but other aspects of the dominant "Western" discourse of homosexuality have not. Foucault's genealogy of homosexuality in the "West" locates the intersection of power and knowledge at the confession.[59] Identity reveals and renders intelligible an interior, private self but is not authentic until exteriorized to an interlocutor who interprets and acknowledges this confession. Only then is the person "out of the closet," even in the remarkable case of the "intralocutor" operative in "coming out to yourself." Many theorists have shown how this model construes homosexual identity as a constant, iterative process of articulation and reception, an incitement to discourse that contributed to the "reverse discourse" of the lesbian and gay rights movement.[60]

But when the terms *lesbian* and *gay* moved to Indonesia, the conjunction of sexuality and confession neither preceded nor followed it. As a result, the ontological status of *lesbi* and *gay* subjectivities does not hinge on disclosure to spheres of home, workplace, or God. *Gay* men and *lesbi* do not "come out of the closet" but speak of being "opened" [*terbuka*] or "shut" [*tertutup*]. Construed not in terms of moving from one place to another but in terms of opening oneself, these subjectivities are additive rather than substitutive; opening them does not necessarily imply closing others. In addition, *lesbi* and *gay* Indonesians open not to the whole universe but to the *gay* world; confessing to other worlds in society is irrelevant. We find not an epistemology of the closet but an epistemology of life worlds, where healthy subjectivity depends not on integrating diverse domains of life and having a unified, unchanging identity in all situations but on separating domains of life and maintaining their borders against the threat of gossip and discovery.

This may call to mind the work of George Chauncey and other scholars on the history of homosexual identities in the "West."[61] In early-twentieth-century New York, for instance, the term *coming out*, derived from the notion of a debutante ball, implied coming out to a select community, not to all spheres of life. Furthermore, many homosexually identified people married and did not see their doing so as incongruous. Nonetheless, I would caution against a teleological reading of Indonesians as followers in these footsteps and against a structuralist reading of contemporary Indonesia and historical New York as presenting a mutual set of necessary and sufficient conditions. Such interpretations beg the question of how sameness and difference are measured in the first place. Contemporary *lesbi* and *gay* subjectivities

diverge in important respects from earlier homosexual identities in the "West," not least because they imagine themselves situated in an actual transnational archipelago of established lesbian and gay movements. As Ikbal's story reveals, moreover, the epistemology of the gay world coexists mysteriously with a narrative self exhibiting a tropism toward unity.

The fallacy of seeing contemporary *gay* and *lesbi* subjectivities as living fossils is highlighted by what we know about homosexual identities in Indonesia before national independence in 1945. It may seem that people started hanging out in *tempat ngeber* like *Texas* only after the emergence of *gay* and *lesbi* subjectivities. But the following episode from Sucipto's text *The Perfect Path*, mentioned at the beginning of this essay, suggests otherwise. The year is 1926, and Sucipto, young and homeless in Surabaya, has been walking along the river at night. He pauses to rest on a bridge near the Gubeng train station, near present-day *Texas*. While he is lost in thought, a voice calls out to him. It is a Dutchman, who invites Sucipto to his house and pays Sucipto to have sex with him. After leaving the house, Sucipto returns to the bridge, "thinking about what had just happened. . . . it was completely impossible that a Dutch person could desire things like that. . . . he was of a different race than myself. Apparently my assumptions had been turned upside down. . . . How did he know that I like this kind of thing? This was what astonished me."[62]

The "Westerner" of Sucipto's imagination did not have same-sex desires prior to this encounter. Even after learning that a colonial "Westerner" can have these desires, Sucipto does not identify with him; he sees him as interested only in commodified sex, incapable of the love that distinguishes the desire Sucipto has shared with other Javanese men. Sucipto sees his homosexuality in the 1920s as a local, Javanese phenomenon; he also sees it as incompatible with marriage and has discouraged his Javanese friends from marrying. Living at the high point of Dutch colonialism, he does not imagine himself as part of a national or transnational community, but in some ways his subjectivity is closer to "Western" gay or lesbian subjectivity than to contemporary Indonesian *gay* subjectivity, since normative *gay* Indonesians marry and normative gay "Westerners" do not. It is not coincidental that the sociologist who discovered Sucipto's text published it as *Path of My Life*, which seemed "more fitting with its character as an autobiography," rather than as *The Perfect Path*. From his perspective, Sucipto's story could represent not a perfect path but only the path of his life. From this standpoint, self-identity is personal and Sucipto's text an auto-biography – particular, not universal.[63] Clearly, a theory of globalization that holds that things become more similar as time marches on is insufficient. Contemporary *lesbi* and *gay* subjectivities are not just the evolutionary end points of Sucipto's subjectivity. They represent a dubbing culture, the production of translocality, the reterritorialization of "Western" discourses of homosexuality in the context of already existing notions of same-sex desire.[64]

Conclusion

The term "post-colonial" is not merely descriptive of "this" society rather than "that," or of "then" and "now." It re-reads "colonization" as part of an essentially transnational and transcultural "global" process – and it produces a decentered, diasporic or "global" rewriting of earlier, nation-centered imperial grand narratives. Its theoretical value therefore lies precisely in its refusal of this "here" and "there," "then" and "now," "home" and "abroad" perspective.

Stuart Hall, "The Question of Cultural Identity," 247

In this essay I have taken in earnest Hall's interpretation of postcoloniality as a flexible, provocative problematic. In doing so, I have produced the beginnings of a decentered, archipelagic rewriting of what might otherwise be interpreted as imprints on a perfect path: the emergence of *lesbi* and *gay* subjectivities in Indonesia. Refusing the perspectives of samness-difference and local-global, I hope that my analysis opens avenues of inquiry beyond the Indonesian case.

In reference to nationalism, Chatterjee asks: "If nationalisms in the rest of the world have to choose their imagined community from certain 'modular' forms already made available to them by Europe and the Americas, what do they have left to imagine? History, it would seem, has decreed that we in the postcolonial world shall only be perpetual consumers of modernity.... Even our imaginations must remain forever colonized."[65] For Chatterjee, postcoloniality provides a rough starting point from which to deconstruct this dilemma. Such a framework, I argue, proves worthwhile in the context of *gay* and *lesbi* subjectivities as well.

Transposing Chatterjee's question to sexuality, I would answer that there is a vast, archipelagic space in which *gay* and *lesbi* Indonesians might imagine new subjectivities and communities, despite conditions of inequality, oppression, and contradiction. When some Indonesians began to identify as *lesbi* and *gay*, they articulated subjectivities that apparently rejected local traditions and lay outside Indonesian history. But in fact these Indonesians have reconfigured local, national, and transnational discourses in a way that challenges the modernist single trajectory for lesbian and gay identity. Were Sucipto and Minke to meet a contemporary *lesbi* or *gay* Indonesian, they would have difficulty understanding a postcolonial subjectivity that has transformed the boundaries by which one decides who is "the same." The specter of LGQ identities as either homogenized or fractured beyond recuperation by the forces of globalization must give way to a more nuanced postcolonial and translocal perspective, informed by a rubric of postcolonial LGQ studies. There is no perfect path.

Notes

To protect their confidentiality, I have changed the names, as well as details of locations and personal histories, of all Indonesians mentioned in this essay except Dédé Oetomo. My research in Indonesia in 1992, 1993, 1995, and 1997–8 was generously supported by a Social Science Research Council International Dissertation Research Fellowship, a National Science Foundation Doctoral Dissertation Improvement Grant, the Department of Social and Cultural Anthropology at Stanford University, the Morrison Institute for Population and Resource Studies, and the Center for the Teaching of Indonesian. During the writing of this essay I received support as a

MacArthur Fellow at the Center for International Security and Cooperation at Stanford University. I thank the following individuals for commenting on earlier drafts: Kathleen Coll, Shelly Errington, Erich Fox Tree, Akhil Gupta, David Murray, Dédé Oetomo, and Sylvia Yanagisako. Particular thanks are due George Chauncey, Bill Maurer, and Elizabeth Povinelli for their supportive editorial guidance and to Purnima Mankekar for a careful reading of a final draft. All errors, of course, are my sole responsibility.

1   Throughout this essay the terms "West" and "Western" are quoted to indicate that they are hegemonic norms. Like Akhil Gupta, "in speaking of 'the West,' I refer to the effects of hegemonic representations of the Western self rather than its subjugated traditions. Therefore I do not use the term to refer simply to a geographic space but to a particular historical conjugation of place, power, and knowledge" (*Postcolonial Developments: Agriculture in the Making of Modern India* [Durham: Duke University Press, 1998], 36). It is precisely this homogeneous image of the "West" that *gay* and *lesbi* Indonesians experience as *the* West. Throughout the essay the terms *gay* and *lesbi* are italicized to distinguish them from "gay" and "lesbian" as analytic concepts.

2   Pramoedya Ananta Toer, *Footsteps*, ed. and trans. Max Lane (New York: Penguin, 1990), 15.

3   Arjun Appadurai, "Disjuncture and Difference in the Global Cultural Economy," in *Modernity at Large: Cultural Dimensions of Globalization* (Minneapolis: University of Minnesota Press, 1996), 31. In contradistinction to what he terms a priori difference, Daniel Miller describes the "new forms of difference" as a posteriori differences: "This is the sense of quite unprecedented diversity created by the differential consumption of what had once been thought to be global and homogenizing institutions. . . . The idea of *a posteriori* diversity . . . seeks out new forms of difference, some regional, but increasingly based on social distinctions which may not be easily identified with space" ("Introduction: Anthropology, Modernity, and Consumption," in *Worlds Apart: Modernity through the Prism of the Local*, ed. Daniel Miller [London: Routledge, 1995], 2–3). Excellent examples of the burgeoning literature on globalization and difference include Arjun Appadurai, "The Production of Locality," in *Modernity at Large*, 178–200; Mike Featherstone, "Global and Local Cultures," in *Mapping the Futures: Local Cultures, Global Change*, ed. Jon Bird et al. (London: Routledge, 1993); Featherstone, "Localism, Globalism, and Cultural Identity," in *Global/Local: Cultural*

Production and the Transnational Imaginary, ed. Rob Wilson and Wimal Dissanayake (Durham: Duke University Press, 1996), 46–77; J. K. Gibson-Graham, *The End of Capitalism (as We Knew It): A Feminist Critique of Political Economy* (Cambridge, Mass.: Blackwell, 1996); Paul Gilroy, "Route Work: The Black Atlantic and the Politics of Exile," in *The Post-Colonial Question: Common Skies, Divided Horizons*, ed. Iain Chambers and Lidia Curti (London: Routledge, 1996), 17–29; Akhil Gupta and James Ferguson, "Beyond 'Culture': Space, Identity, and the Politics of Difference," *Cultural Anthropology* 7 (1992): 6–23; Stuart Hall, "The Local and the Global: Globalization and Ethnicity" and "Old and New Identities, Old and New Ethnicities," in *Culture, Globalization, and the World-System: Contemporary Conditions for the Representation of Identity*, ed. Anthony D. King (London: Macmillan, 1991); Hall, "When Was 'the Post-Colonial'? Thinking at the Limit," in Chambers and Curti, *Post-Colonial Question*, 242–60; Hall, "The Question of Cultural Identity," in *Understanding Modern Societies: An Introduction*, ed. Stuart Hall et al. (Cambridge, Mass.: Blackwell, 1995), 596–633; Ulf Hannerz, "Scenarios for Peripheral Cultures," in King, *Culture, Globalization, and the World-System*; Hannerz, *Transnational Connections: Culture, People, Places* (London: Routledge, 1996); Fredric Jameson, "Notes on Globalization as a Philosophical Issue," in *The Cultures of Globalization*, ed. Fredric Jameson and Masao Miyoshi (Durham: Duke University Press, 1998), 54–77; Philip McMichael, "Globalization: Myths and Realities," *Rural Sociology* 61 (1996): 25–55; and Malcolm Waters, *Globalization* (London: Routledge, 1995).

4   See Richard Parker, *Beneath the Equator: Cultures of Desire, Male Homosexuality, and Emerging Gay Communities in Brazil* (New York: Routledge, 1999), 218–21; Appadurai, "Production of Locality"; Jonathan Friedman, "Being in the World: Globalization and Localization," *Theory, Culture, and Society* 7 (1990): 311–28; and Gupta, *Postcolonial Developments*.

5   E.g., Aijaz Ahmad, *In Theory: Classes, Nations, Literatures* (London: Verso, 1992); Arif Dirlik, "The Postcolonial Aura: Third World Criticism in the Age of Global Capitalism," *Critical Inquiry* 20 (1992): 328–56; Ella Shohat, "Notes on the 'Post-Colonial,'" *Social Text*, nos. 31–2 (1992): 99–113. For useful discussions of postcoloniality debates see Bart Moore-Gilbert, *Postcolonial Theory: Contexts, Practices, Politics* (London: Verso, 1997); and Hall, "When Was 'the Post-Colonial'?" In response to fears about

the term's potential to efface cultural specificity, Hall notes that "Australia and Canada, on the one hand, Nigeria, India, and Jamaica on the other, are certainly not 'post-colonial' *in the same way*. But this does not mean that they are not 'post-colonial' *in any way*" (246).

6 I use the term *LGQ studies* to refer to gay, lesbian, bisexual, queer, transgender, and intersex studies.

7 For an excellent critique of the concept of the "indigenous" see Gupta, *Postcolonial Developments*, chaps. 3–4.

8 Kath Weston, "Lesbian/Gay Studies in the House of Anthropology," *Annual Review of Anthropology* 22 (1993): 344. Examples of the growing literature of lesbian, gay, and bisexual identities outside the "West" include Dennis Altman, "Global Gaze/Global Gays," *GLQ* 3 (1997): 417–36; Evelyn Blackwood, "Tombois in West Sumatra: Constructing Masculinity and Erotic Desire," in *Female Desires: Same-Sex Relations and Transgender Practices across Cultures*, ed. Evelyn Blackwood and Saskia E. Wieringa (New York: Columbia University Press, 1999), 181–205; Donald L. Donham, "Freeing South Africa: The 'Modernization' of Male–Male Sexuality in Soweto," *Cultural Anthropology* 13 (1998): 3–21; Peter Drucker, "'In the Tropics There Is No Sin': Sexuality and Gay-Lesbian Movements in the Third World," *New Left Review*, no. 218 (1996): 75–101; Peter A. Jackson, "*Kathoey* ⟨ ⟩ Gay ⟨ ⟩ Man: The Historical Emergence of Gay Male Identity in Thailand," in *Sites of Desire, Economies of Pleasure: Sexualities in Asia and the Pacific*, ed. Lenore Manderson and Margaret Jolly (Chicago: University of Chicago Press, 1997), 166–90; Mark Johnson, *Beauty and Power: Transgendering and Cultural Transformation in the Southern Philippines* (Oxford: Berg, 1997); Martin F. Manalansan IV, "In the Shadows of Stonewall: Examining Gay Transnational Politics and the Diasporic Dilemma," in *The Politics of Culture in the Shadow of Capital*, ed. Lisa Lowe and David Lloyd (Durham: Duke University Press, 1997), 485–505; Parker, *Beneath the Equator*; and Saskia E. Wieringa, "Desiring Bodies or Defiant Cultures: Butch–Femme Lesbians in Jakarta and Lima," in Blackwood and Wieringa, *Female Desires*, 206–29.

9 See Gayatri Chakravorty Spivak, *In Other Worlds: Essays in Cultural Politics* (New York: Methuen, 1987), 202; Arturo Escobar, *Encountering Development: The Making and Unmaking of the Third World* (Princeton: Princeton University Press, 1995); and James Ferguson, *The Anti-Politics Machine: "Development," Depoliticization, and Bureaucratic Power in Lesotho* (Minneapolis: University of Minnesota Press, 1994).

10 Homi K. Bhabha, *The Location of Culture* (London: Routledge, 1994), 86. For one example of this first type of reductionism see Barry D. Adam, Jan Willem Duyvendak, and André Krouwel, eds., *The Global Emergence of Gay and Lesbian Politics: National Imprints of a Worldwide Movement* (Philadelphia: Temple University Press, 1999): "There are impressive parallels in the names of organizations: many countries have known 'gay liberation fronts,' 'revolutionary leagues,' and so on, indicating that movements follow more or less comparable paths, pass through the same phases, and draw names from other social and political movements with which there is some resemblance in terms of ideology, goals, or methods of resistance" (369–70; see also 352, 357). Cf. my discussion of GAYa Nusantara and GAYa Dewata, below.

11 Important examples of this literature include Benedict Anderson, *Imagined Communities: Reflections on the Origin and Spread of Nationalism* (London: Verso, 1983); Anderson, *Language and Power: Exploring Political Cultures in Indonesia* (Ithaca: Cornell University Press, 1990); John R. Bowen, *Muslims through Discourse: Religion and Ritual in Gayo Society* (Princeton: Princeton University Press, 1993); Suzanne Brenner, "Reconstructing Self and Society: Javanese Muslim Women and 'the Veil,'" *American Ethnologist* 23 (1996): 673–97; Brenner, *The Domestication of Desire: Women, Wealth, and Modernity in Java* (Princeton: Princeton University Press, 1998); Amen Budiman, ed., *Jalan Hidupku: Autobiografi Seorang Gay Priyayi Jawa Awal Abad XX* (1927; rpt. Jakarta: Apresiasi Gay Jakarta, 1992); Robert W. Hefner, "Islam, State, and Civil Society: ICMI and the Struggle for the Indonesian Middle Class," *Indonesia* 56 (1993): 2–35; Robert W. Hefner and Patricia Horvatich, eds., *Islam in an Era of Nation-States: Politics and Religious Renewal in Muslim Southeast Asia* (Honolulu: University of Hawaii Press, 1997); John Pemberton, *On the Subject of "Java"* (Ithaca: Cornell University Press, 1994); Michel Picard, *Bali: Cultural Tourism and Touristic Culture* (Singapore: Archipelago, 1996); Geoffrey Robinson, *The Dark Side of Paradise: Political Violence in Bali* (Ithaca: Cornell University Press, 1995); Danilyn Rutherford, "Of Birds and Gifts: Reviving Tradition on an Indonesian Frontier," *Cultural Anthropology* 11 (1996): 577–616; Laurie J. Sears, *Shadows of Empire: Colonial Discourse and Javanese Tales* (Durham: Duke University

Press, 1996); James T. Siegel, *Solo in the New Order: Language and Hierarchy in an Indonesian City* (Princeton: Princeton University Press, 1986); Siegel, *Fetish, Recognition, Revolution* (Princeton: Princeton University Press, 1997); Mary Margaret Steedly, *Hanging without a Rope: Narrative Experience in Colonial and Postcolonial Karoland* (Princeton: Princeton University Press, 1993); Anna Lowenhaupt Tsing, *In the Realm of the Diamond Queen: Marginality in an Out-of-the-Way Place* (Princeton: Princeton University Press, 1993); and Adrian Vickers, *Bali: A Paradise Created* (Hong Kong: Periplus, 1989).

12 See Dédé Oetomo, "Patterns of Bisexuality in Indonesia," in *Bisexuality and HIV/AIDS: A Global Perspective*, ed. Rob Tielman, Manuel Carballo, and Aart Hendriks (Buffalo: Prometheus, 1991); and Oetomo, "Gender and Sexual Orientation in Indonesia," in *Fantasizing the Feminine in Indonesia*, ed. Laurie J. Sears (Durham: Duke University Press, 1996), 259–69.

13 That is, men who self-identify as *gay* in some contexts at least.

14 My thanks to Lisa Rofel for helping me develop this point. I explore the implications of cogendered friendships and activities in Tom Boellstorff, "The Gay Archipelago: Translocal Identity in Indonesia," manuscript, 1999.

15 Globalization generally is highly gendered. See Gibson-Graham, *End of Capitalism*; and Maila Stivens, "Theorizing Gender, Power, and Modernity in Affluent Asia," in *Gender and Power in Affluent Asia*, ed. Krishna Sen and Maila Stivens (London: Routledge, 1998), 1–34.

16 See Evelyn Blackwood, "Falling in Love with An-Other Lesbian: Reflections on Identity in Fieldwork," in *Taboo: Sex, Identity, and Erotic Subjectivity in Anthropological Fieldwork*, ed. Don Kulick and Margaret Willson (London: Routledge, 1995); Blackwood, "Tombois in West Sumatra"; B. J. D. Gayatri, "Coming Out but Remaining Hidden: A Portrait of Lesbians in Java" (paper presented at the International Congress of Anthropological and Ethnological Sciences, Mexico City, July 1993); Gayatri, "Indonesian Lesbians Writing Their Own Script: Issues of Feminism and Sexuality," in *Amazon to Zami: Towards a Global Lesbian Feminism*, ed. Monika Reinfelder (London: Cassell, 1996), 86–97; Alison Murray, "Femme on the Streets, Butch in the Sheets (a Play on Whores)," in *Mapping Desire: Geographies of Sexualities*, ed. David Bell and Gill Valentine (London: Routledge, 1995), 66–74; Murray, "Let Them Take Ecstasy: Class and Jakarta Lesbians," in Black-

wood and Wieringa, *Female Desires*, 139–56; and Wieringa, "Desiring Bodies or Defiant Cultures." In my larger project I also examine the male-to-female transgendered identity known as *waria* (Boellstorff, "Gay Archipelago," chap. 2).

17 Michel Foucault, *The Order of Things: An Archaeology of the Human Sciences*, trans. (New York: Pantheon, 1970). For a discussion of the strengths and weaknesses of Foucault's archaeological method see Hubert L. Dreyfus and Paul Rabinow, *Michel Foucault: Beyond Structuralism and Hermeneutics* (Chicago: University of Chicago Press, 1982).

18 Here I reference a discussion of sameness, difference, and postcoloniality whose detailed enumeration is beyond the scope of this essay. For examples see Akhil Gupta, "Blurred Boundaries: The Discourse of Corruption, the Culture of Politics, and the Imagined State," *American Ethnologist* 22 (1995): 375–402; Gloria Anzaldúa, *Borderlands/La Frontera* (San Francisco: Spinsters/Aunt Lute, 1987); Renato Rosaldo, *Culture and Truth: The Remaking of Social Analysis* (Boston: Beacon, 1989); and Craig Calhoun, ed., *Habermas and the Public Sphere* (Cambridge, Mass.: MIT Press, 1992).

19 See Pheng Cheah and Bruce Robbins, eds., *Cosmopolitics: Thinking and Feeling beyond the Nation* (Minneapolis: University of Minnesota Press, 1998).

20 Robert J. C. Young, *Colonial Desire: Hybridity in Theory, Culture, and Race* (London: Routledge, 1995), 25.

21 This is true not only in Indonesia. See, e.g., Donham, "Freeing South Africa"; Johnson, *Beauty and Power*; Parker, *Beneath the Equator*; and Took Took Thongthiraj, "Toward a Struggle against Invisibility: Love between Women in Thailand," in *Asian American Sexualities: Dimensions of the Gay and Lesbian Experience*, ed. Russell Leong (New York: Routledge, 1996), 163–74.

22 I have also come to realize that the neglect of *gay* and *lesbi* subjectivities in Indonesian studies stems less from a putative homophobia than from the equivalencies drawn in the "Western" academy between disciplines, methodologies, and discursive constitutions of the "field" as a unit of analysis. Historically, anthropologists in these islands have tended to study "ethnicities," the Javanese or Balinese or Minangkabau, rather than "Indonesians."

23 Given the limitations of space, I do not discuss conflicts in these communities in terms of gender, class, region, and so on (see, e.g.,

Murray, "Let Them Take Ecstasy"; Blackwood, "Tombois in West Sumatra"; Boellstorff, "Gay Archipelago"; and Oetomo, "Gender and Sexual Orientation in Indonesia"). Instead, I focus on processual formations of imagined *lesbi* and *gay* communities (i.e., the conditions of possibility for imagining intercommunity conflict in the first place).

24 For a broader discussion of the "privatization" of public spaces by lesbian, gay, bisexual, and transgendered communities see Gordon Brent Ingram, Anne-Marie Bouthillette, and Yolanda Retter, eds., *Queers in Space: Communities, Public Places, Sites of Resistance* (Seattle: Bay, 1997); and Bell and Valentine, *Mapping Desire*.

25 The distinction between "organizations" and other spaces is less clear than it might seem. Organizations tend to be small (three to ten members), and many cease to exist after three or four years. Those that survive for longer periods have usually obtained international funding, but since the primary impetus of such funding is HIV/AIDS prevention, and since international HIV/AIDS prevention discourse commonly ignores lesbians, *lesbi* groups are rarely able to access such funding, so they find it particularly difficult to sustain themselves. Only a few specifically *lesbi* magazines have ever existed: one, *GAYa LEStari*, was published four times between February and August 1994 as a supplement to the magazine *GAYa Nusantara*. A specifically *lesbi* magazine, *MitraS*, published three issues beginning in December 1997, but it is currently on hiatus.

26 During colonial times it was hardly unusual for Indies "natives" to have greater knowledge of the "West" than "Westerners" had of them. This imbalance persists today and represents a strong thread of continuity in the postcolonial context. At issue is the relationship that this knowledge bears to the *gay* or *lesbi* self.

27 Alfred Russel Wallace, *The Malay Archipelago, the Land of the Orang-utan and the Bird of Paradise: A Narrative of Travel, with Studies of Man and Nature* (1869; rpt. New York: Dover, 1962). The centrality of nationalism to postcoloniality has been explored thoroughly in Partha Chatterjee, *Nationalist Thought and the Colonial World: A Derivative Discourse* (Minneapolis: University of Minnesota Press, 1993); and Chatterjee, *The Nation and Its Fragments: Colonial and Postcolonial Histories* (Princeton: Princeton University Press, 1993).

28 At the First International Conference of the Law of the Sea in Geneva in 1958, Indonesia argued that its borders did not lie only a certain distance from the coast of each island, as was the norm, but included all of the waters "within" the archipelago. The Second International Conference in 1960 recognized the notion of an "archipelagic state" and with it the archipelago concept. See Mochtar Kusumaatmadja, "The Concept of the Indonesian Archipelago," *Indonesian Quarterly* 10, no. 4 (1982): 19.

29 Ibid., 25.

30 The framing of diversity in unity is common in postcolonial nationalisms (including the United States's own motto, E Pluribus Unum). See, e.g., Akhil Gupta, "The Song of the Nonaligned World: Transnational Identities, Late Capitalism, and the Reinscription of Space," *Cultural Anthropology* 7 (1992): 63–79.

31 Gayatri, "Indonesian Lesbians Writing Their Own Script," 94; Murray, "Let Them Take Ecstasy," 142. I explore the significance of the fact that this labeling was linked specifically to femininity in Boellstorff, "Gay Archipelago" (see also Tan beng hui, "Women's Sexuality and the Discourse on Asian Values: Cross-Dressing in Malaysia," in Blackwood and Wieringa, *Female Desires*, 289–97). But there is no a priori reason that greater oppression will not appear in Indonesia in the future. A disturbing precedent has been set by the antihomosexual group Pasrah, to my knowledge the first of its kind in Southeast Asia, which was formed in Malaysia in 1998 following the arrest of former deputy prime minister Anwar Ibrahim on sodomy and corruption charges. At present Pasrah appears to be a front organization with a manifesto but no record of activity.

32 The link between mass media and postcolonial states has been commented on in many contexts. For the case of television in India, for example, see Purnima Mankekar, *Screening Culture, Viewing Politics: An Ethnography of Television, Womanhood, and Nation in Postcolonial India* (Durham: Duke University Press, 1999).

33 For "public" Darta used the term *umum*, the same term used by my Balinese informant to distinguish *tempat umum* [public places] from *tempat ngeber*.

34 That Darta and Darta's mother knew of *lesbi* first was probably due to the wide publicity given the marriage of two women in Jakarta in 1981. See Boellstorff, "Gay Archipelago."

35 About two-thirds of my informants learned of these terms through mass media. Almost all the rest learned of them from friends or by wandering into a *tempat ngeber*. Of course, there is a high probability (which I have documented in some instances) that the people who provided them

with the information had themselves learned of the terms through mass media.

36 See Pierre Bourdieu, *Outline of a Theory of Practice*, trans. Richard Nice (Cambridge: Cambridge University Press, 1977).

37 *Republika* (Jakarta), 2 May 1996.

38 *Kompas* (Jakarta), 25 July 1997.

39 But the law is regularly flouted. See *Republika*, 7 March 1998.

40 Novel Ali, "Sulih suara dorong keretakan komunikasi keluarga," in *Bercinta Dengan Televisi: Ilusi, Impresi, dan Imaji Sebuah Kotak Ajaib*, ed. Deddy Mulyana and Idi Subandy Ibrahim (Bandung: PT Remaja Rosdakarya, 1997), 341–2. My translation.

41 See Dédé Oetomo, "Ketika Sharon Stone Berbahasa Indonesia," in Mulyana and Ibrahim, *Bercinta Dengan Televisi*, 333–7.

42 Even if they learn (from a non-Indonesian like me, from a mass-media source, etc.) that gay men in the "West" usually do not marry women, most Indonesian *gay* men continue to assume that they themselves will. In other words, the "Western" norm is not framed as a necessary component of *gay* subjectivity in Indonesia.

43 See Shelly Errington, *Meaning and Power in a Southeast Asian Realm* (Princeton: Princeton University Press, 1989); Clifford Geertz, "From the Native's Point of View: On the Nature of Anthropological Understanding," in *Local Knowledge: Further Essays in Interpretive Anthropology* (New York: Basic, 1983), 55–72; Marilyn Strathern, *The Gender of the Gift: Problems with Women and Problems with Society in Melanesia* (Berkeley: University of California Press, 1988); and Strathern, *Reproducing the Future: Essays on Anthropology, Kinship, and the New Reproductive Technologies* (New York: Routledge, 1992).

44 The term Ikbal used for "unified," *nyatu*, is derived from "one," *satu*.

45 Sexual dysfunction like Ikbal's is far from universal. Some married *gay* men claim that their sexual experiences with their wives are mutually satisfying.

46 For example, high-status women who are unable to find suitable partners may remain single and childless for life without compromising their femininity. See Nancy K. Florida, "Sex Wars: Writing Gender Relations in Nineteenth-Century Java," in Sears, *Fantasizing the Feminine in Indonesia*, 207–24; and Errington, *Meaning and Power*.

47 There is an extensive literature on the relationship between the postcolonial state and marriage in Indonesia. See, e.g., Sylvia Tiwon, "Models and Maniacs: Articulating the Female in Indonesia," Julia I. Suryakusuma, "The State and Sexuality in New Order Indonesia," Daniel S. Lev, "On the Other Hand?" and Benedict Anderson, "'Bullshit!' S/he Said: The Happy, Modern, Sexy Indonesian Married Woman as Transsexual," in Sears, *Fantasizing the Feminine in Indonesia*, 47–70, 92–119, 191–202, 270–94; Evelyn Blackwood, "Senior Women, Model Mothers, and Dutiful Wives: Managing Gender Contradictions in a Minangkabau Village," in *Bewitching Women, Pious Men: Gender and Body Politics in Southeast Asia*, ed. Aihwa Ong and Michael G. Peletz (Berkeley: University of California Press, 1995), 124–58; Brenner, *Domestication of Desire*; and Barbara Hatley, "Nation, 'Tradition,' and Constructions of the Feminine in Modern Indonesian Literature," in *Imagining Indonesia: Cultural Politics and Political Culture*, ed. Jim Schiller and Barbara Martin-Schiller (Athens: Ohio University Center for International Studies, 1997), 90–120.

48 Rosalind C. Morris uses this term to refer to a similar configuration of state and marriage in Thailand ("Educating Desire: Thailand, Transnationalism, and Transgression," *Social Text*, nos. 52–3 [1997]: 53–79).

49 Here I draw on a long tradition that explores the relationship between the state, capitalism, and the family. See Dennis Altman, *Homosexual: Oppression and Liberation* (New York: Outerbridge and Dienstfrey, 1971); Michael Bronski, *Culture Clash: The Making of Gay Sensibility* (Boston: South End, 1984); Bronski, *The Pleasure Principle: Sex, Backlash, and the Struggle for Gay Freedom* (New York: St. Martin's, 1998); Chatterjee, *Nationalist Thought and the Colonial World*; Chatterjee, *Nation and Its Fragments*; John D'Emilio, "Capitalism and Gay Identity," in *Powers of Desire: The Politics of Sexuality*, ed. Ann Snitow, Christine Stansell, and Sharon Thompson (New York: Monthly Review Press, 1983), 100–13; Frederick Engels, *The Origin of the Family, Private Property, and the State, in the Light of the Researches of Lewis H. Morgan*, ed. Eleanor Burke Leacock, trans. Alec West (1884; rpt. New York: International, 1942); Richard K. Herrell, "Sin, Sickness, Crime: Queer Desire and the American State," in *The Nation/State and Its Sexual Dissidents*, ed. David Murray and Richard Handler (Newark, N.J.: Gordon and Breach, 1996), 273–300; Guy Hocquenghem, *Homosexual Desire*, trans. Daniella Dangoor (London: Allison and Busby, 1978); Andrew Parker et al., eds., *Nationalisms and Sexualities* (New York: Routledge, 1992); Linda Singer, "Sex and the Logic of Late

Capitalism," in *Erotic Welfare: Sexual Theory and Politics in the Age of Epidemic*, by Linda Singer, ed. Judith Butler and Maureen MacGrogan (New York: Routledge, 1993), 34–61; and Eli Zaretsky, *Capitalism, the Family, and Personal Life* (New York: Harper and Row, 1976).

50 See Hal Hill, *The Indonesian Economy since 1966: Southeast Asia's Emerging Giant* (Cambridge: Cambridge University Press, 1996); and Jeffrey A. Winters, *Power in Motion: Capital Mobility and the Indonesian State* (Ithaca: Cornell University Press, 1996).

51 Quoted in Richard Tanter and Kenneth Young, eds., *The Politics of Middle Class Indonesia* (Clayton, Australia: Monash University Centre of Southeast Asian Studies, 1990), 26. There is a burgeoning literature on the new middle class and consumerism in Southeast Asia, including, besides Tanter and Young's work, Michael Pinches, ed., *Culture and Privilege in Capitalist Asia* (London: Routledge, 1999); Richard Robison and David S. G. Goodman, eds., *The New Rich in Asia: Mobile Phones, McDonalds, and Middle-Class Revolution* (London: Routledge, 1996); and Krishna Sen and Maila Stivens, eds., *Gender and Power in Affluent Asia* (London: Routledge, 1998).

52 Quoted in Tanter and Young, *Politics of Middle Class Indonesia*, 64. Pinches emphasizes the importance of understanding middle classes in Asia in terms of "the processes of status formation through the shared symbols of lifestyle and consumption" rather than solely in terms of raw income *(Culture and Privilege in Capitalist Asia*, 8). See also Gibson-Graham's processual theory of class *(End of Capitalism*, 46–71).

53 See, e.g., Marcel Mauss, "A Category of the Human Mind: The Notion of the Person; the Notion of Self" (1938), in *Sociology and Psychology: Essays*, trans. Ben Brewster (London: Routledge and Kegan Paul, 1979), 57–94; and Michel Foucault, *The History of Sexuality*, trans. Robert Hurley, 3 vols. (New York: Pantheon, 1978–86).

54 More generally, Arjun Appadurai notes that "until recently . . . a case could be made that social life was largely inertial, that traditions provided a relatively finite set of possible lives" ("Global Ethnoscapes: Notes and Queries for a Transnational Anthropology," in *Modernity at Large*, 53).

55 See Jane F. Collier, Bill Maurer, and Lilana Suárez-Navaz, "Sanctioned Identities: Legal Constructions of Modern Personhood," *Identities* 2 (1995): 1–27; John L. Comaroff, "Images of Empire, Contests of Conscience: Models of

Colonial Domination in South Africa," in *Tensions of Empire: Colonial Cultures in a Bourgeois World*, ed. Frederick Cooper and Ann Laura Stoler (Berkeley: University of California Press, 1997), 163–97; and C. B. Macpherson, *The Political Theory of Possessive Individualism: Hobbes to Locke* (Oxford: Clarendon, 1962).

56 Nor are apparent contradictions inevitably a site of resistance. Stuart Hall notes: "In our intellectual way, we think that the world will collapse as the result of a logical contradiction: this is the illusion of the intellectual – that ideology must be coherent, every bit of it fitting together, like a philosophical investigation. When, in fact, the whole purpose of what Gramsci called an organic (i.e., historically effective) ideology is that it articulates into a configuration different subjects, different identities, different projects, different aspirations. It does not reflect, it constructs a 'unity' out of difference" ("Gramsci and Us," in *The Hard Road to Renewal: Thatcherism and the Crisis of the Left* [London: Verso, 1988], 166). David M. Halperin makes precisely this point with respect to "Western" homophobia: "Homophobic discourses are incoherent, then, but their incoherence, far from incapacitating them, turns out to empower them. In fact, homophobic discourses operate strategically by means of logical contradictions" (*Saint Foucault: Towards a Gay Hagiography* [New York: Oxford University Press, 1995], 34).

57 It is in this context that the existence of the term *biseks* in Indonesia is so interesting. While its range is much smaller than that of *lesbi* or *gay*, *biseks* is known to a substantial number of men and women. Men and women who identify as *biseks* almost always identify as *lesbi* or *gay* as well; it is a dual subjectivity lexicalizing simultaneous same-sex and opposite-sex interests (i.e., a *gay* man who is married to a woman will sometimes say that he is "*gay* and *biseks*," but not *biseks* alone). While there are *biseks* subjectivities, there is no "*biseks* world," no *dunia biseks*; these men and women see themselves as part of the *gay* world. In the Indonesian context, what is significant is not that this subjectivity calls into being a different community but that it implies, contrary to the dominant view, that *gay* and *lesbi* subjectivities exclude marriage.

58 "A productive question is to ask how culturally-specific domains have been dialectically formed and transformed in relation with other cultural domains, how meanings migrate across domain boundaries, and how specific actions are multiply constituted. In other words, we need to historicize our domains and trace their effects"

(Sylvia Yanagisako and Carol Delaney, introduction to *Naturalizing Power: Essays in Feminist Cultural Analysis*, ed. Sylvia Yanagisako and Carol Delaney [New York: Routledge, 1995], 11).

59 Foucault, *History of Sexuality*, vol. 1.

60 E.g., Judith Butler, *Bodies That Matter: On the Discursive Limits of "Sex"* (New York: Routledge, 1993); Foucault, *History of Sexuality*, vol. 1; Halperin, *Saint Foucault*; Eve Kosofsky Sedgwick, *Epistemology of the Closet* (London: Harvester Wheatsheaf, 1991).

61 See George Chauncey, *Gay New York: Gender, Urban Culture, and the Making of the Gay Male World, 1890–1940* (New York: Basic, 1994).

62 Budiman, *Jalan Hidupku*, 111–14. My translation.

63 Sucipto himself never terms his writings "auto-biography" or "memoir."

64 Generalizing from a single historical source is precarious but necessitated by the fact that Sucipto's is the only known text of its type from the colonial era. Interviews with informants in their fifties and sixties, although they do not extend quite so far into the past, corroborate important aspects of Sucipto's narrative.

65 Chatterjee, *Nation and Its Fragments*, 5.

15

A Man in the House
The Boyfriends of Brazilian
Travesti Prostitutes

Don Kulick

A recurring and extremely serious problem with scholarly studies of prostitution is that they generally only ever tell us about the professional lives of the women who earn their living through sex work. Unlike most other people, who are readily acknowledged to have a life outside or beyond what they do at work, a prostitute tends to be defined completely in terms of the work that she does.[1] She is generally thought of as a prostitute twenty-four hours of the day, even when she is not working. This understanding of prostitutes is reinforced by study after study that either makes no mention of a prostitute's private life or that discusses her private life in a way that only serves to highlight her identity as a prostitute. Often we are told, or led to believe, for example, that the boyfriends of prostitutes are their pimps and that the prostitutes are together with them out of necessity, or delusion, or fear – or for all those reasons at once (e.g., Barry 1979, 86–120; Barry 1995, 198–219; Høigård and Finstad 1986, 203–69).

Even work that is sympathetic to prostitutes and committed to nuanced understandings about them and their lives tends to mention their private lives cursorily, and then primarily to draw contrasts with their professional lives.[2] So in Sophie Day's (1990) sensitive writing about London prostitutes, or in the careful monograph by McKeganey and Barnard (1996) on prostitutes in Glasgow, for example, discussion of boyfriends is restricted to an account of how the women interviewed reserve specific parts of their bodies (e.g., their mouths) and specific sexual activities (e.g., kissing and oral sex) for their boyfriends, whereas other parts and activities can be made available to clients. We are told nothing about how the prostitutes' boyfriends are chosen or how the women interact with them in nonsexual contexts. Similarly, in Shannon Bell's (1995) respectful and revealing interviews with prostitutes, in Gail Pheterson's (1989, 1996) theoretical and activist writings, and in the important special issue of this journal that concerned prostitutes (*Social Text*, no. 37 [winter 1993]), what is discussed is the practice and politics of sex work, not private lives.

What all this means is that in study after study, interview after interview, and book after book about prostitutes, we learn an enormous amount about how prostitutes think about, interact with, and relate to their clients. But with only a few exceptions – such as Serena Nanda's (1990) work on Indian *hijras*, Annick Prieur's (1994; 1998) writings on Mexican *jotas*, or Jeferson Bacelar's (1982) monograph on the domestic lives of Brazilian female prostitutes – we learn next to nothing about how they think about their private relationships, how they make themselves attractive for the individuals they wish to have as partners, and what role those partners play in the prostitutes' lives more generally.

This essay explores the role that boyfriends play in the lives of transgendered prostitutes living in the city of Salvador, in northeastern

Brazil. Transgendered prostitutes are called *travestis* in Brazilian Portuguese, a word derived from *transvestir* (cross-dress). Travestis are males who, sometimes at ages as young as eight or ten, begin modifying their bodies and their self-presentational styles in an increasingly feminine direction, through the use of cosmetics, feminine clothing, and, as they grow older, the ingestion of massive quantities of estrogen-based hormones. By the time they reach their mid-teens, many travestis have also begun paying other travestis to inject several liters of industrial silicone directly into their bodies, in order to give those bodies prominent hips, buttocks, thighs, and, sometimes, breasts. Most travestis in Salvador have injected between two to five liters of silicone, but one well-known travesti in the city had twelve liters, and there are reports among travestis of travestis in other cities who have injected up to twenty liters over the course of several years. All travestis self-identify as homosexual, and despite the dramatic and often irrevocable modifications they perform on their bodies, they do not consider themselves to be women. They want to be feminine, they maintain, not female.

Travestis exist in Brazilian cities of every size, and in the large southern cities of São Paulo and Rio de Janeiro they number in the thousands. Salvador, which is Brazil's third largest city, with a population of over 2 million, has a population of travestis that fluctuates between about 80 to 250. Many of these travestis live together in the center of the city, in dilapidated houses that have been divided up into tiny cell-like rooms. During 1995 and 1996, I conducted anthropological fieldwork among travestis in Salvador, living with them in such a house and visiting them nightly at their various points of prostitution.

In my work with travestis, I discovered very quickly that boyfriends (generally referred to as *maridos*, which literally means "husbands," but also called *bofes*, *ocós*, *homens*, and *machos*) are a continual and central consideration in their lives. Boyfriends take up an enormous amount of a travesti's thought, time, and talk – not to mention her money. Travestis are forever orienting themselves to their current boyfriends, their ex-boyfriends, and their prospective boyfriends. The activities of boyfriends provide

endless fodder for gossip and conflict among travestis. When talking to other travestis, they discuss various men, commenting on what qualities a male must possess in order to be considered eligible as a boyfriend. They are forever trying to figure out how to attract some male who they have decided has those qualities, or they are trying to get over their bitterness at having been left and possibly robbed by some male who they *thought* had those qualities. When they are courting a potential boyfriend, or have snagged one they want to keep, a great deal of their life and their income revolves around him and his comfort, and they shower him with money, presents, and drugs – until the day they tire of him, at which point they send him packing and install a new man in their room. If there is one topic about which all travestis have strong opinions, it is boyfriends. Without understanding the role that boyfriends play in the lives of travestis, it is impossible to understand any dimension of their lives.

Keila's Passion

Keila Simpsom, a robust and heavyset travesti in her early thirties, and my teacher and coworker in Salvador, was in the throes of passion. During Carnival week she had suddenly begun falling in love with Tiane, a tall, muscular, tattooed, illiterate, thirty-year-old man who looked and acted like a nineteen-year-old adolescent – spending every day playing soccer on a nearby beach and getting high with his friends. Keila knew Tiane well – for six years he had been the live-in boyfriend of her best friend Marília, who had died after a long illness a few months previously – but she had never felt anything for him. She had lived in the same house with him, seen him daily, and spoken to him occasionally without contemplating the possibility of having him as her boyfriend. Now, though, for some completely inexplicable reason, she felt herself to be experiencing what she told me was desperate, sincere, and blind passion.

It had begun with an electric exchange of looks as they passed one another on the street during Carnival, and quickly progressed into brief, meaningful greetings as Tiane passed by Keila while she was working on the street at night. From Tiane's mother, who lived in a windowless room the size of a cupboard in the same house as Keila, Keila began hearing that Tiane wondered if Keila could spare a few *reais* (a few dollars) for him to buy himself food and beer on the street. Keila gave the mother the money to pass onto her son. She also bought him several new shirts and pairs of shorts, which she conveyed to him through his mother.

Tiane's mother was the intermediary between the two at this point because, initially, Keila's passion for Tiane had to be kept secret. The reason for this was partly because Keila shared her tiny room with Edilson, her boyfriend of the past seven years, and partly because Rita Lee, a toothless, older travesti living in a room in the same house as everyone else, had recently let it be known that Tiane was hers. She demonstrated this by ostentatiously buying and preparing food for him and calling him into her room to eat, closing the door behind him, and emerging later with a content smile, even when it had been obvious to everyone living in the house that all she and Tiane had done in her room was argue.

For the first few weeks of her infatuation, Keila didn't know what to do – she couldn't openly speak to Tiane, not near the house where she lived, because her boyfriend Edilson or Rita Lee or someone else would surely see, nor could she talk to him on the street where she worked at night, because one of the other travestis working the same street would certainly observe such a conversation and report it to others. All she could do was keep sending him small sums of money and presents through his mother and exchange brief, coded words as they passed one another on their way to or from the communal bathroom, or to or from the communal refrigerator at the back of the house, where they both had rooms (Tiane had been sleeping in his mother's room since the death of his travesti girlfriend Marília). During these quick encounters, Keila twice whispered times and places for Tiane to pass by on backstreets near where she worked. Both times she waited in vain – once he didn't show, and once he passed by with friends saying he would return later, but never did. A third time she asked *him* to suggest a time when he knew he would be able to come. He didn't show up that time either.

Keila began to despair. After having unsuccessfully attempted to meet with Tiane three times, she was tired and annoyed. She was going to drop him, she told me firmly – well, maybe after she gave him one more chance. She would ask him straight out next time she saw him: Did he want her or not? She needed a definite answer. "It will hurt me if he says no," she explained to me, "because I am impassioned with him – I'm going crazy, I think about him all the time. But the hurt will go away. And if he definitely says no, he doesn't want me, then I can stop thinking about him. If he gives me the answer I want, though," she continued, "then he will have to stop playing with me."

The next day, Keila, beaming, told me that she had asked Tiane straight out whether he wanted her. And he had given her, she laughed, "the correct answer." With that much now decided, Keila told him that they needed to meet somewhere and have a real talk. So they had arranged to meet later that night outside a backstreet hotel to which Keila sometimes took clients.

I heard the denouement to Keila's passion the following day. Keila had arranged to meet Tiane outside the hotel at eight o'clock the previous evening. At nine o'clock, he passed by in the company of a friend. "Where are you going?" Keila hissed at him discretely. "Up the street for a drink," he shrugged nonchalantly.

He returned at eleven o'clock. Keila was still waiting. They took a hotel room and sat talking for several hours. They did not have sex, Keila told me, they just talked about whether Tiane truly wanted to begin having a relationship with Keila. He assured her he did. He also told her, before they left the hotel room, that his birthday was coming up in a few weeks' time, and he would really like a present of an expensive pair of stylish overalls that he had had his eye on for quite some time.

The end of this story is both happy and sad. A few days after her discussion in the hotel room with Tiane, Keila announced to her boyfriend Edilson that it was over and that she was leaving him. She installed herself in another room in the same house for a couple of days, then she moved her belongings to a room in a house several blocks away from where she had been living. Tiane began to sleep and take his meals with her regularly. After several weeks of living isolated from other travestis, and from the milieu she had lived in for seven years, Keila decided that she wanted to return to her old house. She rented a small room right above Edilson, who was now her ex-boyfriend, and she moved in there with Tiane. Edilson took all this very badly, and he began to drink heavily and spread rumors that Keila had AIDS. He made several attempts to find another travesti girlfriend, but no one was interested. Edilson did what he could to make Keila's life miserable for a few months, then he had to move, because he had sold the last of his belongings and could no longer pay his rent. Rita Lee, who had only been together with Tiane for less than a week, but who continued to regard him as her boyfriend whom Keila had maliciously snatched from her, grew enormously bitter and began, too, to drink continually. Her health failed, she grew increasingly desiccated, and she was unable to work the streets at night. She too eventually became unable to pay her rent and was duly evicted. Unable to support herself, and unwanted by her family, who live in a suburb on the outskirts of Salvador, Rita Lee ended up in a hospice for AIDS patients, where she died in early 1996.

The Selection of Boyfriends

The story of Keila's passion reveals a number of characteristic features of travesti–boyfriend relationships. First of all, there is the object of Keila's passion – Tiane, a handsome young man with no apparent means of income, who spent all his days getting stoned and playing soccer on a nearby beach. For six years he had been the boyfriend of Marília, a travesti who had lived in the same house as Keila. This relationship ended only when Marília died in late 1994.

Tiane could be the pattern from which all other travesti boyfriends are cut. The men that travestis choose to be their boyfriends are always handsome, muscular, and usually tattooed young men between the ages of about sixteen to thirty. They almost never work, and if they do, they virtually invariably seem to work as security guards for buildings or parking lots. Just as invariably, the majority of them who do work stop working soon after they establish a relationship with a travesti – sometimes they stop

working at the insistence of the travesti; most often they don't need to be told, and they quit on their own accord.

Travestis usually meet these men because they live in the same area as the travesti herself, because they are the brother or the cousin or the friend of a man who is already the boyfriend of a travesti, or, finally, because the man is himself already the boyfriend of a travesti. Once a male becomes the boyfriend of a travesti, he immediately sparks the interest of the others, who will wonder what he has that his travesti girlfriend wants. If whatever he has is some quality or characteristic that other travestis also find attractive, then the boyfriend will be the object of much attention from other travestis, who may try to win him over by giving him presents and money. There is thus continual, and sometimes quite fierce and brutal, competition among travestis over a limited number of boyfriends. (The only fights I have witnessed between travestis have all been about boyfriends). Many of these boyfriends, once they have formed a relationship with a travesti, remain in the boyfriend pool for many years, where they circulate among travestis until they either settle down with one or, as in the case of Keila's ex-boyfriend Edilson, they grow too old and unattractive to be of much interest to anyone, in which case they disappear from the travesti milieu.

The most unusual way for a travesti to meet a male who later becomes her boyfriend is as a paying client. This apparently sometimes happens – in her recently published autobiography *a Princesa* [Princess], the Brazilian travesti Fernanda Farias de Albuquerque (1994) mentions that several of her boyfriends were men whom she first met on the streets as clients. But in this, Fernanda seems somewhat exceptional. I know of no travesti in Salvador who has formed a relationship with a man whom she met as a paying client. Travestis can meet their boyfriends while working on the street, but usually only in the capacity of what they call *vícios*, a word that means "vice" or "addiction," and which signifies men with whom they have sex for free because they are attracted to them. A particularly manly and breathtaking *vício* can eventually become a boyfriend – it would seem, but not a man from whom the travesti has accepted money for sex.

There are three reasons why travestis are not interested in making their clients into boyfriends. The first is that they are suspicious of a man who has paid for sex and then attempts to develop a relationship with them. They think that he is only interested in free sex and in ingratiating himself so that he will become part of the pool of boyfriends who circulate among travestis. In addition, the very fact that the travesti accepted money from him in the first place (instead of treating him as a *vício* and having sex with him for free) means that she does not find him desirable enough to enter into consideration as a boyfriend. And finally, a great number of clients pay travestis to penetrate them. While travestis often enjoy penetrating clients and some of their *vícios*, they will not tolerate, for reasons to be discussed in detail below, a male who enjoys being anally penetrated *dentro de casa* (in the house).

Another very characteristic feature of Keila's passion for Tiane is the fact of her being *apaixonada* (impassioned). This is an emotion that travestis feel that they share with women. Like themselves, women can become *perdidamente apaixonadas* (desperately impassioned) with men and do anything and everything to attract and keep the object of their passion. Men, travestis say, rarely become impassioned, and when they do, it is always for a woman – never for a travesti. As far as I was able to determine, this is a viewpoint shared by all travestis; I never heard a travesti describe her boyfriend's feelings for her in terms of passion, even though they regularly used that word in talking about their own emotional engagement. Quite the opposite – I repeatedly heard travestis tell one another that, in fact, boyfriends don't even particularly like travestis. During a conversation that Keila had with a travesti friend right after she had left Edilson and had begun living with Tiane, the friend advised Keila to be careful: "Men don't love us," she warned Keila, "men don't love us" (*Homem não ama a gente, homem não ama a gente*). Another travesti, thirty-four-year-old Banana, told me something very similar. "Men don't like us," she said, "They like women. For a woman they'll go out and sell popsicles on the street if they have to, and for us, even if we're on our deathbed, they won't work." Forty-year-old Martinha bemoaned that "men are mean and spiteful [*maldoso*] to travestis. Unfortunately,

we're homosexual, we like them. But they create a lot of malevolence [*maldade*] around us."

Travestis posit a concrete, tangible reason for this malevolence and for why men do not become impassioned with them. The reason habitually cited to explain this is: "God made woman for man and man for woman" (*Que Deus fez a mulher pro homem e o homem pra mulher*).

This phrase is a surprisingly recurrent one in travesti talk. I heard it used in discussions about gay marriage, which many travestis dismiss as a *safadeza* (a strongly condemnatory word meaning something like "an atrocity" or "an abomination"), and in discussions about lesbianism, which travestis find unnatural and threatening. It also regularly appears in discussions about boyfriends. At one point during the conversation that Keila was having with her travesti friend about her fresh relationship with Tiane, for example, the friend told Keila not to delude herself into thinking that the relationship would last forever. Keila's response was:

> I know it won't last [forever], I know it won't, I know that nothing lasts forever. When men and women, who were born for one another, since God determined that men should be for women, separate sooner or later, imagine two men with the same [male] head who think differently. I know it won't last [forever], of course not.

Because travestis believe that men were not "determined" for them and, hence, do not become impassioned with them, it is useless for them to try to appeal to a man's emotions when they are trying to hook him. In other words, a travesti does not assume that a man to whom she is attracted will also become attracted to her if she flirts demurely and tries to ingratiate herself with him. Her assumption is the opposite – that the man she is after will never fall in love with her. So instead of attempting to seduce him through sex appeal, a travesti will travel a much more direct road to her man's heart (to the extent that he has one, in this understanding of male emotions). That road is one paved with money and material goods.

From its inception, any travesti–boyfriend relationship will be characterized by the transfer of money and presents from the travesti to the male who is in the process of becoming the travesti's boyfriend. Money and gifts began to flow from Keila to Tiane, for example, via his mother, before the two had even had their first long conversation. Words were not needed at this point, however – the fact that Tiane requested money from Keila, and the fact that she gave it, signaled that a relationship was in the offing. Indeed, gift giving from a travesti to a male both marks a relationship and signals to others that a relationship is underway. After Keila had left him, Edilson, her ex-boyfriend, told me that he began to suspect something was amiss when he noticed that Tiane suddenly had begun sporting expensive-looking new clothes. Who bought them for him? he wondered to himself, suspecting that it might have been Keila. And when Keila was still in the very initial stages of her relationship with Tiane, before anyone actually knew that she was in fact interested in him, Rita Lee confided to me that she thought that Keila was after "her man." The reason she cited for this suspicion struck me as ridiculously trivial and paranoid, but I later realized that within the travesti framework for understanding relationships with boyfriends, it was actually profoundly meaningful. The reason was this: One evening when he was staying in Rita Lee's room, Tiane demanded a soda pop. Rita Lee had no money and told him so. He left the room, and returned a few minutes later with a soda pop. "Where did you get that?" she asked him; "Keila gave it to me" was his portentous response.

How much a travesti gives her boyfriend depends entirely on what she earns. Rita Lee, who was too old and sick to earn much money on the street as a prostitute, courted Tiane by giving him the only thing she had to offer – a place to sleep and one cooked meal a day. At the other end of the continuum are travestis who spend enormous sums on their boyfriends. One travesti who had earned a sizeable amount of money working as a street prostitute in Italy bought her boyfriend of the time a car when she returned to Salvador. Another travesti, who was renowned for her daring assaults on clients, and who sometimes returned from an evening of prostitution with more than the equivalent of $500 – all of it stolen – showered the young men she was courting with beer and marijuana and

clothes and cocaine. Keila was my coworker throughout the period of my fieldwork in Salvador; and, because I was working so intensely with her during the first few months of her relationship with Tiane, we talked a lot about the relationship. It quickly became very clear that she bought him some kind of present almost every single day. The present could be a slice of fancy cake for the equivalent of $2, or it could be a little hand-held video game for $5, or a shirt for $10, or a wallet for $12, or some soccer socks for $15. In two particularly expensive weeks several months into their relationship, Keila bought Tiane a pair of soccer boots with spikes ($60); a pair of pants and a shirt ($60); another pair of tennis shoes that he had asked her for ($119); a wallet and a baseball cap ($30); several T-shirts and shirts ($40); and a ticket to a rap concert ($30). In other words, in two weeks, Keila spent the equivalent of over $300 on Tiane – this in a country where the average salary at the time was just over $100 *a month*, and this in addition to paying the rent for the room, washing Tiane's clothes, preparing him meals, and providing him pocket money for entertainment, beer, snacks, and marijuana.

It is important to note here that despite this unidirectional flow of money and goods from the travesti to her boyfriend, it would be misleading to view the boyfriends of travestis as their pimps. Boyfriends are not pimps. They do not force unwilling individuals out into a life of prostitution and out onto the street in order that they may live the high life. Nor do they keep tabs on their travesti girlfriends while the travestis are working; indeed, the vast majority of boyfriends maintain no active involvement at all in the professional life of the travesti. As long as the travesti keeps paying the bills, boyfriends seem happy to leave the work side of life completely to the discretion of their travesti girlfriends. Many boyfriends go so far as to get up, turn off the television, and leave the room they share with their travesti girlfriend if she suddenly enters with a man and announces, "I'm gonna work" (*vou trabalhar*). The only problems that can arise in this arrangement occur if a travesti claims to have no money despite the fact that she has been going to work nightly. At this point the boyfriend will suspect either that his travesti girlfriend has been doing *vícios* and having sex for free with attractive males (something which in fact occurs quite frequently while travestis are on the streets working) or that she is paving the way for a relationship with another male by siphoning money off her income in order to begin the flow of presents and cash that will eventually result in a new boyfriend. In either case, the boyfriend will feel his own status threatened, and he will react and protest.

Socialization and Domination

Whenever travestis talk about their relationships with their boyfriends, and the presents and money that they give them, they always stress their own agency. They all emphasize that they chose their boyfriends, not vice versa, and they all maintain that they choose to support them and give them things because they want to, not because they feel forced to. "I *like* giving," Keila insisted whenever I expressed dismay at the fact that she was forever buying Tiane presents. She and other travestis commonly denote their giving using the verb *agradar,* which means "to please" – they give to please their boyfriends, not because they feel forced to.

But is this magnanimity really entirely uncoerced? Are travestis really so generous by nature that they happily give a substantial amount of their hard-earned income to males who not only are not impassioned with them, but who don't even do anything to help them either at work or around the house? An outsider coming from a culture where intimate relationships are supposed to be based on love, mutually felt emotions, and reciprocal efforts at generating incomes might easily see travesti accounts and practices of giving as delusions – fantasies of agency that travestis spin in order to mask the harsh fact that they are, in actual fact, being exploited by greedy, manipulative gigolos.

There are two reasons why a perspective that portrays travestis as the deluded victims of mercenary males would be too simplistic. The first is that travestis actively socialize young men into expecting money and goods from them. The majority of travestis I know in Salvador all have a great weakness for adolescent boys, whom they refer to as *boys,* or *boyzinhos.* The *boyzinhos* who are most attractive to travestis are often muscu-

lar youths between the ages of about fourteen to seventeen. There is no shortage of such youths in Salvador, and in any of the areas in which travestis live, there will be scores of shirtless, tough-looking young men hanging around on the streets, doing little except socializing with one another and smoking and/or selling marijuana and other drugs. In many cases, these young men have grown up in the area, and travestis may have known them since they were children. What happens when a travesti sees a *boyzinho* to whom she feels attracted is that she will call him into her room and offer him a beer and/or some marijuana, and then she will have sex with him. Afterwards, she will give him the equivalent of a couple of dollars, to buy himself a *lanche* – a hot dog or some other light snack – or some marijuana.

Although not all *boyzinhos* whom the travestis beckon into their rooms follow them there, many do, often warning the travesti afterwards not to mention a word of the encounter to anyone else (she, of course, agrees, and then immediately blabs all the details to any other travesti willing to listen). Through interactions like these, travestis treat themselves to a steady supply of attractive young men. And those attractive young men come to learn at least two things. First, some of them undoubtedly learn that sex with a travesti can be erotically fulfilling. But second, they all learn that sex with travestis translates into cash. Keila's former boyfriend Edilson told me during an interview that he learned early on that *"viado dá dinheiro"* (homosexuals pay):[3]

Edilson: Eu sempre gostei de dinheiro. É porque, a gente, pobre – no bom sentido – sem formação. Viado pra a gente, é uma fonte de renda.

Don: É.

E: Sempre, desde pequeno que eu aprendi, que me ensinaram assim, eu, eu aprendi assim –

D: Quem ensinou você?

E: Eu num sei, talvez outros colegas, talvez comentários, né? Viado pra a gente sempre foi uma fonte de renda, uma fonte, um jogo de interesse.

D: An-rã, an-rã.

E: Desde pequeno que eu aprendi isso. Num sei se eu aprendi por mim próprio, mais sempre que alguns viados se interessava por mim, eu também, queria ganhar alguma coisa.

D: N-rã. Então sempre quando você transou com um viado, você recebeu algum.

E: Eu sempre recebi alguma coisa.

D: Algum, dinheiro, ou qual?

E: É, alguma coisa, sempre procu-rando fazer um tipo de amizade pa poder ganhar uma camisa, um reló-gio, uma calça.

D: É verdade?

E: É, sempre querendo exigir um presente, não exigindo, mas sabendo pedir, né?

E: I always liked money. It's because one is poor – don't get me wrong – without education. *Viados* [i.e., homosexuals] for us are a source of income.

D: Yeah.

E: Always, since I was little I knew, who taught me, that I learned that –

D: Who taught you?

E: I don't know, maybe friends, maybe I just heard comments, you know? *Viados* for us were always a source of income, a source, a scheme.

D: Uh-huh, uh-huh.

E: I learned this when I was a kid. I don't know if I just picked it up on my own, but whenever any *viados* were interested in me, I also wanted to get something out of it.

D: Uh-huh. So whenever you had sex with a *viado* you got something.

E: I always got something.

D: Some money or what?

E: Yeah, something, [I was] always trying to make some kind of friendship to be able to get a shirt, a watch, a pair of pants.

D: Really?

E: Yeah, always wanting to demand a present – not demand, but knowing how to ask, you know?

It is not merely coincidental that Edilson; knowing this, later formed attachments only to travestis.

The second, related, reason why it would not do justice to travestis to see their relationships with their boyfriends simply in terms of them being exploited or deluded (or both) is that travestis are not unaware of the power that they exert over *boyzinhos* and, later, their boyfriends, by virtue of the goods and money that they bestow on them. The coercive nature of the gifts that travestis bestow on their boyfriends was pointed out to me by Keila on many occasions. She maintained that travestis give in order to dominate their boyfriends. At first, I was surprised at this assertion. But when I objected to its stark Machiavellian undertones and suggested that many travestis perhaps gave out of affection, Keila – who at this point was, of course, herself deeply embroiled in the process of supporting Tiane and giving him some new present virtually every single day – was dismissive. "No, it's not that," she told me, "because with everyone I talk to, they say this: 'Ah, I like to give money [to my boyfriend] because then I can humiliate him, I can order him around.' So it's something we do to feel good. To feel powerful in relation to another person." She continued with a concrete example:

Keila: Ele vai achar que não vai encontrar mais uma pessoa como eu pra ficar com ele, porque ele tinha Marília, Marília morreu, ficou eu, agora ele não vai encontrar uma outra pessoa, então ele não quer isso. É por esse motivo de ele se sentir assim, um pouco receoso de nos perder, eles ficam submissos à gente. A gente lá pode dominar eles um pouco, pode falar mais alto que ele, pode dar um ordem, e eles tem que aceitar.

Don: [laughs]

K: É. O problema todo é esse. . . . Por a gente ser uma classe muito humiliada na rua vítima de muitos preconceitos na rua – a gente tem que ter uma pessoa sempre pra a gente se montar em cima dela. E a gente procura botar em quem? Nos casos da gente. Como a gente pode montar em cima deles? Sustentando eles, dando dinheiro a eles, para que a gente possa dominá-los, pelo menos dizer assim: "Na rua eles podem me criticar, mas em casa, pelo menos, tem uma que eu mando nele, ele faz o que eu quero, na hora que eu quero."

K: He [Tiane] will think that he will never meet another person like me to be with him, because he had Marília, Marília died, then it was me, now he'll never meet another person – so he won't want [to lose everything]. This is the motive – for him to feel like that, a little afraid to lose us; they become submissive to us. We can dominate them a little, we can talk louder than them, give orders, and they have to listen.

D: [laughs]

K: Yeah. That's what it's all about. . . . Because we're a group that gets really humiliated on the street – really. We're the victims of a lot of prejudices on the street – we need to have a person who we can always straddle and be on top of. And we try to be on top of who? Our boyfriends. How to be on top of them? Supporting them, giving them money, so that we can dominate them, at least be able to say this: "On the street they can criticize me, but at home, at least, I have someone to boss around, he does what I want, when I want."

Keila draws attention here to an important dimension of travesti–boyfriend relations that would be missed if one examined them only from the point of view of an outsider observing the flow of cash and presents from travestis to the men with whom they live. She foregrounds the respect and even fear that travestis feel that their boyfriends will have for them, because the boyfriends understand all they will lose if they do anything to displease the travesti. Keila also draws an explicit connection between boyfriends and a travesti's professional life as a prostitute, pointing out that their interactions on the street have a significant relation to the type of relationship that they wish to maintain at home with their boyfriends.

I suspect that in highlighting domination as austerely as she does here, Keila is enunciating an insight granted her by virtue of her relative age and maturity (she is in her early thirties). I am uncertain whether travestis in their late teens, for example, who support their boyfriends explicitly see themselves as dominating them in

the manner Keila describes here. I also suspect that the majority of newly "impassioned" travestis, no matter what their age, do not interpret their giving of money and gifts in terms of domination. My guess is that they see their giving primarily in terms of being impassioned and wanting to "please" the object of that passion. As a relationship wears on, however, the subtext of dependency and domination that Keila foregrounds may become increasingly apparent – one older travesti regularly announces publicly to her boyfriend of many years, "I support you, I can humiliate you" (*Eu te sustento, eu te humilho*). And the awareness that giving implies power is never totally absent even in the case of young travestis, for during conflicts, even adolescent travestis will remind their boyfriends that they give them things: once during a fight with her boyfriend that had all of the house awake at three o'clock in the morning, nineteen-year-old Erica screamed at her boyfriend, "I took you off the street, sleeping in the gutter – you hear?! You're a beggar!" (*Eu peguei você na rua, dormindo no relento, tá?! Você é mendingo!*).

In addition to not shying away from reminding their boyfriends that they are dependent on them, travestis know that they can stop giving whenever they want, and they do stop supporting their boyfriends when they tire of them or when their boyfriends betray them in some way (such as when the boyfriend has an affair with another travesti). Dismissing a boyfriend is not entirely without problems, however. One of the biggest risks for travestis within the framework in which they establish and maintain intimate relationships is that a boyfriend who is sent packing may not go. Having grown accustomed to a life of relative comfort and extreme ease, he may resist the travesti's attempts to dislodge him, and it is not uncommon for boyfriends in this situation either to rob the travesti of everything she owns when she is out working (some boyfriends go so far as to haul off refrigerators) or to begin threatening and harassing the travesti. "If I can't be with you, no one will" seems to be something that these soon-to-be-ex-boyfriends fairly often announce to their travesti girlfriends who tell them to get out.

Travestis deal with this threat in one of four ways: (1) they threaten the boyfriend right back, telling him they are not afraid of him and they will stab him if he tries anything; (2) they make sure that they already have established a relationship with another (bigger, stronger, and meaner) man, and hence can count on his support to eject the old boyfriend who refuses to go; (3) they skip town (an option that tends to hinge on how many belongings a travesti has and whether she wants to abandon them); or (4) they acquiesce to the boyfriend's threats and remain living with him until they can either meet someone new or skip town. This latter option results in relationships that are clearly oppressive and abusive, and I know several travestis in Salvador who remain with their boyfriends only because they are afraid of them. Relationships like this are not common, however, and when they do occur they are generally the object of much discussion among other travestis, who regard them with concern and distaste. Most travestis who find themselves in a conflict with an ex-boyfriend opt for the second or third options, and young travestis, especially, who have very little possessions and who rent their rooms by the week, will leave town at a moment's notice because of a dispute with a boyfriend. Nineteen-year-old Stefani's boyfriend Ulysses, for example, hit her one evening during a fight they were having over a rumor that Stefani had done a *vício* with a *boyzinho* earlier in the day when he was away. In a rage, he left the room they shared. The next morning, when Ulysses returned to change his clothes and eat his breakfast, he found the room empty and Stefani gone.

Boyfriends and Sex

Travestis win their boyfriends over with money and material goods, and if we take Keila's arguments about domination seriously and grant that many travestis may construe their giving as a way of dominating their boyfriends (even if it may not always work out that way in practice), then it becomes somewhat clearer what they get out of a relationship that otherwise might appear rather empty and one-sided. In addition to domination, however, it quickly becomes very clear from the way that travestis talk about and interact with their boyfriends that boyfriends are also important for their own identity and self-

esteem. Remember that travestis are biological males who live their lives in women's clothing, assume women's names, and dramatically alter their physiological forms to make their bodies look more feminine.

In doing all that, travestis are not trying to become women; indeed, there is a widespread conviction among travestis in Salvador that any biological male who claims to actually *be* a woman is mentally disturbed. Instead of considering themselves to be women, travestis feel that they are *like* (heterosexual) women in their feelings, tastes, emotions, interests, and erotic desires. These similarities between women and travestis are foregrounded through the modifications travestis undergo to make their bodies more feminine. And they are also underscored by the fact that travestis, like heterosexual women, maintain intimate relationships with men. Not just any men, however.

In order to enter into consideration as a boyfriend, a male has to meet certain specific criteria. The first thing he has to do is to look like a man. Travestis are drawn to men who are classically masculine in their appearance. When I asked various travestis what an ideal man was for them, many responded by listing a number of stereotypically masculine physical traits that they found attractive, such as pronounced muscles and a big penis. Very soon after such a list, however, or even instead of it, another criterion immediately arose when travestis began talking about men. That criterion focused on how the man behaved in bed.

Fifty-eight-year-old Angélica told me that she likes "the type of man who is, like, macho (*retado*). Who has a woman. . . . Who fucks the cunt of a woman (*que fode tabaco de mulé*)." Twenty-seven-year-old Tina responded to my question about the kinds of men she liked by telling me that for her, the most important thing was "for him to be a man." That meant, she explained, that he would not "turn into a woman at the Moment of Truth [*Hora H*]." When I pressed for clarification of that somewhat cryptic pronouncement, Tina elaborated. A "real man" (*um homem mesmo*), she told me, was a male who didn't engage in "certain types of sex." Chief among those prohibited types was receptive anal sex. There are men who you think are men, Tina recounted with distaste, and then you get them into bed, and what do they do? Give their ass. "This is a man?" she snorted dismissively. "This is no man. This is a *viado* [a homosexual]."

> Erica: Eu gosto de comer. Eu nunca tive homem que me desse o cu, entendeu? Se por acaso ele me der eu vou achar uma coisa estranha, né, ficar com homem que dá cu dentro de casa, né?
>
> Don: É.
>
> E: Eu vou achar uma coisa estranha, né? Porque ó – eu posso também comer, e no outro dia botar pra fora também, né? Eu vou achar uma coisa estranha, ńe? Um homem que dá cu dentro de casa é viado, né?
>
> E: I like to penetrate. I've never had a boyfriend who gave me his ass, you know? If by chance he did, I'd find it strange, you know, being with a man who gave his ass in the house, you know?
>
> D: Yeah.
>
> E: I'd find it strange, you know? Because, look – I can penetrate him, but the next day I'd probably put him out. I would find it strange, you know? A man who gives his ass in the house is a *viado*, right?

Erica told me something similar, explicitly ruling out a man who "gives his ass" from all consideration as a boyfriend.

Thirty-five-year-old Mabel, in her answer to my question about men, repeated many of the same themes that travestis like Angélica, Tina, and Erica developed when I interviewed them. She also suggested a reason why travestis are so appalled at the thought of having a boyfriend who "gives his ass."

> Mabel: Eu num gosto de ter homem pa morar comigo que seja bicha, seja maricona não. Prefiro homem galinha com mulher tá entendendo, do que ter ... badalado por bicha, que a pior coisa é cê ter um homem badalado por viado.
>
> Don: Verdade?
>
> M: É
>
> D: Por quê?

> M: Porque é, porque uma chega: "A, aquele homem foi meu, eu fiz aquilo com aquele homem, eu botei na bundinha dele, ele fez uma pa mim, uma gulosa, ele bateu uma punhetinha pra mim. Saiu com a outra, fez aquela mesma coisa." E o homem galinha, ele é aquele homem galinha que ele não dá a bunda, que ele não faz chupeta pa ninguém, que ele não bate punheta, não pega no pênis de ninguém. É aquele galinha que vai, cê vira, virou pra ele, tá pondo, POU, tá gozando, "inté, tchau."
>
> M: I don't like to have the man living with me be a *bicha* or a *maricona* [i.e., a homosexual]. I prefer a womanizer, you know, than to have . . . a man who is chased after by homosexuals, 'cause the worst thing is to have a man who is chased after by *viados* [homosexuals].
>
> D: Really?
>
> M: Yeah.
>
> D: Why?
>
> M: Because some fag will come to you and [say]: "That man was mine, I did that with that man, I stuck it in his little behind, he sucked my dick, he jerked me off. He went with another [homosexual], did the same thing." And a man who chases after women, he's the kind of man who won't give his behind, he won't suck anyone's penis, he won't jerk anyone off, won't touch anyone's penis. [What I want] is a womanizer who goes [to bed with you], you turn, turn [your back to him], he puts it in, POW, cums, "Later on, bye."

The concern expressed here by Mabel that a man who "gives his ass" will give it to any homosexual who wants it also emerged in a discussion between Angélica, me, and Angélica's female prostitute friend Boca Louca about the kind of man a travesti wants. Angélica insisted that a travesti would never live with a man who allowed anyone to penetrate him, because, she said, "if you live with a man, and you penetrate his ass, you'll feel disgust (*nojo*) towards him." When I wanted to know why, Boca Louca spelled it out for me. "Because then he's a *viado*," she ennunciated clearly, "and he can give his ass to other people, too."

All these responses indicate that travestis are extremely preoccupied with the sexual behavior of the men they take as their boyfriends. A male's status as a man, it would appear, is crucially dependent on what he does in bed. Even if he is in bed together with a *viado*, a travesti, or some other homosexual, a man is someone who will always assume the penetrative role, and not suddenly "turn into a woman" at "the Moment of Truth." This understanding of men is something shared by every travesti in Salvador.

Within the understandings of gender that travestis draw on to understand and create their relationships, males are thus not naturally and self-evidently men. Manhood is the result of particular interests and particular acts. And one of the defining attributes of being an *homem*, being a man, in the gendered conceptions that the travestis draw on and invoke is that a male classified as a man will not be interested in another male's penis. A man, in this interpretive framework, will happily penetrate another male's anus. But he will not touch or express any desire for another male's penis. For him to do so would be tantamount to relinquishing his status as a man. The sexual act freighted with the most significance here is to *dar o cu*, as it is called in Brazilian Portuguese – to "give the ass," to allow penetration. That act is transformative – it is like the wave of a magic wand, changing a man into a *viado*, a homosexual: a person who shares a sexuality with travestis.

The disturbing nature of this transformation for travestis hinges on the fact that they are uninterested in males who share their own sexual desire. This is one of the profound differences between travestis and the people who travestis refer to as *os gays* or as *as bichas gay* (gay males). Whereas gay relationships are understood to be based on sameness (both partners in a relationship desire males), travesti–boyfriend relationships, in order to function and exist at all, must be founded on deep and dividing *difference*. Here, one partner will desire males and the other will desire females. This configuration of desire is not merely a Brazilian version of the insistence of North American and European male-to-female transsexuals that the relationships they maintain with men are definitionally heterosexual even before they undergo sex reas-

signment surgery, because they feel themselves to be women. As I have already made clear, travestis do not define themselves as women, and, hence, they do not define their relationships with their boyfriends as heterosexual. To the extent that they would apply such terminology at all to their relationships, they would say that their boyfriends are heterosexual, but that they themselves are homosexual. Or, as Keila's ex-boyfriend Edilson put it succinctly when I asked him to define his own sexuality, "I'm heterosexual. I won't feel love for another heterosexual, because, to do that [i.e., for two males to be able to feel love], one of the two has to be gay. . . . Between a heterosexual and a gay there can exist a kind of sincere love."

Edilson articulates the basis of the gender system with which travestis and their boyfriends understand and coordinate their relationships. In this system, a heterosexual male – that is, a male who desires the "opposite sex" – is definitionally a man. And a homosexual male – that is, a male who desires the "same sex" – is definitionally the "opposite sex" in relation to a "man." "Between a heterosexual and a gay there can exist a kind of sincere love," Edilson says, which is a statement that can only make sense from the point of view of a set of understandings that perceives such love as generated from two completely different natures and perspectives. Furthermore, it can only make sense from the point of view of a system that conceptualizes desire as meaningful only in relation to difference. The underlying assumption that gives this system form and makes it sensible is that it configures *all* desire as heterosexual desire. Homosexual desire in the sense of desire between two males *as males* (or between two females, as females) is not recognized here, or is only recognized as an aberration, a farce, and it is regarded as vaguely repellent by many travestis (many travestis find gay male pornography offensive and "disgusting" (*nojento*), for example, because images of two stereotypically macho men engaging in intercourse make no sense to them). Desire, here, is only meaningful in relation to difference. Desire is also what *produces* that difference – a male is a man *because* he desires a female; a travesti can feel like a woman *to the extent that* she desires a man and is desired, in return, by a man. It is this relationship between desire and the production of difference that excludes other homosexuals from consideration as partners for travestis. It takes a man to make a travesti feel like a woman. A homosexual would short-circuit the conceptual system and make a travesti feel like – what? (The answer: a lesbian).[4]

What all this means is that the gendered status of males is not given but must be produced through the appropriate desires, which are manifested through the appropriate practices. And the single most significant of these practices is sexual behavior. The bed is the arena where some males make themselves into "men," by penetrating their partner, and where other males make themselves "women," by allowing themselves to be penetrated by those men. It is thus in bed where gender is truly established. But it is also in bed where the risk for gender slippage is most acute. It is in bed where one experiences, as Tina so poignantly put it, *Hora H* – the "Moment of Truth." Edilson, as the boyfriend of a travesti, was aware of this: He told me that he has never, in all his fifteen years of sex with various travestis, touched a travesti's penis or allowed a travesti to penetrate him. He believes that "if I did that type of thing, I'd stop being a man, right?" And in order to prevent such a fate, Edilson explained that "I have to control myself."

Edilson has had two long-term relationships with travestis, one that lasted for six years, and one, with Keila, that lasted for seven. One of the main reasons for the longevity of both these relationships was precisely his ability to "control himself." Because when it comes to the sexual behavior of boyfriends, travestis have eyes as sharp as hawks, and they are alert to any lapse of self-control. While they enjoy penetrating other males, and do so regularly while they are working, or when a *boyzinho* they have called into their room makes it clear that he is willing to "give his ass," no travesti will tolerate a male who is interested in her penis at home (*dentro de casa*). As Erica explained, "I'd find it strange, you know, being together with a man who gave his ass in the house." Nineteen-year-old Adriana was even more decided. She told me that the only reason her current boyfriend was still *dentro de casa* was because "he's penetrating me" (*ele tá me comendo*). If he had wanted Adriana to pen-

etrate him, she would have already sent him away: "I'd look at his face and I'd keep seeing that he isn't a man. I'd see that he is a *viado* just like us, and I'd think 'I'm having sex with, supporting, giving food to, all that – a *viado*?' No."

Travestis feel so strongly about not wanting men who "give their ass in the house" that they will act as Adriana says she would do and expel any boyfriend who begins to do so. The reasons that they themselves give for ridding themselves of such a male are several.

First, they will, as they say, "lose respect" (*perder respeito*) for their boyfriend. From being held in high esteem as a man, a boyfriend who expresses interest in his travesti girlfriend's penis becomes nothing more than *um viado igual a gente* (a viado, just like us). And this change in gendered status is accompanied by a plunge in respect; I have heard many travestis express how they would feel in relation to such males in very strong affective terms, including *nojo* (disgust), as Angélica puts it in the quote above, and *vergonha* (shame). One travesti told me that a man who expressed an interest in her penis would, in her estimation, be "*reduzido a nada*" (reduced to nothing). This reduction to "nothing" will be expressed in the way that the travesti addresses her boyfriend. Many different travestis told me that they were certain that they would begin publicly humiliating their boyfriend the moment he allowed them to penetrate him. They would *jogar na cara dele* (throw it in his face) that he was a *maricona*, a soft faggot. "The whole house will know the day my boyfriend gives me his ass," Erica told me. "I already call him *maricona*, even though he isn't one – imagine what I would call him if he really did give me his ass!"

Second, if a boyfriend whom they thought was a man turns out to be a *viado* just like themselves, travestis will wonder why they should support him. Why should they be out on the streets working to support someone who desires the same thing (sex with men) as they do? What is preventing that person from working the streets as well?

Third, travestis strongly believe that boyfriends who begin to allow themselves to be penetrated will never again want to penetrate. Travestis are unanimous in agreeing that they would never decline a boyfriend's offer to be penetrated. "Who would pass up an ass?" they all ask (*Quem é que dispensa um cu?*). Banana even told me that she has requested her past boyfriends to give her their ass. "Come on daddy, let mommy penetrate your ass" she urged them (*Vá painho, deixa mainha comer teu cu*). But this request was a kind of test. Because the concern is that a boyfriend who begins to *dar*, to "give" (i.e., allow penetration), will become so smitten with the joys of anal penetration that he will never want to return to his old ways. And some travestis can happily penetrate their boyfriends for several weeks, or months, or in exceptional cases even years, but they will all eventually *enjoar* – a word that all travestis use when talking about this situation, and which means they will "grow tired of" or "get sick of" this sexual behavior. "It would be like eating chicken every day," one travesti told me with an expression of repugnance on her lips. (It is both interesting and significant that the reverse situation – that is, the desired state of affairs, in which the boyfriend only ever penetrates the travesti – is never spoken about in this way. No one ever suggested that they would *enjoar* of only ever being penetrated by their boyfriend, and whenever I suggested that I would find such behavior tiresomely repetitive, they looked at me with curiosity and surprise, then waved my objections aside, saying, "Ah, that's because you're a gay.")

The belief that boyfriends who begin to "give" won't be able to stop giving is also tied to the idea, expressed by both Mabel and Angélica, that a male who begins to *dar* will engage in a frenzy of anal promiscuity and seek out travestis everywhere to penetrate him. One travesti said she wouldn't dare bring clients to her room if her boyfriend was interested in "giving," because the boyfriend would probably want to have sex with the client.

Travestis also suspect that a male who begins to "give" has always really wanted to "give" all along, which means that he has probably been "giving" to other travestis in secret. And that her boyfriend has "given" to other travestis, but not to her, is the gravest and most bitter humiliation that a travesti can face, as Mabel makes clear in her comments about boyfriends. The extreme mortification a travesti feels upon hearing news that her boyfriend has "given" to others does not

hinge on the fact that the boyfriend has been unfaithful. On the contrary, part of the expectations that travestis have of their boyfriends as men – as both Mabel and Angélica underscore – is that the boyfriends will be sexually promiscuous with women. Travestis are fully aware that some of the money they give to their boyfriends gets spent by them entertaining their girlfriends. The disgrace centers entirely on the fact that the travesti has been deceived – she has been supporting someone whom she thought was a man, but who in reality suddenly turns out not to be a man at all, but instead a *viado* just like her, a person who "gives his ass on the street," just like her. Fernanda Farias de Albuquerque calls this *a pior das traições* (the worst of treasons) in her book a *Princesa* (1994, 74–5). The extreme power of this "treason" seems to derive from the gender configuration that travestis draw on and elaborate: the revelation that one's boyfriend is not a man also implies that one is not as much of a woman as one would like to believe.

A final reason why travestis will end relationships with males who allow themselves to be penetrated is because they feel as though the boyfriend, by "giving his ass," has desperately played out the last card in his hand to try to hold on to a travesti who is on her way out. Erica expressed this understanding when she told me one night on the street that one of her most recent boyfriends, a young man universally referred to and adressed as *Negão* – "Big Black Man" – had "given his ass" to her early on in their brief relationship. She pondered this for some time, and came to the conclusion that he did it in order to try to prolong the relationship that he somehow sensed was doomed. Keila also elaborated this thought, asserting that any boyfriend who "gives his ass" always does so with *segundas intenções* – with a hidden agenda. She told me many times that boyfriends who suddenly begin to *dar* do so because they realize they are losing their travesti girlfriend:

Men, because they have a head that is more . . . mistaken [*errada*] than a travesti's, will think that a travesti will only be happy when things are going his [the travesti's] way – which, in the majority of times, is true – and so he'll think what?[5] "I have a travesti and I have everything he gives me – everything I want he gives me. But we're not 100 percent OK sexually. So sooner or later I'm gonna lose the travesti. So what do I do? To not lose the travesti? I'm gonna try to do something for him, that I can, that it's possible for me to do, so that I'll succeed in being with him [the travesti] always. So that I won't lose my comfort, the advantages [*minha mordomia*] that I have." And so what does he do? To try to make the travesti dependent on him? He goes to bed with the travesti and inverts the roles [*inverte os papéis*], lets the travesti penetrate him [*deixa que o travesti coma ele*], sucks the travesti ['s penis], and sure – at that exact moment, that month, for the days to follow, the travesti, because it's a new thing, because it's a new experience – because every travesti is curious – will like the new arrangement. But there will come a certain moment when the travesti will get sick of it [*vai enjoar daquilo*]. And then he [the boyfriend] won't have another chance to win over the travesti again, because he already did the last thing that he had left to do [*a última coisa que ele tinha que fazer*].

As soon as the boyfriend starts misunderstanding the situation [*perde a noção da coisa*] and starts thinking that by being passive in bed he'll be able to dominate the travesti more than he could when he was active – as soon as he thinks he can secure the travesti through sex – he's roundly mistaken, because that way he'll end up falling out of the picture completely. A travesti doesn't get attached to anyone for sex, because a travesti doesn't need a boyfriend to cum [i.e., ejaculate (*O travesti não vai se prender a ninguém por sexo, porque o travesti não precisa de homem em casa pra gozar*)].

What emerges very clearly from the ways in which travestis talk about and interact with their boyfriends is that relationships between them are structured along a very strictly upheld schema. Brazilian Portuguese is felicitous here, because the verbs it uses to denote socioeconomic relationships of giving and consuming are *dar* (give) and *comer* (eat). These exact same verbs are used to denote the sexual practices of being penetrated (*dar*) and penetrating (*comer*). Thus, a male who penetrates another person (male or female) is said to *comer* (eat) that person, and that person is said to *dar* (give) to the male who is penetrating him or her.

The schema along which travesti–boyfriend relationships are structured is one in which travestis should "give," in both the economic and the sexual sense, and the boyfriends should "eat" – again, in both the sense of consumption and the sense of sexual penetration. The boundary between giving and eating is very heavily patrolled and upheld by travestis, and any boyfriend who "starts misunderstanding the situation," as Keila so slyly expresses it, and attempts to "invert the roles," does so at the cost of his relationship with his travesti girlfriend.[6]

In both the economic and the sexual senses, the controlling agent here is the "giver," because she can, at any moment, decide to cut off the flow of goods and services that she supplies to the "eater." She may not always be successful in achieving this, and travestis' predilection for tough, strong, macho men can result in them having to leave town to escape them, or, in the worst cases, it can result in them discovering themselves to be entangled in an oppressive and abusive relationship. In the vast majority of cases, however, travestis can and do sever relationships with boyfriends that they wish to be rid of.

If one examines travesti–boyfriend relations in terms of the normative gender expectations that exist in Brazil, what one sees very clearly is that boyfriends, for all their masculine props, are feminized. Rather than working and supporting their spouse, as Brazilian males are normatively exhorted to do, the boyfriends of travestis are supported by their spouses. They are economically dependent on them, living in their rooms, eating food bought with their money, and wearing clothes purchased by them. Furthermore, it is they who are expected to (and often do) stay at home while their spouses are out making a living on the street. Once when I was walking home with Tina after a night on the streets, and before I realized the extent to which travestis support their boyfriends, I asked her if her boyfriend worked. She looked at me incredulously and laughed out loud. "No," she told me, "he's laying in my room, watching television, waiting for me to come home from work." And Keila's ex-boyfriend Edilson complained to me that whereas the boyfriends and husbands of women "sleep away from home, have other women, hang out with other men and everything," travestis want "to have a man in the house, always at their disposal" (*o todo tempo à disponibilidade*).[7] In addition, in stark contrast to the majority of heterosexual relationships in Brazil, where it appears that the one in a relationship who runs the greatest risk of being abandoned is the woman, in travesti–boyfriend relationships, the one who runs this risk is the "man": both the travesti and her boyfriend are aware that the travesti can up and go anytime she wants to – leaving the boyfriend, unless he has managed to rob her before she leaves, with nothing.

It is perhaps because boyfriends are so undisguisedly feminized in relation to travestis (and travestis, hence, so clearly masculinized in relation to their boyfriends) that many travestis regularly employ a number of pronouncements and practices that encourage misrecognition of this fact. It is the case very frequently, for example, that a travesti will publicly proclaim to everybody that her boyfriend has not allowed her to do something or go somewhere or wear some particular article of revealing clothing. Erica once told me, for example, with a proud smile on her face, that because of her boyfriend's objections, "I can't wear short skirts, I can't wear off-the-shoulder blouses because they show my breasts, I can't go to any parties, he won't let me go to the beach." Even more dramatically, Chica spent the entire week of Carnival 1995 inside the house on São Franciso Street. She couldn't go out, she told everybody who wondered, because "the man won't allow it" (*o bofe não deixa*).

I was dumbfounded at announcements like this, because I knew that travestis like Erica and Chica were economically supporting the men who were issuing such restrictive edicts. What did they mean their boyfriends wouldn't allow them to do something they wanted to do?

It was Keila who, in her usually incisive way, cut to the heart of the matter for me. Travestis, she told me, love for boyfriends to order them around, because when they do, they can *se sentir amapô* – they can feel like a woman. Travestis think that men should dominate women, Keila explained, "so how are they going to feel like a woman? With a man dominating her." And with this in mind, travestis can broadcast this domination to other travestis, who, they reckon, will envy them because they have a boyfriend who

cares enough about them to order them around and make pronouncements about their clothing and their behavior.

But even infinitely perceptive Keila did not identify the misrecognition involved in the sexual relationships between travestis and their boyfriends. One of the main reasons why travestis insist that their boyfriends restrict themselves to the role of penetrator, Keila explained to me, is that travestis are so dominating in every other dimension of their relationship that they enjoy relinquishing their dominance when they are in bed. Sex is the one context in which boyfriends *really* dominate travestis, Keila said.

As ought to be clear by now from the way in which travestis police the sexual conduct of their boyfriends, however, it would perhaps be more reasonable to interpret sex between a boyfriend and a travesti not as a case where the travesti relinquishes her dominance over her boyfriend, but, on the contrary, as a case where the travesti resolutely and absolutely *exerts* her dominance, even in bed. Especially in bed. Rather than constituting an exception to the rule of travesti control of boyfriends, sexual behavior in bed is an enactment of the rule; indeed, it is a concentration of it.

One important practical outcome of this exertion of power in bed is that the majority of travestis do not normally have orgasms when they have sex with their boyfriends. Sex with a boyfriend consists, for the most part, of the travesti sucking the boyfriend's penis and of her boyfriend penetrating her, most often from behind, with the travesti on all fours or lying on her stomach on the bed. If the boyfriend touches the travesti at all, he will caress her breasts and perhaps kiss her. But no contact with the travesti's penis will occur. Several travestis I know wear panties whenever they have sex with their boyfriends and whenever they sleep next to their boyfriends, so that the boyfriends will not be confronted with the fact that the travesti has a penis. One travesti told me that she had been living with her boyfriend for almost two years, but that the only way he could possibly have seen her penis is if he peeked under her panties at night while she slept.

Whatever else travestis may get out of their boyfriends, then, it is not sexual fulfillment.[8] As

Mabel explained in her description of what kind of man she wants, sex with a boyfriend involves him "go[ing to bed with you], you turn, turn [your back to him], he puts it in, POW, cums, 'Later on, bye.'" And as Keila stated explicitly, "A travesti doesn't get attached to anyone for sex, because a travesti doesn't need a boyfriend to cum." The point of having a boyfriend, instead, is to help a travesti feel like a woman, by looking like a man, and most of all, by upholding the sexual behavior of a man in bed. The reasons why boyfriends of travestis do little else than that is because that is all they are supposed to do. And as long as they continue looking like men and being men, boyfriends can remain relatively secure, and travestis can remain happy (until the time, of course, when they find somebody else who does it better). That these rigid expectations and demands result in relationships in which travestis get very little sexual fulfilment is, for them, beside the point. They do not want boyfriends for sex. They don't get sex from their men – what they get, instead, is gender. Sexual pleasure is something that travestis obtain elsewhere, with their *boyzinhos*, their *vícios*, and the clients they meet on the street at night.[9]

Notes

1 This is not quite true for the literature on male prostitution (e.g., West 1993; McNamara 1994; Davies and Feldman 1997). Indeed, one of the most significant differences between how male and female prostitution is treated in the literature is that whereas female prostitution is portrayed as an identity, male prostitution is often seen as an activity. Even though the transgendered prostitutes I discuss in this essay are biologically male, this essay builds on and draws contrasts primarily with the literature on female prostitutes. This choice has to do partly with the fact that travestis self-identify and live as feminine homosexuals, and partly with the fact that it is in the literature on female prostitution where one finds the strongest claims made about the partners of prostitutes.

2 This is not to suggest that researchers like Barry and Høigård and Finstad are unsympathetic to prostitutes as individuals. It is just that their vocal political opposition to prostitution naturally influences the way in which they understand the private relationships of prostitutes, and it results

in them classifying boyfriends almost definitionally as pimps. Høigård and Finstad's (1986, 215) typology of pimps, for example, which ranges from "boyfriend-pimp" (*kjærestehallik*) to "sex club pimp" (*sexklubbhallik*), leaves it unclear whether it is ever possible for a boyfriend of a prostitute to *not* be a pimp.

3 Travestis refer to themselves, and are commonly refered to throughout Brazil, by this word *viado*, but the word also signifies "male homosexual" in the broadest sense of the term. Edilson is speaking about travestis here, but his use of the word *viado* should be understood in its broad sense of "homosexual," and not just as travesti. It would seem that the system to which Edilson refers is widespread throughout Brazil. Teresa Adada Sell's 1987 book *Identidade Homossexual e Normas Sociais* [Homosexual identity and social norms], for example, is a series of interviews with homosexual men living in Florianópolis, a city located at the opposite end of the country from Salvador. Many of those men mention that macho men often expect to be (and usually are) paid if they have sex with a *viado* (35, 51–2, 155).

4 Two travestis living together as a couple are talked about as a *lesbian* couple, and one of the words used to describe the kind of sex they are publicly imagined as having is *roça-roça* (rub-rub) – the same word used to describe lesbian sex. Travesti understandings of, and opinions about, lesbianism are discussed in detail in Kulick (1998b).

5 Although travestis habitually use feminine pronouns, articles, and adjectival endings when referring to themselves and one another, Keila uses masculine forms here. Pronoun usage among travestis is a complicated issue, but in a nutshell the principle is this: when Keila discusses travestis as an impersonal, general phenomenon, she uses the masculine pronoun, because the word *travesti* is grammatically masculine in Portuguese (*o travesti*). Whenever she discusses any particular travesti, however, she uses feminine grammatical forms. I consistently use feminine forms, partly out of deference to travesti usage, but also because I believe that travestis' linguistic practices perceptively and incisively enunciate core messages that are generated by their culture's arrangements of sexuality, gender, and biological sex (Kulick 1997).

6 At least some boyfriends are aware of this. When we were talking about whether he would ever allow a travesti to penetrate him, Edilson told me that "one likes travestis, right? And so one wants to make that person happy, too, make them feel pleasure. But at the same time, one holds oneself back (*a gente se segura*) because if one does that [i.e.,

253

"gives" to a travesti], that person [i.e., the travesti to whom one has "given"] is gonna discriminate against one, think that one is a *viado* too (*vai discriminar a gente, achar que a gente é viado também*) And then one will be seen in a bad light by them (*já fica mal visto por elas mesmos*)." And here, Edilson began quoting abuse that he had heard many travestis hurl at boyfriends they were in the process of leaving: "Ah, who do you think you are? You gave me your ass! I penetrated your ass, you sucked my dick! You think you're so great, but the other day you were on top of my dick! Giving all night long!" (*Ah quem é você? Você me deu o cu! Comi seu cu, cê chupou minha pica! Porque você é muito bom, mas um dia desse cê tava na minha pica! Deu toda noite!*).

7   In an interesting choice of words, Edilson explained that this was a sign that travestis wanted to be "more than women" (*elas quer ser mais do que uma mulher*). By this, he meant that whereas a woman would accept (or would be forced to accept) the infidelities and social life of her man, travestis don't. I think that Edilson here comes intriguingly (and, for him, probably, dangerously) close to articulating my own argument that boyfriends are feminized in their relationships with travestis.

8   Stephen O. Murray has pointed out to me that this formulation equates sexual pleasure with ejaculation and seems to disallow the possibility that travestis might derive great pleasure from being anally penetrated, whether they actually ejaculate or not. Let me therefore state explicitly that my discussion of sexual pleasure here is based on how travestis talk about sex, not on my own personal assessment about what constitutes good sex. Although individual travestis undoubtedly derive erotic pleasure from being penetrated, even when they don't ejaculate, whenever travestis talk among themselves about thrilling or fulfilling or incredibly fun sex, that talk usually focuses on how they *penetrated* their sexual partner, and it unfailingly includes detailed descriptions of how many times they themselves ejaculated.

9   Travestis differ dramatically from most other prostitutes described in the literature in that they regularly derive sexual pleasure from their contacts with their clients. They invert the division between "private" and "commercial" sexuality that researchers on prostitution hold to be virtually axiomatic. (For a recent summary of the arguments for such a division see McKeganey and Barnard 1996, 83–98). The sexual pleasure that travestis derive from their clients is mentioned in Kulick 1997 and discussed in detail in Kulick (1998a).

References

de Albuquerque, Fernanda Farias, and Maurizio Janelli. 1994. *a Princesa: Depoimentos de um travesti brasiliero a um líder das Brigadas Vermalhas*. Rio de Janeiro: Nova Fronteira.

Bacelar, Jeferson Alfonso. 1982. *A família da prostituta*. São Paulo: Ática.

Barry, Kathleen. 1979. *Female sexual slavery*. New York: New York University Press.

——. 1995. *The prostitution of sexuality*. New York: New York University Press.

Bell, Shannon. 1995. *Whore carnival*. Brooklyn, N.Y.: Automedia.

Day, Sophie. 1990. Prostitute women and the ideology of work in London. In *Culture and AIDS*, edited by Douglas A. Feldman. New York: Praeger.

Davies, Peter, and Rayah Feldman. 1997. Prostitute men now. In *Rethinking prostitution: Purchasing sex in the 1990s*, edited by Graham Scambler and Annette Scambler. London: Routledge.

Høigård, Cecilie, and Liv Finstad. 1986. *Bakgater: Om prostitusjon, penger og kjærlighet*. Oslo: Pax.

Kulick, Don. 1998a. *Travesti: Sex, Gender and Culture among Brazilian Transgendered Prostitutes*. Chicago, Ill.: University of Chicago Press.

——. 1998b. Fe/male trouble: The unsettling place of lesbians in the self-images of Brazilian *travesti* prostitutes. *Sexualities* 1, no. 3: 299–312.

——. 1997. The gender of Brazilian transgendered prostitutes. *American Anthropologist* 99.3: 1–13.

McKeganey, Neil, and Marina Barnard. 1996. *Sex work on the streets: Prostitutes and their clients*. Buckingham and Philadelphia: Open University Press.

McNamara, Robert P. 1994. *The Times Square hustler: Male prostitution in New York City*. Westport, Conn.: Praeger.

Nanda, Serena. 1990. *Neither man nor woman: The hijras of India*. Belmont, Calif.: Wadsworth.

Pheterson, Gail, ed. 1989. *A vindication of the rights of whores*. Seattle: Seal.

——.1996. *The prostitution prism*. Amsterdam: Amsterdam University Press.

Prieur, Annick. 1994. *Iscensettleser av kjønn: Transvestiter og machomenn i Mexico by*. Oslo: Pax.

——. 1998. *Mema's house, Mexico City: On transvestites, queens, and machos*. Chicago: University of Chicago Press.

Sell, Teresa Adada. 1987. *Identidade homossexual e normas sociais: Histórias de vida*. Florianópolis: Editora da Universidade Federal de Santa Catarina.

West, Donald J., in association with Buz de Villiers. 1993. *Male prostitution*. New York: Harrington Park.

Index

Index